THE CAMBRIDGE COMPANION TO AMERICAN UTOPIAN LITERATURE AND CULTURE SINCE 1945

Providing a comprehensive overview of American thought in the period following World War II, after which the United States became a global military and economic leader, this book explores the origins of American utopianism and provides a trenchant critique from the point of view of those left out of the hegemonic ideal. Centering the voices of those oppressed by or omitted from the consumerist American Dream, this book celebrates alternative ways of thinking about how to create a better world through daily practices of generosity, justice, and care. The chapters collected here emphasize utopianism as a practice of social transformation, not as a literary genre depicting a putatively perfect society, and urgently make the case for why we need utopian thought today. With chapters on climate change, economic justice, technology, and more, alongside chapters exploring utopian traditions outside Western frameworks, this book opens a new discussion in utopian thought and theory.

SHERRYL VINT is Professor of Media and Cultural Studies and of English at the University of California, Riverside. She is a recipient of the Science Fiction Research Association's Lifetime Achievement and Innovative Research awards. She has published widely on speculative fiction and culture, including most recently *Biopolitical Futures in Twenty-First-Century Speculative Fiction* (2021).

A complete list of books in the series is at the back of the book.

THE CAMBRIDGE COMPANION TO AMERICAN UTOPIAN LITERATURE AND CULTURE SINCE 1945

EDITED BY

SHERRYL VINT

University of California, Riverside

CAMBRIDGE
UNIVERSITY PRESS

Shaftesbury Road, Cambridge CB2 8EA, United Kingdom

One Liberty Plaza, 20th Floor, New York, NY 10006, USA

477 Williamstown Road, Port Melbourne, VIC 3207, Australia

314–321, 3rd Floor, Plot 3, Splendor Forum, Jasola District Centre, New Delhi – 110025, India

103 Penang Road, #05–06/07, Visioncrest Commercial, Singapore 238467

Cambridge University Press is part of Cambridge University Press & Assessment, a department of the University of Cambridge.

We share the University's mission to contribute to society through the pursuit of education, learning and research at the highest international levels of excellence.

www.cambridge.org
Information on this title: www.cambridge.org/9781009180061

DOI: 10.1017/9781009180078

When citing this work, please include a reference to the DOI 10.1017/9781009180078

First published 2024

A catalogue record for this publication is available from the British Library.

A Cataloging-in-Publication data record for this book is available from the Library of Congress

ISBN 978-1-009-18006-1 Hardback
ISBN 978-1-009-18005-4 Paperback

Contents

List of Figures — *page* vii
List of Contributors — viii

Introduction: Utopianism in Dark Times — 1
Sherryl Vint

1 Pandemics and the Lesson of History — 23
Priscilla Wald

2 American Futures — 41
Phillip E. Wegner

3 Engendering Utopia: The Force of Gender and the Limits of Feminism — 62
Jennifer A. Wagner-Lawlor

4 America and/as White Supremacy — 82
Edward K. Chan and Patricia Ventura

5 American Spirituality — 100
Andrew Tate

6 Black Escapes and Black Wishlands — 115
Jerry Rafiki Jenkins

7 Latinx Belonging in New World Borders: Mestiz@ Rhetoric and Critical Utopian/Dystopian Dialectics of Ambivalence — 133
Rubén R. Mendoza

8 Educating Desire: Young Adult Utopian Fiction — 152
Jonathan Alexander

9 Utopia after American Hegemony — 167
Peter Boxall

10 Technological Fantasies 185
Matthew Wolf-Meyer

11 Utopian Spaces 201
Roger Luckhurst

12 Environmentalism and Ecotopias 217
Gerry Canavan

13 Economic Justice 237
Hugh C. O'Connell

14 Renewing Democracy 254
Mathias Nilges

15 The Time of New Histories: Utopian Possibility in America's Twenty-First Century 271
John Rieder

Works Cited 287
Index 310

Figures

2.1	Cover of *The Iron Heel*	*page* 42
2.2	Panel from "Judgement Day"	49
12.1	Crumb's "A Short History of America"	218
12.2	Deurbanized Utopia	233

Contributors

JONATHAN ALEXANDER is Chancellor's Professor of English at the University of California, Irvine. He has published twenty-two books, the most recent of which is *Writing and Desire: Queer Ways of Composing* (2023).

PETER BOXALL is Goldsmiths' Professor of English Literature at the University of Oxford. He has written a number of books on the novel, including *Twenty-First-Century Fiction* and *The Value of the Novel* (2013) and *The Prosthetic Imagination: A History of the Novel as Artificial Life* (2020). He is editor of the journal *Textual Practice* and series editor of Cambridge Studies in Twenty-First-Century Literature and Culture. He has a volume of collected essays forthcoming entitled *The Possibility of Literature* (2024) and is currently writing a book entitled *Fictions of the West.*

GERRY CANAVAN is a professor in the English Department at Marquette University, specializing in twentieth- and twenty-first-century literature. An editor at *Extrapolation* and *Science Fiction Film and Television,* he has also coedited *Green Planets: Ecology and Science Fiction* (2014), *The Cambridge Companion to American Science Fiction* (2015), *The Cambridge History of Science Fiction* (2019), and *Uneven Futures: Strategies for Community Survival from Speculative Fiction* (2022). His first monograph, *Octavia E. Butler,* appeared in 2016 in the Modern Masters of Science Fiction series at University of Illinois Press.

EDWARD K. CHAN is Professor of American Studies at Waseda University (Japan). His research/teaching interests cut across transnational perspectives on American culture in relation to race and utopia. Selected publications include *White Power and Neoliberal American Culture* (2023, coauthored with Patricia Ventura), "Race" (2022, in the

Palgrave Handbook of Utopian and Dystopian Literature), "Race in the *Blade Runner* Cycle and Demographic Dystopia" (2020), "The White Power Utopia and the Reproduction of Victimized Whiteness" (2019), *The Racial Horizon of Utopia* (2016, Ralahine Utopian Studies), and "Utopia and the Problem of Race" (2006). He also coedited with Patricia Ventura a special issue of *Utopian Studies* on race (2019).

JERRY RAFIKI JENKINS is Professor of English at Palomar College and a lecturer in the English and Comparative Literature Department at San Diego State University. His research focuses on Black speculative fiction and film, with an emphasis on horror and science fiction, and he is the author of *The Paradox of Blackness in African American Vampire Fiction* (2019) and the forthcoming *Anti-Blackness and Human Monstrosity in Black American Horror Fiction* (2024). Rafiki also coedited, with Martin Japtok, *Authentic Blackness/Real Blackness: Essays on the Meaning of Blackness in Literature and Culture* (2011) and *Human Contradictions in Octavia E. Butler's Work* (2020).

ROGER LUCKHURST is Geoffrey Tillotson Chair at Birkbeck College, University of London.

RUBÉN R. MENDOZA is Associate Professor of Chicana/o Studies at East Los Angeles College, where he has taught since 2009. He holds an MA in Chicana/o Studies and a PhD in English/Rhetoric Studies from the University of California, Riverside. His work applies rhetoric studies in the development of critical pedagogy through a focus on contemporary Chicana/o art, Latin American cultural production, and speculative fiction. He has presented at conferences throughout the Americas in Latinx studies, rhetoric, Latin American studies, comparative literature, and science fiction studies and has published in *Paradoxa*, *Science Fiction Studies*, *Confluencia*, and *Science Fiction Film & Television*.

MATHIAS NILGES is Professor of English at St. Francis Xavier University. His most recent books are *How to Read a Moment: The American Novel and the Crisis of the Present* (2021) and (coedited with Mitch R. Murray) the collection of essays *William Gibson and the Futures of Contemporary Culture* (2021).

HUGH C. O'CONNELL is an associate professor of English at the University of Massachusetts–Boston. His current research examines the relationship between speculative fiction and speculative finance. He is the editor of Darko Suvin's *Disputing the Deluge: Collected 21st-Century Writings on*

Utopia, Narration, and Survival (2021) and coeditor with David M. Higgins of *Speculative Finance/Speculative Fiction*, a special issue of *CR: The New Centennial Review* (2019).

JOHN RIEDER, Professor Emeritus of English at the University of Hawaiʻi at Mānoa, is the author of three books and dozens of essays and book chapters on science fiction. He was awarded the Science Fiction Research Association's award for Lifetime Achievement in 2019. He currently serves on the editorial board of *Extrapolation*.

ANDREW TATE is Reader in Literature, Religion and Aesthetics at the University of Lancaster. He has published widely in the field of nineteenth-century and contemporary literature. His books include *Contemporary Fiction and Christianity* (2007), *The New Atheist Novel* (coauthored with Arthur Bradley, 2010) and *Apocalyptic Fiction* (2017). He also coedited, with Jo Carruthers and Mark Knight, *Literature and the Bible: A Reader* (2014).

PATRICIA VENTURA is Associate Professor of English at Spelman College, Atlanta. She teaches classes in American cultural studies, media studies, and critical theory. She wrote the monograph *Neoliberal Culture: Living with American Neoliberalism* (2012). With Edward Chan, she cowrote *White Power and American Neoliberal Culture* (2023) and edited the collection *Race and Utopian Desire in American Literature and Society* (2019). Among her book chapters and articles are "Scandal: A Melodrama of Social Death" (2019) and "Dystopian Eating, Queer Liberalism, and the Roots of Donald Trump in HBO's *Angels in America*" (2018).

SHERRYL VINT is Professor of English and of Media and Cultural Studies at the University of California, Riverside. She has published widely on speculative fiction, including most recently *Biopolitical Futures in Twenty-First Century Speculative Fiction* (2021) and, with Jonathan Alexander, *Programming the Future: Politics, Resistance and Utopia in Contemporary Speculative Television* (2022).

JENNIFER A. WAGNER-LAWLOR is Professor of Women's, Gender, and Sexuality Studies at Penn State University and the editor of *Utopian Studies: The Journal of the Society for Utopian Studies*. Her research focuses on feminist and utopian literatures, the theory of utopia and dystopia, and gender theory. Wagner-Lawlor is currently completing a book project that considers the relationships of plastic materiality and especially of conceptual plasticity, as developed by philosopher Catherine Malabou, with utopian figurations of subjectivity, temporality, and narrativity.

PRISCILLA WALD is R. Florence Brinkley Professor of English and Professor of Gender, Sexuality, and Feminist Studies at Duke University and author of *Constituting Americans: Cultural Anxiety and Narrative Form* (1995) and *Contagious: Cultures, Carriers, and the Outbreak Narrative* (2008). She is currently at work on a monograph entitled *Human Being after Genocide*.

PHILIP E. WEGNER is Marston-Milbauer Eminent Scholar and Professor of English at the University of Florida, where he has taught since 1994, and the director of the Working Group for the Study of Critical Theory. He is the author of numerous essays and five books, including *Invoking Hope: Theory and Utopia in Dark Times* (2020) and the forthcoming *Late Theory: Jameson, or the Persistence of Reading*.

MATTHEW WOLF-MEYER is Professor of Science and Technology Studies at Rensselaer Polytechnic University and is the author of *The Slumbering Masses: Sleep, Medicine and Modern American Life* (2012), *Theory for the World to Come: Speculative Fiction and Apocalyptic Anthropology* (2019), *Unraveling: Remaking Personhood in a Neurodiverse Age* (2020), and *American Disgust: Racism, Microbial Medicine, and the Colony Within* (2024). He is the editor, with Denielle Elliott, of *Naked Fieldnotes: A Rough Guide to Ethnographic Writing* (2023). His research focuses on the biology of everyday life, affective approaches to subjectivity, and posthuman bioethics.

Introduction
Utopianism in Dark Times

Sherryl Vint

The opening decades of the twenty-first century are not, at first glance, an auspicious time for a book on utopian thought. Indeed, during the period from the postwar era to the present, utopianism has been regarded in some circles with an air of suspicion, dismissed as either an impossible fantasy or feared as a worldview that inevitably tends toward overly rigid interpretations of the good society that become totalitarian demands for conformity. Not only has the speculative fiction genre associated with the utopian as a literary form turned all but exclusively toward dystopias in the late twentieth and early twenty-first centuries, but the world itself seems to take its cues from such fiction. The period between the conception of this collection in mid-2020 through to its publication has seen a global pandemic that intensified existing inequalities within and between countries; a worsening immigration crisis that regularly results in fatalities at both the southern US and southern European borders; the return of extreme-right and fascist political figures across the globe and a related rise in incidents of racist violence; increasingly frequent and more intensively destructive storms, fires, extreme temperatures, droughts, floods, and other evidence of massive climate change; the Russian invasion of the Ukraine; and the looming specter of a major recession in 2024.

Walter Benjamin's second Thesis on history quotes Hermann Lotze, who comments on "the freedom from envy which the present displays toward the future."[1] Benjamin's theses famously culminate with the image of the backwards-facing angel of history who sees the catastrophes of historical violence piling up behind him as a "storm" "we call progress" propels him nonetheless into the future.[2] In a moment in which we see the storm quite clearly even when facing forward, I want to pause not with the angel's dilemma, but instead with this entanglement of the present with a future that we may well fear rather than envy. Reflecting on Lotze, Benjamin tells us that "our image of happiness is thoroughly colored by the time to which the course of our own existence has assigned us."[3]

Benjamin earlier focuses on the relations between present and past, the claim the past has on the generations who follow, an anticipation of redemption, which "cannot be settled cheaply."[4] He links this force of redemption to class struggle, which we might broaden to the struggle against the dispossession and immiseration produced by racial capitalism from its colonial incarnation onward. Through "courage, humor, cunning, and fortitude," Benjamin argues, the marginalized continue to call into question every victory "of the rulers,"[5] and our critical task is to articulate the past not as nostalgia but as a kind of vital energy that insists that no oppression is every total, no foreclosure of utopian futurity ever complete. Benjamin's thoughts are similar to the ideal of the utopian articulated by Ernst Bloch. For Bloch, the utopian is not a blueprint for the perfect society, but an impulse toward a better world that emerges from a sense of dissatisfaction with the present, which he also calls a "rejection of deprivation."[6] Just as Benjamin cautions against identifying with the victors of past historical struggles and seeing their achievements as an unblemished record of progress, Bloch recognizes that utopian sensibilities need to be educated and directed such that one's unhappiness is channeled toward hope for a collectively better future, not a fearful nostalgia focused on an idealized past.

Although utopianism looks toward the future, Bloch locates it in the here and now, in the moments of daydreams or the affects inspired by artistic works, evidence of a discontent with the status quo that is a symptom of a widespread longing for greater justice and universal thriving, of a recognition that the world as shaped by the hegemony of the victors is not enough. Drawing on Bloch, José Muñoz focuses especially on the affect to be found in queer communities of color, insightfully insisting that this kind of utopianism is most likely to emerge from those subjects most marginalized in the existing order of things.[7] Bloch recurrently uses the term Not-Yet (*Noch Nicht*) to refer to the anticipatory consciousness that longs for this better world and shifts towards actualizing it in materiality, not via a strict program but instead through the cultivation of different ways of being and feeling. Caroline Edwards glosses the Not-Yet as "a temporal mode that names the utopian content hidden within ordinary daily life, works of art, religious belief systems, political ideas and the imaginary worlds of fiction."[8] It is this Blochean sensibility that animates the utopian within this volume: a sense of utopia as improvised, contingent, and always in-progress, of utopianism embodied in living spaces of counterhegemonic resistance that persist despite the power of racial capitalism. In other words, this is not a book about the utopian understood as fiction about the perfect society, although it will focus on utopianism as embodied in cultural texts. Within the larger framework of the utopian, the chapters collected here consider texts emerging from dystopian settings as well: these two are part of the broader utopian project in that they document the dystopian not as exemplar but as cautionary tale, aiming at the utopian in their critique of the given.

Benjamin tells us that any image of happiness is shaped by the contours of the historical moment into which an individual is born. If we link this ideal of happiness to the utopian-as-impulse we take from Bloch, we begin to recognize how a certain idea of happiness – a certain Not-Yet sensibility – might thus emerge from what is often experienced as a dystopian present. The degree of present immiseration calls for more utopianism, not for abandoning the idea as irrelevant or unrealistic, precisely because – to take some liberty with Benjamin's phrasing – the fact that the future as embodied in our current historical trajectory inspires more fear than envy demonstrates our urgent need to nurture the utopian, understood as traces of past historical struggles for a just society that remain latent in the present. Although hegemonic discourse has insisted, at least since Francis Fukuyama's naive "end of history" thesis,[9] that the triumph of global capitalism (conflated with liberal democracy) has put an end to all need for social struggle over what constitutes the good society, those expelled from this triumphal collective have persisted nonetheless, have nurtured visions of a social order premised on values other than those of extractive capitalism and colonial hierarchy. Such peoples inhabit and keep alive versions of happiness that do not rely on Western privilege or consumerist excess. And it is this utopian sensibility that the world could still be otherwise than its current trajectory that most needs cultivation in these darkest times, not least because those most harmed by our present configurations of power are those most marginalized by recent histories.

The volume is itself something of a provisional utopianism in another sense as well. The idea for this volume emerged in a conversation between me and Cambridge editor Ray Ryan, near the beginning of the Covid lockdowns, regarding how scholarship might best respond to the exigencies of the moment. Informed by another set of conversations with my colleague Anindita Banerjee, which resulted in the publication of a series of short responses by speculative-fiction (sf) scholars to the historical openings made available by the unprecedented situation we were living through,[10] I became convinced of the importance of looking at traditions of utopian thought and experiment in US literature and culture over the past seventy years as a way of providing context to the moment we were experiencing, but also of reminding us of the tools of collective resistance that remain within our grasp. The vision for this volume that emerged was not merely to review the recent history of such work in American culture, but also to foreground voices and perspectives that run counter to the mainstream story of America's identity, to recognize that times of intense crisis – such as the pandemic – are also moments of opening to new possibility, if we allow this. This volume collects utopian visions that mainly run against the grain of the nostalgic nationalism of current polarized US political discourse or the technological solutionism of Silicon Valley's promises to save the world by transcending the human condition entirely.[11]

The provisional and unfinished quality of Blochean utopianism is relevant as well to the process by which this volume came together, a final project that is not a perfect version of what was initially planned. The very crises to which we responded in our work in this volume inevitably had an impact on the work itself: the final roster of chapters unfortunately omits some that were initially planned but could not be completed, and the timeline for the volume has expanded beyond the period of lockdowns into the new endemic phase of Covid infection. Consistent with Bloch's work, however, these changes embody the appropriate spirit of a utopianism that is contingent, in progress, and flexible, eschewing the rigidity of the putatively perfect society that is often associated with dismissive accounts of utopianism either as unrealistic or as tending toward authoritarianism. Utopianism, however, is about the process of always seeking the horizon of a better world, not about a rigid picture of what this world looks like in a final instance, which, in any case, can never arrive, as life is not static. While this volume does not represent all the voices and perspectives that I had hoped to make part of the conversation, it starts important dialogues about how we can cultivate the needed utopian impulse, rethink the trajectory of twenty-first century America, and bring into prominence voices and perspectives that have not historically been associated with American utopianism.

Whose Utopianism?

Most of the works discussed in the chapters collected here are utopian in this Blochean sense and thus represent visions of a better world shared by fiction and chapter authors alike. But this volume also seeks to chart the influence of utopian rhetoric in US culture since the end of World War II, a period during which the United States came to occupy a dominant global role and mythologize its unique historical mission as part of what Henry Luce dubbed the American Century in a 1941 editorial for *Life* magazine.[12] In many ways, the chapters collected here document the degree to which this military-industrial complex American utopianism, resting on a foundation of settler colonial utopianism, produced the dystopian worlds that demanded new utopian traditions from those oppressed by or excluded from mainstream hegemony. The importance of utopianism as we near the end of the first quarter of the twenty-first century is related to the question of futurity: if we cannot accept another "American century" in this mold, what alternatives should we cultivate, and how?

Each chapter in this volume charts its own set of theoretical and conceptual influences, and I want simply to emphasize the broad canvas of utopian theorizing that informs the volume. While the focus remains on cultural works, this is not a book about utopianism as merely a literary form, much less about a form that documents a perfect world. Rather, rooted in Bloch, we follow scholars who emphasize the utopian as method for political imaginings and collective activism. Even the images of perhaps-better worlds that the fiction embodies can be understood as utopian not in the classical sense of the model society but rather, as Kathi Weeks suggests about political demands for changes such as Universal Basic Income, not as concrete plans but as prompts to think otherwise, "potentially effective mechanisms by which to advance critical thinking, inspire political imagination, and incite collective action."[13] Crucial to this way of thinking about utopianism is the recognition that the utopian and dystopian are not opposites but are two ways of thinking about the social and its future trajectories: just as the utopian emerges in response to dystopian experiences, imaginative visions of dystopia are modes of critique and resistance. The utopian is thus more often found in the midst of disaster than in success and often diagnoses what is wrong and what elements have been omitted to the detriment of our current social orders, rather than offering fully developed versions of what the alternative will entail. For example, we can see a latent utopianism in Ruth Wilson Gilmore's critique of prisons; as she shows, they are constituted by a new kind of state that "depends on ideological and rhetorical dismissal of any agency or capacity that 'government' might use to guarantee social well-being";[14] and we can couple this with the overt naming of abolition as utopian by Dylan Rodriguez, understanding abolitionism not merely as the removal of prisons, but more importantly as the cultivation of how we must change to make prisons irrelevant: "Abolition, as a practice of speculative futurity" or as a "counter-Civilizational practice of freedom that defies the modern disciplinary (and generally militarized) orders of the citizen, the nation-state, jurisprudence, politicality, and – most importantly – the gendered racial ascendancy of the white human."[15]

Avery Gordon describes this mode of utopianism as being-in-difference, "a standpoint and a mindset for living on better terms than what we're offered, for living as if you had the necessity and the freedom to do so."[16] In language that echoes Weeks's notion of the utopian demand as an invitation toward activism and imagination, Gordon argues that "to refuse to live as if there is no other choice shifts the terrain of struggle to the more difficult and delicate work of living autonomously," a refusal of the given that might be "imposed on you by the impossibility of being assimilated and rewarded by the dominant order or chosen by you against all the odds."[17] Gordon draws on Herbert Marcuse to talk about longings for the better world that exist in attenuated form but must be transformed into "'vital needs,' into things that we cannot and will no longer live without,"[18] but this sense of the utopian as a longing that emerges from full human experience and that exists – if repressed and marginalized – in the interstices of quotidian experience mirrors the Blochean idea of the utopian impulse, a framework that has been developed extensively by scholars such as Ruth Levitas, Fredric Jameson, and Tom Moylan. In her book *Utopia as Method*, Levitas uses the term the Imaginary Reconstitution of Society to identity the utopian as a kind of sociological method, arguing that the utopian is about both reconstituting the social orders that shape and contain us, but also reconstituting ourselves as different subjects in this different future. The utopian "requires us to think about our conceptions of human needs and human flourishing in those possible futures."[19] Thus, *contra* those who suggest the utopian is impossible due to the limitations of a fixed human nature, Levitas insists, "what really is impossible is to carry on as we are, with social and economic systems that enrich a few but destroy the environment and impoverish most of the world's population. Our very survival depends on finding another way of living."[20]

We see this kind of utopianism embodied in M. E. O'Brien and Eman Abdelhadi's creative critical work *Everything for Everyone: An Oral History of the New York Commune, 2052–2072*. Published as if it were a work of sociology from the future, the book appears to be interviews with a range of people who lived through a socialist transformation of global society in the second half of the twenty-first century. The first interview, with Miss Kelley, concerns the Hunts Point insurrection in New York in 2052, one of the flashpoints for a global reconfiguration of power and sociality that the book charts via its remaining chapters/interviews with a range of characters who experienced this transformation from multiple embodied experiences over a twenty-year period. While the book contains an implicit argument about the need for utopian transformation related to issues of property, abolition, grassroots assembly, and reestablishing the commons, the book is utopian in its form as well as its content, in the sense that it does not present these matters through grand theory or coordinated revolutionary strategy. Instead, as we see again and again through the interviews, the new global order emerges repeatedly and unevenly. It emerges through improvisation and mainly through acts that Levitas describes as refusals: "the refusal to accept that what is given is enough . . . the refusal to accept that living beyond the present is delusional, the refusal to take at face value current judgements of the good or claims that there is no alternative."[21] O'Brien and Abdelhadi also repeatedly show that political change is necessarily bound together with changes in social reproduction, and especially with broadening queer possibilities for kinship. The book begins with an epigraph from the interview with Miss Kelley: "we took something that was property and made it life."[22]

Everything for Everyone is the perfect case study for recognizing why we need the utopian today, not *despite* but *because* we seem to be living out some dystopian script. As its stories/histories make clear in a range of vignettes, the utopian future emerges not because of some grand program but as a result of people improvising as they try to survive dark times, try to live within systems premised on the erasure of people like them, to forge solidarities in a world structured against their vitality and futurity. The interviews offer glimpses of the better world that exists on the other side of their struggle, but the main focus is on the difficulties people lived through, the trauma transformation entailed, the ways that these traumas were not seeds of despair but instead the kind of refusal that Levitas champions. As one interviewee, Aniyah Reed from the Harlem Common, puts it, thinking back to the 2030s, "I remembered these pamphlets that people would hand out on the subway or on the street or that people would forward to me. Things about how the system was broken, how it was capitalism, etc. I always thought, 'I don't have time for this,' or 'I don't have energy for this.' But then I realized, 'I don't have time because of this. I don't have energy because of this.'"[23] Theorists such as Weeks, Levitas, and Gordon all recognize this relationship between limits and imagination as a political question. The utopian demands a kind of excess, whether this be excess of how Weeks theorizes the demand as a provocation, as "excessive, defying what are proclaimed to be reasonable limits on what we should want and demand,"[24] or what Gordon describes as the surplus that refuses the parameters of the world as given: "an accumulated excess or surplus available to help make living more sustainable, more sociable, more anticipatory, and to help with the scandalous shape-shifting – the subject work and public works – necessary for any change that will make a qualitative difference."[25] Although the better world might lie in the future, the utopian exists here, in the midst of the dystopian, in "all those things we are and we do that exceed or are just not expressions of what is dominant and dominating us."[26]

Everything for Everyone, in using fiction as a mode of critique and analysis, joins with a range of recent critical works that take seriously the capacity of the imagination as a critical and political technique. Laura Horn, Aysem Mert, and Franziska Müller, in their *Palgrave Handbook of Global Politics in the 22nd Century* (2023), adopt a similar strategy, asking their contributors to write entries on how politics *might be* in a world organized otherwise, presenting a range of visions that draw on both utopian and dystopian narrative methods to help jar us out of our habituated ways of perceiving and thinking. The utopianism lies precisely in this method – prompting us to reconceive the natural, the possible, and the desirable – more than in any specific vision offered by a contributor.[27] While the chapters contained in this volume focus on cultural texts embodying utopian (and dystopian) visions of the American future, these texts similarly function simultaneously as works of political theory and activism, as arguments for the kinds of futures we can and should strive to materialize as we move toward the twenty-second century.

Rethinking American through the Utopian

Many of the works discussed in this volume are global in their address, but what anchors this collection is a specific focus on American authors and on works that address the issue of American futurity. Thinking about the utopian in relation to American culture brings with it a distinct set of challenges related to the nation's mythology about itself as a state that emerged from a utopian project of freedom, which was later extended in the period of concern here to a mission of global leadership understood in moral terms, not simply as an expression of US military and economic dominance. This mythology is often embodied in the image of "the city upon a hill," a phrase taken from Christ's sermon on the mount by a colonialist clergyman as inspiration for Puritans who viewed their settler project as a utopian escape from religious oppression by a corrupt church and state leadership. In the twentieth century, the phrase was repurposed as justification for US hegemony and alibi for US exceptionalism, most notably by Ronald Reagan, whose 1980 presidential victory inaugurated a new chapter of right-wing Christian political influence and neoliberal policy, both of which lie at the heart of the difficult political and environmental crises facing the United States today.[28] Thus the question of whose utopia is especially fraught in a US context in which mainstream culture fosters an anemic notion of the utopian premised on racial genocide – of Indigenous peoples to appropriate their land; of African Americans to extract their labor – and capitalist excess (as entailed by the reinvention of the American Dream from equality of opportunity to a fantasy of being entitled to achieve tremendous wealth).[29]

The doubleness of the utopian within the American context is visible throughout this book, which includes chapters documenting the persistent strains of utopian thought as American exceptionalism *and* chapters that draw attention to counterhegemonic perspectives that persist within – indeed, are made necessary by – the exclusions and oppression essential to this "city on a hill" version of American utopianism. A central argument pursued across the chapters collected here, then, is the need to rethink the utopian in American culture in order to come to terms with the persistence of white supremacy and capitalist accumulation as dimensions of utopian thought within US culture. The operative definition of the utopian, then, encompasses some discussion of texts embodying those views, although they would not be endorsed as utopian by the authors of the chapters or by me. Yet to simply erase them from the discussion entirely would make it impossible to offer an overview that adequately assesses the possibilities for political change in the United States today; particularly, it would make it impossible to assess the barriers and challenges we face in any utopian project of creating a more just and liveable future.[30]

But while such perspectives are documented and discussed in what follows, they are not consistent with the Blochean utopianism that informs this volume. Bloch differentiates real from false utopias, suggesting that the former are future-oriented and motivated by hope, while the latter are backward-focused and infused by fear. Critics building on his work have emphasized that desire alone does not enable a utopian vision, that desire has to be shaped or educated such that our dissatisfaction with the present is channeled toward a world that is collectively better, not simply toward our own betterment within the status quo. This kind of utopianism thus entails transforming not just the world but also humans as subjects in it. In Levitas's terms, "Utopia as method must address the transformation of needs, wants and satisfactions entailed both in a new society and the transition to it. The process of making and communicating imagined alternative futures must be both affective and cognitive."[31] The project of utopianism, then, is as much about resisting or countering the "bad utopian" as it is about the contours of the better world. And in American mainstream culture, "bad utopias" abound, from the escapist, consumerist fantasies of Disney to the technological solutionism of World's Fairs or Tech Crunch. The bad utopia can absorb or dissipate utopian energies, evacuating the public sphere as a space of political agency by conveying the impression that all conflicts can easily be resolved through homogeneity, displacing real antagonisms onto minor frustrations so they are dissipated without real political change.

Related to the problem of the "bad utopia" are texts that appear to be dystopias but are better characterized as antiutopias, that is, they are depictions of "bad futures" not intended to warn against our current trajectory – as in the classical dystopia – but that function instead as expressions of hopelessness regarding the utopian. As Lucy Sargisson explains, antiutopianism "is a phenomenon that resists the utopian impulse" and is a perspective adopted by both "conservatives and liberals, for quite different reasons."[32] While conservatives worry that utopianism is impossible or, worse, a precursor to the authoritarian insistence on a single definition of perfection, liberals scoff at the naivete of utopian longing or – worse in my estimation – insist that we have already come as close to the utopian as is feasible under conditions of liberal democracy. Yet this insistence that the liberal world is the best of all possible worlds skirts dangerously close to American exceptionalism and its dark, white supremacist underpinnings. Taking note of the rise of right-wing, reactionary tendencies in some utopian thought, David Bell argues that we need to understand them not as the opposite of "liberal post-utopianism" but rather as the "extrapolation of some of its tendencies."[33] For him, antiutopianism, then, is not simply a resistance to utopian thinking; it is "a form of material violence that clamps down on the (possibility of generating) utopian alternatives to the status quo."[34] Sargisson uses the title of her book on twenty-first century utopianism, *Fool's Gold*, to reframe this resistance to utopianism. This common name for iron pyrite generally connotes the foolishness of mistaking it for gold, but she points out that "pyrite has its very own beauty, so long as we don't mistake it for something else."[35] If we take the utopian to mean the discovery of the blueprint for a perfect society, we inevitably will be disappointed, will be fools; but if we understand the utopian as the contingent and perpetual work of seeking better forms of solidarity and flourishing, then we have found something very valuable indeed. This is a Blochean version of the utopian in which the world as we experience it is the product of human agency, and thus the "fabric of reality itself is utopian in the sense of being literally not yet 'there', incomplete."[36] The current order of things is neither necessary nor eternal, and in this we can always find hope – if never closure. The antiutopia represents another way of siphoning off the energy or excess necessary for the utopian, transforming political refusals of the present into cynicism or despair rather than activism.

Varieties of Utopian Experience

Within literary studies, and especially in relation to the genre of science fiction, a rich vocabulary has emerged to describe the nuances of various utopian narrative techniques and their political efficacy. The two most influential thinkers in this space are Fredric Jameson and Tom Moylan, both of whom work in a largely Marxist cultural studies tradition and something of a Blochean sense of the utopian. Moylan has complicated our sense that utopia and dystopia function as a binary pair denotating "good" and "bad" models respectively. For him, the utopian is less about the specific image of another world and more about the fact of its existence *as an other*: "utopia opposes the affirmative culture maintained by dominant ideology" and "negates the contradictions in a social system by forging visions of what is not yet realized either in theory or practice."[37] He later adds the term "critical utopia" to denote narratives that represent not the static "good" place but the ongoing attempt to create such a place, works that resist the limitations of stasis and closure that compromise the classical utopia. The critical utopia, moreover, refuses the commoditized utopianism that I have described as the "bad utopia." Relatedly, Moylan emphasizes that dystopia is not merely about the "bad" place but is a method "to reflect upon the causes of social and ecological evil as systemic."[38] *Contra* the antiutopia's focus on the individual – who may escape or transcend the coercive power system – the true dystopia foregrounds collective resistance. In these reframings, the point is not the *place* as model, but rather the imaginative means such texts provide to enable historical struggle for the better world.

As with Levitas – and consistent with Blochean materialism – the utopian is an ontological mode for Moylan, requiring us to ask what kind of capacities we need to cultivate to move in the direction of the utopian, a responsibility named in the title of his most recent book, *Becoming Utopian*. Jameson approaches these matters from the perspective of a negative dialectic, which serves the doubled function of "denaturalizing the current social order and offering the mind, in a photographic negative, the 'preconcept vial' figuration of a radically 'other' order."[39] Jameson's work emphasizes repeatedly that the function of the utopian is to keep alive the dream of something else, not to provide a specific model of the new order. Thus, he suggests, the utopian is "the negative mirror image of the social order, but in that negativity is also the precondition of its transformation."[40] Across his works, he returns to this ideal of the utopian as impulse or desire, a move toward "something not yet realized, something altogether different from the present, and hence capable of transforming it,"[41] or the "conviction that our own present is not all there is."[42] It is the dialectical form of the utopian that is central to Jameson's work, the tension between realism and the utopian enables us to reflect on our present with a sense of historicity, that is, with the recognition that human agency makes the world and can always remake it, that the current order of things is not inevitable nor natural nor eternal. In *Valences of the Dialectic*, he most overtly theorizes this dialectical element of utopianism, insisting on the necessary relationship between utopianism and the political, that "utopia is the motor and energizing force of praxis itself."[43]

It is with this sense of the necessary relationship between utopianism and political change that I wish to conclude this introduction by focusing attention on two vital and connected spaces of utopian activism today: work to mitigate climate change by rethinking the energy infrastructures of modernity, and the related fights for Indigenous sovereignty that seek to halt the entwined harms of colonial oppression and capitalist extraction. In an article published in *Utopian Studies*, Kim Stanley Robinson – who once studied with Jameson – notes that in the context of climate change "utopia has gone from being a somewhat minor literary problem to a necessary survival strategy."[44] Discussing his career-long commitment to issues of environmentalism, Robinson notes that the difficulty of utopianism is trying to imagine the space of transformation between the world as we find it and the world as we believe it might be. Calling this period of transformation the Trench, he connects this difficulty of concretely imagining the utopian future with Jameson's notion of the utopian:

> We can't imagine the bridge over the Great Trench, given the world we're in and the massively entrenched power of the institutions that shape our lives – and the guns that are still there under the table, indeed right on the table. The bridge itself is what we can't imagine – and maybe that's what Jameson means: but then it's not utopia we can't imagine but history – future history, the history yet to come.[45]

Faced with this difficulty, Robinson emphasizes that we need to adjust our sense of temporality, to focus not on the specific details of the bridge, but simply to move history onto a slightly different trajectory, to begin to move in the right direction and realize that our ancestors will build on the work that we have done, that while we might not see utopian change in our lifetimes, our actions and political commitments are not futile.

From a science-fictional perspective, we might think of this sense of temporality as future history, an idea Jameson has also explored in relation to the genre as giving us a capacity to see the present as if from a future vantage point and thus recognize that our choices are always shaping what the future can be.[46] Connecting the techniques of speculative fiction with approaches to temporality, story, and creativity that are central to Indigenous cultures – and which give them distinct ontological and epistemological frameworks that do not enable the destructive colonialist extractivism of modernity – Grace Dillon suggests that "all forms of Indigenous futurisms are narratives of *biskaabiiyang*, an Anishnaabemowin word connoting the process of 'returning to ourselves,' which involves discovering how personally one is affected by colonization, discarding the emotional and psychological baggage carried from its impact, and recovering ancestral traditions in order to adapt in our post-Native Apocalypse world."[47] The framework of the post-apocalyptic world here connects this decolonial practice to utopianism as much as to sf, while the concept of *biskaabiiyang* suggests a practice that shares some resemblance to the utopian improvision documented in O'Brien and Abdelhadi's *Everything for Everyone* and remembered in the traces of past revolutionary praxis in the documents (partly fictional, partly historical) assembled by Gordon in *The Hawthorn Archive*.

David Bell also highlights the ongoing decolonial practices of Indigenous peoples globally as evidence of a utopian praxis that survives uninterrupted, despite the genocidal violence of colonial modernity that has sought to usher everyone into a universal modernity premised on the Western liberal values so foundational to the United States' narrative of its exceptionalism. Bell insists that these decolonial "struggles to defend their ways of life" are "inseparable from the places in which they live."[48] Thus utopianism must be decolonial, a perspective Mark Rifkin proposes as well when he suggests that speculative imaginaries are a crucial political tool when focused on "disrupting processes of reification through which trajectories of racial and colonial violence continue to be materialized."[49] This connection between the decolonial and the utopian has a fraught history, not only in the ways in which the United States as a settler state imagined itself as a utopian new beginning for its Puritan residents, but also in the long shadow cast by Thomas More's *Utopia* (1516), which grounds the emergence of a utopian place in colonial politics.

Yet as the chapters collected here document, the field has grown and changed substantially and feels no fidelity to the contours of this eponymic text. The future of utopian thinking and activism lies rather in Indigenous practice and may require the adoption of other vocabularies, such as Glen Coulthard's notion of *grounded normativity*, which he defines as "the modalities of Indigenous land-connected practices and longstanding experiential knowledge that inform and structure our ethical engagements with the world and our relationships with human and nonhuman others over time."[50] Grounded normativity emerges from a land-back political framework that puts Indigenous sovereignty at the center of its politics: from this centering of Indigenous knowledge, new relations of social reproduction, including the social reproduction of other species and of the environment in which we live, follow. Although Coulthard does not use the term utopianism, I see his framework as consistent with the Blochean utopianism championed in this book, as similar to the abolitionist utopianism encouraged by Rodriguez, as a place from which to start to orient our historical trajectory in a new direction, one that seems more promising for enabling us to build a bridge across what Robinson calls the Trench separating our presenting institutions from a future in which human and other life might thrive. The decolonial perspectives that emerge repeatedly across the chapters collected here, then, are the core of a new generation of utopian studies. This book seeks to begin the project of charting where utopian thought needs to go next, especially in relation to the US nation-state project and its possible futures.

The Chapters

In *Becoming Utopian*, Moylan begins to emphasize what he calls the utopian problematic rather than the utopian text:

> The utopian *problematic*, therefore, must always enable further openings, further movement, so that its mobilization of desires and needs for a better world will always exceed any utopian formulations that arise from that very process, always look through any utopian answers, and always seek for more.[51]

Each of the chapters collected here embraces this spirit of seeking for more, and each addresses a specific area of social and cultural reproduction that demands political engagement today.

Priscilla Wald opens the volume with a chapter on pandemic narratives and how they have been mobilized for political ends, opening with a reflection on the recent experience of living through a global pandemic to add historical context that enables us to better see the risks and opportunities that disruption created. Ultimately, she reveals, contagion foregrounds questions of what it means to live as a human community, a mingle of risk and promise. Such narratives equally "can inspire radical change or retreat into the *status quo*" (Chapter 1, p. 28).

Phillip Wegner follows with an overview essay on utopianism and American exceptionalism, with an emphasis on the discontents challenging cozy certainties about America's role in the world. This chapter in many ways establishes the narrative against which texts discussed in the following chapters contend. As Wegner points out, the "notion of the US as single homogenous nation uniquely exempt from history" (Chapter 2, p. 43) is a dangerous fantasy, and sf has long served as a cultural mode that refuses to naturalize this hegemonic ideal.

Jennifer Wagner-Lawlor (Chapter 3) focuses on the traditions of feminist and queer utopian activism in the United States, sites of urgent enquiry in the era ushered in by the *Dobbs* decision and multiple bills at state and federal levels seeking to restrict gender-affirming care and LGBTQI rights. The recent downgrading of the US bond credit rating – sure to exacerbate rising economic inequality – was prompted by standoffs over the debt ceiling debate that largely had to do with riders targeting queer and transgender people, evidence of how intense the issue of gender identity is within the United States at this moment. Wagner-Lawlor charts the history of how feminist sf addresses these questions, underlining the need for greater attention to race in social reproduction activism.

Edward Chan and Patricia Ventura (Chapter 4) interrogate the troubled terrain of racial identity as it intersects with American utopianism, demonstrating the degree to which the mainstream ideal of the good life in the United States has always been founded on the fantasy of white supremacy and racial homogeneity. While critiquing recent texts that continue to celebrate and center whiteness, they simultaneously show that this ideology has never gone unchallenged.

Andrew Tate (Chapter 5) examines the utopianism attached to religion in the US context, a challenging topic given the degree to which alt-right versions of Christianity are central to many of the oppressive forces troubling US politics today, especially attacks on gender expression and women's bodily autonomy. Yet he also reminds us that the Puritan ideal of the "city on a hill" was not always focused on exclusion and material accumulation. He recovers a buried tradition of communitarianism that refused the project of wealth accumulation that now substitutes for the American Dream.

Jerry Rafiki Jenkins turns our attention to one of the most central questions that troubles American utopian projects, the experience of Black people in the country. Utopianism for Black people frequently has the horizon of escape from the dystopia that is Black life in America, resulting in a mode of utopianism within Black communities that stresses the quotidian present over the promised future. Yet as Jenkins argues, this positions Black culture as a productive space for rewriting the utopian, insisting that it must be a project of "liberating black life from social death at the dawn of the twenty-first century" (Chapter 6, p. 118). In a powerful analysis, Jenkins reveals how Black utopianism and Afro-pessimism are both necessary to address the afterlives of slavery, thereby opening a door toward a utopian future.

Addressing Indigenous and Latinx experience, Rubén Mendoza similarly reframes how we think about utopianism as he works through how Latinx cultures have created new modes of utopian praxis in the wake of the dystopian disruptions of their lifeworlds enacted by the (utopian) project of Euroamerican colonialism. In Latinx cultures, Mendoza charts a complex engagement with elements of precolonial culture, not as simple returns to a lost past, but as a dialectical engagement with the world as changed by modernity. In contrast with the totalizing visions often associated with the classical Western notion, Latinx utopian texts "present partial, fragmentary utopian visions that are deeply ambivalent, precarious, and focused on process" (Chapter 7, p. 134).

Jonathan Alexander (Chapter 8) takes up the question of young adult (YA) utopian texts, emphasizing the multiple ways in which a focus on youth intersects with the range of crises their generation is compelled to navigate, including the climate crisis, economic precarity, and attacks on gender identity. Yet YA texts can often convey a sense of quotidian utopianism in the sense that they present the existence of queer desire as normal, creating worlds in which the dystopian attacks on queer people so prevalent in recent US politics are absent from the protagonists' experiences.

Peter Boxall's chapter (Chapter 9) is in many ways a bookend companion piece to Wegner's, examining what becomes of utopian energies in mainstream American literature in a twenty-first century that lacks the smug assurance of American exceptionalism that characterized the twentieth century. We could suggest that the waning affect and faltering energy that Boxall diagnoses in the texts he discusses have gone elsewhere, infusing texts from feminist, queer, Black, Latinx, and Indigenous communities, as we see in the preceding chapters. Boxall's chapter skillfully explores how American culture responds when the fantasy of a homogeneous and hegemonic white American identity unravels.

Continuing the dialectic approach to utopianism, Matthew Wolf-Meyer explores the uneven relationship between technology and utopianism in US culture. As he argues, technology exists as "a blurred line that brings the utopian and dystopian into vibrant proximity, with one hand promising a possibility and with the other revealing that the promise comes at a deadly cost" (Chapter 10, p. 187). Much like the exceptionalism that has defined America's sense of itself among nations, the fantasy of technological utopianism often functions to suggest that humans alone among the living world need not face vulnerability and morality.

Roger Luckhurst (Chapter 11) examines a history of utopian spaces in US history, documenting how they often ended up being complicit in the very capitalist fantasies whose consequences they sought to escape. Although the period of communes in the United States had mostly ended before the period covered by this volume, Luckhurst demonstrates that many of their ideas persist in architectural projects to this day and indeed often inform the design of the kinds of technological utopian projects interrogated by Wolf-Meyer.

Gerry Canavan wrestles with the urgent topic of environmentalism, documenting how an emergent sense of environmental utopianism that took shape in the postwar period has declined into an overwhelming sense of dystopian inevitability. Environmentalism, he notes, is often suspicious of the kinds of techno-utopian fixes promoted by US corporations and green energy discourse. Yet he finds hope in the decolonial projects of Indigenous land activism, celebrating communities that "attempt with varying levels of success to put into practice the communitarian, anarchist, de-technologized, pastoralist, and Indigenous Futurist vision of many of the ecotopias" (Chapter 12, p. 232).

Hugh C. O'Connell (Chapter 13) turns to the equally urgent and related issue of economic justice, recovering a lost tradition of utopian economic reform articulated in the late twentieth century, but focusing strongly on the period after the 2008 crash. As he observes, utopianism has struggled with how to respond to a neoliberal moment that sought to present its policy choices as simply scientific operations of natural (hence inevitable) markets. Yet despite difficulties in addressing economic systems directly through utopian modes, there is a strong utopian tradition contesting the social changes caused by neoliberalism, especially the ecological crisis. A key utopian project, then, is connecting these social issues with economic conditions, especially in relation to contesting the rise of debt culture.

Continuing a critique of capitalism as a central agent of our dystopian present, Matthis Nilges turns more directly to the question of politics itself, which Jameson has argued is the aim of utopian praxis. While noting the limitation of liberal democracy as the horizon of political form – a perspective shared by many earlier chapters – Nilges finds a utopian kernel in the ideal of democracy as the voice of the demos, especially in a context of rising authoritarianism and emerging fascism. Yet this new democracy cannot be attached to the nation state, he insists, but instead "the power of the people [must bind] itself to the power of stories that are able to bring us together in the attempt to imagine ways to address the forms of injustice whose grip on our present and imagination seems so very difficult to loosen" (Chapter 14, p. 268).

Finally, John Rieder brings the volume to a close with a focus on new histories and what utopianism might mean into the twenty-first century and beyond. His chapter celebrates traditions of thinking and living that have mainly been marginalized in US culture up to this point, but whose utopian persistence in the face of such exclusion has been documented by the preceding chapters. Looking forward to an American utopianism that can overcome its parochial past, Rieder foregrounds a new and more diverse generation of American thinkers, who offer a utopianism that embodies "an array of different temporal frameworks that afford radically different possibilities for human agency and cohere with radically different political and ethical demands" (Chapter 15, p. 273).

The trajectory of this volume thus runs from opportunities for rethinking what we take to be the "good" society opened by the crisis of the Covid pandemic to the promise that American utopianism of the twenty-first century must be radically different from a static sense of the utopian as perfect society that came before. This volume does not aim to be the final word on the shape of this utopianism to come, but merely to insist on the need for the utopian now more than ever, and to begin to chart the pathway toward the utopianism needed for our times.

Notes

1. Walter Benjamin, "Thesis on the Philosophy of History," from *Illuminations: Essays and Reflections*. Edited and introduction by Hannah Arendt; translated by Harry Zohn (New York: Schocken Books, 1968), 253–254.

2. Benjamin, 258.
3. Benjamin, 258.
4. Benjamin, 254.
5. Benjamin, 255.
6. Ernst Bloch, *The Principle of Hope*, vol. 1, translated by Neville Plaice, Stephen Plaice and Paul Knight (Cambridge: MIT Press, 1986), 11.
7. José Estaban Muñoz, *Cruising Utopia: The Then and There of Queer Futurity* (New York: NYU Press, 2009).
8. Caroline Edwards, *Utopia and the Contemporary British Novel* (Cambridge: Cambridge University Press, 2019), 24–25.
9. Francis Fukuyama, *The End of History and the Last Man* (New York: Simon and Schuster, 1992).
10. Anindita Banerjee and Sherryl Vint, "Thinking through the Pandemic: A Symposium," *Science Fiction Studies* 47.3 (2020); 321–376.
11. The phrase technological solutionism is from Evgeny Morozov, *To Save Everything Click Here: The Folly of Technological Solutionism* (New York: Public Affairs, 2013). For a discussion of the faux utopianism of Silicon Valley, see Douglass Ruskoff, *Survival of the Richest: Escape Fantasies of Tech Billionaires* (New York: W. W. Norton, 2022). There is a left-wing version of technological utopianism, most influentially described by Aaron Bastani in *Fully Automated Luxury Communism* (London: Verso, 2019). Bastani is clear, however, that technology may be the means of a better future, but only through concerted political action, not merely as some inevitable outcome of better tools: "Nothing is certain about where these technologies will end, nor whose benefit they will serve. What is discernible, however, is that a disposition can be drawn from them – if only they are allied to a political project of collective solidarity and individual happiness . . . This is why Fully Automated Luxury Communism (FALC) is a politics rather than some inevitable future" (12).
12. Henry Luce, "The American Century," *Life* (February 17, 1941).
13. Kathi Weeks, *The Problem with Work: Feminism, Marxism, Antiwork Politics, and Postwork Imaginaries* (Durham, NC: Duke University Press, 2011), 224.
14. Ruth Wilson Gilmore, *Golden Gulag: Prisons, Surplus, Crisis, and Opposition in Globalizing California* (Berkeley: University of California Press, 2007), 11.
15. Dylan Rodriguez, *White Reconstruction: Domestic Warfare and the Logics of Genocide* (New York: Fordham University Press, 2020), 306, 303.
16. Avery F. Gordon, *The Hawthorn Archive: Letters from the Utopian Margins* (New York: Fordham University Press, 2017), v.
17. Gordon, 50.
18. Gordon, 63.
19. Ruth Levitas, *Utopia as Method: The Imaginary Reconstitution of Society* (London: Palgrave Macmillan, 2013). Kindle edition. Kindle location 96–99.
20. Levitas, Kindle location 122–124.
21. Levitas, Kindle location 560–561.

22. M. E. O'Brien and Eman Abdelhadi, *Everything for Everyone: An Oral History of the New York Commune, 2052–2072* (New York: Common Notions, 2022), 1.
23. O'Brien and Abdelhadi, 140.
24. Weeks, 146.
25. Gordon, 286.
26. Gordon, 64.
27. Laura Horn, Aysem Mert, and Franziska Müller (eds.), *Palgrave Handbook of Global Politics in the 22nd Century* (London: Palgrave Macmillan, 2023). They adopt a speculative notion of multiple parallels worlds in their introduction, drawing on Ted Chiang's sf, to explain how their contributors can write about a range of futures that often contradict one another. One innovative chapter, "Planetary Politics in the Twenty-Second Century" by Ian Manners (pp. 271–290), adopts a strategy similar to that used by Kim Stanley Robinson in his Three Californias trilogy (discussed in several chapters that follow). Robinson imagines three different futures for Orange County based on a catastrophe, a continuation of then-current hegemonic views, and a utopian transformation. Manners similarly analyses the political structure of three entangled worlds that he labels the status quo, the capitalist, and the symbiotic universes, showing how political science and human possibilities for thriving differ across each.
28. See Melinda Cooper, *Family Values: Between Neoliberalism and the New Social Conservatism* (New York: Zone Books, 2017) for an in-depth analysis of the long-term consequences of these shifts, specifically on how the rise of the new conservatism undid the achievements of social activism for equality during the 1960s and 1970s, especially her discussion of economic policies that targeted the social welfare programs that mitigated the inequalities fostered by generations of racism.
29. These issues – accumulation and racial hierarchization – are really a single problem. As Robyn Maynard notes in her exchange of letters with Leanne Betasamosake Simpson, *Rehearsals for Living* (Chicago: Haymarket Books, 2022), "Du Bois warned, after all in 1935 – nearly a century ago now – that the privileges of whiteness (the 'wages of whiteness') are most importantly psychological privileges, even as they are undoubtedly lived in a material sense as well. He warned that only precious few, even white, would escape the ravages and violence of an economic system predicated on the exploitation of nearly all of us, if unevenly distributed across racial lines. It is absurd, monstrous, that it has taken a global pandemic of all things to bring this reality to light, and even then, only partially" (71). This exchange of letters is another example of the kind of everyday utopianism that can incrementally shift things toward a more radical transformation. Maynard and Simpson offer one another mutual support, cultivate solidarity by sharing their histories, and document daily practices of thriving despite state violence. Their publisher, Haymarket, is named for an important labor uprising that took place in Chicago in 1886, another reminder that every day people practice and insist upon other ways of living.

30. For example, although I would by no means want to amplify or otherwise engage with these documents, it is difficult to fail to take note of the fact that online manifestos composed by racist mass shooting criminals often evoke utopian language to describe their actions. While not specifically American, we see similar logics at work in projects to construct putatively utopian habitations in locations such as Dubai, where opportunities to experience great luxury are built on the backs of exploited labor and dispossessed locals, an imitation of American exceptionalism as utopia. See Simon Spiegel, *Utopias in Nonfiction Film* (London: Palgrave Macmillan, 2022), chapter 7 on what Spiegel calls utopian propaganda; and Lucy Sargisson, *Fool's Gold? Utopianism in the Twenty-First Century* (London: Palgrave Macmillan, 2012), especially chapter 8 on architecture and utopianism.
31. Levitas, Kindle location 4742.
32. Sargisson, 22.
33. David Bell, *Rethinking Utopia: Place, Power, Affect* (London: Routledge, 2017), 10.
34. Bell, 9.
35. Sargisson, 5.
36. Cat Moir, *Ernst Bloch's Speculative Materialism: Ontology, Epistemology, Politics* (Leiden: Brill, 2019), 13.
37. Tom Moylan, *Demand the Impossible: Science Fiction and the Utopian Imagination*, reprint edition, edited by Raffaella Baccolini (Oxford: Peter Lang, 2014), 1.
38. Tom Moylan, *Scraps of Untainted Sky: Science Fiction, Utopia, Dystopia* (New York: Routledge, 2000), xii.
39. Greg Forter, *Critique and Utopia in Postcolonial Historical Fiction* (Oxford: Oxford University Press, 2019), 10.
40. Fredric Jameson, *Postmodernism, or, The Cultural Logic of Late Capitalism* (Durham, NC: Duke University Press, 1992), 385.
41. Fredric Jameson, *Archaeologies of the Future: The Desire Called Utopia and Other Science Fictions* (London: Verso, 2007), xi.
42. Fredric Jameson, *Marxism and Form* (Princeton, NJ: Princeton University Press, 1974), 68.
43. Fredric Jameson, *Valences of the Dialectic* (London: Verso, 2010), 197.
44. Kim Stanley Robinson, "Remarks on Utopia in the Age of Climate Change," *Utopian Studies* 27.1 (2016), 2–15 (8).
45. Robinson, 8.
46. Jameson explores this in his essay "Progress versus Utopian; Or, Can We Imagine the Future?" *Science Fiction Studies* 9.2 (1982), 147–158. This is most likely the essay Robinson has in mind when he talks about what we struggle to imagine.
47. Grace Dillon, "Imagining Indigenous Futurism," from *Walking the Clouds: An Anthology of Indigenous Science Fiction* (Tucson: University of Arizona Press, 2012), 1–14.
48. Bell, 65.

49. Mark Rifkin, *Fictions of Land and Flesh: Blackness, Indigeneity, Speculation* (Durham, NC: Duke University Press, 2019), 65–66.
50. Glen Sean Coulthard, *Red Skins, White Masks: Rejecting the Colonial Politics of Recognition* (Minneapolis: University of Minnesota Press, 2014), 24.
51. Moylan, *Becoming*, 38–39.

CHAPTER I

Pandemics and the Lesson of History

Priscilla Wald

White letters appear ominously, soundlessly against a black screen: "The single biggest threat to man's continued dominance on the planet is the virus." The epigraph opens Wolfgang Petersen's 1995 cinematic medical thriller *Outbreak*, in which epidemiologists race to contain a potentially species-threatening pandemic. Five years later, the author of the quotation, the Nobel Laureate microbiologist Joshua Lederberg, would forecast in the journal *Science* that "the future of humanity and microbes likely will unfold as episodes of a suspense thriller that could be titled *Our Wits Versus Their Genes*."[1] Lederberg's keen understanding of popular culture as an effective way to draw attention to the urgent problem of what he called "emerging infections" had led him to leak the story of a close call with an Ebola virus to the journalist Richard Preston, resulting in a widely circulating, sensational *New Yorker* article in 1994 that became the best-selling book *The Hot Zone: A Terrifying True Story*. In turn, *The Hot Zone* inspired *Outbreak*, which drew its chilling reproduction of a Biosafety Level 4 lab and the effects of a hemorrhagic virus from Preston's vivid descriptions. Preston's work and Petersen's film had the desired effect: emerging infections – catastrophic communicable diseases and the potentially species-threatening pandemics they could cause – became part of a cultural vocabulary, inspiring, in the process, the proliferation of pandemic novels and films.

Lederberg and his colleagues had helped to generate what would become the plotline of a familiar story following a 1989 conference, principally organized by the epidemiologist Stephen Morse, on "Emerging Viruses: The Evolution of Viruses and Viral Diseases" at the end of the decade in which HIV/AIDS had brought the phenomenon of newly emerging catastrophic communicable diseases to the attention of medical communities worldwide. The phenomenon, especially HIV/AIDS, had punctured the sanguinity of a medical establishment that had begun to imagine communicable disease as no longer posing a serious threat to humanity, serving as a harbinger of what would happen if humans failed to change the way they were inhabiting the world (in geopolitical terms) and the planet (its environment). The scientific and journalistic publications in the wake of the meeting warned that a growing population moving into previously uninhabited areas – and hence encountering microbes unfamiliar to human populations – combined with an increasingly interconnected world produced the ideal conditions for outbreaks of these infections and for the outbreaks to become pandemics. These works – notable among them, Laurie Garrett's best-selling *The Coming Plague*, which included an account of the 1989 meeting – became the basis for a storyline with enormous mass appeal, as evinced by the rapid proliferation of journalistic, fictional, and cinematic treatments of what I have called "the outbreak narrative."[2]

These medical thrillers conventionally begin with an outbreak of a catastrophic communicable disease in a jungle in the Global South that quickly explodes or threatens to explode into a species-threatening event until contained by heroic researchers and epidemiologists in the Global North. They are, however, but one manifestation of a longer literary fascination with pandemics. As the Covid-19 pandemic quickly dramatized, humans are social beings. We depend on each other for survival – physical, social, even spiritual. But implicit in that dependence is also considerable risk. Whether deliberate or unwitting, humans pose a threat to one another. Contagion makes that risk starkly visible. An analogue for what it means to be human, contagion manifests our social being.

A long tradition of pandemic – or plague – literature, dating back at least as far as classical Greece, has accordingly used catastrophic communicable disease as a backdrop to explore the human condition: what it means to live in a community of other humans, and, as awareness of the crises of environmental devastation and climate change grows, on a planet with other living organisms. The message Lederberg and his colleagues hoped to convey following the 1989 meeting was that humans were not just characters in the episodes of the forecasted suspense thriller, but also the authors of it. In different ways, and with differing resolutions, works of pandemic fiction expose the terms of that authorship, showing how the crisis stems not only from human practices, but also from the values, beliefs, and stories about the past – the histories – in which they are rooted. Whether dystopic or utopic, apocalyptic or resolved, literary pandemics warn that in order to change the way humans collectively inhabit the world, we need to change the dominant stories we tell about it.

Historians, observes the historian William McNeill, assemble facts into patterns they then fashion into stories. In turn, those stories circulate values and beliefs as unquestioned truths that facilitate groups' coherence. These stories of the past – histories – are, McNeill explains, "the great secret of human power over nature and over ourselves as well. Pattern recognition is what natural scientists are up to; it is what historians have always done, whether they knew it or not."[3] McNeill calls these stories mythistories to mark the distinction between how they appear to insiders (as truths) and to outsiders (as beliefs), but the term also conveys the enchanting transportive quality that inspires group coherence. Literary pandemics throw into relief the vulnerabilities in social structures and global infrastructures – the priorities, the inequities, the power and risk differentials, all upheld by values and beliefs – that turn local outbreaks into global pandemics.

As a crisis such as a pandemic elucidates the need for change, it may bring the terms of the mythistory into view. In Laura Van Den Berg's 2015 pandemic novel *Find Me*, a doctor studying the disease explains "that the smallest alteration can create the perfect atmosphere for a new disease to emerge," noting, "the world is a very fragile place." But the narrator, Joy, finds the explanation in a book about the Mayans more persuasive: "the author says they were wiped out by a plague, that every so often 'incurables' appear and civilizations are reset."[4]

Literary pandemics, ranging from verisimilitude to fabulation, offer a variety of resolutions. In many, the crisis is averted or contained, and the social order is maintained, even affirmed. In others, the effect of the pandemic, hence the reset, is more extreme. Some usher in a dystopic future, but many offer the possibility of rebuilding a more just and sustainable world. Some of the most fantastical culminate in a revolutionary transformation of society or even an evolutionary metamorphosis of the species. Whatever the resolution in the fiction, literary pandemics manifest a world out of order and the need for a reset. Where Lederberg and his colleagues recognized the need for humans to change our practices, literary pandemics often show how such transformations would require a radical change in our stories and the values and beliefs they circulate.

In Peng Shepherd's 2018 *The Book of M*, the leader of a group making its way through a world radically transformed by a mysterious disease insists on saving as many books from the Library of Congress as they can carry. Contrary to expectation, he orders them to collect not the "medical textbooks and technical manuals" his followers assume would contain the information they may need in the future, but rather "novels, story collections, biographies, history, memoir," including his infected husband's poetry.[5] As his dubious interlocutors come to understand, those works contain the most information about who we (humans) are, or have been, and who we might become. Perhaps in the contemporary moment – in the third decade of the twenty-first century and in the wake of a global pandemic – our pandemic novels may offer that much-needed insight.

Plagues and the Sacred

Early progenitors of contemporary literary pandemics, plagues in the ancient world magnified the disruption of other forms of natural disaster because of their duration and mystery. In literary works, they often signaled a pollution of some kind: an offense against a god or a disruption in the social order. Oedipus did not need knowingly to kill his father, marry his mother, and sire their children to embody such a pollution and to plunge Thebes into a multiyear plague. As literary descriptions suggest, the irrationality of a sudden sickness visited on a population led to collective introspection as community leaders – political, medical, religious – searched for answers.

Then, as now, there is something sacred about the experience of a pandemic, something that accords particularly with the original meaning of the word "sacred," which, as the early twentieth-century German philosopher Rudolf Otto contends, preceded its subsequent religious, theological, even moral designations. The term in early Greek, Hebrew, or Latin, argues Otto, names a feeling of "daemonic dread"[6] or "creature-feeling": "the emotion of a creature, submerged and overwhelmed by its own nothingness in contrast to that which is supreme above all creatures."[7] "It is this feeling," for Otto, "which, emerging in the mind of a primeval man, forms the starting-point for the entire religious development in history. 'Daemons' and 'gods' alike spring from this root, and all the products of 'mythological apperception' or 'fantasy' are nothing but different models in which it has been objectified."[8] It is Oedipus crying out against the inexplicable forces that led to his unthinkable – and unpardonable – transgressions.

Such plagues offer a chance for expiation and an opportunity for cleansing. *Oedipus Rex* follows the arrogant king's growing, and humbling, realization that he is the source of the pollution, the defilement that has caused the plague. Oedipus's actions have resulted in a troubling confusion of kinship categories on which his social order rests: his mother is his wife;

his children are his siblings. For Sigmund Freud, his patricide and incest violate the two prohibitions absolutely necessary for maintaining the social order. But these are explanations, and, as Otto insists, the true meaning of "*heilig*" (sacred or holy) is that "creature feeling" of being helpless in the face of the irrational. "The fact is," he explains, "we have come to use the words 'holy,' 'sacred' (*heilig*) in an entirely derivative sense, quite different from that which they originally bore." We take the term to mean "the absolute moral attribute, denoting the consummation of moral goodness," something "imperative upon conduct and universally obligatory." But such is "a clear overplus of meaning."[9] The feeling certainly can inform morality, which in turn may well correspond to the exigencies of social order, but the feeling is more primal. Plagues are reminders of human fragility and the impending chaos of the natural world that haunts the social order.

As they capture that experience, literary pandemics can inspire retreat from that insight into affirmation of the social order and its mythistory or acceptance of the insight, with the possibility for change. Stories told by the young people who take shelter from a plague in Giovanni Boccaccio's late medieval *Decameron* offer lessons reaffirming social values. Albert Camus's plague, by contrast, manifests the fundamental irrationality of existence and fruitless desire for meaning; selflessness emerges and community forms in the absence of such meaning, not because of it: "creature-feeling," an acceptance of the irrational, conjoins Camus's survivors. Literary plagues have often culminated in a renewed commitment to – even a utopian aspiration for – a more communitarian spirit.

Contemporary plague narratives, journalistic as well as fictional and cinematic, highlight the conditions that have produced pandemics. We (humans) are defiling the planet, producing those conditions – social, geopolitical, and environmental, as Lederberg and his colleagues had warned – through which these disease-causing microbes thrive. We are the "traffic engineers" moving them around the globe as goods and people circulate.[10] The deadly Shen fever spreads on exports from China in Ling Ma's 2018 pandemic novel *Severance*, leaving few human survivors and a collapsed social order. "If the End was Nature's way of punishing us so that we might once again know our place," muses Ma's narrator, Candace, "then yes, we knew it. If it was at all unclear before, it was not now."[11] After all, observes the virologist Karl M. Johnson in a publication following the "Emerging Viruses" conference, "our earth is, in fact, a progressively immunocompromised ecosystem."[12]

Yet even as growing scientific insight into disease-causing microbes increasingly unravels the mysteries of contagion, the experience of a pandemic has retained something of the primal affect Otto describes. In *The Hot Zone*, Preston recounts the response of a researcher who, realizing he had unwittingly exposed himself to an Ebola virus, is both terrified and mesmerized by the "breathtaking . . . beauty" of "the life form thing." As he contemplates the "virus particles shaped like snakes . . . white cobras tangled among themselves, like the hair of Medusa . . . the face of Nature herself, the obscene goddess revealed naked," he has the bewitching sensation of being drawn "out of the human world into a world where moral boundaries blur and finally dissolve completely."[13] Although an ecstatic world of pure being is unsustainable, it is a moment of visionary possibility and Benjaminian danger; the insights it offers can inspire radical change or retreat into the status quo.[14]

Utopianism and Its Discontents

An apparently ineluctable animation of microbes is evident in the metaphors of scientific and journalistic works in which, for example, "enemy" microbes declare "war" on humanity. These metaphors become plotlines in some of the more fantastical medical thrillers that bring mystical viruses to life. Some vilify the microbe, as in Chuck Hogan's *Blood Artists* and Robin Cook's *Invasion* (a rewriting of Jack Finney's *The Body Snatchers*), which cast them as spokes-beings for an aggrieved planet. "Innocent plants and sinless animals will be spared," intones Hogan's human/viral hybrid, explaining his intention to seed outbreaks of a nearly 100 percent fatal virus in order to annihilate "only the criminal man. The planet will rejoice as I rid its crust of his plague."[15] Humanity's defeat of the microbes affirms the status quo.

Whether a chastened humanity will learn to live more harmoniously in its habitat, however, remains a question that draws readers into humanity's complicity. Although pandemics are endemic to human history, pandemic fiction typically forecasts a future to which contemporary readers have therefore in some fashion contributed. Carl Freedman identifies a "science-fiction tendency," which he sees as not only integral to, but "the precondition for the constitution of fictionality – and even of representation" that acts as a reminder of readers' historicity.[16] Science fiction (sf) "turns the actual present – the empirical present of the reader – into a potential and historicized past."[17] Istvan Csicsery-Ronay, Jr., calling sf a "direct heir" of history, notes "by maintaining a sense of the integral connection between the present and the future, science fiction constructs micromyths of the historical process, establishing the audience's present as the future-oriented 'prehistory of the future.'"[18] Works of sf put on display the consequences of contemporary actions, showing how contemporary readers are not just historical actors, but also authors, how we are not just living in, but actually making history, authoring the episodes of Lederberg's medical thriller that future humans will live.

A pandemic throws into relief both the systemic and structural problems of the social order – the inequities, for example, that find expression in the differential morbidity and mortality rates across populations and the practices that are making the planet increasingly unlivable – and the role of history in perpetuating them. As they offer an opportunity to reflect on those problems, they raise questions about what actions might be taken to change that self-perpetuating history and, in the process, to forestall such catastrophes – how, to draw on Lederberg's terms, "our wits" might prove victorious over "their genes." In the fictional outbreak narratives that proliferated in the 1990s following the "Emerging Viruses" conference, "our wits" typically meant science and medicine; those narratives end with heroic medical researchers and epidemiologists developing vaccines and pharmaceuticals that contain the threat or, in the case of the more fantastical bioterror, discovering and thwarting the viral villain or its human conspirators. In so doing, that version of the pandemic narrative works, contra the explicit message of the conference, against the need for more widespread changes.

Not all past literary pandemics adhere to that formula, however; some have been apocalyptic and world changing, ending either in a reboot of society, as in George R. Stewart's *Earth Abides*, in which the few survivors of a global pandemic hopefully begin human society anew, or in an entirely new order, as in Richard Matheson's *I Am Legend*, in which the virus ends the human species. The main protagonist of *Earth Abides*, a geography graduate student named Isherwood Williams, bears witness – as the remnants of the complex civilization he hopes to rebuild gradually fail – to a new generation of humans who grow up with knowledge and communitarian values that leave them better equipped than Ish's generation to thrive on the planet. By contrast, the virus in *I Am Legend* turns all but one immune human being into vampiric creatures. The novel follows Robert Neville on his daily killing sprees to rid the world of the "monsters" until he is captured. It ends with his realization that he was now the anomaly who had to be exterminated and transformed into a "legend" that would help to form the basis for the emerging (literally posthuman) society.

The implications of Matheson's novel are not easily digested. Of its three cinematic adaptations – *The Last Man on Earth* (1964), *Omega Man* (1971), and *I Am Legend* (2007) – only the first followed Matheson in making the disease both the result of naturally occurring bacteria and the evolutionary beginning of a new species on earth. Both *Omega Man* and *I Am Legend* hold out hope for a possible cure, hence humanity's survival. In an essay penned in the wake of the 1989 conference, Lederberg acknowledges the difficulty of accepting the significance of the microbial challenge: "It is scary to imagine the emergence of new infectious agents as threats to human existence, especially threatening to view pandemic as a recurrent, natural phenomenon," not least because of its challenge to human exceptionalism. "Many people find it difficult," he observes, "to accommodate to the reality that Nature is far from benign, at least it has no special sentiment for the welfare of the human versus other species."[19]

If the survival of the human species is not preordained, its finitude definitively is: as part of the organic world, the species will inevitably either go extinct or evolve into something unrecognizable hence, to many, threatening. But the evolutionary theme can also take a more utopic turn, as it does at least in part in novels such as Nicola Griffith's *Ammonite* and Larissa Lai's *The Tiger Flu* and, in a different vein, Greg Bear's *Darwin's Radio* and *Darwin's Children* and Mike Carey's *The Girl with All the Gifts* and *The Boy on the Bridge*. Both *Ammonite*, which takes place on another planet, and *The Tiger Flu*, set on a ravaged future earth, begin with the premise that a virus has killed off all (*Ammonite*) or most (*The Tiger Flu*) of the men and some of the women. All of the women in *Ammonite* and some in *The Tiger Flu* have evolved to reproduce through parthenogenesis. While that ability is no guarantee of the utopic community that Charlotte Perkins Gilman had imagined in *Herland*, communitarianism is a characteristic of some of the communities in *Ammonite* and in the single all-female community in *The Tiger Flu*, which has developed a more communal and naturopathic existence in an otherwise dystopic (violent and polluted) world.

Greg Bear, by contrast, builds on the scientific theory that viruses cause saltational evolution as he explores humanity's resistance to evolutionary change. The children born following the virus are gifted with telepathic communication and other skills, including a capacity for empathy, that far exceed those of their progenitors. Offering the promise of a much-improved social order, they are nonetheless hunted, persecuted, and incarcerated by governments that perceive them as a threat. The evolutionary leap in Carey's novels is the result of *Ophiocordyceps unilateralis*, a fungus that turns humans into zombie-like creatures but transforms the babies born of women infected while pregnant into a new intelligent and fully functional species. Viewed as "monsters" by the uninfected humans who seek to destroy or contain them, the new species is more physically robust than their human progenitors, and, like the succeeding (human) generations in *Earth Abides* and the evolved species of Bear's novels, more communitarian and more respectful of, and adapted to survival on, the planet.

Changing the Story

The viral-induced metamorphoses in these novels variously elucidate the human exceptionalism that is fundamental to the mythistory of many contemporary cultures. While the conventional outbreak narrative often demonizes the environmental perspective, the evolved beings of these works manifest more enlightenment. They embody the advice Lederberg offers for a more salutary way of inhabiting the planet when he counsels, "our most sophisticated leap would be to drop the manichaean view of microbes – 'We good; they evil' . . . Perhaps one of the most important changes we can make is to super[s]ede the 20th-century metaphor for describing the relationship between infectious agents" and to replace it with "a more ecologically informed metaphor, which includes the germs'-eye view of infection."[20]

From a germs'-eye view, the world is a system of interconnected networks, of pathways linking all living organisms to each other and to their environments. Through a germs'-eye view, we can see more clearly the opportunities humans create for germs to traverse the globe. A germs'-eye view is also a lesson in evolution, showing how human practices and behaviors – including prophylaxes – can contribute to the microbial transformations that enable them to survive: another episode of *Our Wits Versus Their Genes.* Remarkably, the Nobel Laureate microbiologist sees the key to humanity's survival as a change in metaphor, which for Lederberg corresponds to a different way of understanding the world. The war metaphor perpetuates an understanding of microbes as a pernicious threat to human health: humans at war with our microbes – good versus evil; us versus them. Thinking more ecologically and less militaristically is, for him, better science. The human body is a microbiome composed of microbiota without which we cannot survive. Working with beneficial microbes is more effective than focusing only on the ones that cause disease in humans.

But the metaphor has social and geopolitical implications as well. Implicit in Lederberg's formulation is the assumption that language registers a world view, or mythistory. Mythistories not only create order out of the chaos of the world, but also create a coherent inside against a discernible outside: "'us' versus 'them.'"[21] "Finding the right things to lump together and the right words to focus attention on critical transitions," notes McNeill,

> is the special work of human intelligence – whether applied to history or to everyday encounters with the world. Nearly everything is done for us by the language we inherit that generalizes and organizes the flow of sensory experience with every noun and verb we employ. But myth makers and myth breakers are entrusted with the task of adjusting and improving received ways of understanding and reacting to the world.[22]

Lederberg is acting as a myth breaker in his injunction to replace the military metaphors with ecological ones.

Mythistories become most visible at moments of collective crisis – turning points in which a group's survival is literally or metaphysically at stake. While Lederberg intends, in the metaphor exchange, to offer a lesson in microbiology, he effectively also suggests two ways of looking at evolution, both derived from Charles Darwin. The Malthusian influence on Darwin's *On the Origin of Species* finds expression in a depiction of life as struggle, competition, and warfare. This animated and brutal zero-sum game between "us-es" and "thems" has so permeated the concept of natural selection that it may seem "unscientific" to tell this story in a different way. It is a *truth* in a scientific mythistory of humanity. But Darwin's origin story offers an alternative depiction, following Alexander von Humboldt, of the interconnection of all living organisms, "plants and animals, most remote in the scale of nature ... bound together by a web of complex relations" in which "cattle absolutely determine the existence of ... Scotch fir" and "insects determine the existence of cattle."[23] Cooperation is at least as beneficial to survival as competition, and natural selection is as at least as miraculous as it is violent.

Not Warriors but Historians

Pandemics confront humanity with our finitude. They can be meditations on individual mortality, as in Katherine Anne Porter's *Pale Horse, Pale Rider* and Camus's *The Plague*, or on the impermanence of the species, as in Mary Shelley's nineteenth-century *The Last Man*. They might end hopefully, if mournfully, with a small band of survivors seeding, or hoping to seed, a new way of inhabiting the world, as in *Earth Abides* and Emily St. John Mandel's *Station Eleven*, or uncertainly in the midst of the plague, as in Boccaccio's *The Decameron*. Or they might inaugurate the dystopic worlds of *The Tiger Flu*, Geoff Ryman's *The Child Garden*, and Margaret Atwood's Maddaddam trilogy. The recent proliferation of more fantastical metamorphoses, from the evolutionary emergence of a new and better adapted species, as in Bear's and Carey's novels, or the vampires and zombies of *I Am Legend*, Colson Whitehead's *Zone One*, and Del Toro and Chuck Hogan's *The Stain* trilogy, suggest a growing tendency to challenge human exceptionalism and suggest the species' inevitable finitude.

As the twenty-first century unfolds, both realist and fantastical pandemic novels are increasingly less sanguine about the possibility of a return to the status quo and more likely to stress the need for a reset of civilization if the species survives. Lawrence Wright's *The End of October*, which came out in the midst of the Covid-19 pandemic in 2020, ends with the dystopic scenario, which Lederberg also predicted, in which a "microbial war" becomes a global biowar. The deadly Kongoli virus, having ravaged the world, reignites the Cold War, which turns hot when the superpowers open the freezers in which they have stored the world's deadliest communicable diseases: "the first great biowar was underway, and unlike all other wars, no one could stop it."[24]

The end of the novel finds the epidemiologist protagonist, Henry Parsons, boarding the USS *Georgia*, the submarine in which he plans to ride out the war with his children and the boat's crew. But he has a final mission on land: to track down the source of Kongoli, which they have traced back to October Revolution Island, where Henry knew the Soviet Union had had a bioweapon facility. As he tells the Navy SEALS who accompany him, "We are not acting as warriors but as historians. … One day, people will ask, 'Who did this to us?' And we will have the evidence. History will make its judgments based on what we find."[25]

The evidence he finds, however, is not what he expects. Having learned some polar bears had been relocated to October Revolution Island after an ice floe deposited them in a Russian town, Henry suspects they had found their way into the abandoned laboratory where they were exposed to the products of abandoned bioweapons research. Instead, he discovers the bears died after feasting on an extinct woolly mammoth, which had been exposed by melting permafrost and which was carrying Kongoli, the ancient deadly progenitor of influenza. In turn, cranes feasting on the dead bears carried Kongoli to China, where the first human cases had appeared. Both the bears' relocation to this desolate spot and the deadly meal on which they feasted were the result, not of bioterror, even incidentally, but of the human-induced catastrophe of climate change. "Well, doc, what are we going to tell history?" asks the leader of the SEAL team. "Henry looked up. The last flock of Siberian cranes had taken flight, headed for China. 'We're going to say that we did this to ourselves.'"[26]

Although the ending is bleaker than the resolution of the classic outbreak narrative, there is still a hint of hope. At one point in the novel, Henry ponders how "survivors [of the 1918 pandemic] rarely talked about it afterward." While survivors of the Great Depression, world wars, and terrorist attacks all "lived their lives with one eye on the past even as they moved on . . . [writing] books . . . join[ing] societies . . . ha[ving] reunions . . . [bringing] their grandchildren to view the battled fields . . . [getting] therapy . . . survivors of the 1918 flu did their best to purge the episode from their memories – and, therefore, from history."[27] And he wonders if this lack of remembering might be propelling a "sleepwalking [humanity] toward a pointless, civilization-annihilating conflict, astride another great pandemic."[28]

Perhaps in thinking of himself as a historian rather than a warrior, Henry imagines the history he documents could break the pattern in the future world he anticipates and be the necessary "reset" for civilization. Despite the unleashing of "the instruments of the apocalypse,"[29] Henry clearly does not believe he is witnessing the end of humanity as he prepares for his and his children's survival on the *Georgia*, assuring them, as he leaves for his mission, he will "be back in time for dinner. And then we'll stay underwater until the war is over. We'll be safe."[30] Henry's faith in the future is matched by his faith in history, evidently subscribing to the philosopher George Santayana's famous aphorism, "those who cannot remember the past are condemned to repeat it."[31]

Remembering the past, however, does not inevitably forestall its repetition. On the contrary, history – mythistory – often has the opposite effect, endlessly recirculating beliefs and values as unquestionable truths. Literary pandemics make clear the need for change not only in how humans inhabit the world, but also in the stories we tell about ourselves, past as well as present. *Severance*, *Find Me*, and *The Book of M* – all contemporary first novels written within the half-decade before SARS-CoV-2 realized Lederberg's warnings – suggest a trend in outbreak narratives away from reestablishing the status quo and instead revisiting the past in order to reimagine the future.

Memory, individual as well as collective, is a problem in all three novels. The infected in *Severance* are literally stuck in the past; a fungus that attacks the brain leaves them mindlessly performing habitual practices – setting a table, lifting a fork, reading a book, even operating dead machinery, or endlessly pickling moldy or desiccated produce – until their bodies wear down completely, and they die. The "fevered," Candace explains, "were creatures of habit, mimicking old routines and gestures they must have inhabited for years, decades."[32] Nostalgia, a longing for the comforts of the habitual and familiar, is a predisposing factor in the infection. Ma describes Shen Fever as "a disease of remembering," in which "the fevered are trapped indefinitely in their memories."[33]

The diseases in *Find Me* and *The Book of M* cause memory loss, especially the attributes of identity and kinship. The narrator of *Find Me*, Joy, describes "an epidemic of forgetting" in which the infected lose any sense of self and, gradually, even "sight betrays them. They see things that aren't there. The once solid world dissolves like a brick of sugar left out in the rain."[34] "What is a memory but the telling of a story," she muses, thinking of the entire period of her childhood she cannot recall, the traumatic result, we learn, of sexual abuse. Maybe "we stop remembering," she considers, because "there is a part of our story that we do not know how to tell to ourselves and we will away its existence for so long that finally our brain agrees to a trade: I will let you forget this, but you will never feel whole."[35] She imagines her own missing memory as "a little black spot . . . eating away at [her] brain like a fungus," and she wonders if "the sickness" similarly "takes those dark stains that exist within us and melts them down into a lake of forgetting."[36] She considers, moreover, that her dark spot may even account for her immunity to the disease; maybe "the sickness circled [her] and took a whiff and decided that [her] own memory was already doing the work it wanted to do, the work of forgetting."[37] Perhaps a traumatized humanity urgently needed a "reset of civilization."

The narrators of both *Severance* and *Find Me* are survivors. Although the pandemic has ended in *Find Me* and is still underway in *Severance*, the narrators are both pregnant and moving at once hopefully and tentatively into uncertainty: Joy in search of a mother she never knew; Candace in search of a place she can put down roots "for Luna, the child of two rootless people . . . [who] will be born untethered from all family except [Candace], without a hometown or a place of origin."[38] In *The Book of M*, the disease known as The Forgetting forces a more radical reset. The transformations caused by The Forgetting require a new way of inhabiting not only the world, but memory itself.

Those Who Cannot Remember the Past

"Sometimes science seemed like magic," observes one of Shepherd's characters.[39] The Forgetting begins subtly in a spice market in Pune, India on Zero Shadow Day, the semi-annual phenomenon in which, in locations between the Tropics of Cancer and Capricorn, the sun is directly overhead at noon, briefly causing the disappearance of all shadows. There is, however, no scientific explanation when the shadow of one man in the Pune spice market, Hemu Joshi, does not return. No one can explain why "Hemu Joshi stayed shadowless and free," and "for three magical days the entire world watched Hemu Joshi dance around untethered to the earth, captivated by the ununderstandable beauty of it. Magic."[40] Until the magic becomes dark, as Hemu begins to forget, failing to recognize his surroundings, his brothers, his name. And the dark "magic" quickly spreads as groups repeat Hemu's experience, first on successive Zero Shadow Days and soon randomly worldwide.

"Remembering [a] false memory," Joy remarks in *Find Me*, "can make you feel like you are rewriting the past, reordering the laws of physics, which of course you are not."[41] In *The Book of M*, the shadowless do just that, literally altering the material world as they misremember it. A buck appears with wings on its head in place of antlers; streets are reordered, and when Hemu fails to remember the Pune spice market, it disappears, along with the people in it. Shadowed and shadowless alike must negotiate the chaotic terrain of an endlessly metamorphosing world.

The initial joy at Hemu's "untethering" from the earth suggests humanity's widespread sense of being bound to a planet – or a fate (mortality) – it wishes to escape. It is a dangerous wish, as the philosopher Hannah Arendt warned in her 1958 study of *The Human Condition*. Arendt was troubled by the media's response to the first successful launching of Sputnik, not "pride and awe at the tremendousness of human power and mastery," but "relief about 'the first step toward escape from men's imprisonment to the earth.'"[42] It is disturbingly escapist to believe survival is not only desirable, she cautions, but even possible beyond "the earth [that] is the very quintessence of the human condition."[43] Such escapism obviates the need for change. Hemu confesses that the loss of his shadow does not make him forget, but "makes it *possible*" to do so. He is drawn to a "*feeling*" or "pull" that gets "better and better" as he goes "toward it." Even the memory loss is worth what he gets in return: "*Magic*," he whispers furtively to a trusted interlocutor.[44]

At the same time, Hemu, struggling to make sense of the phenomenon, shares with the interlocutor – an amnesiac from New Orleans who had lost his retrograde memory in a car accident shortly before The Forgetting – two stories he remembers even when he cannot remember his name. In the first, a variant of a myth he attributes to the *Rigveda*, Sanjna, goddess of the clouds, marries Surya, god of the sun, only to find she cannot tolerate his brightness; she leaves Chhaya – her mortal likeness, sometimes referred to as her shadow – in her place and hides in the forest as a mare. Her father enables her return by sufficiently reducing Surya's brightness.

The second is the account of a famous elephant, Gajarajan Guruvayur Keshavan, who was captured as a young calf and lived most of his life in the Guruvayur temple. A group of elephants is called "a memory of elephants," Hemu explains, and they have collective memories.[45] In Hemu's telling, Gajarajan (meaning Elephant King) had a sister, born after his capture, whom a biologist taught to paint. The "magic" happens when Gajarajan, having gained access to some paint, furiously paints the biologist who was the subject of most of his sister's paintings, despite never having met either one.

Gradually, the amnesiac makes sense of the stories, as he comes to understand the importance of both collective memories, which for humans are shaped by the circulation of stories – myths and histories – and personal memories, which, located in the shadow, are necessary for an expression of selfhood that "tethers" us to the world. Because the amnesiac is liberated from the constraints of his earliest socialization by his retrograde amnesia, he experiences the world of The Forgetting with less mediation than most, and he becomes the near-mythical figure "The One Who Gathers," as all who wish to remember – shadowed and shadowless alike – find themselves inexorably drawn to the assisted living residence for dementia patients in New Orleans, where he is working with his doctors to help the afflicted retain their memories. Blinded during a storm, in classical mythic tradition, he completes his radical metamorphosis; his shadow becomes Gajarajan while remaining attached to his human body: "two things completely independent of each other except for the point where their two pairs of feet met."[46] He becomes – literally – two conjoined beings, human and elephant. Unlike the shadowless who give in to the pull of magic, he remains tethered to the earth, the material world; but, unlike the shadowed, he is not bound by the procrustean limitations of an inherited mythistory. He can, that is, draw on collective memories and a collective imagination to forge a new kind of community.

Two premises govern the New Orleans community: an acceptance of the irrational mystery of the world – Otto's "creature-feeling" – and the importance of both personal and collective memory. Forged from the collective imagination, however, that memory is most powerful when it encompasses the most diverse perspectives possible. The collective imagination in New Orleans draws not only on the varied experiences of the community members, but also on their libraries, notably the salvaged books from the Library of Congress. Building on his combined human and elephant perspectives, The One Who Gathers realizes books have both memories and shadows. From books he learns to forge shadows for the shadowless, giving them "*some* memories, so they can have some concept of self to start from." He thereby allows them to remain tethered to the world, hence to survive, but gives them a reset:

> because the shadow will now be made from a past that never existed, because the source of the shadow has never been alive in the real world, there will be no chance of discovering later that the memories are an accidental perversion of nature—a recycling of a person already in existence. . . . No one would ever become someone else by mistake.[47]

Gajarajan learned the lesson painfully, after he had mistakenly attached the memories of a private journal to the wrong person. Selfhood, the (nameless) amnesiac understands, must be unique. But, Gajarajan knows, memories must also be shared. If the shadowless need to be tethered, the shadowed must be liberated, so both become capable of the balance the amnesiac has achieved. Although they do not yet exist in a world devoid of warfare, their worldview, rooted in connection and cooperation, shows their interest in enacting Lederberg's metaphor exchange as the basis for a more communitarian society at the end of the novel.

As it has made clear the inequities and vulnerabilities of the contemporary world, the Covid-19 pandemic has shown the urgent need for a reset as we move further into the third decade of the twenty-first century. Lederberg's metaphor exchange will not, of course, usher in a utopian world in which warfare and environmental devastation are bad memories of the past, but it might disrupt an entrenched – and naturalized – worldview sufficiently to shift focus long enough for "our wits" to imagine cooperation rather than competition as an equally "natural" and significantly more effective way of cohabiting the planet. Perhaps we might follow the lesson of *The Book of M* and turn to our own literary memories – particularly our pandemic novels – to help us do so.

Notes

1. Joshua Lederberg, "Infectious History," *Science* 288(5464) (2000), 287–293 (290).
2. For a discussion of the phrase and concept, see my *Contagious: Cultures, Carriers, and the Outbreak Narrative* (Durham, NC: Duke University Press, 2008).
3. William H. McNeill, "Mythistory, or Truth, Myth, History, and Historians," from *Mythistory and Other Essays*, edited by William H. McNeill (Chicago: University of Chicago Press, 1986), 3–22 (5).
4. Laura Van Den Berg, *Find Me* (New York: Farrar, Straus and Giroux, 2015), 14.
5. Peng Shepherd, *The Book of M* (New York: William Morrow, 2018), 261.
6. Rudolf Otto, *The Idea of the Holy: An Inquiry into the Non-rational Factor in the Idea of the Divine and Its Relation to the Rational*, translated by John W. Harvey (New York: Oxford University Press, 1958), 16.
7. Otto, 10.
8. Otto, 14–15.
9. Otto, 5.
10. Stephen S. Morse, "Examining the Origins of Emerging Viruses," from *Emerging Viruses*, edited by Stephen S. Morse (New York: Oxford University Press, 1993), 10–28 (21).
11. Ling Ma, *Severance* (New York: Farrar, Straus and Giroux, 2018), 6.
12. Karl M. Johnson, "Emerging Viruses in Context: An Overview of Viral Hemorrhagic Fevers," from *Emerging Viruses*, edited by Stephen S. Morse (New York: Oxford University Press, 1993), 46–57 (51).
13. Richard Preston, *The Hot Zone* (New York: Random House, 1994), 197.
14. In his lyrical meditation, "Theses on the Philosophy of History," the cultural critic Walter Benjamin describes how (historical) memory flashes up at a moment of danger. It is a fleeting insight that poses either the "danger" of insight – the recognition of the repetitions through which power reproduces itself structurally – or, more likely, the "danger" through which the fleeting nature of the insight forecloses on that recognition and the cycle continues. See Walter Benjamin, "Theses on the Philosophy of History," from *Illuminations: Essays and Reflections*, translated by Harry Zohn, edited by Hannah Arendt (New York: Schocken, 1969), 253–264.
15. Chuck Hogan, *The Blood Artists* (New York: Avon Books, 1998), 338.
16. Carl Freedman, *Critical Theory and Science Fiction* (Hanover, NH: Wesleyan University Press, 2000), 21.
17. Freedman, 49.
18. Istvan Csicsery-Ronay, Jr., *The Seven Beauties of Science Fiction* (Hanover, NH: Wesleyan University Press, 2008), 4, 6.
19. Joshua Lederberg, "Viruses and Humankind: Intracellular Symbiosis and Evolutionary Competition," from *Emerging Viruses*, edited by Stephen S. Morse (New York: Oxford University Press, 1993), 3–9 (3–4).
20. Lederberg, "Infectious History," 292–293.

21. McNeill, “Mythistory,” 11.
22. William H. McNeill, “The Care and Repair of Public Myth,” from *Mythistory and Other Essays*, edited by William H. McNeill (Chicago: University of Chicago Press, 1986), 23–42 (35).
23. Charles Darwin, *On the Origin of Species*, 3rd edition, edited by Barbara Bordalejo (Darwin Online, 1861), 76, 75.
24. Lawrence Wright, *The End of October* (New York: Alfred A. Knopf, 2020), 371.
25. Wright, 373.
26. Wright, 376.
27. Wright, 348.
28. Wright, 348.
29. Wright, 349.
30. Wright, 373.
31. George Santayana, *The Life of Reason.* Volume One: *Reason in Common Sense.* Second Edition. (New York: Scribner’s, 1922 [1905]), 284.
    NB: the original pub was 1905 London: Constable, but I can’t find a copy of the original that includes page numbers so can’t confirm the page number from that edition. I can confirm from the 2nd edition.
32. Ma, 28.
33. Ma, 160.
34. Van Den Berg, 30, 31.
35. Van Den Berg, 243.
36. Van Den Berg, 147.
37. Van Den Berg, 275.
38. Ma, 287.
39. Shepherd, 38.
40. Shepherd, 39.
41. Van Den Berg, 150.
42. Hannah Arendt, *The Human Condition* (Chicago: University of Chicago Press, 1958), 1.
43. Arendt, 2.
44. Shepherd, 156.
45. Shepherd, 152.
46. Shepherd, 402.
47. Shepherd, 481.

CHAPTER 2

American Futures

Phillip E. Wegner

il y a icy un nouveau monde?

Is there here a new world?[1]

One year after the 2016 US national election, I attended a conference panel on the challenges faced by intellectuals and teachers in the age of President Donald Trump. A concern that quickly rose to the forefront was the discomfort people would feel a few weeks hence when they would attend Thanksgiving dinners with family members who had voted for and continued to support Trump's radical policies. In response to such complaints, a scholar from Greece stood up and angrily asserted that all this indicated how out of touch so many American academics continue to be. He pointed out that in his country he knew of families where members betrayed kin on the other side of political divides to the authorities. Moreover, he maintained, from the perspective of much of the rest of the world, the election of Trump might be the best thing that could have happened. This is because the United States would be so tied up with internal struggles that it would be forced to curtail its meddling in the affairs of other nations.

More recently – and as the political situation in the United States has continued to deteriorate – I had the privilege to participate with scholars from Brazil in a discussion of the literary dystopia. When the conversation turned to the genre's reception, one of the members of the group keenly observed that, whereas audiences in the United States and Great Britain often understand dystopia's figure of the "bad place" to be located somewhere else – and hence read these texts as warnings of paths not to follow – for readers in Brazil and other places on the so-called peripheries of the modern world-system, the bad place is located in the past, or even the present. For this latter audience then, what becomes most vital in dystopias are the visions they offer of resistance and struggle.

Support for this observation can be found in the 1977 Lawrence Hill republication of one of the founding works of the literary dystopia: Jack

Figure 2.1 Cover of *The Iron Heel.*

London's *The Iron Heel* (1908). This edition features a striking wraparound cover, with a front illustration of a black boot standing on a placard with a picture of the twenty-eighth president of Chile and the words "Viva Allende" printed across the top. In Figure 2.1, the back cover shows the companion boot and the muzzle of a rifle pointed at this passage from London's text: "This, then, is our answer. . . . We will grind you revolutionists down under our heel, and we shall walk upon your faces."[2] The cover translates London's story into a premonition not of a potential US future, but rather of what had already occurred in Chile, with the September 11, 1973 military coup that deposed the democratically elected Salvador Allende and installed Augusto Pinochet as the nation's dictator. A report released in September 2000 notes that the "CIA actively supported the military Junta after the overthrow of Allende" and that "many of Pinochet's officers were involved in systematic and widespread human rights abuses following Allende's ouster. Some of these were contacts or agents of the CIA or US military."[3]

Both anecdotes underscore the persistence in the United States of a foundational commonsense notion – what Roland Barthes terms *myth*, a narrative that "transforms history into nature"[4] – at work in the period

Giovanni Arrighi identifies as "the long twentieth century" and Yanis Varoufakis as the ages of the "Global Plan" and "Minotaur": *American exceptionalism.*[5] While a number of influential Cold War scholars trace the roots of the notion to Alexis de Tocqueville, American exceptionalism is first explicitly referenced in 1920s debates among American communists over the possibility of revolution in the United States. Following World War II, the concept is deployed for very different purposes, stressing not only the nation's unique "difference from the historical trajectories that it attributed to Europe, to the Soviet Union, and to the Third World" but its status "as qualitatively better" than these other nations and hence entrusted with a divine mission to impose its way of life worldwide.[6] In this moment, Donald Pease contends, American exceptionalism serves at once as "an academic discourse, a political doctrine, and a regulatory ideal assigned responsibility for defining, supporting, and developing the U.S. national identity."[7] He further points out that "throughout the Cold War, U.S. dominance was sustained through its self-representation as an exception to the rules through which it regulated the rest of the global order."[8]

The notion of American exceptionalism is structured around things the nation is posited as uniquely lacking: "a landed aristocracy, a feudal monarchy, a territorial empire, a society hierarchized by class, a deeply anchored socialist tradition."[9] Events that are counter to the exceptionalism paradigm – settler colonialism; wide-scale labor unrest; the closure of immigration to Asians; interventions in Mexico, the Philippines, Cuba, Korea, and elsewhere; regional and generational political conflicts; gender and sexual inequality; and, most of all, slavery and the ongoing legacies of post-Reconstruction segregation – are cast as temporary and incidental "exceptions" to the normal exceptional order of things.[10] The end product of this discourse is thus an "image of a hardworking, unified national monoculture," one exempt from the conflicts and traumatic breaks that plagued all other nations around the globe.[11] In short, American exceptionalism presents a vision of the nation as outside of history – history here understood as what Fredric Jameson describes as the unsymbolizable Real, "what hurts . . . what refuses desire and sets inexorable limits to individual as well as collective praxis."[12]

The notion of the United States as a single homogenous nation uniquely exempt from history will also be foundational for and further reinforced by what became, in the years after World War II, the dominant and effective literary aesthetic of the period, which Mark McGurl identifies as the "Program Era." McGurl argues that the Program Era privileges a realism shaped by the triple mandates of *experience* ("write what you know"), *craft* ("show don't tell"), and *creativity* limited to the development of a singular individual mode of expression ("find your own voice").[13] The consequences for other forms of fiction writing would be monumental:

> Formula in the unconscious of craft: only in the most highly mediated way can the science fiction writer be said to deploy the faculties of memory or observation in her work, and this violation of the law of "write what you know" would become part of the modernist brief against the shoddy inauthenticity of genre fiction of all kinds.[14]

This reality is borne out in the experiences of the young Vietnam veteran and science-fiction (sf) writer Joe Haldeman during his time at the Iowa Writers' Workshop, long the Era's preeminent writing program. Haldeman recalls, "Jack Leggett [director of the Workshop from 1970 to 1987] would never have accepted me if he'd known I was writing science fiction. He detested commercial fiction, genre fiction – anything normal people read for pleasure."[15] Haldeman helps bring into focus a significant elision that takes place in Program Era ideology: the collapsing together of *all* sf into the category of formulaic commercial genre fiction. While there is of course always the possibility of sf sliding into formula, the same is equally true for Program Era realism – indeed, McGurl observes that this is an accusation regularly leveled against it.[16]

Jameson points out that "realism requires a conviction as to the massive weight and persistence of the present as such, and an aesthetic need to avoid recognition of deep structural social change as such and of the deeper currents and contradictory tendencies within the social order."[17] In this way, Jameson elsewhere argues, realisms produce group ideologies – but ideology in this sense is not to be thought of in terms of

> error (false consciousness) to be replaced by a more appropriate form of truth (or better still, of science); but rather that ideology is always with us, that it will be present and necessary in all forms of society, including future and more perfect ones, since it designates the necessary function whereby the biological individual and subject situates himself/herself in relationship to the social totality.[18]

While such realism is the dominant literary practice in Great Britain in the late nineteenth century, it does not exist in the United States, as Richard Chase demonstrates in his classic study *The American Novel and Its Tradition*, until the moment of Henry James[19] – and, not surprisingly, Program Era realism represents a formalization of the notions of "good fiction" first formulated by James.[20]

Jameson argues that in the very moment of the waning of the historical novel, there arises another genre that will take up in a wholly original manner its earlier vocation:

> We are therefore entitled to complete Lukács' account of the historical novel with the counter-panel of its opposite number, the emergence of the new genre of SF as a form which now registers some nascent sense of the future, and does so in the space on which a sense of the past had once been inscribed.[21]

Jameson maintains that the while sf turns its attention to the future, the practice "does not seriously attempt to imagine the 'real' future of our social system. Rather, its multiple mock futures serve the quite different function of transforming our own present into the determinate past of something yet to come."[22]

Crucially then both Program Era realism *and* sf develop representations of the present. However, sf's mirror is a distorting anamorphic one, presenting imaginary futures that help its readers more effectively cognize the contradictions, conflicts, and struggles that are always at work in any historical situation, and which naturalizing formulations such as American exceptionalism occlude. Program Era realism, as was the case with its nineteenth-century British predecessors, takes the stability of the present as the precondition for the portrayal of the psychology and lived experiences of people inhabiting a particular historical moment. Realisms slide into myth only when they confuse the historical specificity of these experiences with "human nature" itself. Through its portrayal of imaginary futures, sf calls into question any such notions of a fixed nature, human or otherwise, and thereby raises the specter of our collective responsibility for the current state of the world – and our capacity to change it.

Jameson finds a textbook case of this labor in *Time Out of Joint*, an early novel by one of the most influential writers to emerge in this period, Philip K. Dick.[23] It offers a vision of late-1950s US small-town life as a fantasy reconstruction in the very different "reality" of a future 1997. On this basis, Jameson argues,

> the very structure of the novel articulates the position of Eisenhower America in the world itself and is thereby to be read as a distorted form of cognitive mapping, an unconscious and figurative projection of some more "realistic" account of our situation . . . the hometown reality of the United States surrounded by the implacable menace of world communism (and, in this period to a much lesser degree, of Third World poverty).[24]

Such a reality is one very much mired in historical struggle, and embracing this truth is the first step in moving beyond the present impasse.

The futures presented in post–World War II US sf vary tremendously. All challenge the placid posthistorical myth of American exceptionalism and show change as the norm in the United States as well as anywhere else: what form that change will take then becomes the central concern. The visions of imaginary futures found in many of these texts also would be profoundly influenced by British author George Orwell, whose *Nineteen Eighty-Four* would serve as a paradigm for writers of dystopia the world over. Whereas readers blinkered by American exceptionalism focus on Orwell's vision of the total state – hence interpreting the novel as an allegory of the political "totalitarianism" in the elsewheres of Nazi Germany and the Soviet Union – *Nineteen Eighty-Four* also offers, in its figures of the protagonist Winston Smith's place of employment, the Ministry of Truth, and the omnipresent telescreens, an effective estranging portrait of an emerging industrialized mass culture, whose leading producer is the United States.[25]

It is this latter aspect of Orwell's vision that would have the greatest impact on US sf.[26] For example, in his debut novel *Player Piano* – retitled *Utopia 14* for a paperback release – Kurt Vonnegut Jr. draws upon his own experiences working in a General Electric factory to develop a vision of a future where corporate elites have created a fully automated mass-production society wherein most workers have been rendered redundant and, as a result, social unrest has increased dramatically.[27] The extreme class divisions in Vonnegut's future world also will be present in later American dystopian fiction, memorably in the near-future New York City portrayed in Thomas M. Disch's *334*. Ray Bradbury's *Fahrenheit 451* gives its readers a future America where books have been made illegal and most people spend their time consuming mass-produced television shows.[28] Frederick Pohl and C. M. Kornbluth's *The Space Merchants* is even more direct in its critique of an emerging consumer society. The novel's imaginary future is one where corporations have taken control of the state and advertising has become an immensely powerful profession. In an overpopulated future world where basic resources are scarce, the public is bombarded with continuous intrusive advertisements aimed at convincing them that the surfeit of shoddy commodities offered to them is proof that American exceptionalism's dream of endless prosperity remains a reality.[29]

The work of these early 1950s writers is significant for another reason: while this is the moment that the Program Era division between "literary" and "genre" fiction begins to ossify into common sense, sf writers too would further develop and refine their practice. An outstanding example of such an attention to craft and formal experimentation can be found in Alfred Bester's mid-fifties *The Stars My Destination*. Bester's novel focuses on the accidental discovery of the human technology of teleportation, or jaunting, and its profound effects on society:

> within three generations the entire solar system was on the jaunte. The transition was more spectacular than the change-over from horse and buggy to gasoline age five centuries before. On three planets and eight satellites, social, legal, and economic structures crashed while the new customs and laws demanded by universal jaunting mushroomed in their place.[30]

The Stars My Destination bears out the fact that technological developments, even the most extreme ones, are not the same as meaningful change. Its twenty-fifth-century world is one where characteristic aspects of contemporary everyday life – social conformism, class hierarchies, corporate power, rampant consumerism, and the postwar relocation of women back to their "proper" place in the domestic sphere – are reflected back to the reader in a dramatic estranging light:

> After a thousand years of civilization (it says here) we're still property. Jaunting's such a danger to our virtue, our value, our mint condition, that we're locked up like gold plate in a safe. There's nothing for us to do ... nothing respectable. No jobs. No careers. There's no getting out, Gully, unless you burst out and smash all the rules.[31]

This last line emphasizes the critique that is at heart of all of these novels: the real promise of American exceptionalism is stagnation, a swap of freedom for material comfort. Such a situation cannot last, Bester assures his readers, and the novel's final pages give expression to an undercurrent of discontent that will come to full fruition in the 1960s.

The 1950s also witness a flourishing of postapocalypse fiction. The postapocalypse represents an inversion of the dystopia. At the heart of these fictions lies a deep ambivalence: while the apocalyptic event – be it a natural disaster or the result of human agency – appears a negative one, often the new social order that emerges is understood to be far superior to the present, sometimes even a utopia. Formally, the event of the apocalypse serves as the device Jameson refers to as *world reduction* – "a kind of surgical excision of empirical reality, something like a process of ontological attenuation in which the sheer teeming multiplicity of what exists, of what we call reality, is deliberately thinned and weeded out"[32] – pruning away aspects of contemporary society that the author finds most problematic and thereby highlighting them in a critical estranging manner.

An early masterpiece of the form is George R. Stewart's *Earth Abides*.[33] Stewart's narrative follows the adventures of Ish, one of the few survivors of a devastating plague, as he travels across the depopulated nation before voyaging back to his home in California. Upon his return, Ish marries, begins a family, and gathers around himself a small community, which will slowly adopt a way of life more in balance with the land. Richard Matheson's *I Am Legend* – the basis of four film adaptations, as well as the inspiration for George A. Romero's *Night of the Living Dead* – also treats the theme of a survivor of a biological catastrophe. However, Matheson's protagonist is a far more ambiguous figure, as he both fights to restore the old order and resists the new world coming into being in its aftermath.[34] *I Am Legend* thereby gives effective expression to the generational tensions of its moment.

Bernard Wolfe's *Limbo* portrays a post–World War III United States where men, in order to keep from repeating war, voluntarily have their limbs removed and replaced by cybernetic prostheses; this, however, only makes them even more dependent on machines.[35] Conversely, Pat Frank's *Alas, Babylon* envisions nuclear war as a means to clear away the debilitating and emasculating aspects of contemporary American culture.[36] Judith Merril's "That Only a Mother" emphasizes the destructive aspects of radiation-induced mutations; while Theodore Sturgeon's *More Than Human* reframes such mutations as a positive aspect of human evolution and thereby encourages its readers to embrace rather than fear change.[37] This latter trope would be taken up with great relish a decade later in the superhero renaissance begun in Stan Lee and Jack Kirby's Marvel Comics – indeed, the children of Sturgeon's novel read like precursors to Lee and Kirby's *X-Men*.

It is no coincidence that Lee and Kirby refined their craft in 1950s sf comics, the high point of which came from another publishing firm, EC Comics, with its brilliant if short-lived titles *Weird Science* and *Weird Fantasy*. One of the most celebrated stories published in *Weird Fantasy*, "Judgment Day" by writers William M. Gaines and Al Feldstein and artist Joe Orlando, deploys another strategy through which sf estranges the present. The story tells of the visit of a future representative of Earth to a planet populated by two groups of sentient machines, identical except for their coloring. Discovering systematic segregation and rampant inequalities, the visitor determines that these beings are not advanced sufficiently to join "Earth's great galactic republic."[38] When the inhabitants express despair, the visitor assure them, "Of course there's hope for you, my friend. For a while, on Earth, it looked like there was no hope! But when mankind on Earth learned to live together, real progress first began. The universe was suddenly ours."[39] In Figure 2.2, the final panel's caption reads, "And inside the ship, the man removed his space helmet and shook his head, and the instrument lights made the beads of perspiration on his dark skin twinkle like distant stars . . . "[40] The impact of the story thus relies on an estranging reversal: while the future utopian Earth has become for the reader an alien other, the alien world mirrors back the shameful realities of the reader's own present.

These two trends – visions of postapocalypse and dystopian futures dominated by corporations and consumer culture – come together in the work of the Philip K. Dick, the writer Jameson nominates as the "the Shakespeare of Science Fiction."[41] Dick's diverse visions of dystopian near future worlds – *Martian Time-Slip*, *The Three Stigmata of Palmer Eldritch*, *Do Androids Dream of Electric Sheep?*, *Ubik*, and *Flow My Tears, The Policeman Said* – deeply influence both the later development of the genre and popular culture at large, especially through film adaptations of his work beginning with Ridley Scott's *Blade Runner*.[42] Dick also made a significant contribution to the vitally important subgenre of the alternate history with his Hugo-Award winning *The Man in the High Castle*.[43]

Figure 2.2 Panel from "Judgement Day."

Dick's novel – which was also the basis of a popular recent television series – is set in an alternate present in which the United States lost World War II and is now split between German and Japanese occupiers. Although the alternate history is not concerned with American futures, its portrayal of alternate presents develops an equally effective critique of American exceptionalism. The alternate history confronts the reader with the prospect that "what is" is in fact surrounded by a dizzying number of "what ifs," of other possible worlds, other collective destinies, whose lack of substantiality in the here and now is the result of chance, or of our actions or inactions in the past. The alternate history will remain a vitally important part of American sf and includes such other classics as Ward Moore's *Bring the Jubilee*; Ursula K. Le Guin's *The Lathe of Heaven*; Norman Spinrad's *The Iron Dream*; Chris Claremont, John Byrne, and Terry Austin's comic book series *X-Men*: *Days of Future Past*; Terry Bisson's *Fire on the Mountain*; William Gibson and Bruce Sterling's *The Difference Engine*; Kim Stanley Robinson's *The Years of Rice and Salt*; Philip Roth's *The Plot against America*; Michael Chabon's *The Yiddish Policemen's Union*; and Colson Whitehead's *The Underground Railroad*.[44]

In the decades that follow, sf authors will continue to draw upon these forms of imagining the American future, while also refining and expanding the possibilities of their practice. The next generation of sf writers, the New Wave, drew energy from the radical political movements of the 1960s and 1970s and would further challenge the assumptions of American exceptionalism through fictional futures that brought into focus the gender disparities, environmental despoilment, generational struggles, and contemporary global military conflicts, while also encouraging readers to work for change. Harry Harrison's *Make Room! Make Room!* explores the dystopian effects of overpopulation in a near-future New York City.[45] Harlan Ellison's Hugo-winning short story "I Have No Mouth, and I Must Scream" – whose themes would be further taken up in James Cameron's *The Terminator* – presents a future where humanity has been all but exterminated by its military technology.[46] Thomas Disch's *Camp Concentration*, set in a world where a Robert McNamara-led United States has declared war on the world, is, along with Le Guin's *The Word for World Is Forest* discussed later, and Haldeman's *The Forever War* – a brilliant rewriting of Robert A. Heinlein's popular tale of a future utopian society dominated by the military, *Starship Troopers* – among the great sf responses to US imperialism and the Vietnam War.[47] Barry N. Malzberg's *Beyond Apollo* centers on an ill-fated expedition to Venus and offers a vicious satirical attack on the dehumanizing hypermasculinity of both the US space program and American culture at large.[48]

It was in this period too that women writers began to have both greater visibility and centrality in the genre. As a result, sf futures would increasingly turn their critical estranging gaze on to the realities of gender and sexual inequality. Emblematic of this shift is Joanna Russ's Nebula Award winning short story "When It Changed," first published in Ellison's groundbreaking anthology of experimental sf, *Again, Dangerous Visions.* Russ's story focuses on the arrival of a group of "aliens" – men from Earth – on the planet of Whileaway, a former Earth colony where six centuries earlier all human males died as the result of a plague and the surviving women built a flourishing society without them. At the conclusion of the story, the narrator acknowledges that this event will alter their lives irrevocably, and she fears that the result will be the reinstallation of the hierarchies and oppressions they had lived without for more than a half-millennium: "Men are coming to Whileaway. When one culture has the big guns and the other has none, there is a certain predictability about the outcome."[49] Even in utopia, Russ reminds the reader, history is inescapable.

The same radical feminist energy will be at work in the vital tradition Tom Moylan identifies as *critical utopias*: texts that unveil "the limitations of the utopian tradition" and "reject utopia as a blueprint while preserving it as a dream."[50] Among the most prominent of these critical utopias are Le Guin's *The Dispossessed* and *Always Coming Home*, Russ's *The Female Man*, and Marge Piercy's *Woman on the Edge of Time* and *He, She, and It.*[51] Another significant figure from this moment and the first major African American and queer sf writer, Samuel R. Delany, produced both an experimental dystopia, *Dhalgren*, and two significant critical utopias, in *Triton* and *Stars in My Pocket Like Grains of Sand.*[52]

The most celebrated writer to emerge in this period was Ursula K. Le Guin. The daughter of the American anthropologists Arthur and Theodora Kroeber, Le Guin brought a new depth of attention to the portrayal of cultures that differed in fundamental ways from those on Earth. Le Guin's *The Left Hand of Darkness* is exemplary in this regard, as it tells of a race whose sexual biology is radically different from our own, and who as a result lack our gender divisions.[53] However, while many of Le Guin's most celebrated novels are set in her intergalactic Hainish universe, a future Earth does appear in her novels. For example, in her critical utopia, *The Dispossessed*, Le Guin repeats the formula at work in

"Judgement Day." On the one hand, a future Earth is presented in distinctly dystopian terms:

> we had saved what could be saved, and made a kind of life in the ruins, on Terra, in the only way it could be done: by total centralization. Total control over the use of every acre of land, every scrap of metal, every ounce of fuel. Total rationing, birth control, euthanasia, universal conscription into the labor force. The absolute regimentation of each life toward the goal of racial survival.[54]

On the other hand, the alien planet Urras is divided into first, second, and third worlds, as on contemporary Earth. Finally, the moon world of Anarres offers a working model, an "ambiguous utopia" itself in the tides of change, as an alternative to both our present and any dystopian future.

The residents of the future dystopian Earth appear even more prominently in Le Guin's earlier Hainish novel *The Word for World Is Forest*, which was also first published in *Again, Dangerous Visions*. *The Word for World Is Forest* would impact on later sf film, inspiring both George Lucas's *Star Wars: Return of the Jedi* and James Cameron's *Avatar*. As in Cameron's film, Le Guin's novella tells the story of the attempt by a resource-depleted Earth to exploit a distant forest-covered world, Athshe, and the ultimately successful efforts by the planet's Indigenous people to expel the invaders. The fact that Le Guin's novella is also in part an allegory of the United States' then ongoing involvement in Vietnam is made explicit when the Terran Colonel Dongh declares, "You can't disable a guerilla type structure with bombs, it's been proved, in fact my own part of the world where I was born proved it for about thirty-five years fighting off major super-powers one after the other in the twentieth century."[55]

In his essay "Periodizing the 60s," Jameson maintains that the US defeat in Vietnam, along with "a whole series of other, seemingly unrelated events in the general area of 1972–74 suggests that this moment ... signals the definitive end of what is called the 60s."[56] Be that as it may, the radical energies of both sf's New Wave and the counterculture more generally were largely spent by the early 1980s. Some sf novels in this moment, such as Larry Niven and Jerry Pournelle's *Oath of Fealty*, would develop futures that were explicit critiques of the 1960s political countercultures.[57] Moreover, the final two decades of the Cold War – the 1980s and the transitional moment I term the "between two deaths" of the 1990s – witness a resurgence of American exceptionalism and an increasing return to military interventionism.[58]

Indeed in 1989, American exceptionalism returns with new vigor in Francis Fukuyama's "end of history" thesis. Fukuyama argues that the fall of the Soviet Union signaled the "unabashed victory of economic and political liberalism" the world over.[59] The "universal homogenous state" that was emerging could best be described "as liberal democracy in the political sphere combined with easy access to VCRs and stereos in the economic"[60] – American exceptionalism achieved on the global stage. A few years later, a group of conservative intellectuals associated with the two Bush presidential administrations built on Fukuyama's claims in their formulation of the Project for the New American Century. The Project was based on "a few fundamental propositions: that American leadership is good both for America and for the world; that such leadership requires military strength, diplomatic energy, and commitment to moral principle; and that too few political leaders today are making the case for global leadership."[61] David Harvey argues, "though recognized as distinctive American values, these principles are presented as universals, with terms like freedom and democracy and respect for private property, the individual, and the law bundled together as a code of conduct for the whole world."[62]

This changed situation would require new strategies on the part of US sf writers. Emblematic of the shift was a series of novels released in 1984. That year saw the publication of one of the final masterpieces of the New Wave in Delany's *Stars in My Pocket Like Grains of Sand.* While he had planned it as the first part of a diptych, Delany felt that a number of recent events – including the intensification of the AIDS crisis, Reagan's reelection, and the neoliberal remaking of urban space – made the project feel out of step with the contemporary situation, and he never completed the second manuscript.[63] However, another 1984 novel would give expression to key aspects of an emerging American reality: William Gibson's debut *Neuromancer.* First published in the influential New Ace Science Fiction Specials series edited by Terry Carr, *Neuromancer* is the opening novel of a trilogy that continues in *Count Zero* and *Mona Lisa Overdrive.*[64]

Although it would also include well-known writers such as Bruce Sterling, Pat Cadigan, John Shirley, Lewis Shiner, Rudy Rucker, and Neal Stephenson, Gibson remains the preeminent figure in the movement known as *cyberpunk*, which also quickly came to be recognized as a privileged symptom of contemporary or postmodern culture more generally. Jameson testifies to cyberpunk's importance when he notes that it "is fully as much an expression of transnational corporate realities as it is of global paranoia itself: William Gibson's representational innovations, indeed, mark his work as an exceptional literary realization within a predominantly visual or aural postmodern production."[65] Gibson's fiction, with its sharp prose redolent of *noir* detective novels, also marks the beginning of the erosion of the Cold War binary of "literary" and "genre" fiction, as well as the hegemony of the Program Era.

The near future represented in Gibson's trilogy is a decidedly ambivalent one. *Neuromancer* remains critical of the standardized corporate life. Moreover, the decaying urban reality presented in the novel recalls that of earlier New Wave dystopias: "a blasted industrial landscape," with "dead grass tufting the cracks in a canted slab of freeway concrete" and "broken slag and the rusting shells of refineries."[66] At the same time, the novel celebrates new possibilities that were emerging in what would soon be referred to as neoliberalism: while the labor of the novel's protagonist, the freelance computer hacker Case, is decidedly without the day-to-day monotony of those employed by postwar corporations, he also lacks the securities such employment made available – lifetime employment, housing, high wages, guaranteed recreation time, schooling, and health insurance. While the price of failure in this brave new world is high – "Night City was like a deranged experiment in Social Darwinism . . . Biz here was a constant subliminal hum, and death the accepted punishment for laziness, carelessness, lack of grace, the failure to heed the demands of an intricate protocol"[67] – the rewards, the novel promises, are equally tremendous.

The other major debut published in 1984, also in the New Ace Science Fiction Specials, was Kim Stanley Robinson's *The Wild Shore*. Differing from Gibson and other cyberpunk writers, Robinson's work combines a hard sf sensibility, superb characterization, and immense worldbuilding talents with a deep commitment to the radical sensibilities of the 1960s New Wave. Robinson's inaugural trilogy portrays three possible futures for his childhood home in California's Orange County. *The Wild Shore* is set in a postapocalypse west coast, sixty years after thousands of neutron bombs had been exploded across the United States, reducing the nation to a scattering of isolated agricultural communities. The fantasy of returning to an imaginary past of American greatness – of restoring what, in 1984 at least, would readily be understood as a Cold War global hegemony – is voiced by the imperious leader of what remains of the one-time city of San Diego: "You tell them they can make this country what it used to be. They can help. But we all have to work together. The day will come. Another Pax Americana, cars and airplanes, rockets to the moon, telephones. A unified country. . . . You go back up there and tell your valley that they join the resistance or they oppose it."[68]

The Wild Shore was soon followed by *The Gold Coast*, an early example of the practice Moylan identifies as the *critical dystopia*, texts that "negotiate the necessary pessimism of the generic dystopia with an open, militant, utopian stance that not only breaks through the hegemonic enclosure of the text's alternative world but also self-reflexively refuses the antiutopian temptation that lingers like a dormant virus in every dystopian account."[69] Robinson then concludes his Three Californias trilogy with the green utopia of *Pacific Edge*, a work comparable in its scope and vision to Ernst Callenbach's pioneering *Ecotopia*.[70] In these three novels, Robinson reverses and retraces the chronology of modern sf, moving from a Cold War nuclear postapocalypse; back through the late nineteenth-century's precursor to modern sf, the dystopia; before finally bringing the trilogy to a rousing climax with a contemporary reworking of the form founded by Thomas More nearly half a millennium earlier, the narrative utopia.

Another major writer to emerge in this moment – and also hailing from Southern California – is Octavia E. Butler, the first sf writer to receive a MacArthur Foundation Genius Grant. Butler's most celebrated trilogy, "Lilith's Brood" or "Xenogenesis" – *Dawn*, *Adulthood Rites*, and *Imago* – tells the story of the encounter between the future human survivors of a nuclear war and an alien species, the Oankali, who initiate genetic exchanges they deem necessary for humanity's survival.[71] Through this figure of a postapocalyptic future, Butler ingeniously develops a complex allegory of the experience of forced desegregation in the US South and white resistance to the changes it demanded.

In her subsequent critical dystopia *Parable of the Sower*, Butler offers a devastating critique of the violence of neoliberalism in a future world of widespread environmental disaster and social disorder, where the federal government has apparently dissolved away, fundamental services are privatized or have disappeared, corporate-run townships reintroduce wage slavery, and the remnants of the lower-middle class retreat into barricaded neighborhood enclaves wherein they provide whatever schooling their children receive and fight an ongoing battle with the anarchic predators pressing down on them.[72] The sequel *Parable of the Talents* shifts focus to a nation beset by a rising tide of fundamentalism, which takes root through a promise of returning some semblance of order to this chaotic world: "People struggled toward it, hoping for a still civilized place of jobs, peace, room to raise their children in safety, and a return to the mythical golden-age world of the mid-twentieth century."[73] A presidential candidate in the novel prophetically invokes what will become the slogan of the Trump campaign: "making America great again. He seems to be unhappy with certain other countries. We could wind up in a war. Nothing like a war to rally people around flag, country, and great leader."[74] In this way, Butler develops an astonishing estranging vision of the dialectic of neoliberalism and neoconservatism that continues today to define the nation. However, as a critical dystopia, the two novels also explore the possibility of more utopian alternate kinship structures and communities emerging from the wreckage of the present.

The events of September 11, 2001 would mark both the end of the post–Cold War 1990s and the beginning of a new period in American life. This moment – ours – is defined by a sense of perpetual crisis: 2001 was followed by the new forever War on Terror, the global economic meltdown of 2008, the worldwide protests in 2011, the 2016 election of Trump, the Covid-19 pandemic and nationwide protests of 2020, the January 6, 2021 storming of the US Capitol, unprecedented threats to democratic institutions, increasing polarization and fragmentation of the nation, and a seemingly endless wave of mass shootings – all of which have deeply challenged whatever remains of the notion of American exceptionalism. At the same time, this period is one in which the divisions of the Program Era seem to have run their course, as more work formerly dismissed as sf is given serious attention and mainstream "literary" writers turn to the practices of sf to grapple with the changing realities of the present.

Emblematic of this shift is Cormac McCarthy's *The Road*, which combines the minimalism favored by Program Era fiction and sf postapocalypse to critically diagnose contemporary neoliberal culture. McCarthy's novel presents a future where Margaret Thatcher's adage, "there's no such thing as society. There are individual men and women and there are families," is taken to its logical conclusion:[75]

> Someone's coming.
> Is it bad guys?
> Yes. I'm afraid so.
> They could be good guys. Couldnt they?
> He didn't answer. He looked at the sky out of old habit but there was nothing to see.[76]

It is precisely the death sentence of this way of life that the coming generation rejects in the novel's hopeful, open-ended climax.

Colson Whitehead's *Zone One* similarly uses the figure of a zombie apocalypse to offer a scathing commentary on the effects on our society of endless catastrophes – it turns out everyone in this near-future world suffers from "PASD, or Post-Apocalyptic Stress Disorder"[77] – as well as the unwillingness to acknowledge these realities on the part of political and economic elites, who instead fall back on empty promises of restoring American exceptionalism: "one had reason to dust off the old optimism. You had only to look at the faint movement in the ashes: surely this is the American Phoenix Rising. At least that's what the T-shirts said, lifted from biodegradable cardboard boxes fresh from Buffalo. Toddler sizes available."[78] This novel too ends on a note of hope.

Global climate change represents another rebuke to the ideology of American exceptionalism – and not surprisingly, those who remain most wedded to this outmoded notion are also very often climate-change deniers – and the effects of these changes on everyday life in the nation and around the world have become major concerns in contemporary sf. Climate change is central to Robinson's Science in the Capital trilogy – *Forty Signs of Rain, Fifty Degrees Below*, and *Sixty Days and Counting* – and he returns to these issues in two of his most recent novels, *New York 2140* and *The Ministry for the Future*.[79] Gibson's alternate history trilogy, *The Peripheral*, *Agency*, and *Jackpot*, concerns a future world where the challenges of our present – climate change, pandemic, and political violence – come together to kill off a majority of the planet's human population and devastate the environment in which the survivors are forced to live.[80]

Paolo Bacigalupi's debut novel *The Windup Girl*, his Ship Breaker trilogy – *Ship Breaker*, *The Drowned Cities*, and *Tool of War* – and *The Water Knife* are all set in as future world where fossil fuels have been exhausted and a climate-change-induced rise in sea levels has devastated the US Gulf Coast states.[81] Tobias S. Buckell's technothrillers *Arctic Rising* and *Hurricane Fever* explore the effects of climate change in the polar region and Caribbean and show the ways humans may adapt to them.[82] Finally, one of the most celebrated American sf writers to appear in the last decade has been N.K. Jemisin. Her Broken Earth trilogy – *The Fifth Season*, *The Obelisk Gate*, and *The Stone Sky*, all winners of the Hugo Award – explores the devastating effects on the nation of both climate change and the legacies of racism.[83] All these works testify to sf's undiminished power to help us see with new eyes the, thankfully, unexceptional realities we always already inhabit – and, perhaps, to move us toward making new worlds together, now and here.

Notes

1. François Rabelais, *Pantagruel*, chapter 32.
2. Jack London, *The Iron Heel* (New York: Macmillan, 1908), 96–97.

3. "CIA Acknowledges Ties to Pinochet's Repression," *National Security Archive* (September 9, 2000), online.
4. Roland Barthes, *Mythologies*, translated by Richard Howard and Annette Lavers (New York: Hill and Wang, 2012), 240.
5. Giovanni Arrighi, *The Long Twentieth Century: Money, Power, and the Origins of Our Times* (New York: Verso, 1994); Yanis Varoufakis, *The Global Minotaur: America, Europe and the Future of the Global Economy* (London: Zed, 2015).
6. Donald E. Pease, "Exceptionalism," from *Keywords for American Cultural Studies*, edited by Bruce Burgett and Glenn Hendler (New York: NYU University Press, 2007), 108–112 (109).
7. Pease, 109.
8. Pease, 110.
9. Pease, 109.
10. Pease, 110.
11. Pease, 111.
12. Fredric Jameson, *The Political Unconscious: Narrative as a Socially Symbolic Act* (Ithaca: Cornell University Press, 1981), 102.
13. Mark McGurl, *The Program Era: Postwar Fiction and the Rise of Creative Writing* (Cambridge, MA: Harvard University Press, 2009), 23.
14. McGurl, 103.
15. Quoted in Eric Olsen and Glenn Schaeffer, *We Wanted to Be Writers: Life, Love, and Literature at the Iowa Writers' Workshop* (New York: Skyhorse, 2011), 25.
16. McGurl, 26.
17. Fredric Jameson, *The Antinomies of Realism* (New York: Verso, 2013), 145.
18. Fredric Jameson, *Signatures of the Visible* (New York: Routledge, 1990), 165.
19. Richard Chase, *The American Novel and Its Tradition* (New York: Doubleday, 1957).
20. McGurl, 49.
21. Fredric Jameson, *Archaeologies of the Future: The Desire Called Utopia and Other Science Fictions* (New York: Verso, 2005), 285–286.
22. Jameson, *Archaeologies*, 288.
23. Philip K. Dick, *Time Out of Joint* (Philadelphia: J.P. Lippincott, 1959).
24. Fredric Jameson, *Postmodernism, or the Cultural Logic of Late Capitalism* (Durham, NC: Duke University Press, 1991), 283.
25. George Orwell, *Nineteen Eighty-Four* (New York: Harcourt Brace, 1949). It is worth recalling that the currency in Winston Smith's Airstrip One, formerly Great Britain and now a minor outpost of the transatlantic empire of Oceania, is the dollar (*Nineteen Eighty-Four* 81).
26. In the following overview, I draw on *Shockwaves of Possibility: Essays on Science Fiction, Globalization, and Utopia* (Oxford: Peter Lang, 2014), chapter 1.
27. Kurt Vonnegut Jr., *Player Piano* (New York: Charles Scribner's Sons, 1952).
28. Thomas M. Disch, *334* (London: MacGibbon and Kee, 1972); Ray Bradbury, *Fahrenheit 451* (New York: HarperCollins, 2012 [1953]).

29. Frederick Pohl and C. M. Kornbluth, *The Space Merchants* (New York: Ballentine, 1953).
30. Alfred Bester, *The Stars My Destination* (1956) (New York: Vintage, 1996), 13.
31. Bester, 74.
32. Jameson, *Archaeologies*, 271.
33. George R. Stewart, *Earth Abides* (New York: Random House, 1949).
34. Richard Matheson, *I Am Legend* (New York: Gold Medal Books, 1954).
35. Bernard Wolfe, *Limbo* (New York: Random House, 1952).
36. Pat Frank, *Alas Babylon* (Philadelphia: J. P. Lippincott, 1959).
37. Judith Merril, "That Only a Mother," *Astounding Science Fiction* (June 1948); Theodor Sturgeon, *More Than Human* (New York: Farrar, Straus, and Young, 1953).
38. William M. Gaines, Al Feldstein, and Joe Orlando, "Judgment Day" *Weird Fantasy* 18 (April 1953), 1–7 (2).
39. Gaines et al., 7.
40. Gaines et al., 7.
41. Jameson, *Archaeologies*, 345.
42. Philip K. Dick, *Martian Time-Slip* (New York: Ballantine, 1964); Philip K. Dick, *The Three Stigmata of Palmer Eldritch* (New York: Doubleday, 1964); Philip K. Dick, *Do Androids Dream of Electric Sheep?* (New York: Doubleday, 1968); Philip K. Dick, *Ubik* (New York: Doubleday, 1969); Philip K. Dick, *Flow My Tears, The Policeman Said* (New York: Doubleday, 1974).
43. Philip K. Dick, *The Man in the High Castle* (New York: Putnam, 1962).
44. Ward Moore, *Bring the Jubilee* (New York: Ballantine, 1953); Ursula K. Le Guin, *The Lathe of Heaven* (New York: Avon, 1971); Norman Spinrad, *The Iron Dream* (New York: Avon, 1972); Chris Claremont, John Byrne, Terry Austin, *The Uncanny X-Men* 141–142 (Jan.–Feb. 1981); Terry Bisson, *Fire on the Mountain* (Oakland, CA: PM Press, 1988); William Gibson and Bruce Sterling, *The Difference Engine* (London: Victor Gollancz, 1990); Kim Stanley Robinson, *The Years of Rice and Salt* (New York: Bantam, 2002); Philip Roth, *The Plot against America* (London: Jonathan Cape, 2004); Michael Chabon, *The Yiddish Policemen's Union* (New York: HarperCollins, 2007); Colson Whitehead, *The Underground Railroad* (New York: Doubleday, 2016).
45. Harry Harrison, *Make Room! Make Room!* (New York: Doubleday, 1966).
46. Harlan Ellison, "I Have No Mouth, and I Must Scream," *Worlds of If Science Fiction* (March 1967), 24–36.
47. Thomas Disch, *Camp Concentration* (London: Rupert, Hart-Davis, 1968); Ursula K. Le Guin, *The Word for World Is Forest* (New York: Berkley Books, 1976); Joe Haldeman, *The Forever War* (New York: St. Martin's Press, 1974); Robert A. Heinlein, *Starship Troopers* (New York: G. P. Putnam's Sons, 1959).
48. Barry N. Malzberg, *Beyond Apollo* (New York: Random House, 1972).
49. Joanna Russ, "When It Changed," from *Again, Dangerous Visions*, edited by Harlan Ellison (New York: Doubleday, 1972), 248–262 (259).

50. Tom Moylan, *Demand the Impossible: Science Fiction and the Utopian Imagination*, edited by Raffaella Baccolini (Oxford: Peter Lang, 2014), 10.
51. Ursula K. Le Guin, *The Dispossessed: An Ambiguous Utopia* (New York: Harper, 1974); Ursula K. Le Guin, *Always Coming Home* (Berkeley: University of California Press, 2001); Joanna Russ, *The Female Man* (New York: Beacon Press, 1986); Marge Piercy, *Woman on the Edge of Time* (New York: Fawcett Crest, 1976); Marge Piercy, *He, She, and It* (New York: Fawcett, 1991).
52. Samuel R. Delany, *Dhalgren* (New York: Bantam, 1975); Samuel R. Delany, *Triton* (New York: Bantam, 1976); Samuel R. Delany, *Stars in My Pocket Like Grains of Sand* (New York: Bantam, 1984).
53. Ursula K. Le Guin, *The Left Hand of Darkness* (New York: Ace Books, 1987).
54. Ursula K. Le Guin, *The Dispossessed: An Ambiguous Utopia* (New York: HarperPrism, 1994), 348.
55. Le Guin, *Word*, 133.
56. Fredric Jameson, *The Ideologies of Theory* (New York: Verso, 2008), 510.
57. Larry Niven and Jerry Pournelle, *Oath of Fealty* (New York: Timescape Books, 1981).
58. Phillip E. Wegner, *Life Between Two Deaths, 1989–2001: U.S. Culture in the Long Nineties* (Durham, NC: Duke University Press, 2009).
59. Francis Fukuyama, "The End of History?" *The National Interest* 16 (Summer 1989), 3–18 (3).
60. Fukuyama, 8.
61. Quoted in David Harvey, *The New Imperialism* (Oxford: Oxford University Press, 2005), 191.
62. Harvey, 192.
63. Charlie Jane Anders, "Samuel Delany Answers Your Science Fiction Questions!", *Gizmodo* (June 9, 2009), online.
64. William Gibson, *Neuromancer* (New York: Ace, 1984); William Gibson, *Count Zero* (London: Victor Gollancz, 1986); William Gibson, *Mona Lisa Overdrive* (London: Victor Gollancz, 1988).
65. Jameson, *Postmodernism*, 38.
66. Gibson, *Neuromancer*, 85.
67. Gibson, 7.
68. Kim Stanley Robinson, *The Wild Shore* (New York: Ace, 1984), 106.
69. Kim Stanley Robinson, *The Gold Coast* (New York: Tom Doherty Associates, 1988); Tom Moylan, *Scraps of the Untainted Sky: Science Fiction, Utopia, Dystopia* (Boulder, CO: Westview, 2000), 195.
70. Kim Stanley Robinson, *Pacific Edge* (New York: Tom Doherty Associates, 2013). Ernest Callenbach, *Ecotopia* (Berkeley, CA: Banyan Tree, 1975).
71. Octavia E. Butler, *Dawn* (New York: TOR, 1987); Octavia E. Butler, *Adulthood Rites* (New York: TOR, 1988); Octavia E. Butler, *Imago* (New York: TOR, 1989).
72. Octavia E. Butler, *Parable of the Sower* (New York: Warner Books, 1993).
73. Octavia E. Butler, *Parable of the Talents* (New York: Warner Books, 1998), 52.

74. Butler, *Parable of the Talents*, 26.
75. "Margaret Thatcher: a life in quotes." *The Guardian* (April 8, 2013), online.
76. Cormac McCarthy, *The Road* (New York: Alfred A. Knopf, 2006), 101.
77. Colson Whitehead, *Zone One* (New York: Doubleday, 2011), 67.
78. Whitehead, 136.
79. Kim Stanley Robinson, *Forty Signs of Rain* (New York: Bantam, 2004); Kim Stanley Robinson, *Fifty Degrees Below* (New York: Bantam, 2005); Kim Stanley Robinson, *Sixty Days and Counting* (New York: Bantam, 2007); Kim Stanley Robinson, *New York 2140* (London: Orbit, 2017); Kim Stanley Robinson, *The Ministry for the Future* (London: Orbit, 2020).
80. William Gibson, *The Peripheral* (New York: G. P. Putnam, 2014); William Gibson, *Agency* (New York: Berkley, 2020); William Gibson, *Jackpot* (forthcoming).
81. Paolo Bacigalupi, *The Windup Girl* (San Francisco: Night Shade, 2009); Paolo Bacigalupi, *Ship Breaker* (New York: Little, Brown, 2010); Paolo Bacigalupi, *The Drowned Cities* (New York: Little, Brown, 2012); Paolo Bacigalupi, *Tool of War* (New York: Little, Brown, 2015); Paolo Bacigalupi, *The Water Knife* (New York: Knopf, 2015).
82. Tobias S. Buckell, *Arctic Rising* (New York: Tom Doherty, 2012); Tobias S. Buckell, *Hurricane Fever* (New York: Tom Doherty, 2014).
83. N. K. Jemisin, *The Fifth Season* (London: Orbit, 2015); N. K. Jemisin, *The Obelisk Gate* (London: Orbit, 2016); N. K. Jemisin, *The Stone Sky* (London: Orbit, 2017).

CHAPTER 3

Engendering Utopia
The Force of Gender and the Limits of Feminism

Jennifer A. Wagner-Lawlor

In a January 2008 *New York Times* op-ed, Gloria Steinem flags – once again – the essential(ist) sexism of American life: "Gender is probably the most restricting force in American life, whether the question is who must be in the kitchen or who could be in the White House."[1] Two months later, *Washington Post* commentator Ruth Marcus responds with a correction: "Gender isn't the most restricting force in American life. It remains a force to be reckoned with."[2] Marcus is not saying the famous feminist is wrong, exactly, but rather is reminding us of where Steinem's own celebrity in American life comes from: the force of opposition in second- to third-wave feminism. Marcus's op-ed title, "The Force of Gender," is striking in its conjuring of a revolutionary spirit "in American life," a certain promise of a "reckoning" – both an accounting (of and for), and a *response*. The force of gender is oppressive *and* oppositional, a restriction *and* a reckoning. Neither Steinem nor Marcus says anything about the "force" of race being *at least* as restricting as gender in American life; indeed, in the days before the 2008 election, the question was asked: Who would Americans be more likely to elect, a black man or a white woman? Thus the American double bind: the inseparability of gender and racial injustice stands in the way of any American utopia in which liberty and justice for all is possible.

Whether or not Marcus intended this, her notion of gender as "a force to be reckoned with" is a suggestively flexible framework for considering the evolution of "gendered worlds" in feminist utopian texts. The "conceptual privilege" of heterosexism[3] and the oppositional consciousness raised by feminist movements is an obvious through-line for a survey of feminist utopian imaginary. The 1970s are often deemed a high-water mark for feminist utopian visioning, in alignment with the activism of second-wave and lesbian feminisms and the judicial victory of *Roe v. Wade*. Literature surveys often focus on classic touchstones of second-wave feminist speculation, starting with separatist and reverse-gender utopias and speculative worlds from Joanna Russ, Suzy McKee Charnas, Sally Miller Gearheart, Starhawk (Miriam Simos), Joan Slonczewski[4] – and Shulamith Firestone, whose *The Dialectics of Sex* includes the irritable charge that "there is not even a utopian feminist literature in existence."[5] Indeed, as Marguerite Duras once observed, and as author Lidia Yuknavitch quotes as an epigraph to *The Book of Joan*, "Heterosexuality is dangerous. It tempts you to aim at a perfect duality of desire. It kills the other story options."[6]

As if in answer to Duras, Yuknavitch argues that "we've got to reimagine ourselves, we've got to reinvent ourselves. Like I'm doing in [*The Book of Joan*], we've got to wrench ourselves out of old narratives that are going to keep us in perpetual war with one another."[7] Critic Joe P. L. Davidson asks, "What has happened to the feminist *utopia*?": "Imaginative attempts to construct social orders defined by liberation and freedom have been overshadowed in the last decade by tales of horror, feminist horizons of expectation filled not with fundamentally better worlds but instead the intensification of the worst tendencies of the present."[8] The SCOTUS Dobbs decision in 2022 may give the clearest answer to "what has happened": the bad faith of a political movement against women's bodily autonomy, along with the politicization of that central figure of social reproduction, the human child. Despite Firestone's objections to heterosexist reproductive futurism, the figure of the child remains central to contemporary "gendered worlds" of feminist speculation. However, the nature and function of that figure, I will argue, has shifted in the last twenty-five years.

The relationship of oppositional gender consciousness *to narrative* is the particular focus of this chapter's attention to "gendered worlds" in postwar utopian writing, including the fragile embedded utopias of Janet Russ's Whileaway in *The Female Man* and Marge Piercy's Mattapoisett in *Woman on the Edge of Time*; Margaret Atwood's and Sherri Tepper's unsettling dystopias of eugenics, controlled fertility, and sex slavery in *The Handmaid's Tale* and *The Gate to Women's Country*, respectively; in Octavia Butler's many stories of miscegenation and posthuman reproduction; and in contemporary speculative and Afrofuturist imaginaries. In broad brushstrokes, this chapter reviews feminist writers' efforts to (re)work the double bind of gender binarism and racial hierarchy, not simply to recover women from history, but to dislocate them as well. Of the figuration of Joan of Arc in her most recent novel, Yuknavitch argues she is "trying to relocate her ... in some other kind of narrative," a narrative that does not "settle into old binaries"; Yuknavitch is trying to queer the narrative.[9] As the brilliant (British) science-fiction writer China Miéville puts it, "if we take utopia seriously, as a total reshaping, its scale means we can't think it from this side. It's the process of making it that will allow us to do so. . . . We should utopia as hard as we can" (ellipsis in original).[10]

In the specific context of "gendered worlds" of postwar American utopian literature, "the process of making it" might propose a different kind of "reproduction" and/as history: an *engendering* of other histories and other forms of being beyond the conventionally heterosexual and beyond even the conventionally human figure of the child. Social reproduction in utopia, today, means the becoming of *difference* rather than sameness. Narratologically, then, the task of utopia is no longer "transcendence" (of opposites, of war, of anything nonharmonious); it becomes an achievement of the "immanence" of difference emerging from the moment. To put it another way, some recent writers are returning utopia to its own queerness by thinking through what it means to engender utopia – rather than settle what gender is, was, can be, or should be, we might imagine ways of being *as we are* in all our multiplicitous difference. This is a far cry from thinking American utopianism in terms of governance; it is a cry for the existential freedom *to be as one is* in the here and now.

A "Defeating Circularity"

By the 1950s, there existed already a tradition of women's speculative writing tapping into the generic possibilities and thematics of predominantly male-authored utopian and science fictions. Carol Farley Kessler's important anthology, *Daring to Dream,* indexes many of the themes recognizable to this day in the gendered worlds of contemporary speculative fiction: the disruption of gender-role expectations; resistance to male control over and narrow proscription of women's labor; women's financial independence; the possibilities of technology; a drive for self-autonomy. Kessler outlines these texts' critical look at the "defeating circularity" of what Charlotte Perkins Gilman, author of "A Woman's Utopia" and *Herland,* describes as a mutually enforcing "narrowing" of women by men, and men by women.[11] While contemporaneous technological efficiencies promise women "time and thoughts" beyond domestic, especially *reproductive,* labor, domestic roles remain the moral anchor of good housekeeping in Gilman's "remodeled" American homeland.[12]

The final piece in Kessler's anthology, however, Gertrude Short's story, "A Visitor from Venus," seems to gesture in another direction. Published in the immediate aftermath of World War II, the story registers the discontent of American women forced to return from work at the "home front" to the work of the home itself. Social histories of this period agree that the retrenchment of women's agency created the conditions under which second-wave American feminism would take hold. "A Visitor from Venus" takes place *during* wartime and follows a female transport aviator, Roberta, whose in-flight thoughts revolve around her love of professional independence, grateful not to be confined to domestic work (though her fiancé wishes she *had* stayed home). Forced by blizzard conditions, she lands in a wilderness area she cannot find on her military maps: there are no coordinates. In a scene anticipating today's online meetings, Roberta hears a "real-time" audio-visual report on a "*mission of goodwill and planetary neighborliness*" by an ambassador from the planet Venus to Earth.[13] The speaker, "Zua," finds this ever-warring planet "*strange and confused.*"[14] Sexual difference and hierarchy are responsible "in large part," with women "*held in slavery as a sex-creature,*" confined to procreation; the "darker skinned races" are similarly regarded as children to be controlled.[15] Zua's "queer (re)reading" of modern human history as fatally hierarchized ends with a hope, if not a prediction, that there will emerge a "free agent" among women or among the racially oppressed populations who will reject "unfreedom" (as Simone de Beauvoir put it, also in 1949).[16] At the moment, though, humanity lacks the intelligence to do so, Zua concludes, too immature as a civilization to evolve toward the ethical mutuality Venusians have already attained.

"A Little Criminal Conversation": Le Guin to Piercy

The linking of gender and race emerges in Ursula K. Le Guin's work as well, the exploration of gender and genre, kind and kinship, extending across nearly her entire career. Her fourth novel and first critically admired work, *The Left Hand of Darkness*, began as a thought experiment: "I eliminated gender, to find out what was left. Whatever was left would be, presumably, simply human. It would define the area that is shared by both men and women alike."[17] The novel dismantles the foundational fictions of gender dualism: "there is no division of humanity into strong and weak halves, protective/protected, dominant/submissive, owner/chattel, active/passive. In fact the whole tendency to dualism that pervades human thinking may be found to be lessened, or changed."[18] Le Guin reverses the orientation of Short's narrative frame, as human envoy Genly Ai arrives at the frigid planet Gethen (or Winter), where ambisexual inhabitants, unconscious of gender difference, experience no mass warfare, though plenty of political machination; no rape; "no psycho-sexual relationship to his mother or father," according to interpolated anthropological field notes ("The Question of Sex") from an early human investigator.[19] A forced survival journey with a Gethenite ally across a depopulated, politically neutral ice field finally prompts Ai's admission: "And I saw then again, and for good, what I had always been afraid to see, and had pretended not to see in him: that he [Estraven] was a woman as well as a man. . . . What I was left with was, at last, acceptance of him as he [*sic*] was."[20] Such scenes epitomize Le Guin's talent for stripping down characters to bare life and, as the author says, "opening the door to imagination, and the possibility of things being other than they are"; sex and sexuality offer "a tremendous playground, and it doesn't do any harm to have people's ideas shook up."[21]

Samuel R. Delany plays on a similar field but attends provocatively to entanglements of gender *and* race in terms of power relations. Dubbed the "first African-American science-fiction writer," Delany adds "queer," emphasizing his focus on the "rhetoric [of sex] and the discourse [of desire]" as well as race, and citing not only Le Guin, but also Toni Morrison, Octavia Butler, and others who trouble power, race, and sexual desire. This "darker and more dangerous tale" weaves through his stories, shapeshifting his characters, and sharpening his style of realism.[22] Delany was also an outspoken fan and friend of lesbian feminist Joanna Russ, whose *The Female Man* (1975) broke new ground in the field of feminist fabulation.[23]

Russ's "Female Man" is a splintered entity of four, epigenetically different versions of the author: "Joanna," "Jeannine," "Janet," and "Jael," each of whom inhabits one of an "infinite number of possible universes," brought together in space-time by Jael, who lives furthest in the future.[24] Jael's world is a battleground for which, she coyly hints, she recruits her earlier epigenetic selves as warriors. Sexual relations are understood simply as forms of power (as Delany appreciates), their technologies of sex including a variety of weaponized bioenhancements. Jael's war is precipitated by an Us and Them understanding of human interaction unchanged over the course of her civilization's history. "When I say Them and Us I mean . . . the two sides, there are always two sides, aren't there? I mean the men and the women." Her war exploits Manland's "fear" (of duality, of "themselves") and growing contempt of "real women."[25] Jael's world does feature males who are not "real-men," either surgically "changed," popularly called "the cunts"; or "half-changed," typically "artists, illusionists, impressionists of femininity who keep their genitalia but who grow slim, grow languid, grow emotional and feminine, all this the effect of spirit only."[26] Neither group seems remotely political in their turn away from an originally assigned sex; and the change appears to go just one way, M2F.

Janet's world, Whileaway, is an all-female utopia a millennium in the future, filled with highly intelligent, technologically advanced, extremely "workful," largely peaceful women, supported by a social "kinship web" that is flexible and constant.[27] After the male population is decimated by viral pandemic, genetic scarcity prompts a sudden evolutionary return to parthenogenic reproduction. (Self-)Generations later, Whileaway, graced with an "eternal optimism,"[28] celebrates community, family, and above all pleasure, sexual and otherwise; it represents a utopia far more appealing than, say, Charlotte Perkins Gilman's more severe *Herland.* Among the four Js, only Janet loves her community, and only she has children, which Whileawayans generally treasure. By novel's end, Jael's recruitment plan is revealed, and Janet – the only one of the other three Js who has ever fought for anything (she has won several duels) – demurs. While not one to step away from a fight, Jael's blatant militarism does not interest Janet. The characteristically abject Jeannine, "plucked" from a parallel history in which feminism never happened, is the only one who signs on to Jael's sex war: "You can bring in all the soldiers you want. You can take the whole place over; I wish you would."[29] As for Joanna, the feminist author-scholar reporting all this, the book of *The Female Man* is itself offered, in a Renaissance-type *envoi,* a flight-line toward possibility, toward a future where her tale of gender discrimination is simply ancient history.

Donna Haraway admires Russ's treatment of gender itself as a technology and praises the novel specifically for making "a patent scandal of the imagination, the intellect, nature, language, and history ... [its] linguistic and genetic miscegenation ... provoking a little technical and political intercourse, or criminal conversation, or reproductive commerce, about what counts as nature, for whom, and at what cost."[30] Marge Piercy's classic *Woman on the Edge of Time*, published within a year of *The Female Man*, focuses on gender and race, with sexual and social reproduction coming into sharper focus. Protagonist Connie is a poor, Hispanic woman whom we watch fall in and out of institutionalized treatment for drug abuse, child abuse, and psychiatric disorders. Her weak grip on self-control and sanity makes her "receptive" to Luciente, a time-traveler from Mattapoisett, located in the year 2137 in what had been the eastern United States. Like Jael, Luciente seeks contact with a historical "crux-time" that may have molded the shape of their own present.[31] The reason: Luciente's world is under attack from a parallel historical plane in which "corps," "multis," and "richies" (presumably the late-capitalist evolution of corporations, multinational industry, and the 1 percent) are bent on destroying her gentle society with their superior technologies of dimension-hopping and military control.

For its part, Mattapoisett has broken down the opposition between the natural and the technological, indeed of "all the old hierarchies," by intentionally removing from women the "original production" of giving birth.[32] With fetuses cultivated in long test-tubes, Mattapoisettians are no longer "biologically enchained" to their parents.[33] Morphological shifts (males capable of breast-feeding, for example) and linguistic shifts to ungendered nouns and pronouns are strange enough, but Connie recoils from the "brooders," condemning "the bland bottleborn monsters of the future, born without pain, multicolored like a litter of puppies."[34] Yet finally, understanding that gender categories are "not useful,"[35] Connie acknowledges these "monsters" are "without the stigmata of race and sex" and admits that her own child would have been better cared for in Mattapoisett.[36] *Woman on the Edge of Time* offers a more complex account-(ing) of gender, class, *and* race rooted in capitalism's ruthless logics than *The Female Man*, though both novels are regarded as the high-water mark in feminist speculative writing in the 1970s, along with Sally Gearhart's *The Wanderground.* With the advent of Reaganism in 1980, however, a sudden right-wing political swerve seemed to shut down expectations, or even hope, for progress toward a utopian feminist reality. Enter Margaret Atwood's *The Handmaid's Tale*, not set in any wilderness or time-space dimension, but in the here and how of a sexist carceral America.

"What's Going On"

Atwood's unsettling portrait of a Boston-based, ultra-right theocracy where fertile women are reduced to sex slaves reflects the urgent sense of feminist crisis during the years of the Reagan administration. Following its original publication, some feminists critiqued the novel's move away from endorsing a radical feminist agenda, leaving the central handmaid Offred, it appeared, at the mercy of her lover Luke, an underofficer of the Gilead command. The novel leaves the posthumous construction of her history to a smug, (still) sexist, future academic in the "Historical Notes" appended to the "tale," which the scholar had himself constructed from a cache of audiotapes found randomly strewn in a locker. If the novel's Offred fails to wrest political agency from her situation, however, it is another story in the five-season Hulu production of *The Handmaid's Tale* launched on April 26, 2017. In this adaptation, it's time for *payback*, a theme Atwood develops in her 2007 Massey lectures at Harvard University. Her focus is ethical decision-making and obligation: "simply the way human beings have thought about what is owed, who owes it, and how it should be repaid – the balancing of the scales, in religion, literature, the criminal underworld, the revenge tragedy, and in Nature."[37] The increasing violence enacted by the handmaids in the Hulu series, culminating in the "particicution" of Offred's former ritual rapist, Commander Fred, made some viewers uncomfortable enough to stop watching.[38] But the US Supreme Court's unsettling of reproductive rights in 2022, striking down women's constitutional right to choose abortion, renewed popular appreciation of the novel and the series, as now-familiar scenes of political protests in Handmaid costume at courthouses and government buildings worldwide signal that the force of regressive sex/gender ideologies of "the past" was only temporarily muted.

From a purely literary standpoint, the novel's legacy is more complex. A cluster of dystopian novels in the last ten years respond to the erosion of reproductive rights and the build-up of conservative strategies to control social reproduction by reenacting, again and again, Atwood's scenario: Hillary Jordan's *When She Woke*, Louise Erdrich's *Future Home of the Living God*, Jennie Melamed's *Gather the Daughters*, Leni Zumas's *Red Clocks*, Bina Shah's *Before She Sleeps: A Novel*, Kim Liggett's *The Grace Year*, and Joanne Ramos's *The Farm*. All are viewed as contemporary responses to Atwood's 1985 novel. Several texts highlight the racial logics of reproduction that Atwood leaves unremarked; but as a group, the texts are uneven in quality, and most are not as compelling, with one or two exceptions, to which I turn.

Queer Generations and Radical Imagining: Erdrich and Yuknavitch

Two novels appeared in 2017 that recover the imaginative force of utopian disruption. National Book Award winner Louise Erdrich's *Future Home of the Living God* is marketed as "captur[ing] the essence of *The Handmaid's Tale*,"[39] but this is misleading. Set in an ecologically damaged present (again) that is facing birth-rate collapse, the novel recalls the Bush-era US Patriot Act's surveillance practices "in order to protect national security" by tracking fertility records and rounding up pregnant women into "gravid detention centers."[40] Unlike Offred, who is kept from writing and from any sort of text that would let her know "what's going on,"[41] Erdrich's protagonist Cedar maintains at all cost the archives of her own life in precisely dated journal entries comprising a proleptic love letter to her unborn child. Living at the confluence of ecological precarity, depopulation, and infrastructural breakdown, Cedar eschews Offred's abject despair. As "an insecure Ojibwe, a fledgling Catholic ... maybe a walking contradiction, maybe two species in one body. Nobody knows," she appreciates (like Erdrich herself) mystery and strangeness, particularly the Christian incarnation.[42] Considering the Virgin's experience of carrying "the embodiment of God's word," she wonders whether "we are experiencing a reverse incarnation. ... I want to see past my lifetime, past yours, into exactly what the paleontologist says will not exist: the narrative. I want to see the story. More than anything, I am frustrated by the fact that I'll never know how things turn out."[43]

Cedar avoids retrospective blame for what the present is become: "*Now* is all we have, I tell myself. Work on the *now*, the hereness, the present" and on exercising "extreme hyperawareness."[44] Her narrative of carefully dated journal entries evolves into queer autotheory, seeing reality "from another side" of both Christianity and Ojibwe spirituality: "Without act or will on my part, I am creating a collage of DNA and dreams, all those words made flesh, and I am doing it even in my sleep."[45] Kaylee Jangula Mootz reads this novel through Grace Dillon's theorization of Native Apocalypse as "encompassing futuristic narratives that imagine a reversal of historical events" and "facilitat[ing] a return to balance through apocalyptic upheaval."[46] Cedar's maternal body is "an archive," she argues: *biological* ("millions of years of evolutionary data within its DNA"); and *linguistic* ("an archive of memory, story, song and words").[47] Cedar's body is also an archive of the historical "link between race and reproduction" and "a legacy written on the body of both violence and survivance, violation and adaptation."[48] Moreover, a Native "spirit-mother," which according to Mootz Cedar represents, is regarded as a "life-giving force bringing together human and non-human life."[49]

Cedar herself regards the pregnancy as "a wilderness of being," without pathways of time or space.[50] The frequency of malformed and stillborn children signals degraded genetic pathways too, but Cedar's investment in her growing fetus suggests another possibility: "maybe we aren't just copying ourselves" but returning to the juncture of "the evolutionary forked road": "At any time our bodies could change their minds" and return to parthenogenesis, no longer "outsourcing fertilization."[51] In this case everything that Cedar is, every aspect of her history and her present experience, so carefully documented as both personal and tribal archives, becomes "the DNA" of the unborn child who, Cedar believes, is not the end of the line but is the beginning of another way of being. Following Mootz's argument, a utopian hope, however speculative, remains: the child comes into being as a figuration of the Native Apocalypse's vision of a return to balance. Given Cedar's Christian upbringing, Cedar also anticipates the child as a reappearance of "the Living God": born on Christmas Day ("For once in my life, I am right on time"), the infant marks the immanence of "the living Word" – but *not* "the word uttered by God to make life, but by the baby who recognizes the being on whom life depends" – that is, "Ma, ah, oh, mama. Mother. . . . I know the Word. It is the oldest word in any language, first utterance."[52] "The story" has a new beginning: not at the word of the Father – but at the word *for* the Mother. The shift is subtle but transformative: from a model of *lineage* to a *relationality* of care and kin, of the human and more-than-human. The child finally born, glimpsed only momentarily, appears of another "kind": with copper hair that "glows" and eyes "darker, already burning to live. . . . I looked into the soul of the world" – a child simultaneously ancient and new.[53] Following Dillon again, Mootz calls both the childbirth and the narrative itself "a return to ourselves."[54]

Lidia Yuknavitch's *The Book of Joan* is similarly situated as a contemporary *Handmaid's Tale*, although it boasts a grotesque scene of organ breeding to restore reproduction that Atwood herself only came to in the later MaddAddam trilogy. *The Book of Joan*'s narrative scaffolding derives from the hagiographic history of Joan of Arc, whose name, disruptive spirit, and martyred body are reprised in the figure of a second Joan, also of mystical abilities. The mythic narrative shape of "romance" is ironically critiqued in the depredations of the novel's Jean de Men, whose medieval namesake, Jean de Meun, had completed *The Romance of the Rose*. Contemporaneous author Christine de Pizan, who objected to the de Meun's misogyny and authored the roughly contemporary female utopian vision *The City of Ladies*, is the namesake of a third central character, Christine. By the time *this* history is set centuries later (in 2049), the affluent-only remnants of "Mother" Earth's population remove themselves to CIEL, a "floating space world" ensuring not just humanity's survival but "an actual evolution of the mind and soul."[55]

Within several decades, however, a morphological "*de*volution" is occurring, with race and gender markers fading into a dull colorlessness and toward "asexual systems" of reproduction. The genitalia are first to lose their shape: as a consequence, "there are no births here."[56] In response to this fatal threat, the tyrannical de Men insists on preserving heterosexual reproduction by performing vivisectional open-vagina surgeries. By experimenting with hormone treatments to *regrow* ovaries in young girls and experimenting with hormonal treatments, all females are relegated to "rape, death, insanity, prison, or marriage."[57] This juxtaposition of medieval and futuristic misogyny, symbolized by reprize of romance characters, offers an ironical protest to de Men's savage perversion of romance narrative; that is, de Men's discourse functions "to sanction, validate, and accelerate that act [of rape]."[58] According to narrator Christine/Chris, "the idea of men and women – or the distinction between men and women – was radically and forever dead. . . . Perhaps we were some new species, some new genus with alternative sexual opportunities."[59] Only Joan, "through some genetic act of grace, has retained her body intact," remaining fertile, and she becomes the "savior" of CIEL-dwellers above the Earth; she is "the force of life we could never return to. . . . our only remaining connection to the material world"[60] – but she has remained on Earth, refusing De Men's cultish following.

Like Cedar, Christine wants a "new form of storytelling" to record a new kind of human. In this novel, that figure has a name: an *engendrine*, defined as "someone whose mutation has resulted in a kind of human–matter interface."[61] Joan is such a figure, "the rarest of engendrines, more than a breeding gold mine. Her body is of the earth more uniquely than any other in human existence . . . closer to matter and elements than to human."[62] As a reproductive interface within one body, "she has the power to regenerate the entire planet and its relationship to the sun. She can bring the planet back to life,"[63] for which purpose de Men hopes to enslave Joan as the sole hope for human survival. This second Joan is "for us, the force of life we could never return to," says Christine.[64] In apparent devotion to this Joan, Chris becomes expert in "skingrafting" the history of Joan (first *and* second incarnations) onto her own flesh: "my skin coming alive under my fingers."[65] As a flesh-text artist, the word is literally made flesh, "and thus the gap between representation and living, collapsed. In the beginning was the word, and the word became our bodies."[66] Christine's body, in short, *is The Book of Joan.*

There is a second engendrine, but not a mutated one; rather a sculpted one. Her name, Nyx, indicates the level of her negative morality as compared to Joan's positive: when Nyx, sent by de Men to capture her, meets Joan on Earth, Nyx warns that Joan is alive only "because I haven't decided who you are. Saviors are dead. God is dead. Are you about power or love? It's a simple choice I'll have to make."[67] Hearing Nyx's history of torture and surgeries, which leaves her with both a "truncated and crooked worm of a penis" *and* "a partially sutured half-open gash" for a vagina ("Another attempt at genitalia. Botched"), Joan understands Nyx's icy stare, her "equality of hate" ("Rage, wedged between us like the ghosts of the girls we were"), and her "brutal will toward death" – which raises in Joan "a kind of radical compassion to exist as a self in relation to others."[68] Nyx puts it simply: "I am proof of what happens when power turns its eye toward procreation. I am a monstrosity" – and worse yet for Nyx, one who seeks love rather than seeks power.[69] Assured of Joan's commitment to love and "radical compassion," Nyx receives the answer she wants to her original question. They form an alliance, then, to bring down de Men.

Like so many other resistant women in feminist fiction, the engendrines possess special powers: Nyx teaches Joan to ride a "telluric current," their "combined energies [able to] dematerialize us and rematerialize us anywhere."[70] As with Roberta in "A Visitor from Venus," Earth's landmarks evaporate as Joan and Nyx travel, "so radically changed that they look like different continents, mountain ranges," "Geology unbound."[71] In a denouement too complex to unravel here, the figures of Joan, Nyx, and Christine unite as a single energy to defeat and "ravage" de Men – but "this killing scene has another side. Creation" as hundreds of children, "of all colors ... materialize from nothingness and rise."[72] Of this event, modern Christine's longtime lover Trinculo summarizes: "we are the proud parents of what's going to happen down there"; though they will not see the new story unravel, their constant resistance to brute power has kept possibility open. Joan is reunited with her lover, Leone, and they too are creators, two women "going down into [*sic*] one another": "We will not conceive this way. Reproduction will become another kind of story ... A different story, leading whoever is left toward something we've not yet imagined," a *rebecoming*.[73] The ending of *The Book of Joan* leaves the reader with a final message: that the "wound" that is woman will heal itself, and on *that* day, existence ends and begins again. With a new story, "*some new myth*": "*there's no other way to say this. Whoever we are becoming is not part of any narrative I've ever known. ... Could the story go someplace as yet unknown?*"[74] Just as Joan and Nyx travel the "energy lines" that connect Earth to CIEL, Christine rides narrative lines of flight toward a "someplace as yet unknown," a portal of possibility.

"What Would Be on the Other Side? What on Earth Would It Be? What on Earth?"

American Afrofuturism today itself *is* such a portal.[75] Nearing the first quarter-century mark of the third millennium, such speculative vibrancy is less about "realizing our dreams of freedom and justice,"[76] more about doing the "endless work"[77] of taking utopia – and especially the queer crux of utopian thought and writing – seriously. Works by Samuel Delany and Octavia Butler – I would add Toni Morrison's masterpiece *Paradise* – cleared pathways elsewhere, altering genetics and genres along the way. Sheree Renée Thomas's important anthology, *Dark Matter: A Century of Speculative Fiction from the African Diaspora*, offers an early collection of such short fiction, including not only Delany and Butler but also Jewelle Gomez, Tananarive Due, Nalo Hopkinson, Nisi Shawl, Ishmael Reed, and others; important essays on racism, blackness, and science fiction by Delany, Butler, and others close the volume. Nalo Hopkinson and Uppinder Mehan's edited collection, *So Long Been Dreaming: Postcolonial Science Fiction & Fantasy*, features Thomas, Shawl, Andrea Hairston, Larissa Lai, and others. Hopkinson's own career was already well on the rise, buoyed by the early success of the now classic *Brown Girl in the Ring* and *Midnight Robber*, with *The Salt Roads* as well as collected short stories following.

The infusion of black and queer speculative fiction into American utopian writing includes N. K. Jemisin's astonishing work (the *Inheritance* and *Broken Earth* trilogies; the *Great Cities* series inaugurated by *The City We Became*), as well as Nnedi Okorafor's *Who Fears Death*, *Lagoon*, the Young Adult "Nsibidi Scripts" series, and the Binti trilogy. The "Black Pages" and "Black Stars" series of short speculative fiction from Amazon Publishing includes not only Jemisin and Okorafor, but also Chimamanda Ngozi Adichie, in addition to Shawl and Hopkinson. Relative newcomer Rivers Solomon, author of *An Unkindness of Ghosts*, *The Deep*, and *Sorrowland*, joins all of these writers in reimagining the force of race and gender, generativity, and genre. The resources of Indigenous knowledges ground these narratives in foundations alien to Western conceptions, including forms of conjuring, loud dreaming, and in-seeing that emphasize the essential plasticity of narrative and make visible Miguel Abensour's notion of utopia as "the various forms of alterity to which the desire for freedom . . . has given birth through the course of history."[78]

To be "given birth" by a desire for *freedom*: this is a convenient bridge, backward and forward, to the image of the child and the theme of reproduction and reproductive rights that have persisted as dominant tropes in postwar utopian literature. Queerly conceived children begin to populate speculative literature, often by authors appealing to similar resources of Indigenous knowledges and cosmologies. Hopkinson's Caribbean-inflected *Midnight Robber* is exemplary: only in the novel's last pages do we realize that the narrative voice throughout the novel is that of a virtual *eshu*, part of an Anansi-web entity "Granny Nanny" who via "earbug" devices, guides and protects inhabitants of Toussaint, a planetary utopia for black populations willing to leave the toxicity (environmental as well as racial) of a dying Earth. The novel follows Tan-Tan, a nine-year-old girl who stows away on a ship taking her father to exile on a penal planet for raping that same daughter. Once Tan-Tan is discovered there, her father continues the abuse, impregnating her at the very moment when her former house *eshu* and Granny Nanny have finally located her, having tracked her through multidimensional space. At that moment, they attempt contact with the girl's earbug in order to reconnect her to the home planet's network. As Tan-Tan's fetus develops, Nanny figures out a new calibration:

> She instruct the nanomites in your mamee blood to migrate into your growing tissues, to alter you [. . .] so all of you could *feel* nanny song at this calibration. [. . .] You will be a weave in she web. Flesh people talk say how earbugs give them a sixth sense . . . Not a fully functional perception. You now; you really have that extra limb.[79]

Tubman, the name given the infant on the last page of the novel, is not a "monster" born from rape (as Tan-Tan feared), but a "little bit of person in her arms," "one living connection with the Grande Anansi Nanotech Interface"; minutes old, he is already singing the "nanny-song" understood by Toussaint citizens – and by the exile planet's Indigenous inhabitants, bird-creatures who save Tan-Tan from harm and nurse her to health.[80] Tubman is literally a new kind of human, whose kinship promises to extend to beings both human and more-than-human. "***Tubman: the human bridge from slavery to freedom. . . . A seer woman might have name you that.***"[81]

Nnedi Okorafor's narrator in *Who Fears Death*, Onyesonwu, is also a child of rape, marked and shunned as "Ewu" (the word means risk, danger, hazard) in a far-future Nigeria. Her mother and rapist-father, however, are sorcerers, the former gifting magical abilities to Onye; the latter determined to destroy her nascent powers. In years-long training to control her magic, which includes shapeshifting, regeneration of life and limb (including her own clitoris, years after its excision), and the ability to travel at will among other spatiotemporal planes (the so-called wilderness of unorganized space-time), Onye is joined by Mwita, a young man and fellow trainee, also Ewu, as not a rape-child but a sorcerer child. "What will our child be?" Onye asks Mwita, as they commit themselves to each other: "*Ewu*" is his response.[82] In a last battle against her father, Onye draws power to herself by drawing *together* her own egg and Mwita's sperm inside her. This moment of self-generated conception creates a surge of power that overwhelms the evil that is her father.

Following the pattern of a "new kind" of child born, this *ewu* child, about to be born, stands as a potent challenge to the forms of intolerance rampant in this version of Nigerian society.

In a final example, African American writer Rivers Solomon's most recent novel, *Sorrowland*, centers on Vern, a queer, partially sighted young woman driven from a cult enclave and an abusive husband/cult leader. Barely out of childhood herself, Vern flees deep into the woods (another wilderness) and births twins. All three are sustained through the hospitality of the forest, enhanced by an unexpected strength Vern seems to gain there. Their eventual return to Vern's home constitutes a final reckoning with the crimes of that community; at the same time as Vern continues to change physically. In a radical instance of cross-species intercourse, Vern learns she is host to a fungus that gradually morphs her body, building up an exoskeleton such that she is becoming more of the wilderness that hosted her in safety, than of humankind. Again a self-generating transformation is at work; according to critic Roxane Gay, the change is "beyond human . . . something terrifying and powerful that just might allow her to break free from all that haunts her."[83] From Octavia Butler to Rivers Solomon is a clear line: both mothers and children are *ewu*, their very existence a threat to the social reproduction of sameness. In each example, we see mobilized the powers of a more radical imaginary of difference, the engendering of another way, another being: a queer generativity.

Conclusion

If gender in America is "a force to be reckoned with" still, these texts propose that the intransigent binarism of gender and race opposition continues to limit any mutual "self-actualization"[84] of males and females in a just and harmonious commonwealth. *To utopia hard*, as Miéville demands, means taking up the hard work of critique and reckoning, including self-reckoning, with the entangled forces of gender and race within American biopolitics, "even," as Miéville adds, in the "absence of an alternative."[85] Why the word "even" here? Because that absence is only apparent; it may not yet be possible – but, as queer theorizing of utopia proposes, it always already exists as a virtual imagining, which, I increasingly believe, is exactly as concrete as utopia needs to be. The force generated by critical intelligence *is* utopia's praxis, theoretically inventive and imaginatively creative. To be otherwise risks reinforcing our enthrallment to dominant social mythologies. The queer force of utopia itself as a *genre* of textual narrative, or as mode of thinking, re-presents itself throughout the postwar period in faithful, and increasingly frequent, resistances to the logics of gender, race, and sexuality.

When feminist writers do engage the queer resources of utopia, even that most persistent figuration of "humanity's future" and hope – the child – is recast. This chapter touches on those literary moments where the radical utopian work of *engendering* otherwise erupts into being, at once highlighting the limits of feminist narratives that attempt to derail the social reproduction of a monolithic patriarchy, and signalling the possibilities of utopian (queer) generativity. The *engendrine* is perhaps the best term of all to characterize the contemporary version of the disruptive germ that Darko Suvin calls the *novum*: a break in history, a radical Event, a contingency of the moment that offers a "shift" (Hopkinson), a "portal" (Morrison), a "reverse Incarnation" (Erdrich). I have argued elsewhere,[86] that there has always been something "queer" about utopia. As Amalia Ziv observes, in reeducating the imagination, utopia twerks "resignifications of sex, gender and identity – and the cultural context in which some things and practices signify, and some don't" and thereby offers "repertoire[s] of cultural notions, narratives, and roles."[87] Similarly, Caterina Nirta thus proposes "a new ethics of utopianism" deriving from "a difference in being," specifically answering to Lee Edelman's and Leo Bersani's nihilistic descriptions of reproductive futurism, whereby "reproduction of the same" under a heteronormative imperative "kills the potentiality of queer [transformation] in the present."[88] Nirta's contribution to utopian theory here is to recover utopia *in* the present – rather than wait for it in the future. In her reading, it is the queer, transgender body that captures the immanence of utopia: "a condition of actualization,"[89] as hooks had hoped – but not in the temporality of Ernst Bloch's "not-yet"; following a Deleuzian conception of "the temporality of the present," Nirta would relocate utopia of the future into the *now* of the present: "queer utopia – transgender – is a futurity of the *here* and of the *now*, a *virtuality* that does not belong to the past nor does it lend itself to projections of the future, but it is totally immersed in the very now of the present."[90] This makes perfect sense as a reading, too, of the latest novels treated in this chapter, by Erdrich, Yuknavitch, Morrison, Hopkinson, Okorafor and Solomon, who create "new DNA strands" for new genders and narrative genres, "made from everything we see."[91]

Notes

1. Gloria Steinem, "Women Are Never Front-Runners," *The New York Times* (January 8, 2008), online.
2. Ruth Marcus, "The Force of Gender," *The Washington Post* (March 5, 2008), online.

3. Eve Kosofy Sedgewick, *Epistemology of the Closet* (Berkeley: University of California Press, 1990), 31.
4. There is a substantial list of excellent critical appreciations of feminist utopian writing from the mid-1970s and onwards, including monographs and edited collections: Angelica Bammer, *Partial Visions: Feminism and Utopianism in the 1970s* (London: Routledge, 1992); Marleen Barr, *Feminist Fabulation: Space/Postmodern Fiction* (Iowa City: University of Iowa Press, 1992) and *Future Females, The Next Generation: New Voices and Velocities in Feminist Science Fiction Criticism* (New York: Rowman and Littlefield, 2000); Tom Moylan, *Scraps of the Untainted Sky: Science Fiction, Utopia, Dystopia* (Boulder, CO: Westview Press, 2000), *Dark Horizons: Science Fiction and the Dystopian Imagination* (New York: Routledge, 2003), and *Demand the Impossible: Science Fiction and the Utopian Imagination*, edited by Baccolini and Moylan (Oxford: Peter Lang, 2014); Lisa Yaszek, *Galactic Suburbia: Recovering Women's Science Fiction* (Columbus: The Ohio State University Press, 2008); Jenny Wolmark, "Alternative Futures? Science Fiction and Feminism," *Cultural Studies* 2.1 (1988), 48–56; Jennifer Wagner-Lawlor, *Postmodern Utopias and Feminist Fictions* (New York: Cambridge University Pres. 2013) – and hundreds of essays by these and many other utopian, speculative-fiction, and feminist scholars.
5. Shulamith Firestone, *The Dialectic of Sex: The Case for Feminist Revolution* (New York: Bantam Books, 1973), 227.
6. Lidia Yuknavitch, *The Book of Joan* (Edinburgh: Canongate Books, 2019).
7. Amy Wang, "In 'The Book of Joan,' Lidia Yuknavitch Blends Dystopia with a Redefinition of Hope," *The Oregonian* (April 15, 2017), online.
8. J. P. L. Davidson, "Retrotopian Feminism: The Feminist 1970s, the Literary Utopia and Sarah Hall's *The Carhullan Army*," *Feminist Theory* 24.2 (2021), online.
9. Wang.
10. China Miéville, "The Limits of Utopia," *Salvage: Journal of Revolutionary Arts and Letters* (August 1, 2015), online.
11. Carol Farley Kessler, *Daring to Dream: Utopian Fiction by United States Women before 1950*, second edition (Syracuse, NY: Syracuse University Press, 1995), xiv.
12. Kessler, xxvii.
13. Gertrude Short, "The Visitor from Venus," from *Daring to Dream*, edited by Kessler, 212–246 (221).
14. Short, 240. The meaning of the Arabic name "Zua" is "a truly pure heart"; the Hebrew word means "to shake (with fear)."
15. Short, 223, 231.
16. The concept of queer (re)reading is from Veronica Hollinger, "(Re)reading Queerly: Science Fiction, Feminism, and the Defamiliarization of Gender," *Science Fiction Studies* 26.1 (1999), 23–40.
17. Ursula K. Le Guin, "Is Gender Necessary?", from *The Language of the Night: Essays on Fantasy and Science Fiction*, revised edition, edited by Susan Wood (New York: HarperCollins, 1989), 155–172 (160).

18. Ursula K. Le Guin, *The Left Hand of Darkness*, fiftieth anniversary edition (New York: Ace Books, 2019), 100. In 1987, Le Guin was asked to write a jacket blurb for a new anthology of contemporary science fiction, *Synergy: New Science Fiction, Volume 1*, edited by George Zebrowski. In a letter to the senior editor John Radziewicz at Harcourt, Brace Jovanovich, Le Guin turned down the offer, noting the absence of women's writing and the overall "tone" of the volume, "which is so self-contentedly, exclusively male, like a club, or a locker room" ("Gentlemen, I Just Don't Belong Here," *Letters of Note*, online).
19. Le Guin, *Left Hand*, 100.
20. Le Guin, *Left Hand*, 226. Naomi Jacobs, "The Frozen Landscape in Feminist Utopian and Science Fiction," from *Utopian and Science Fiction by Women: Worlds of Difference* edited by Jane L. Donawerth and Carol A. Kolmerten (Syracuse, NY: Syracuse University Press, 1994), 190–204, is apropos: "the frozen landscape is one in which physical growth and decay are stilled; it is also free of those institutions and mores that restrict women in the social world ... a place where radical confrontations and reconceptualizations become possible" (190).
21. Le Guin, qtd. in Wood, 265–266.
22. Samuel L. Delany, *Shorter Views: Queer Thoughts & the Politics of the Paraliterary* (Middletown, CT: Wesleyan University Press, 1999), 20. He continues, "When caught in an actual rhetorical manifestation of desire – a particular sexual act, say, it is sometimes all but impossible to untangle the complex webs of power that shoot through it from various directions, the power relations that are the act and that constitute it" (20). Throughout his long career, Delany pursues a queer realism that is aligned – in novels such as *Babel-17*, *Stars in My Pockets Like Grains of Sand*, and his many stories – with a science-fictional imaginary of what science-fiction theorist Darko Suvin calls "the space of a potent *estrangement*" in *Metamorphoses of Science Fiction: On the Poetics and History of a Literary Genre* (Oxford: Peter Lang, 2016), 2.
23. The term comes from Marleen Barr, *Feminist Fabulation*. Donna J. Haraway singles out *The Female Man* among many stories offering an "elsewhere born out of the hard (and sometimes joyful) work of getting on together in a kin group of cyborgs and goddesses" in *Modest_Witness@Second_Millenium. FemaleMan© Meets OncoMouse™: Feminism and Technoscience* (New York: Routledge, 1997), 3.
24. Joanna Russ, *The Female Man* (Boston: Beacon Press, 1986), 7.
25. Russ, 170.
26. Russ, 167.
27. Russ, 31. Years back, many men were killed off through conflict with women; the rest were killed by a virus toxic only to males.
28. Russ, 52.
29. Russ, 211.
30. Haraway, 75.
31. Marge Piercy, *Woman on the Edge of Time* (New York: Fawcett, 1976), 177.

32. Piercy, 105.
33. Piercy, 105.
34. Piercy, 98.
35. Piercy, 214. In Piercy's later *He, She, and It* (1991), neither are the categories of human and nonhuman, as love and desire come to be shared.
36. Piercy, 106.
37. Margaret Atwood, *Payback: Debt and the Shadow Side of Wealth* (Toronto: House of Anansi Press, 2019), 12.
38. In the official trailer to her HBO MasterClass, Atwood observes that the violence in *The Handmaid's Tale* represents nothing human beings have not already perpetrated on one another: "When I wrote *The Handmaid's Tale*, nothing went into it that had not happened in real life somewhere at some time. The reason I made that rule is that I didn't want anybody saying, 'You certainly have an evil imagination, you made up all these bad things.' I didn't make them up."
39. Louis Erdrich, *Future Home of the Living God* (New York: HarperCollins, 2017). This quote from Roxane Gay is from the book jacket of the first paperback edition of the novel.
40. Erdrich, 73.
41. Margaret Atwood, *The Handmaid's Tale* (New York: Anchor Books, 2017), 224.
42. Erdrich, 66–67.
43. Erdrich, 67.
44. Erdrich, 69.
45. Erdrich, 239.
46. Kaylee Jangula Mootz, "The Body and the Archive in Louise Erdrich's *Future Home of the Living God*," *Journal of the Fantastic in the Arts* 31.2 (2020), 263–276 (264).
47. Mootz, 268.
48. Mootz, 268
49. Mootz, 269.
50. Erdrich, 67.
51. Erdrich, 225.
52. Erdrich, 263.
53. Erdrich, 264.
54. Mootz, 272.
55. Yuknavitch, 7.
56. Yuknavitch, 8.
57. Yuknavitch, 21.
58. Yuknavitch, 20.
59. Yuknavitch, 22.
60. Yuknavitch, 46.
61. Yuknavitch, 94.
62. Yuknavitch, 190, 198.
63. Yuknavitch, 190.

64. Yuknavitch, 46.
65. Yuknavitch, 46.
66. Yuknavitch, 22.
67. Yuknavitch, 209.
68. Yuknavitch, 209.
69. Yuknavitch, 207.
70. Yuknavitch, 211.
71. Yuknavitch, 214, 216.
72. Yuknavitch, 251, 252.
73. Yuknavitch, 259–260.
74. Yuknavitch, 263.
75. Toni Morrison, *Paradise* (New York: A.A. Knopf, 1998), 305.
76. bell hooks, *Feminism Is for Everybody: Passionate Politics*, second edition (New York: Routledge, 2015), xiv.
77. Toni Morrison, *Paradise* (New York: A.A. Knopf, 1998), 318.
78. Miguel Abensour, "Persistent Utopia," *Constellations* 15.3 (2008), 406–421 (407).
79. Nalo Hopkinson, *Midnight Robber* (New York: The Warner Company, 2000), 328.
80. Hopkinson, 328.
81. Hopkinson, 329.
82. Nnedi Okorafor, *Who Fears Death?* (New York: DAW, 2010), 172.
83. Roxane Gay, comment posted on Goodreads, January 21, 2021.
84. hooks, xiv.
85. Miéville.
86. See my section, "The Next 500 Years of Utopian and Dystopian Literature," (15–20) in the introduction by Peter Marks, Fátima Vieira, and Jennifer Wagner-Lawlor to the *Palgrave Handbook of Utopian and Dystopian Literatures* (Cham: Palgrave Macmillan, 2022), 1–21.
87. Amalia Ziv, *Explicit Utopias* (Albany: SUNY Press, 2015), 230–231.
88. Caterina Nirta, "Actualized Utopias: The *Here* and *Now* of Transgender," *Politics & Gender* 13 (2017), 181–208 (192, 191).
89. Nirta, 206.
90. Nirta, 181.
91. Yuknavitch, 260.

CHAPTER 4

America and/as White Supremacy

Edward K. Chan and Patricia Ventura

America – and all that signifies in the United States – has the indelible mark of white supremacy running throughout its past, present, and future.[1] We define white supremacy not only as a social and cultural regime of exploitation and abuse by people of European descent upon others deemed by that system to be outside the category of whiteness, but, importantly, also a process of centering whiteness, often in relation to patriarchal heteronormativity.[2] The utopian, white settler-colonial origin story of the "shining city on the hill" was created by displacing and killing Indigenous peoples, establishing chattel slavery, racializing various ethnic immigrant groups (such as Irish, Italian, and Jewish people), incarcerating Black people since the end of slavery and Japanese Americans during World War II, building a manual labor economy on the backs of workers mostly viewed as nonwhite, and supporting past and continuing police brutality against Black and Brown people.[3] Clearly, the United States has always been a country shaped by racism or, as speculative-fiction (sf) writer Tananarive Due puts it, American "history has been a dystopia,"[4] especially when we study it through the lens of white supremacy.

Racial science from the seventeenth century onward devised racial hierarchies and created notions of white supremacy, which in turn shaped the United States as a racial state.[5] To say that the United States was built on these processes and practices of racialization is not saying anything new, but it does mean that considering utopian thought and writing in the context of America – whether seen as eutopian (a good place) or dystopian (a bad place) – must include notions of race and white supremacy, which have been underexplored in utopian studies, though this has begun to change. So, to bring the United States together with its white supremacist past, present, and possible futures, this chapter necessarily walks the terrain of racist and antiracist formulations of utopia, which have predominantly been dystopic during the time period covered by this collection; however, just as importantly, we must always look to the progressively eutopian horizon expressed in antiracist representations in order to offer a vision of the way we want the world to be. Announcing a long-standing notion in utopian and science fiction studies, sf writer Ursula K. Le Guin writes, "every eutopia contains a dystopia, every dystopia contains a eutopia."[6] Thus, even as dystopia predominates, there is always space for hope.

As for our historical present, we write this chapter in 2021–2022, during a season of white supremacist terror and Covid pandemic exhaustion. As we begin the third decade of the twenty-first century, we saw again the reality of white supremacy and an unceasing American fascism that historian Robin D. G. Kelley categorized, "not as some aberration from the march of progress, an unexpected right-wing turn, but a logical development of Western civilization itself . . . a blood relative of slavery and imperialism, global systems rooted not only in capitalist political economy but in racist ideologies that were already in place at the dawn of modernity."[7] Changing the course of that Western trajectory and creating a new future requires, in the words of sf writer adrienne maree brown, that "we must dream the impossible, dream it together, out loud, until it becomes practice and pathway."[8]

As we look at the relationship between white supremacy and American utopian thinking since 1945, we see two main trends. The first asserts white supremacy either in a default form that implies or assumes the centrality of whiteness or even in an explicit and outright embrace of white supremacist ideology. The second directly challenges white supremacy and envisions at least a glimmer of what a different world might look like, which we see in some notable twentieth- and twenty-first-century texts; however, we start to hear more and more of these challenges from more and more voices in the last few decades. What also becomes clear in the big picture is that there is an ongoing dynamic tension between those representations that, on the one hand, either maintain white supremacy as a status quo or openly call for it through violent revolution and, on the other, those that critique white supremacist ideology or envision the revolution to subvert it. In each of the following sections, we try to give a sense of these larger categories while highlighting a few texts to illustrate the trends. We begin by examining the fundamental premise of American literature – whiteness itself.

Default White Supremacy

Shaped by the presence of Blackness as a pervasive Otherness, whiteness is the norm as Toni Morrison establishes in *Playing in the Dark*. As she states, American readers have been trained to assume characters are white and that whiteness is the default category unless characters are specifically marked as nonwhite through references to skin color, names, and other racialized characteristics.[9] Following on to this, we take white supremacy here not simply as racist movements like the KKK or even everyday acts of racism (intentional or not), but also as the assumption of whiteness as the universal norm and nonwhiteness as the marked, the Other, in structures of power and cultural artifacts such as literature. As a result, whiteness becomes the default assumption of fictional characters and is privileged as the neutral and innocent center of American culture and its representations.

The classic eutopian and dystopian texts mobilize a number of strategies of reinforcing white supremacy: masking it, presuming it, or ignoring it. Some of the major eutopian works in the US tradition ignore race and the way it is situated in white supremacy, as in Edward Bellamy's *Looking Backward* (1888), or presume it as the natural order of things as in Charlotte Perkins Gilman's *Herland* (1915), or simply push it aside as in B. F. Skinner's *Walden Two* (1948).[10] While race functions in different ways in other national contexts, the classic dystopias in world literature such as Yevgeny Zamyatin's *We* and George Orwell's *1984* implicitly reinforce a white supremacist framework by essentially ignoring nonwhiteness.

These canonical texts seem to lay out a model for postwar dystopias by American writers that also effectively ignore or downplay race and by default reinforce the centrality of whiteness, despite other generic, satirical, or aesthetic merits. In Ray Bradbury's *Fahrenheit 451*, for example, the character Beatty notes that no racial or ethnic groups, including the white majority, may be offended. Thus, "colored people don't like *Little Black Sambo*. Burn it. White people don't feel good about *Uncle Tom's Cabin*. Burn it."[11] Even though society must assuage racial animosities, there are no identifiable characters of color in the novel. Moreover, the idea that racial minorities might deserve social justice or be understandably upset about degrading or damaging representations is subsumed under the novel's attack on censorship of all kinds. In many texts, nonwhiteness often takes the form of merely passing references, part of the narrative backdrop – and this is a form of white supremacy by default. In the fundamental absence or marginalization of race, we would argue that these texts participate in the foundational ideology of whiteness.

Indeed, even in mid-century dystopias, where the author is purposely trying to include nonwhite characters as part of an attempt at racial progressiveness, they are essentially marginal, even when appearing frequently. As Jacqueline Foertsch convincingly establishes in *Reckoning Day: Race, Place, and the Atom Bomb in Postwar America*, these nonwhite characters appear in limited positions that support the main white characters in generic roles she calls "servant-savior-savant."[12] As part of a larger trend in postwar sf of either ignoring race or engaging in gestures toward nominal racial progressivism that she calls "half-baked postwar liberalism,"[13] these texts are ultimately recontained within the conservative structures of race in the period. Foertsch sees this "servant-savior-savant" pattern in many representative postapocalyptic dystopias resulting from nuclear war, pandemics, and natural disasters – from George R. Stewart's *Earth Abides* to Philip K. Dick's *Dr. Bloodmoney*. The inclusion of racialized characters in these novels gestures toward a sense of racial progressivism only to fail at actual inclusiveness, reasserting white people as the dominant central figures.

Even texts confronting race head-on, such as Robert A. Heinlein's *Farnham's Freehold*, cannot seem to dislodge the white supremacist frame. Here, a white family with a Black servant is thrown hundreds of years into a future world ruled by Black people, who of course must be cannibals, reviving colonial stereotypes. The novel is notorious because it imagines the worst nightmare of white supremacists – putting Black people in positions of power over whites. But in *Farnham's Freehold*, Heinlein makes an ostensibly bold statement against the very idea of slavery and white supremacist thinking by turning the tables and making white people the oppressed race to show that slavery is bad no matter what race comes out on top. For Heinlein, slavery in the United States or ancient Greece or wherever is *simply* a hierarchical structure of power in which any group could be plugged into the master or slave position with essentially the same outcome.

Thus, at the end of the novel, the white characters Hugh and Barbara discuss Ponse, their Black master:

> Barbara said stubbornly, "Hugh, how many white men of today could be trusted with the power Ponse had and use it with as much gentleness as he did use it?"
>
> "Huh? None. Not even yours truly. And that was a low blow about 'white men.' Color doesn't enter into it."
>
> "I withdraw the word 'white.' . . . " [ellipses in original][14]

Heinlein has a critical reputation as both a racist and an antiracist due to such color-blind treatments of race.[15] Farah Mendlesohn explains that Heinlein did include nonwhite characters in his writing (though mostly not in a significant way) and adamantly claimed he was not a racist. Yet at the same time, we find that he could express, in a letter to F. M. Busby written around the same time as *Farnham's Freehold*, "I don't feel any guilt over the fact that slavery existed in this country from 1619 to the Civil War. *I* didn't do it" (emphasis in original).[16] Heinlein was not able fully to understand race or acknowledge institutionalized racism,[17] so mouthpieces such as his character Hugh express his disentanglement of slavery and other forms of racism from their roots in hundreds of years of white supremacist ideology and colonialism.

What makes texts that ignore or marginalize racial issues different from *Farnham's Freehold* is that they quietly participate in mainstream thinking that centers whiteness, whereas texts like Heinlein's attempt to dismantle US racism against Black people using libertarian logic to suggest that it just so happened that whites were in the position of power, that race had nothing to do with it. Thus, race and racism are explained away as arbitrary or connected only to individuals rather than being systemic. Thus, no matter if the novel ignores racism, by identifying a vague and opaque inequality as the real historical issue, or ignores race altogether, leading to a default white subject position that disregards the deep framework of race in the United States, the end result is that whiteness and white supremacy are left unquestioned and unchallenged.

Certainly, this centering of whiteness does not end in the 1960s, and authors continued to "play in the dark" well past the Civil Rights period and into the current century. For example, Cormac McCarthy's *The Road*, perhaps the most prominent (non-Young Adult) postapocalyptic dystopia in the 2000s, continues this unspoken default whiteness. So much of what might otherwise be prominent information in other novels is unspoken or at best vague; most notable is the cause of the apocalypse, but of critical importance here are the obscured racial identities of "the man" and "the boy" or any of the people they meet during their trek.[18] The novel simply remains silent about race, establishing instead a dominant gray coloration in its diegetic world from the beginning. The ubiquitous ash suggests a grayish cloud through which the man and the boy wander – "gray as his heart."[19] The color gray, which appears at least forty-nine times in the novel, pervades the narrative as the ambient atmosphere of dystopia and reinforces the color-blind approach in its unwillingness to address the reality of racialized subjectivity in the United States.

If we choose to read differently and reject the standard narrative presumption of whiteness in American literature, what happens if we alternatively presume the man and the boy are, say, Latinx? While narratively this would be possible – if we assume these particular Latinos to be thoroughly anglicized – we suspect that readers would have a different experience of reading the novel even without the representation of Latinx identity. If, on the other hand, the man and boy *did* embody Latinx ways of being and moving through the world informed by racialized cultural practices and experiences, would non-Latinx readers effortlessly be able to transidentify with them, as nonwhite readers are normally asked to do with white characters? (Would the novel be as popular? Would it have won a Pulitzer Prize? What audience madness would have ensued if the film adaptation had unilaterally performed this racial substitution?) McCarthy's erasure of racial markers works as a postracial update to Heinlein's attempt to manipulate racial history. But neither move is sufficient to break away from the whiteness embedded at the center of American culture. After all, ignoring race in a race-identified world is not a rejection of racism. It is an erasure of identity.

Outright and Explicit White Supremacy

And yet there has been another stream of utopian thought explicitly foregrounding white supremacy, rather than assuming or implying it as the default. George Lincoln Rockwell, an unapologetic white supremacist who founded the American Nazi Party in 1959, put white supremacy at the forefront in his manifesto *White Power* (1966/1967). While mostly he sounds the alarm of perceived dystopian threats to the white race, such as theories of white replacement that are still current in today's white supremacism, he also expresses a profoundly white supremacist eutopian desire:

> America is the last, the only hope for the salvation of all white people and therefore our civilization. Only in America is there still a large enough pool of raw, Aryan White blood with the wealth and power to lead a revival of our race.
>
> If America falls finally and irretrievably into the hands of the Jews and Blacks, as England, France, Russia, and the rest of the Western world have already done, there will be no patch of ground left on this planet where even a few White men can or could get together and organize any kind of resistance to the final drowning of the White Race by the flood of inferior colored blood.[20]

To get to this racist eutopian hope for white supremacy, white Americans must first live through the "Nightmare" of racial diversity "engulfing" the

United States, a perspective Rockwell shares with other white supremacists up to and including our current historical moment.

An acolyte of Rockwell's, who went on to become an even more visible and influential figure of white supremacy, was William Luther Pierce. His notorious novel *The Turner Diaries*, published under the pseudonym Andrew MacDonald in 1978, has had wide influence among white supremacists, depicting racial and cultural pluralism as a dystopia for white people. Some of the notable white supremacists who drew inspiration directly from the book include Robert Matthews, the leader of The Order, a white supremacist group that assassinated the Jewish radio host Alan Berg in 1984, as well as Timothy McVeigh, the primary terrorist in the Oklahoma City bombing in 1995, which was the single deadliest act of white supremacist terrorism in the United States. *The Turner Diaries* depicts the revolution needed to move toward a real-world, white-only eutopia through its delirious spectacles of violence such as the Day of the Rope, during which thousands of Jewish people and white female "race traitors" are hanged with their bodies left dangling as a testament to white supremacy. That the Day of the Rope has become a meme in current white supremacist discourse bespeaks the horrific longevity of such savage visions.[21]

Prefiguring much of the contemporary rhetoric of white supremacy, Pierce's book catalogues the so-called horrors of white people falling prey to the System, the name he uses for mainstream American society, which promotes and fosters a progressive ideology of racial justice that "brainwashes" white people to lose their "authentic" racial identities. For white supremacists, of course, one of the most egregious outcomes of this brainwashing is interracial sex. Turner, the narrator, comments on one such example: "I understand that the two girls were with the Blacks only because they had been infected with the disease of liberalism by the schools and the churches and the plastic pop-culture the System churns out for young people these days. Presumably, if they had been raised in a healthy society they would have had some racial pride."[22] This healthy (i.e., white) society is the eutopia to which Turner and his fellow white guerilla terrorists aspire:

> We are forging the nucleus of a new society, a whole new civilization, which will rise from the ashes of the old. And it is because our new civilization will be based on an entirely different world view than the present one that it can only replace the other in a revolutionary manner. There is no way a society based on Aryan values and an Aryan outlook can evolve peacefully from a society which has succumbed to Jewish spiritual corruption.[23]

This desire for a white supremacist eutopia has a long history that we can even trace back to the origins of the United States as a sovereign state. However, in its modern radicalized form it encompasses several white supremacist leaders such as Aryan Nation's Richard Butler and White Aryan Resistance's Tom Metzger and has reemerged in the twenty-first century as evidenced by the ethnonationalism of white terrorists such as Anders Breivik, who slaughtered almost eighty people in Norway in 2011, and Dylann Roof, who murdered nine Black people at the Emanuel African Methodist Church in South Carolina in 2015.

Directly citing Pierce as an influence, white supremacist terrorist David Lane wrote the novella *KD Rebel*, which also figures multiracial America as a dystopia inspiring the beginnings of a white supremacist revolution to establish a white ethnonational state in the Colorado region. As proclaimed by one character: "No race of people can indefinitely continue their existence without territorial imperatives in which to propagate, protect and promote their own kind."[24] So too, Harold Armstead Covington's Northwest series of novels, published between 2003 and 2013, establishes multiracial America as a dystopia and imagines a racial civil war that leads to a white supremacist eutopia in the Pacific Northwest – the most fully imagined among those discussed here: "Established as a worldwide home for all persons of unmixed Aryan, that is to say Caucasian, non-Semitic, European descent."[25]

These texts and others by lesser-known authors trace out their white supremacist eutopias, which are also (unsurprisingly) patriarchal fascistic male fantasies, and they illustrate the monstrous parameters of the white supremacist imagination.[26] In their consistent expressions of disgust with the dominant society's progressive racial politics, they also show that white supremacists believe that whiteness is under threat – a belief we see increasingly prevalent today with social media's mainstreaming of white supremacy, combined with white hysteria arising after the election of Barack Obama as the United States' first Black president and emboldened after the election of Trump, who positions himself as the negation of Obama.

Challenging White Supremacy

And yet white supremacy has never gone unremarked or unchallenged by those it oppresses, who bristled under it, spoke out against it, and resisted it despite the dangers. Perhaps one of the earliest notable literary challenges to white supremacism was Frederick Douglass's *Narrative of the Life of Frederick Douglass*, published in 1845.[27] These and other abolitionist texts expressed a powerful eutopian desire for a space of freedom and equality. But in the period covered by this collection, an important subgenre of utopian novels presenting an unambiguous and memorable opposition to white supremacy came from the 1960s and 1970s, texts that Mark Bould labels "black power sf."[28] Many of these texts call for violent revolution against white supremacy. As one example, in Sam Greenlee's *The Spook Who Sat by the Door*, Freeman, a Black man recruited by the CIA, whose job had been to sit by the door in order to show that the CIA had racially integrated, takes his training and organizes a Black Power revolution using a Chicago street gang. Freeman plays the role of the revolutionary with cold hard logic: "We got no time for hate; it's a luxury we can't afford. Whitey just stands in the way of freedom and he has to be moved any damn way we can; he doesn't mean any more than that."[29] He identifies Black pride as the ingredient necessary to effect the revolution:

> We wrapped it [Black pride] up and put it away inside that trunk . . . . White folks been trying to rob that trunk for centuries and maybe they did and we didn't know it, or it shriveled up and disappeared out of disuse. But if we can find it and use it, if we can get that black pride going for us, then nothing is going to stop us until we're free – nothing and nobody. They'll have to kill us or free us, twenty-five million of us![30]

These texts concentrate on revolution, based as they are in a Black apocalyptic/prophetic tradition,[31] while they also express the extreme frustration and need for racial consciousness to move toward the eutopian moment at the end of the revolution.

Much of the revolutionary energy tied to the Black Power movement may have been squashed or dissipated by the end of 1970s after the onslaughts of COINTELPRO, the War on Crime, and other police efforts, but the need and desire for revolutionary change continued. During the 1970s, American feminist utopias by sf writers like Joanna Russ, Marge Piercy, and Samuel Delany, among others, kept up the challenge to white supremacy to envision a nonracist eutopia but, unlike Black Power sf which tends to be hypermasculinist, they focused on its heteropatriarchal dimensions.[32]

Here, we will highlight the critique of white supremacy by Octavia Butler, whose important work has become more and more recognized in the past few decades. Making the case for revolution centered in Afrofuturist feminism, *Parable of the Sower* and *Parable of the Talents* decenter white heteropatriarchal supremacy, most notably through Lauren Olamina – a strong, Black, female protagonist at the core of the narrative.[33] As the world falls apart, Lauren provides her self-created religion, Earthseed, to her family and the stragglers who form the racially and ethnically diverse community that revolves around her as the foundation for a fleeting eutopian community and eventually the future colonization of space. Perhaps the most famous lines from Butler's oeuvre come from Lauren's proclamation:

> All that you touch,
> You Change
> All that you Change,
> Changes you.
> The only lasting truth
> Is Change.
> God is Change.[34]

With these words, Butler's protagonist announces a possibility: a horizon of hope that marks eutopian and dystopian literature. For the followers of Earthseed, the hope is in changing ourselves and, as importantly, the world around us, not worshiping blindly but acting directly. Lauren offers hope but requires that action be taken to focus this hope. Butler's *Parable* series centers on Change and the call to action, the necessity of revolution against structures of oppression like white supremacy.

Butler's novels prefigure a wave of literature explicitly challenging white supremacy – and thus imagining a world without it – that blossomed in the last decade of the period covered in this collection, when the work of Black Lives Matter (BLM) and social media more generally reshaped the popular discourse around white supremacy. If BLM formed in 2013 as a hashtag and statement against American law enforcement and the judicial system that effectively endorses the killing of Black people (in the wake of the murder of a Black teenage boy, Trayvon Martin, by vigilante George Zimmerman), it quickly grew into the central organizing force in response to the police murder of two unarmed Black men, Michael Brown and Eric Garner. By 2015 and in the years after, BLM – in tension with the parallel rise of far-right white supremacy – had altered the political and social landscape, and its impact has rewritten the discourse around white supremacy from both those who endorse it and those, like the authors we are about to discuss, who resist it.

A racialized landscape through which nonwhite characters must find their way is the terrain of American white supremacy, and it is the setting of Matt Ruff's *Lovecraft Country*. Published in 2016 when Trump was running for president and his "Make America Great Again" slogan was in full effect, Ruff's novel looks back at the 1950s, that era when the United States was in the flush of victory over the draconian Axis powers and yet fully operating under the draconian laws of Jim Crow segregation. From this perspective, the novel's name takes on many resonances. H. P. Lovecraft was, of course, a writer who is well known for a body of influential horror fiction that is itself haunted by the author's extreme and vile racism. His stories describe monsters from outer space while his personal letters praise fascist politics, celebrate WASP dominance, and crudely disparage most every American ethnic group. Thus, not surprisingly, in *Lovecraft Country* seemingly every other step the novel's Black characters make is blocked by forces – some supernatural but most very much of the physical world, all representing whiteness and racist brutality.[35]

The narrative, which is presented as a series of interconnected stories, begins as protagonist Atticus Turner drives from Jacksonville, Florida, to his home in Chicago, Illinois. A Black man driving across the country is haunted by an air of danger that looms across the text from its first pages. As Atticus and the other main characters later travel around the country trying to find the "safe negro travel" spots, what becomes clear is that Jim Crow white supremacy was not restricted to the South but was all-encompassing. In short, the entirety of the United States is Lovecraft Country. And if Lovecraft Country is a metaphor for the nation, it is no wonder that white people present obstacle after obstacle at every stage of these Black characters' lives. Here, the white people literally haunt the characters so that even their deaths offer no respite. Establishing racist systems on earth, the very wealthy whites try, like the United States at mid-century, to conquer outer space itself.

The Safe Negro Travel Guide, published by Atticus's uncle George, becomes the guide to navigating the United States as Lovecraft Country, a space that threatens Black people wherever they are. Mobility – the very center of the American Dream of free land and wide-open space – is a cause for potential danger for nonwhite folks. The novel focuses on key sites to stage encounters between its Black protagonists and the ever-menacing whites, such as haunted houses in all-white neighborhoods and streets patrolled by racist cops. The existence of the travel guide points to a clear reality: the very center of that American Dream has always been premised on dystopian nightmares for some – the American Indians who were forcibly removed from the land, the African Americans who were forcibly brought to it, and other groups such as Jewish people, Asians, Latinx people, and Muslims who have been abused and excluded from the promises of equality and access offered to the white majority throughout US history.

The novel's theme of driving shows the danger that mobility has always posed to African Americans – or more precisely, it shows how threatened white supremacy is in the face of Black mobility. In Ta-Nehisi Coates's memoir/letter to his son, *Between the World and Me*, a pivotal moment of his life's journey came in comprehending the police murder of his friend Prince Jones, a brilliant young Black man, who happened to be driving a car past a cop who was searching for a crime suspect and decided any random Black man would do.[36] Black death without legal consequence at the hands of police, who see all Black people as possessed of some essential guilt, remains an ever-present, profound danger since the days of slave patrols centuries ago. It is this, the looming threat of white supremacist violence built into the very structure of the United States and conducted with impunity, that is at the heart of the million injustices endured by Coates and all the central figures in Ruff's novel.

The period after 2015 has seen a wave of short-story collections that provide small, eutopian glimpses while critiquing the dystopia of white supremacy. *Global Dystopias*, edited by Junot Díaz, includes Maria Dahvana Headley's "Memoirs of an Imaginary Country," which inverts Giacomo Casanova's utopia *Icosameron* to tell the story from the perspective of the "lost race" living in the center of the earth: "You called the year your explorers arrived in my country year 1. We called that year 10,077. You called us Utopians. We called you something else."[37] The narrative splices its anticolonialism with feminism: "Imaginary countries and imaginary cunts are in the same category. They are the same story."[38] And part of its challenge to the white supremacist colonial project is taking the power of speech away from the colonizer: "Listen to me tell your story. You've lost the ability to speak."[39] By taking control of the narrative, the inhabitants of the center of the earth are no longer "discovered" and ruled by white Europeans, as in Casanova's original text, and they reclaim their agency.

As with Black Power sf, the theme of violent revolution is carried forth into other dystopian texts written by authors challenging white supremacy. *A People's Future of the United States*, another short-story collection, responds to the growing tide of white resentment in the wake of Trump's election. British-born, Nigerian American writer Lesley Nneka Arimah's "The Referendum" represents this resentment with finesse. Within the dramatic frame of two sisters-in-law having to decide what to do with their children, it imagines a near-future dystopia in which it is illegal for ordinary Black citizens to own guns. Atlanta is the only city left where African Americans can hold political office, and "influential black individual[s]" are disappeared.[40] In this environment, where white supremacy is not only condoned but promoted, the narrator must contend with microaggressions at the supermarket by a white man who won't let her pass by his cart, even after repeated pleas with a "safe-black-person smile."[41] Looming over these degradations is the overturning of the Civil Rights Act and the imminent Congressional vote on the "referendum to repeal the thirteenth amendment and reinstitute slavery."[42] Despite this increasingly dystopic world, the story does provide grounds for hope: the narrator and her husband dream of the unborn son, whom they have already named and who symbolizes "a future we can bring another child into" and who is anachronistically waiting for them to fix the world.[43] To do so, they join the Black Resistance, which amasses weapons for a future race war and operates a modern-day underground railroad.

Many of the stories collected in *The Dystopian States of America* also reflect on the Trump era but importantly call for revolt against white supremacy as part of larger systems of othering that it represents. Thai-born American author doungjai gam's "The Revolution Will Be in Color" involves the incarceration of those deemed undesirable in American society – nonwhites, refugees, LGBTQ+ folks – in various prisons around the country, about which the narrator protests:

> We should not be jailed for the color of our skin.
> We should not be jailed because we seek a better life.
> We should not be jailed for how we live and who we love.[44]

And yet, despite the horrific conditions of the imprisonment, the narrator does not completely despair: "For each fear I hold inside me, there is also a bubble of hope."[45] As the title suggests, white supremacy (along with other forms of oppression) can be dismantled, here by the forces of "resistance [that] are growing outside," fighting back against the structures of white supremacy by destroying the prison system.[46] These critical dystopias provide eutopian desire amidst the bleakness of future systems of white supremacy and other forms of oppression. Especially during the Trump era, we see many writers in these collections responding to renewed white supremacy with a call for revolutionary change, even involving violence. (As we saw at the August 12, 2017, Unite the Right rally and on January 6, 2021, with the Capitol insurrection, violence will indeed be coming from the side of white supremacy.)

While all utopian literature offers a vision for how the world can be different, perhaps the short-writing collection with the most direct commitment to progressive change is *Octavia's Brood: Science Fiction Stories from Social Justice Movements* (2015). Most of the selections are written by social justice activists. The atmosphere of the collection, a mix of short speculative fiction and commentary, can best be summarized, in the words of the introduction, "Whenever we try to envision a world without war, without violence, without prisons, without capitalism, we are engaging in speculative fiction. All organizing is science fiction. Organizers and activists dedicate their lives to creating and envisioning another world."[47]

We see this vision carried through in the selections. In adrienne maree brown's "the river," for example, a magical giant wave suddenly appears in the Detroit River and drowns only select people – hipsters, carpetbagging politicians, and businesses taking over its shores. As the story concludes and the surviving outsiders, having received the message, decide they need to find somewhere else to gentrify, a local Detroit boatwoman whom the River never rose against looks out over the water and sees "through the blue ... something that never died. something alive."[48] This power that survives is the spirit of those unwilling to just give up against the supposed inevitability of exploitation and dislocation.

In an analytical contribution, Mumia Abu-Jamal analyzes *Star Wars*'s father–son dynamic between Luke Skywalker and Darth Vader as an allegory for the United States itself: like Luke, it began life on the anti-imperial side, but as it matured in its power it was expected to assume its place with the "adults."

> That is the meaning of Star Wars: we were rebels; we are Empire.
> And like all rebellious children, we were but going through a phase.
> We are getting ready for adulthood, after we sowed a few wild oats.
> Once grown, we put on our imperial uniform, and bowed to the Empire.
> "It is your destiny."
> Right? Unless – [49]

It is in the "Unless – " that we can find hope for social justice against white supremacist empire. We have tried to show in this chapter that too many American utopian narratives offer only limited horizons for change when it comes to the foundational assumptions of racial identity and the longevity of white supremacy. This is the lesson of all antiracist eutopian visions, even those within dystopian narratives: it is in reimagining the past, present, and future that we can recognize when dominant culture's visions have failed us and then redefine the horizon of possibility. Only then can socially just change occur.

Notes

1. Moon-Kie Jung puts it in postcolonial terms: "the United States has never been a nation-state; the United States has always been an empire-state; the United States has always been a racial state, a state of white supremacy." Moon-Kie Jung, "Constituting the U.S. Empire-State and White Supremacy," from *State of White Supremacy: Racism, Governance, and the United States*, edited by M. Jung, J. H. Costa Vargas, and E. Bonilla-Silva (Stanford, CA: Stanford University Press, 2011), 1–23 (1).
2. George M. Fredrickson, in *White Supremacy: A Comparative Study in American and South African History* (Oxford: Oxford University Press, 1982), adds, "it involves making invidious distinctions of a socially crucial kind that are based primarily, if not exclusively, on physical characteristics and ancestry" (xi). For more views on what terminology to use for white racist ideology, see Betty A. Dobratz and Stephanie L. Shanks-Meile, *The White Separatist Movement in the US: "White Power, White Pride!"* (Baltimore: Johns Hopkins University Press, 2000); C. Richard King and David J. Leonard, *Beyond Hate: White Power and Popular Culture* (New York: Routledge, 2016); Kathleen Belew, *Bring the War Home: The White Power Movement and Paramilitary America* (Cambridge, MA: Harvard University Press, 2018); and Edward K. Chan, "The White Power Utopia and the Reproduction of Victimized Whiteness," from *Race and Utopian Desire in American Literature and Society*, edited by Patricia Ventura and Edward K. Chan (Cham: Palgrave Macmillan, 2019), 139–159. In this chapter, we will primarily use the most commonly recognized term: "white supremacy."
3. George Lipsitz, in *The Possessive Investment in Whiteness: How White People Profit from Identity Politics* (Philadelphia: Temple University Press, 2018), catalogs at length and in detail the notion of "the possessive investment in whiteness," which authorizes many of these practices.
4. Tananarive Due, "History Is a Dystopia," interviewed by Avni Sejpal, *Boston Review* (November 16, 2017), online.
5. For a general history of racial science, the classic study is Stephen Jay Gould 's *The Mismeasure of Man*, revised and expanded edition (New York: W. W. Norton, 1996), though it is not without its critics in scientific and other circles and is now somewhat outdated. For other accounts, see C. Loring Brace, *"Race" Is a Four-Letter Word: The Genesis of the Concept* (Oxford: Oxford University Press, 2005) and Angela Saini, *Superior: The Return of Race Science* (Boston: Beacon Press, 2019), the latter of which is written by a British science journalist and has received positive reviews in publications such as *Nature* and *Scientific American*.
6. Ursula K. Le Guin, "Ursula K. Le Guin Explains How to Build a New Kind of Utopia," *Electric Lit* (December 5, 2017), online. Lyman Tower Sargent expresses a similar idea about the hope embedded within dystopia in "Three Faces of Utopianism Revisited," *Utopian Studies* 5.1 (1994), 1–37 (26).
7. Robin D. G. Kelley, *Freedom Dreams: The Black Radical Imagination* (Boston: Beacon Press, 2002), 56.

8. adrienne maree brown, National Network of Abortion Funds 2016 Keynote, adrienne maree brown website (2016), online.
9. Toni Morrison, *Playing in the Dark: Whiteness and the Literary Imagination* (Cambridge, MA: Harvard University Press, 1992), 72. On the assumption of whiteness in American literary texts and reading practices, see also Rebecca Aanerud, "Fictions of Whiteness: Speaking the Names of Whiteness in U.S. Literature," from *Displacing Whiteness: Essays in Social and Cultural Criticism*, edited by Ruth Frankenberg (Durham, NC: Duke University Press, 1999), 35–59, especially 38.
10. On these texts, see, respectively, Sylvia Strauss, "Gender, Class, and Race in Utopia," from *Looking Backward, 1988–1888: Essays on Edward Bellamy*, edited by Daphne Patai (Amherst: University of Massachusetts Press, 1988), 68–90; Edward K. Chan, *The Racial Horizon of Utopia: Unthinking the Future of Race in Late Twentieth-Century American Utopian Novels* (Bern: Peter Lang, 2016), 10–11; Elinor Bowers, "An Exploration of Femininity, Masculinity, and Racial Prejudice in *Herland*," *The American Journal of Economics and Sociology* 77.5 (2018), 1313–1327; and Susan X. Day, "*Walden Two* at Fifty," *Michigan Quarterly Review* 38.2 (1999), 247–259.
11. Ray Bradbury, *Fahrenheit 451* (New York: HarperCollins, 2012), 78.
12. Jacqueline Foertsch, *Reckoning Day: Race, Place, and the Atom Bomb in Postwar America* (Nashville, TN: Vanderbilt University Press, 2013), chapter 1.
13. Foertsch, 62, 67.
14. Robert Heinlein, *Farnham's Freehold* (Riverdale, NY: Baen, 2001), 323.
15. Farah Mendlesohn, *The Pleasant Profession of Robert A. Heinlein* (London: Unbound, 2019), 262–263.
16. Robert Heinlein, *The Virginia Edition: A Sample of the Series* (Houston, TX: The Virginia Edition, 2012), 56.
17. Mendlesohn, 273.
18. Cormac McCarthy, *The Road* (New York: Vintage, 2006). Notably, the film adaptation does include two Black characters: the "thief" and the "archer."
19. McCarthy, 27.
20. George Lincoln Rockwell, *White Power* (Unknown: Gresham, 2017), 249.
21. Andrew MacDonald [William Luther Pierce], *The Turner Diaries*, 2nd edition (Fort Lee, NJ: Barricade Books, 1996). On the phrase "day of the rope" see Justin Ward, "Day of the Trope: White Nationalist Memes Thrive on Reddit's r/The_Donald," *SPL Center Hatewatch* (April 19, 2018) and the Anti-Defamation League's (2002) entry on the term.
22. MacDonald, Kindle loc. 1366.
23. MacDonald, Kindle loc. 1987–1999.
24. David Lane, *KD Rebel* (Solar General Online Archive, 2015), 69. This work was first published in 2001. This statement also appears in Lane's philosophical tract "88 Precepts" (undated), also published online.
25. Harold Armstead Covington, *The Hill of the Ravens*, Kindle edition (Bloomington, IN: AuthorHouse, 2003), Kindle loc. 124–127. This specific

novel in the series provides the most detail on his imagined white supremacist eutopia.

26. Another notable example is Kenneth Molyneaux's *White Empire* (2000), whose publisher is not clearly identified, although the book is associated with the World Church of the Creator. It is available online.
27. On the utopian dimensions of this and other texts by Douglass, see David Lemke, "Frederick Douglass's Utopia: Searching for the Space of Black Freedom," from *Race and Utopian Desire in American Literature and Society*, edited by Patricia Ventura and Edward K. Chan (Cham: Palgrave Macmillan, 2019), 23–39.
28. Mark Bould, "Come Alive by Saying No: An Introduction to Black Power SF," *Science Fiction Studies* 34.2 (2007), 220–240.
29. Sam Greenlee, *The Spook Who Sat by the Door* (Detroit, MI: Wayne State University Press, 1990), 190.
30. Greenlee, 113.
31. Mark A. Tabone, "Black Power Utopia: African-American Utopianism and Revolutionary Prophesy in Black Power-Era Science Fiction," from *Race and Utopian Desire in American Literature and Society*, edited by Patricia Ventura and Edward K. Chan (Cham: Palgrave Macmillan, 2019), 59–78 (61, 63–72).
32. See, for only a few examples of a much larger body of work, Tom Moylan, *Demand the Impossible: Science Fiction and the Utopian Imagination* (Oxford: Peter Lang, 2014) and Jennifer Burwell, *Notes on Nowhere: Feminism, Utopian Logic, and Social Transformation* (Minneapolis: University of Minnesota Press, 1997).
33. Tom Moylan, in *Scraps of the Untainted Sky: Science Fiction, Utopia, Dystopia* (Boulder, CO: Westview Press, 2000), identifies *Parable of the Sower* as "one of the best examples" of the critical dystopia, which insists on a eutopian vision beyond dystopia more than in previous forms of the dystopian novel (xvi).
34. Octavia E. Butler, *Parable of the Sower* (New York: Warner Books, 1995), 3.
35. Matt Ruff, *Lovecraft Country* (New York: HarperCollins, 2016).
36. Ta-Nehisi Coates, *Between the World and Me* (New York: Penguin Random House, 2015).
37. Maria Dahvana Headley, "Memoirs of an Imaginary Country," from *Global Dystopias*, Kindle edition, edited by Junot Díaz (Cambridge, MA: MIT Press, 2017), Kindle loc. 972–974. *Icosameron* was originally published in 1787.
38. Headley, Kindle loc. 1191–1192.
39. Headley, Kindle loc. 1205–1206.
40. Lesley Nneka Arimah, "The Referendum," from *A People's Future of the United States*, edited by Victor Lavalle and J. J. Adams (New York: One World, 2019), 178–190 (189).
41. Arimah, 184.
42. Arimah, 179.
43. Arimah, 183, 190.

44. doungjai gam, "The Revolution Will Be in Color," from *The Dystopian States of America: A Charity Anthology Benefiting the ACLU Foundation*, Kindle edition, edited by Matt Bechtel (Haverhill, MA: Haverhill House, 2020), Kindle loc. 3782.
45. gam, Kindle loc. 3784.
46. gam, Kindle loc. 3785.
47. Walidah Imarisha, "Introduction," from *Octavia's Brood: Science Fiction Stories from Social Justice Movements*, edited by adrienne maree brown and Walidah Imarisha (Chico, CA: AK Press, 2015), 3.
48. adrienne maree brown, "the river," from *Octavia's Brood: Science Fiction Stories from Social Justice Movements*, edited by adrienne maree brown and Walidah Imarisha (Chico, CA: AK Press, 2015), 40–51 (51).
49. Mumia Abu-Jamal, "Star Wars and the American Imagination," from *Octavia's Brood: Science Fiction Stories from Social Justice Movements*, edited by adrienne maree brown and Walidah Imarisha (Chico, CA: AK Press, 2015), 258.

CHAPTER 5

American Spirituality

Andrew Tate

"If the concept of God has any validity or any use," reflects James Baldwin in *The Fire Next Time*, "it can only be to make us larger, freer, and more loving. If God cannot do this, then it is time we got rid of Him."[1] Baldwin's apocalyptic title is prompted by both the flood narrative in the Book of Genesis and its "re-creation" in a gospel song: "God gave Noah the rainbow sign, No more water, the fire next time!"[2] This strand of imagery is apocalyptic in a double sense: in an echo of the Book of Revelation, the speaker imagines the downfall and destruction of an unjust polity and, to use the primary sense of *apocalypsis*, the elements of water and fire also act as forms of "disclosure or unveiling" of that which has been concealed or hidden.[3] Baldwin's epistle-essay draws on an African American spiritual tradition of dissent that he rewrites to invoke a potentially scandalous idea: for true liberty to reign, the governing idea of divinity, if corrupted by violence and oppression, may need to be forsaken. Baldwin, a contemporary of Dr. Martin Luther King Jr and Malcolm X, was writing in the era of the Civil Rights movement, yet his defiance of conventional theism remains resonant in our similarly turbulent historical moment.

Is it possible to imagine an America in which God is not integral to public discourse? "We are a religiously mad culture, furiously searching for the spirit," Harold Bloom once claimed of a nation that officially enshrines a clear distinction between piety and the state.[4] Religion continues to play a contentious role in the American cultural imagination, especially in conceptions of the good life and aspirations for a more just society. Conservative Evangelical Christianity is the most visible and economically powerful form of institutional religion in contemporary America. Matthew Avery Sutton associates this dominant tradition with "the politics of apocalypse" embodied by fundamentalists who pursue "an absolutist, uncompromising, good-versus-evil faith," one that thrives in the construction of enemies that must be defeated.[5] This is a vividly different account of the possibilities of American Christianity to the one evoked by the novelist Marilynne Robinson, a rare twenty-first-century advocate for the inclusive social virtues of Puritanism: she identifies a "Utopian impulse" that was motivated by "the hope to create a model of good human order, that seems to have arrived on the *Mayflower*, and which flourished through the whole of the nineteenth century."[6] The Pilgrim and Puritan migrations occurred a little more than a century after the statesman and philosopher Thomas More published his influential narrative, *Utopia*. More's fictional island has become synonymous with the dream of perfect, harmonious society. Although the term has been secularized in subsequent centuries, religion was just as crucial to More, eventually canonized by the Roman Catholic Church in 1935, as to the militant Protestants who founded New England. Indeed, the concluding book of the treatise features a detailed reflection on "the Religions of the Utopians." More describes a variety of pantheist-style forms of nature worship but notes that "the vast majority, however, and these by the far the wisest . . . believe in a single power, unknown, eternal, infinite, inexplicable, beyond the grasp of the human mind."[7] This vision idealizes a version of Christianity but, importantly, emphasizes a form of tolerance, a concept that was not widely practiced in the theocratic world of Puritan New England.

Religion frequently figures as a structuring element in North American dystopian fiction: most famously, a familiar strand of fundamentalist Christianity is the foundation of the Republic of Gilead, the theocratic and autocratic regime in Margaret Atwood's *The Handmaid's Tale* and its sequel *The Testaments*. For the supposedly pious men who lead its oppressive social order, Gilead – taking its name from a biblical word meaning "place of witness" – represents a return to the patriarchal values of previous generations rather than a revolution. Its strict hierarchies, occlusions, and violent modes of policing dissent are, in these novels, merely an embodiment of the divinely ordained nature of things. Atwood's Republic of Gilead casts a long shadow over contemporary fiction and film. Popular constructions of utopia, and its undesirable but more common dystopian double, might suggest that religion is primarily a force for repression, occlusion, violence, and exploitation. Spiritual practice, in its broadest sense, including prayer, attendance at worship, and forms of social activism, are, depending on perspective, associated with both emancipation and bondage, pacifism and violence, justice and inequality. American spirituality is a primary element of both utopian and dystopian discourse.

Does the apparent skeptical materialism of late twentieth- and early twenty-first-century fiction militate against strands of theologically oriented utopian fiction? This chapter traces the complex legacies of multiple religious traditions, including Christianity, Islam, and syncretistic spirituality, as they inform twentieth- and twenty-first-century fiction, including the miraculous realism of Toni Morrison, the lyrical historicism of Marilynne Robinson, and the religiously themed science fiction of James Blish and G. Willow Wilson. The chapter draws on postsecular critiques of literature and culture that, in John McClure's terms, indicate "a mode of being and seeing that is at once critical of secular constructions of reality and of dogmatic religion."[8] Vincent Geoghegan also identifies a "growing post-secular turn in political theory" which "reflects the impulse to move beyond the Enlightenment binary of religious and secular."[9] The chapter argues that belief both animates and complicates the ways in which American writing envisions and critiques what Fredric Jameson famously names "the desire called utopia" with reference to both revolutionary hope and conservative religious quietism.[10]

After "the City on a Hill": The Shadow of Puritan Utopianism

One of the most influential American, civic "self-conceptions," to use David Reynolds's term, is the phenomenon widely known as "exceptionalism," the still-popular idea that the country has a unique sacred purpose that sets it apart from other nations.[11] This powerful conceit is, in part, an echo of the long afterlife of seventeenth-century Pilgrim and Puritan settlers, whose belief in a covenantal relationship with God shaped every aspect of their community. This is most vividly articulated in John Winthrop's concept, articulated in *A Model of Christian Charity* and preached to his fellow colonists, of the new settlement as a "city on a hill," an allusion to Jesus's sermon on the mount (Matthew 5:14). Puritanism has a curious cultural legacy that is easily parodied as a metonym for authoritarian, humorless intolerance, but its history and social aspirations are more complex. In his now-paradigmatic sermon, Winthrop, the first governor of the Massachusetts Bay Colony, exhorted his fellow colonists to set aside selfish ambition in favor of communal, fraternal support. Marilynne Robinson argues that the address constitutes a "utopian vision of a society whose relations are based on charity, using the word in the biblical sense, meaning love."[12] There are strong resonances in Winthrop's speech with the New Testament vision for the followers of Jesus. The life of the early church, as recorded in the Book of Acts, is characterized by a commitment to community above individual freedoms, including a disavowal of acquisitiveness and an abandonment of hierarchies signified by wealth:

> All the believers were one in heart and mind. No one claimed that any of their possessions was their own, but they shared everything they had. With great

power the apostles continued to testify to the resurrection of the Lord Jesus. And God's grace was so powerfully at work in them all that there were no needy persons among them. For from time to time those who owned land or houses sold them, brought the money from the sales and put it at the apostles' feet, and it was distributed to anyone who had need. (Acts 4:32–35)[13]

One does not need to be a sociologist of religion to observe that the communitarian practices of the early church, in which private property is effectively abolished, is not a standard to which most iterations of contemporary American Christianity, conservative or liberal, aspire. Fundamentalists who maintain that every word of scripture is the inspired Word of God accommodate a degree of latitude when in relation to this radical element of the Acts of the Apostles, one that would require a much more critical relationship with the dispensation of consumer capitalism. Mark Holloway uses this vivid scriptural quotation as an epigraph for his history of American utopian communities from the seventeenth to the nineteenth century and indicates that many of these "small societies" were inspired by the sermon on the mount, the Beatitudes of Jesus in which the meek will inherit the earth and the peacemakers are called the children of God (Matthew 5:5, 9).[14]

Puritan theocratic ideas collapsed but did not disappear from the cultural imagination with the advent of Enlightenment discourses of freedom and democracy. The first amendment, authorized in 1791, guarantees freedom of religious expression. This apparent privatization of religion and the right to worship, established by the founding fathers and enshrined in the early days of the nation, has not made theological ideas or spiritual practice marginal pursuits in the United States. A belief in the divine – and especially in a God who takes an interest in the everyday life of the nation's citizens – remains relatively common in contemporary US culture, especially when contrasted with European skepticism in which the secularization narrative seems significantly more robust. The UK census of 2021, for example, revealed that for the first time "less than half of the population (46.2%, 27.5 million people) described themselves as 'Christian,' a 13.1 percentage point decrease from 59.3% (33.3 million) in 2011."[15] Although statistics suggest that Christianity is also in decline in America, it remains the dominant form of belief, with one recent Pew Research survey estimating that 63 percent of adults self-identify as Christians, 15 percent lower than in 2007.[16] Significantly, the same survey highlights that approximately three in ten adults in the United States are now "religiously unaffiliated."[17] According to the report, the unaffiliated, known as "nones," are now outnumbered only two to one by Christian believers, compared with five to one in 2007. Other forms of religious affiliation, including Judaism, Hinduism, Islam, and Native American religions, account for 6 percent of the population.[18] America has never been so religiously diverse as it is in the third decade of the twenty-first century. Yet Christianity, especially in Evangelical-Protestant formations, remains a formidably powerful influence in public life, and fiction continues to wrestle with its theological, political, and cultural legacies.

Religion in America has been the source of both violent oppression and hope. This conflict is vividly embodied by Frederick Douglass – abolitionist and author – in his eloquent 1852 rebuke to the racist complacency of the nation in "What to the Slave Is the Fourth of July?" To celebrate "life, liberty and the pursuit of happiness" – enshrined as nonsectarian, sacred values in the Declaration of Independence – is possible only for those included in an ostensible earthly paradise, namely white citizens. This political project, what Douglass sardonically names "the grand illuminated temple of liberty," is violently exclusive: "This Fourth of July is *yours*, not *mine*. You may rejoice, *I* must mourn."[19] Douglass uses an idiom of biblical lament to mock the secular piety of American independence, in which men "in fetters" are called upon "to join . . . in joyous anthems" as a form of "inhuman mockery and sacrilegious irony."[20] The speech compares the injustice of American slavery with oppression of God's people in exile, including an allusion to Psalm 137: "By the rivers of Babylon, there we sat down. Yea! we wept when we remembered Zion." Douglass's homiletic style – one that would have been familiar to the dominantly Christian culture of mid-nineteenth-century America – takes on a distinctively prophetic mood in his warning to those in power: "For it is not light that is needed, but fire; it is not the gentle shower, but thunder. We need the storm, the whirlwind, and the earthquake."[21] Douglass's apocalyptic speech is marked by revolutionary and revelatory hope: the present dispensation is not eternal, and, like other oppressive and corrupt regimes, it will pass away. Although apocalyptic language and ideas are frequently associated with the religious right, scriptural discourse is not the sole preserve of reactionary voices.[22] St. John's Revelation, a key point of reference for Douglass, "has served many agendas, those of revolutionaries and radicals as well as those of quietists and supporters of the status quo."[23] Christian discourse is a threshold in American history: both conservatives and progressives look to scriptural tradition as a ground for their claims and hopes about the social order. Douglass's speech demonstrates the ambiguous position of religious ideas in the American imagination: religion can be used both to imprison and to free, to heal and to wound.

American spirituality is a diverse and slippery term. What do we mean when we invoke this compound, nationalized term? Spirituality both connects and divides; it can unite and engender radical fragmentation. It might be a benign, generous set of disciplines or, from another perspective, a self-serving or deceptive way of thinking. More idiosyncratically, for Harold Bloom, the "American Religion" as practiced by a vast range of spiritual traditions, including Southern Baptists, Mormons, Jewish believers, and Muslims, is more like Gnosticism than the faith practiced by "early Christians."[24] This national spirituality is, he argues, "persuasive and overwhelming, however it is masked" and is flexible enough to include both "secularists" and "professed atheists" who "are more Gnostic than humanist in their presuppositions."[25] This religious sensibility suggests both inwardness and an individualism that is anointed by a kind of special or hidden knowledge. Douglas Coupland, for example, parodies the more consumerist end of contemporary Western spirituality in his Palm Springs-set debut novel, *Generation X: Tales for an Accelerated Culture*, as "Me-ism," a neologism that he defines as:

> A search by an individual, in the absence of training in traditional religious tenets, to formulate a personally tailored religion by himself. Most frequently a mishmash of reincarnation, personal dialogue with a nebulously defined god figure, naturalism, and karmic eye-for-eye attitudes.[26]

Coupland's trinity of 1990s, twenty-something drop-outs, Andy, Dag, and Claire, are exiles from a middle-class world that they find alienating: living on the edge of the Californian desert, they seek a sense of significance in a ritual of "bedtime stories," narratives which might confer meaning in the absence of transcendent religious belief.[27] Their community is a small utopia, provisional, hesitant, and resistant to dogma. In *Life after God* (1994), one of Coupland's narrators reflects on the difficulty of "articulating one's beliefs" in the absence of any fixed worldview.[28] Indeed, the absence of a defining shared story for contemporary Western culture is a recurrent theme in Coupland's writing. In one essay he names this vertiginous loss of a collective story of belonging "denarration":

> It has been said that as animals, one factor that sets us apart from all other animals is that our lives need to be stories, narratives, and that when our stories vanish, that is when we feel lost, dangerous, out of control and susceptible to the forces of randomness. It is the process whereby one loses one's life story.[29]

The protagonists of *Generation X* seek a form of renarration but without reference to the guiding lights of institutional religion or, it should be added, traditional political engagement. Coupland's "denarrated" protagonists frequently express a yearning for the transcendent. In this sense, they resonate with one twenty-first-century theologian's claims that "modern minds seem to have plenty of space for the unexplained, the ineffable, the sublime, worship, awe and wonder."[30]

In *A Secular Age*, Charles Taylor argues that modernity has been characterized by a shift toward understanding the world in an "immanent frame" – what he calls "the sensed context in which we develop our beliefs" – as opposed to the "transcendent frame" of premodern epochs.[31] This does not signify the "end" of religion as such: rather it is a context that emphasizes natural rather than supernatural causation and which assumes that meaning is internally generated – or made by humanity – rather than bestowed by a divine order. For Taylor, as James K. A. Smith puts it, the immanent frame is ubiquitous in contemporary Western culture, and "the question isn't whether we inhabit the immanent frame, but how. Some inhabit it as a closed frame with a brass ceiling; others inhabit it as an open frame with skylights open to transcendence."[32] This "open frame" is visible in different strands of American speculative fiction (sf), including writing that has an ambivalent, if not antagonistic, relationship with organized religion.

"Why Do You Have to Have the God Bit Too?": James Blish and G. Willow Wilson

"What happens when different kinds of world are placed in confrontation, or when boundaries between worlds are violated?" asks Brian McHale in *Postmodernist Fiction*.[33] This question is particularly resonant with James Blish's *A Case of Conscience*, an sf novel that wrestles with utopian thought, legacies of Roman Catholic doctrines of original sin, and the political realities of the Cold War context in which it was written. In 2049, a quartet of scientists – one of whom is both a biologist and Jesuit priest – are sent to a distant planet named Lithia to assess its suitability for contact with Earth. The team encounter an exotic, habitable planet and a peaceful, highly articulate dominant species. The life of the Lithians – technologically sophisticated, bipedal reptilian beings – is characterized by Father Luiz as a kind of perfect godless Christianity. They are vividly contrasted with the fate of humanity in Blish's imagined twenty-first century: the Cold War, in this account, is described as a "shelter race" that ran from 1960 to 1985; as a result, cities such as Manhattan have become subterranean dwellings for vast numbers of human beings. The Lithians, by contrast, appear not to have experienced an equivalent of the Adamic fall from grace: their world is untouched by crime, greed, hatred, or violent rivalry. The "calm sanity" of the Lithian Chtexa, with whom Luiz forms a tentative, respectful bond, is "disquieting" to the Jesuit biologist because it is "derived from reason, none from precept, none from faith."[34] The Lithians seem to exist entirely within what Charles Taylor names "the immanent frame": their sense of virtue is entire self-sufficient, without need for supernatural explanation.[35]

Indeed, in many ways Lithia is an iteration of Eden before the fall, and its intelligent inhabitants dwell harmoniously with each other and the ecosystem. The priest speculates that the Lithians "never in effect having left the Garden ... did not share the terrible burden of original sin."[36] However, this ostensible prelapsarian state leads the Jesuit to a surprising conclusion: far from reassuring him that divine grace is visible throughout the cosmos, the fact that the Lithians have no knowledge of God and, indeed, no category whatsoever for the supernatural, Luiz infers, suggests that their planet is the creation of Satan. The peaceable dwellers of the planet "did not know God. They did things rightly, and thought righteously, because it was reasonable and efficient and natural to do and to think that way. They seemed to need nothing else."[37] The state of evolved concord in which Lithians dwell – there is not even a word for antisocial behavior in their culture – resonates with earthly utopian thought. The absence of transgression ("no criminals, no deviates, no aberrations of any kind") is not a product of state repression, and Blish anticipates and refutes his 1950s readers' anticipated assumption that Lithia is a simple allegory for communism in Luiz's observation that "the people are not standardized – our own very bad and partial answer to the ethical dilemma – but instead are highly individual."[38] The fact that Blish's Lithians "choose their own life courses without constraint" would make them closer to citizens in capitalist democracies than those in countries that were demonized in the popular Western imagination of the 1950s.[39] We might read Luiz's extreme (and, indeed, as he is aware, heretical) interpretation of the Lithians' innate goodness as an echo of long-standing Eurocentric fear of non-Christian peoples. In an introductory essay to the novel, Ken McCleod observes that the Lithians and their civilization, in multiple ways, are hybrids of a variety of colonized native peoples.[40] A frequent assumption of "colonial powers," as James F. McGrath suggests, is that "the conquered lack souls altogether, or that, being presumed inferior in any number of ways, it is perfectly moral for the more advanced society to conquer them."[41]

At one level, Luiz's empathetic connection with the Lithians – and his vivid difference from the aptly named Cleaver's desire to exploit the planet and its inhabitants – resonates with the powerful critique of Bartolomé de

Las Casas, the early modern Spanish Dominican priest and settler who exposed the violence of his fellow colonists in *A Short Account of the Destruction of the Indies*. De Las Casas bore witness to extraordinary violence committed by his fellow Christians; he feared that divine judgment would be visited on the nation for its iniquities. Yet Luiz, for all his sympathy, becomes complicit in the destruction of the planet: the end of the novel, which narrates the sudden destruction of Lithia witnessed from space, is profoundly ambiguous. The planet may be accidentally destroyed by Cleaver's exploitation of it as a source of material for weapons capable of destroying Earth many times over. However, the death of Lithia, with its vivid beauty ("chirruping forests, Chtexa's porcelain house, the barking lungfish, the stump of the Message Tree, the wild allosaurs, the single silver moon") might, the novel suggests, be caused by Father Luiz's prayer of exorcism, an attempt to rid the universe of a malign force in the name of Christ.[42] Blish, it should be said, was not Roman Catholic and, in fact, in a foreword to the novel identified as an "agnostic with no position in these matters."[43] *A Case of Conscience* presents a possible utopia in Lithia, but it is one that human beings, whether devout or mercenary, faithful or pragmatic, cannot accept on its own terms. Blish does not satirize religious dogma – his "intention to write about a man, not a body of doctrine" is evident – so much as he critiques the human capacity to live with a perfect society, even were such a place to be discovered.[44] For Gabriel McKee, "the contemplation of the world as it should be (or how it *must* not be) is at the core of all SF and this utopian impulse parallels the goals of human religion."[45] Christian tradition, including allusion to biblical narratives of Eden and exodus, are vital for a range of sf narratives, but other religions have a strong influence on varieties of twenty-first-century sf.

G. Willow Wilson's *Alif the Unseen* fuses the world of contemporary cybercrime – hacking, security culture, digital surveillance – with elements of Islamic mysticism and fable. Unlike Blish, Wilson's engagement with religious discourse is not ostensibly neutral. She converted to Islam during her undergraduate years. The eponymous antihero is an enterprising hacker living in a relatively poor district in an otherwise wealthy, anonymized (and fictional) city in the Gulf. He makes his living by constructing digital shields for those who wish to evade the state; this coding is represented as a kind of disenchanted magic. Alif is not, initially at least, on a moral crusade; he is an opportunist who uses his skill in a mercenary fashion. However, Alif is drawn into a conflict that connects politics with spirituality when he receives a copy of an enigmatic book called the *Alf Yeom*, "The Thousand and One Days," by his lover, Intisar, whose powerful fiancé he has unwisely angered.[46] This is a book that "humans are not supposed to have."[47] Alif's flight from The Hand – a powerful avatar of state control – brings him into contact with a threshold world caught between the sacred and secular, the mundane and the mystical. He is helped by several people including his friend, Dina, a devout Muslim; a shadowy figure nicknamed "Vikram the Vampire" who, it turns out, is not simply a fixer from the criminal underworld but a djinn; and an American convert to Islam whom Vikram mocks for her inability to "see me as I am."[48] The djinn comments that Americans are "a very spiritual people, but in their hearts they feel there is something shameful about the unseen."[49] This satirical aside might be a glimpse of what Smith, when glossing Taylor's "immanent frame," calls "an open frame with skylights open to transcendence."[50]

The characters who help Alif, as Rachel Aspden notes in her review of the novel, do not "fit easily into the hierarchical, lineage-obsessed society of The City," and the novel "is consistently sympathetic to those caught between two (or more) worlds."[51] *Alif the Unseen* is dedicated to the author's daughter, Maryam, "born in the Arab Spring." The novel is a kind of utopian, magical-realist response to the possibility of change, especially in relation to authoritarian government, which draws creatively and respectfully on aspects of Islamic tradition.

"Endless Work": Toni Morrison and Marilynne Robinson

Toni Morrison's *Paradise* and Marilynne Robinson's *Gilead* offer parallel, but distinct, responses to the failure and potential of American utopian thought. Both narratives are rich with theological allusion, though they have contrasting visions of religious practice. One strong point of connection is a focus on the relationship between present endeavors and after lives, either earthly or spiritual. The final line of Morrison's novel connects eternity with labor: "Now they will rest before shouldering the endless work they were created to do down here in Paradise."[52] This image anticipates the reflections of Robinson's narrator, John Ames, on his failing health. Ames faces the reality of his mortality with a degree of stoicism and attempts to think of heaven "without much success."[53] The strangeness of his earthly body, the fact of human incarnation, presents sufficient mystery for the minister: "Each morning I'm like Adam waking up in Eden, amazed at the cleverness of my hands and at the brilliance pouring into my mind through my eyes – old hands, old eyes, old mind, a very diminished Adam altogether, and it is still just remarkable."[54] In so far as he is able to imagine an afterlife, it is a bodily existence: "I believe the soul in Paradise must enjoy something nearer to a perpetual vigorous adulthood than to any other state we know."[55] Paradise, for both Morrison's and Robinson's protagonists, is connected with agency rather than a passive state of religious contemplation or comfort.

Marianne DeKoven names Morrison's writing "post-utopian utopianism, or utopian post-utopianism."[56] The title, *Paradise*, resonates more readily with religious than political ideas: the lineage of the English term is traced back, via Greek, Latin, and French translations, to the Persian term for a walled garden or orchard. The Greek translation of the Jewish scriptures uses the Persian-derived term for the Garden of Eden. It is also used in both Christian and Muslim holy writings as a synonym for heaven, a place of eternal reward and peace. In European Christian literary culture, paradise is most notably associated with the final section of Dante's medieval *Divina Commedia* and John Milton's early modern rewriting of the temptation and fall of humanity, *Paradise Lost*. Morrison's *Paradise* might be read as a challenge to white, Eurocentric appropriations of religious discourse. It focuses on three utopian communities, all of which either fail or are subject to violent interruption: Haven, a Black town founded in Oklahoma in the 1890s; its successor, Ruby, which was established after the gradual breakdown of Haven following World War II; and, located some miles from this intentionally restricted town, the Convent, an all-female community, which welcomes marginalized women and practices an esoteric, non-Christian form of worship. For Shari Evans, Haven, Ruby, and the Convent are "spaces [that] engage the search for home – for a safe haven – but also the violence that accompanies such a search."[57] The novel has a flashback structure and begins with a group of men from Ruby breaking into the Convent, ready to murder its inhabitants ("Bodacious black eves unredeemed by Mary") because the women are viewed as a threat. The gang is convinced that their actions are sanctified ("God at their side, they take aim").[58] For Channette Romero, the novel emphasizes "the historic importance of Christianity for mainstream American and African American nationhood and community building" and "opens up the possibilities it contains for healing the traumas and injustices of this painful history."[59] The dynamic picture with which the novel ends, a movement from repose to a resumption of the "endless work of paradise,"[60] in Evans's terms, brings together "both the lost and the saved, inside and outside."[61] In this way, *Paradise* resists exclusionary iterations of utopia that are tacitly, and sometimes physically, violent.

Robinson is relatively rare in contemporary American literature in her self-identification as both Christian and liberal, terms that she has sought to reclaim in her long creative life. She is a prolific essayist, and her body of critical work has been particularly concerned with the ways in which contemporary American culture has conspired to forget, and sometimes to denigrate, its best political aspirations. The lyrical historicism of her *Gilead* sequence is haunted by squandered utopian potential, specifically that rooted in a radical antiracist strand of Christianity that she figures as both orthodox and progressive. The eponymous first novel is marked by plural forms of grief, not only that of its narrator for his first wife and their child, but also a subtly politicized mourning for the political radicalism of the titular town's past. Ames observes that "in the old days towns like ours were a conspiracy. Lots of people were only there to be antislavery by any means that came to hand."[62] Elsewhere, Robinson has made it clear that that Gilead is, in fact, inspired by a real historical precedent and is "modeled on Tabor," a town "in the southwest corner of Iowa . . . founded by a group from Oberlin . . . It was intended to serve, and did serve, as a fallback for John Brown and others during the conflict in Kansas."[63] The ostensible theological focus of the narrative – on death and resurrection, trespass and forgiveness, for example – is enacted in a context of political failure and spiritual compromise. The citizens of Gilead, including John Ames whether he knows it or not, silently dishonor the sacrifice of abolitionist figures such as Captain John Brown and the enslaved people who were fighting not just for individual freedom but for collective liberty.

Ames's grandfather was an abolitionist who joined the uncompromising John Brown in his armed struggle against slavery; he "preached his people into the war, saying while there was slavery there was no peace, but only a war of the armed and powerful against the captive and defenseless."[64] The fierce preacher is alienated from his own son, who refuses to join the fight. This estrangement haunts the narrator, and he loves the memory of these two radically different men. Amy Hungerford claims that "[Robinson's] novels imagine belief made capacious, and aim to show us behavior within the life of belief that can heal both family and Republic."[65] Christopher Douglas, by contrast, is more critical of *Gilead*, specifically in relation to its representation of the relationship between mainstream American piety and its complicity with slavery: "in the face of one of the great national sins, what form should Christian resistance take?"[66] Robinson might best be read as a Christian utopian writer, though she is no idealist. Her form of theological belief is neither fundamentalist nor strictly liberal, though her astringent essays frequently defend a politically progressive and inclusive understanding of American polity. "Democracy is profoundly collaborative," she argues in *The Death of Adam*. The powerful word "implies a community," but she notes that it "also seems . . . we have almost stopped using the word in a positive sense, preferring 'capitalism,' which by no means implies community, and for which, so far as I have seen, our forebears found no use at all."[67]

Spirituality, especially in its most mystical forms, might be perceived as an escape from the reality that politicized, revolutionary utopians are committed to transforming into a dynamically, materially better world. Indeed, the image of the pious believer who patiently endures present anguish – and allows others to suffer – because they anticipate compensatory redemption in the afterlife is a common satirical archetype in popular culture. This parodic figure, however, rarely matches the reality of the practical faith that characterizes the lives of many everyday believers from the whole gamut of world religions. As Terry Eagleton argues in *Hope without Optimism,* even if we accept that "there will be no utopia, in the sense of a world purged of discord and dissatisfaction, it is sober realism to believe that our condition could be mightily improved . . . Nothing is more otherworldly than the assumption that the world as we know it is here to stay."[68] Dissident and competing, though often overlapping, spiritualities are found in plural forms in contemporary America. The ethos of Christian Nationalism and its fascistic near deification of the United States is merely the loudest and most power-hungry mode of political theology at play in the twenty-first century. As John A. McClure argues, "there are forms of spiritual life and language that do not shut off inquiry or give birth to violent fervour."[69]

Notes

1. James Baldwin, *The Fire Next Time* (London: Penguin, 2017), 63.
2. Baldwin, 89.
3. Joseph L. Mangina, *Revelation* (London: SCM Press, 2010), 37.
4. Harold Bloom, *The American Religion* (New York: Chu Hartley, 2013), Kindle edition, Kindle location 140.
5. Matthew Avery Sutton, *American Apocalypse: A History of Modern Evangelicalism* (Cambridge, MA: Harvard University Press, 2014), 6–7.
6. Marilynne Robinson, *When I Was a Child I Read Books* (London: Hachette, 2012), 91.
7. Thomas More, *Utopia*. Edited with a revised translation by George M. Logan (New York: W. W. Norton, 2011), 84.
8. John A. McClure, *Partial Faiths: Postsecular Fiction in the Age of Pynchon and Morrison* (Athens: University of Georgia Press, 2007), ix.

9. Vincent Geoghegan, "Utopia, Religion and Memory," *Journal of Political Ideologies* 12.3 (2007), 255–267 (256).
10. Fredric Jameson, *Archaeologies of the Future: The Desire Called Utopia and Other Science Fictions* (London: Verso, 2005).
11. David Reynolds, *America, Empire of Liberty* (London: Allen Lane, 2009), xviii.
12. Marilynne Robinson, *What Are We Doing Here?* (London: Virago, 2018), 153.
13. These verses are cited in Mark Holloway, *Heavens on Earth: Utopian Communities in America, 1680–1880* (London: Turnstile Press, 1951), xvi.
14. Holloway, 18.
15. Office for National Statistics, "The religion of usual residents and household religious composition in England and Wales, Census 2021 data," *Office for National Statistics* (2022), online.
16. Gregory A. Smith, "About Three-in-Ten U.S. Adults Are Now Religiously Unaffiliated," *Pew Research Center* (December 14, 2021), online.
17. Gregory A. Smith.
18. Gregory A. Smith.
19. Frederick Douglass, *The Portable Frederick Douglass* (New York: Penguin, 2016), 204.
20. Douglass, 204.
21. Douglass, 207.
22. See Avery Sutton for a discussion of religious ideas associated with the far right.
23. Judith Kovacs and Christopher Rowland, *Revelation* (Oxford: Blackwell, 2004), 7.
24. Bloom, Kindle location 134.
25. Bloom, Kindle location 134.
26. Douglas Coupland, *Generation X: Tales for an Accelerated Culture* (London: Abacus, 1992), 145.
27. Coupland, *Generation X*, 16.
28. Douglas Coupland, *Life after God* (London: Simon and Schuster, 1994), 178.
29. Douglas Coupland, *Polaroids from the Dead* (London: Flamingo, 1997), 179.
30. Martyn Percy, *The Salt of the Earth: Religious Resilience in a Secular Age* (London: Sheffield Academic Press, 2001), 53.
31. Charles Taylor, *A Secular Age* (Cambridge: Belknap Press, 2007), 549.
32. James K. A. Smith, *How (Not) to Be Secular: Reading Charles Taylor* (Grand Rapids, MI: Eerdmans, 2014), 80.
33. Brian McHale, *Postmodernist Fiction* (London: Routledge, 1987), 10.
34. James Blish, *A Case of Conscience* (London: Gollancz, 2011), 43.
35. Taylor, 549.
36. Blish, *A Case*, 44.
37. Blish, *A Case*, 43.
38. Blish, *A Case*, 85.
39. Blish, *A Case*, 85.
40. Ken McCleod, "Introduction" to Blish, *A Case*, n.p.

41. James F. McGrath, *Theology and Science Fiction* (Eugene: Cascade, 2016), 56.
42. Blish, *A Case*, 229.
43. Blish, "Foreword," n.p.
44. Blish, "Foreword," n.p.
45. Gabriel McKee, *The Gospel according to Science Fiction* (Westminster: John Knox, 2007), Kindle edition, Kindle location 3239–3241.
46. G. Willow Wilson, *Alif the Unseen* (London: Corvus, 2012), 61.
47. Willow Wilson, 101.
48. Willow Wilson, 130.
49. Willow Wilson, 130.
50. James K. A. Smith, 80.
51. Rachel Aspden, "Review of *Alif the Unseen*," *The Observer* (October 7, 2012), online.
52. Toni Morrison, *Paradise* (London: Vintage, 1999), 318.
53. Marilynne Robinson, *Gilead* (London: Virago, 2005), 75.
54. Robinson, *Gilead*, 76.
55. Robinson, *Gilead*, 189.
56. Marianne DeKoven, *Utopia Limited: The Sixties and the Emergence of the Postmodern* (Durham, NC: Duke University Press, 2004), 269.
57. Shari Evans, "Programmed Space, Themed Space, and the Ethics of Home in Toni Morrison's *Paradise*," *African American Review* 46.2/3 (2013), 381–396 (383).
58. Morrison, 18.
59. Channette Romero, "Creating the Beloved Community: Religion, Race, and Nation in Toni Morrison's *Paradise*," *African American Review* 39.3 (2005), 415–430 (415).
60. Morrison, 318.
61. Evans, 394.
62. Robinson, *Gilead*, 180.
63. Robinson, *When I Was a Child*, 180.
64. Robinson, *Gilead*, 115.
65. Amy Hungerford, *Postmodern Belief: American Literature and Religion since 1960* (Princeton, NJ: Princeton University Press, 2010), 121.
66. Christopher Douglas, "Christian Multiculturalism and Unlearned History in Marilynne Robinson's *Gilead*," *Novel* 44.3 (2011), 333–353 (335).
67. Marilynne Robinson, *The Death of Adam: Essays on Modern Thought* (New York: Picador, 2005), 149.
68. Terry Eagleton, *Hope without Optimism* (New Haven, CT: Yale University Press, 2018), 133.
69. McClure, 101.

CHAPTER 6

Black Escapes and Black Wishlands

Jerry Rafiki Jenkins

Life for people of African descent in the United States began as a dystopia, but as Alex Zamalin points out in *Black Utopia*, a "utopian strain of hope," built on the ideas of liberation, justice, and freedom, was also present: "The subjugation of slaves created a transcendent culture in which spirituals embodied the prophetic faith in reaching the promised land of freedom."[1] The "promised land" in this early strain of African American utopianism is like Ernst Bloch's reading of Thomas More's utopia, an already-existing "wishland."[2] As a black wishland, the "promised land" for enslaved black folks was in heaven *and* on earth, a conception of black freedom that led to the "first idea" of African American utopianism – "Black escape to a new world."[3] While emigration to an already-existing black wishland defines the first idea, its back-up plan, what I am calling the *second idea* of African American utopianism, presumes that geographical escape is not possible and, therefore, calls for transforming the United States or parts of it into a utopia for black people. The second idea's approach to the black wishland parallels that of the European utopianists of the eighteenth and nineteenth centuries who, according to Bloch, "transposed the wishland more into the future."[4] Although the transformation of the wishland from the topos of space to that of time insists that the wish is more important than the land, Bloch contends that we should not see this development as nonsensical or esoteric, but as a conception of the "not *yet* in the sense of a possibility; that it could be there if we could only do something for it."[5] Similarly, black escape in this second idea is an ideological endeavor in which the question of the black wishland's location is less important than the beliefs that will govern it. Indeed, part of the "something" that African Americans are required to do to make the black wishland a reality is to discard the ideologies of antiblackness inside and outside African American communities.

The second idea's notion of black escape can be found in the "radical utopian practices" of black preaching women in the early nineteenth century, whose "black radical otherworlds" were realized "in communion and in their dreams and visions,"[6] and in the post–World War II conception of the "Beloved Community" as a not-yet possibility, a conception mostly associated with Martin Luther King Jr. and the civil rights movement.[7] Part of what makes the Beloved Community a not-yet possibility is the status of African American life in postwar America. Even though African Americans served loyally on the battlefield and in war industries during World War II, their status after the war was virtually the same as it was on the eve of the war – "superexploited workers, second-class citizens, and a cultural group despised and reviled by the white majority."[8] Yet, as Anthony B. Pinn points out, the hope that exists in the Beloved Community's not-yet status is tied to America's postwar role in the global arena: "As [King's] thinking on the United States as empire and the consequences of its global reach became more developed, this framing of community served as a cartography of interaction extending beyond the borders of a particular nation-state and beyond racial or ethnic similarity."[9] Since the United States will help shape how people across racial, ethnic, and national differences will interact with each other in the Beloved Community, the first idea of African American utopianism does not make sense in this context. As I discuss in my examination of the texts by Parliament/Funkadelic and Reginald Hudlin later in this chapter, the second idea can lead African Americans to develop an unwillingness to see other places outside the United States as possible wishlands, since it is assumed that this country will set the standard for global interaction. Thus, the second idea's approach to the black wishland raises questions about the role of American exceptionalism and African nonexceptionalism in African American utopianism, questions that direct us to the productive debates between the proponents and critics of Afro-pessimism.

In *Red, White, & Black*, Frank Wilderson III informs us that the term "Afro-pessimism" is a moniker suggested to him by Saidiyah Hartman and is different from the term's use in the 1980s, "when many scholars and journalists in Western countries believed that there was no hope for bringing about democracy and achieving sustainable economic development in [sub-Saharan Africa]."[10] Wilderson's use of Afro-pessimism describes a collection of "theorists of Black positionality who share [Frantz] Fanon's insistence that, though Blacks are indeed sentient beings, the structure of the entire world's semantic field . . . is sutured by anti-Black solidarity."[11] This understanding of antiblackness as a global phenomenon is captured in Calvin Warren's *Ontological Terror*, where he recalls a "terrifying" question posed to him by one of his mentors: "why are blacks *hated* all over the world?"[12] What makes the question terrifying is its assertion that there is *no place* where black people can be truly free. As Warren argues in his answer to his mentor's question, blacks are hated because Western metaphysics "invented" black people to function as the physical manifestation of nothing: "Metaphysics uses blacks to maintain a sense of security and to sustain the fantasy of triumph – the triumph over the nothing that limits human freedom."[13] According to this view, since Western culture continues to deny black people the status of human, blackness cannot be "disaggregated from social death."[14] Christina Sharpe contends that "the crimes and pleasures of slavery persist" in the postbellum world – "reenacted and recirculated in national consciousness through the staging and interpretation of slavery and its excesses, in everyday relations of terror, in literary texts, visual arts, museum exhibitions, and memorials"[15] – precisely because "ongoing state-sanctioned legal and extralegal murders of Black people are normative and, for this so-called democracy, necessary."[16] This means, as Warren argues, that the "free black" does not exist, since "it is impossible for any black to be free in an antiblack world."[17]

Critics of Afro-pessimism might respond to Warren's terrifying question by challenging its premise, as Kevin Quashie does in *Black Aliveness*. According to Quashie, "the definitive fact of black subjection, true as it is, is not exactly sayable because no statement about every black person can be genuinely sayable. Such a claim might be ideologically or conceptually or theoretically or structurally factual, but its truth is and should remain an opacity."[18] While Quashie agrees with the "nuanced insights of black pessimism," his notion of black aliveness challenges "black pessimism's declaration of totality" in which black life is defined primarily in "terms of death."[19] To that end, Quashie seeks to articulate an "aesthetics of aliveness" founded on a "black worldness" in which the expectations of black people are not "blackness," but "beingness."[20] Similarly, Tavia Nyong'o contends in *Afro-Fabulations* that Hartman's "reparative black historiography" in *Scenes of Subjection*, while offering a "scouring critique of the many ruses of the liberal antiracist imaginary," is partly responsible for the rise of Afro-pessimism, which he believes represents "a sharp challenge to the broadly relational and intersectional approach" that he favors because Afro-pessimism "characterizes blackness as a site of accumulation and fungibility, rather than one of identity and resistance."[21] For Quashie and Nyong'o, Afro-pessimism's assumptions about the universality of antiblackness and the totality of white supremacy encourage a black hopelessness that precludes the possibility that free black people do or will exist.

The texts discussed in this chapter – Sun Ra's "Space Is the Place," Parliament's "Chocolate City," Reginald Hudlin's television adaption of Derrick Bell's "The Space Traders," Octavia Butler's "The Book of Martha," and Chesya Burke's "The Teachings and Redemption of Ms. Fannie Lou Mason" – suggest that Afro-pessimists and their critics should not be viewed as adversaries, though their differences are ideologically and materially important, but as two approaches attempting to achieve the same goal – the liberation of black life from social death. While these texts agree with Nyong'o and Quashie that death and its associations do not define the totality of black life – and that black people have always used fabulation and aliveness to thrive, not just survive, in an antiblack world – they do not support what Warren calls the "humanist fantasy," an assumption that "masks subjection in emancipatory rhetoric" by claiming that "freedom can be attained through political, social, or legal action."[22] Read collectively, the works by Sun Ra, Parliament/Funkadelic, Hudlin, Butler, and Burke reveal that the debates between Afro-pessimists and their critics parallel those between Zamalin's "black utopians and antiutopians." While black utopians share many of the ideas and concerns of Afro-pessimism's critics and tend to rehash "elements of Platonic idealism about total social transformation," black antiutopians can be read as Afro-pessimists who are "more critical" about the prospects of Platonic idealism even though their "romantic critiques" tend to embody the utopianism that they criticize.[23] However, as suggested by the texts examined herein, liberating black life from social death at the dawn of the twenty-first century will require "combining the most productive elements of black utopian imagination and black antiutopian critique, rather than accepting the false choice between them."[24] Indeed, by rejecting the "false choice," these works offer approaches to black escape that seek to move the black wishland from the realm of the not-yet to that of the everyday, that is, to make the black wishland, as Jayna Brown puts it in *Black Utopias*, "a state of being and doing."[25]

From "Space Is the Place" to "Chocolate City"

As a founding figure of Afrofuturism, a term coined shortly after his death in 1993, Sun Ra produced music with his Arkestra that was shaped by the "hope impulse," which Isiah Lavender III identifies as one of the guiding principles of Afrofuturism.[26] For example, Ra's "Space Is the Place," which is also the title of the 1974 independent film starring the jazz musician, highlights the hope impulse of the first idea of African American utopianism. One of the lines that is repeated throughout the twenty-one-minute song emphasizes the positives of black people going to space: "There's no limit/to things that you can do. There's no limit/to things that you can be."[27] "Space Is the Place" calls on black people to escape to an already-existing black wishland where black people are free to do and be anything they choose. As Zamalin puts it, "Ra's provocative suggestion was not that black people needed to immigrate or assimilate, but that they needed to undertake space travel in search of new planets."[28] While no one believed that outer space was really the answer, people did recognize that Ra's ideas "probed questions about the ethics and necessity of what was central to the twentieth century: capitalist inequality, ongoing war, white supremacy, de jure and de facto racial segregation, and black ghettoization."[29] Indeed, one can read "Space Is the Place" as an Afro-pessimistic response to the terrifying question posed earlier in this chapter: why are black people hated around the globe? However, black hope is not absent from "Space Is the Place," since the lead vocalist tells us that "outer space is a pleasant place"; rather, it is defined by the desire or willingness to escape an antiblack world. The lack of such desire, as implied by the song, is a sign of hopelessness, since it implies that one believes that black life will always be in the wake, as Sharpe might put it, or that a black wishland can exist in an antiblack world, as presumed by the humanist fantasy.

In contrast to Ra's "Space Is the Place," much of the music of Parliament/Funkadelic focuses on the second idea of African American utopianism in which geographical black escape is not possible nor practical. Parliament/Funkadelic's "P-funk," like Ra's music, sought to "free minds," especially black minds, and it used "liberation-tinged space metaphors," "heartbeat-like bass line[s]," and other rhetorical tools such as irony to create an "astral-liberation party music" that would make Ra's concepts more accessible to popular culture audiences.[30] As declared in Funkadelic's 1974 classic, "Standing on the Verge of Getting It On," the group's music is "designed to free your funky mind" and "to help you cope ... into some other reality" while simultaneously bringing you "hope." Thus, while inspired by Ra's location of the black wishland in outer space or outside the United States, "Chocolate City," like Parliament's songs that feature Clinton's personas Star Child and Dr. Funkenstein, locates the black wishland in the United States.[31]

Parliament's "Chocolate City" is a spoken-word ode to Washington, DC, which is described by Clinton, the song's lead vocalist, as the "capital" of America's chocolate cities, which include Newark, Gary, Atlanta, New York, and Los Angeles. Clinton also notes that some have considered chocolate cities as a form of reparation: "Hey, uh, we didn't get our 40 acres and a mule/But we did get you CC."[32] Obviously, Clinton is being ironic about viewing chocolate cities as reparation payments, since most of the chocolate cities in the 1970s were negatively affected by white flight, deindustrialization, globalization, and scarce public resources[33] (as indicated by Clinton's references to "Vanilla suburbs" and stereotypes of black urban areas as "jive and game and can't be changed"). However, Clinton's irony is not a voice of hopelessness about black life in America, but of opportunity. Insisting that an armed struggle is not required to transform chocolate cities into black wishlands, Clinton tells black people in chocolate cities that "you don't need the bullet when you got the ballot." Thus, when Clinton makes the following claim, "to each his reach and if I don't cop it ain't mine to have," he is suggesting that black people who are not reaching for the chocolate-city dream believe that chocolate cities are unable to become utopic. Such thinking, as alluded to in "Chocolate City," is an example of the black hopelessness that helps to keep the black wishland in the not-yet stage. For Clinton, while the utopic chocolate city is a not-yet possibility, it is "no dream," since there is a feasible way to call it into existence – developing black people's desire to "reach" for it.

The competing images of the black wishland in Ra's "Space Is the Place" and Parliament's "Chocolate City" imply that one's conception of black escape largely determines where one imagines the black wishland. While Ra's outer space, like Martin Robinson Delany's black utopia,[34] implies that the black wishland is located outside the United States, "Chocolate City" identifies the United States as the future site of the black wishland. In Parliament's song, black escape is not practical; thus, the hope impulse in "Chocolate City" is linked with ideological change and is shaped by a willingness to transform an antiblack world into a black wishland. In that understanding of black hope, it is assumed that there are no black wishlands outside the United States, an assumption that uncritically celebrates the idea of American exceptionalism. Indeed, unlike "Space Is the Place" and Ra's other works, which are not concerned with black colonization or Americanization,[35] "Chocolate City" and other songs by Parliament/Funkadelic propose that the US *can* become a utopia for African Americans, if black and nonblack Americans can overcome their social hang-ups (e.g., anxieties over race, gender, class, sexuality, and religion).[36] Put in slightly different terms, while "Space Is the Place" assumes that black emigration is the "something" that must be done for black people to experience the black wishland, "Chocolate City" proposes that black ideological escape is that "something," which implies that geographical black escape is not possible for all black people and, more importantly, that there are no black wishlands to escape to, an assumption that is problematized by Reginald Hudlin's "Space Traders."

"Space Traders" and the Absence of Africa as Black Wishland

Reginald Hudlin's television adaptation of Derrick Bell's short story "The Space Traders,"[37] which Clinton's Dr. Funkenstein hosts, asks us to consider a problem shared by "Space Is the Place" and Parliament's "Chocolate City" – the absence of Africa as a possible black wishland. First aired on HBO in November 1994, "Space Traders" is the first tale of *Cosmic Slop*, an anthology of science-fiction short films produced and directed by Hudlin.[38] According to Hudlin, *Cosmic Slop* was "so controversial that some executives at HBO tried to stop the show from airing."[39] It is, therefore, not surprising that *Cosmic Slop* is absent from HBO's original films archives and is only available on VHS or YouTube. In fact, Bell was surprised that HBO gave the Hudlin the green light to adapt the story for the small screen because the story in its written form "never fails to bring a degree of welcomed enlightenment for blacks, but often upsets whites who see it as threatening and perhaps too revealing."[40] The television film and short story examine what happens when extraterrestrial beings offer to solve America's economic, environmental, and energy problems in exchange for every person in the country who is identified as black. The offer, which ends in five days, is a business proposition that America is free to accept or reject. Moreover, the decision will not be determined by the president, Congress, or the courts, but by a national vote. Since Americans voted to accept the Traders' proposition by a "wide margin" and the vote represents, as one of the president's white cabinet members puts it, the "will of the people," the film suggests that many white and other nonblack Americans believe that America could become a wishland if black people were removed. Given that scenario, we are asked to consider the following question: if antiblackness represents the will of most nonblack Americans, what prevents black folks in late twentieth-century America from imagining Africa as a location for the black wishland?

The film's answer to that question is represented through its depictions of Professor Golightly, the only nonwhite member of the President's cabinet and a longtime critic of Affirmative Action, and the black leaders of the "Coalition to Stop the Trade," who view Golightly as a "big oreo." While Golightly, played by Robert Guillaume, and the Coalition leaders do not agree on how to respond to the Traders' proposal, they all fight to stay in America. Their fight to stay in America is not inspired by the fear of the unknown, but by the belief that America is the only home for African Americans. For example, Golightly creates a secret antitrade committee of wealthy white men, whom he persuades to use their economic power to convince "rank and file" white Americans to reject the trade, because he assumes that these white men are, as he puts it, "capitalists first and Caucasians second." As Golightly sees it, such identification represents black people's hope for America – that it will one day become a nation where one's racial identity is not as important as one's class or other identities. However, as represented by the remarks of the white men at the meeting, while wealthy whites might privilege their class identity over their racial one, their wealth depends on black people being their scapegoats and sources of cheapened labor during times of economic crisis. As stated by one of the white capitalists, while he and his colleagues are frightened by the prospect of an America without black people because they will lose some of its cheap laborers and domestic consumers, the main reason why they are at the meeting is their fear that rank-and-file whites will realize that black people are not responsible for white poverty: "With blacks gone, how many poor whites will stand being at the very bottom of the well? We'll have a revolution before the year is out." Those remarks not only imply that the American Dream continues to be imagined as a white male achievement that comes at the expense of poor whites and nonwhite people, but they also identify antiblack exploitation as the price that black people must pay to stay in America, a price that Golightly and his critics are willing to pay.

After Golightly gives his speech on racism in America, in which he argues that "the major motivation for racism in this country is the deeply held belief that black people should not have anything that white people don't," he asks the Coalition's multiracial members to spread the rumor that black people will be taken to "the wealthiest and most beautiful utopia in the known universe." According to Golightly, if that rumor becomes credible, rank-and-file whites will argue that "to limit the Traders' offer to blacks is unconstitutional discrimination against whites." When the members of the Coalition began to voice approval of Golightly's argument, one of the Coalition's leaders, a black minister who believes that the boycotts and protests explain the rising poll numbers against the Trade, declares that

Golightly is not to be trusted because he has "dedicated his entire life to sabotaging his own people." However, his response to Golightly's argument indicates that he and Golightly are not that far apart in their thinking, since the minister would rather die than leave America: "My people, my people were brought here involuntarily, and involuntarily is the only way they're going to take me out." After that declaration, the minister leads the Coalition in singing "We Shall Overcome." What is noteworthy in this exchange is that Golightly and the minister seem to be guided by the humanist fantasy, since they never consider what the white cabinet member, who proposed to make the Traders' offer a national referendum, asked Golightly near the end of the film: "You knew it was hopeless as soon as the idea was out of the bag. Didn't you?" While Golightly and the minster refuse to accept that reality until it happened, Piggy, Golightly's personal barber who is played by comedian George Wallace, began planning for the trip to space as soon as the Traders' offer became a national referendum. What Piggy represents is an alternative understanding of the black wishland, one that emphasizes content over location.

While Golightly is getting his haircut by Piggy, he proposes that black people could take up arms like the Palestinians to fight the Trade. Piggy quickly tells Golightly that he is not going to get himself killed to stay in America, a place where he is unwanted. Piggy emphasizes this point in his joke about the American Dream, the moment when "all the niggers are swimming back to Africa, with a Jew under each arm." For Piggy, moral, constitutional, or scientific arguments will not persuade rank-and-file white people to reject the Traders' offer precisely because they define the American utopia as the absence of black people, Jews, and other nonwhites. Moreover, while Piggy is uncertain where the Traders will take them, he jokingly states that if he has his favorite brand of cognac and barbering supplies, he will be happy wherever the Traders take him. Unlike Golightly and the church-led Coalition, Piggy believes that wherever he can enjoy his life is a potential black wishland, whether it is in space with the Traders or in another country. In other words, Piggy does not view America as the only place where a black wishland can exist because content, not location, is what makes a black wishland.

Hudlin's "Space Traders," like the urtext, is an Afro-pessimist response to the Traders' offer, implying that white supremacist conceptions of the American utopia are the main reason why America continues to be an antiblack nation. However, the film's Afro-pessimism is not only represented by its depiction of how most white Americans would respond to the Traders' offer, but also by the absence of an Africa-based wishland.

Although Piggy's understanding of the black wishland is in opposition to Golightly's and the Coalition's black utopia, they all are defined by an absence of Africa as a potential utopic space. In this instance, the African Americans in "Space Traders" represent the first iteration of Afro-pessimism in which, as I noted earlier, sub-Saharan Africa is viewed as a place that will always lack democracy and sustainable economic development. Thus, the film suggests that the second idea of African American utopianism, as represented by Parliament's "Chocolate City," can lead to a black unwillingness that is similarly opposed to leaving America and going to Africa. At the same time, while the film favors the first idea, it is also critical of the black wishland offered by Sun Ra's "Space Is the Place," since the song, like Piggy, is willing to accept outer space as a potential black wishland, but not Africa. According to the film, if African American utopianism continues to be shaped by Western Afro-pessimism in which Africa (as an already or near-future black wishland) is devalued, it will be incapable of imagining, creating, or escaping to a black wishland outside the confines of an antiblack world.

Utopic Inequality, God's Will, and Black Women

While Hudlin's "Space Traders" is critical of the conceptions of black escape and the black wishland found in "Space Is the Place" and "Chocolate City," Octavia E. Butler, who is rightly regarded as "a pivotal ancestral figure" in Afrofuturism,[41] suggests in "The Book of Martha" that all three texts have a common problem – the absence of discussions concerning the everyday realities of a wishland. The story centers on a conversation between Martha Bes, a forty-three-year-old black woman who is the author of several novels, and a "powerful entity" called "God" who changes its sex and race throughout the story. During their conversation, God tells Martha, who does not believe in a literal god, that it has a "great deal of work" for her to do.[42] Martha's job is to help humanity "find less destructive, more peaceful, sustainable ways to live,"[43] and God will let Martha "borrow" some of its power to complete her task. However, there is a price that Martha must pay to help humanity – she will "go back and live among [humans] again as one of their lowliest."[44] Although Martha will decide what the "lowliest" will mean, the power to make such a determination will not be an immediate benefit for her because, as God tells her, "whatever [she] decide[s] is to be the bottom level of society, the lowest class, caste or race, that's what [she'll] be."[45] Martha decides that the best way to help humanity is to give them "dreams [that can] teach – or at least promote – more thoughtfulness when people are awake, promote more concern for real consequences."[46]

What stands out in Martha's task is that utopia is understood as an impossibility, not a not-yet possibility. One may not be surprised by Butler's definition of utopia in "The Book of Martha," given that she consistently voiced her problems with utopia stories. In a 1988 interview, for example, Butler states that utopias are "ridiculous" because a "perfect human society" needs a "few perfect humans," who are unlikely possibilities. Moreover, Butler continues, "any true utopia would almost certainly be incredibly boring, and it would be so overspecialized that any change we might introduce would probably destroy the whole system."[47] Fifteen years later, Butler notes that "The Book of Martha" is her only "utopia story" and reminds us that she dislikes most utopia stories because they are not believable. What makes those stories unbelievable is their failure to grapple with what Butler identifies as one of the inevitabilities of all utopias – "that [someone's] utopia would be someone else's hell."[48] This point is captured in Martha's discussion with God about the futility of attempting to create a utopia.

While becoming increasingly frustrated with God's request for her to help humanity, Martha reluctantly asks God if it wants her to create a utopia because she does not "believe it's possible to arrange a society so that everyone is content, everyone has what he or she wants."[49] Implicit in Martha's antiutopianism is that the problem with trying to imagine a perfect human society is that there are multiple ways to be human, which means that a utopia always privileges one version of the human over others and, therefore, one version of the *good life* over others. God shares Martha's antiutopianism and explains that it does not want her to create a utopia because it would last for only "a few moments" due to the human capacity for greed and dominance.[50] This exchange between Martha and God highlights the importance of one question that all utopias must address: who will and will not be content in the proposed utopia? This question maintains that utopias are always attempts to justify certain forms of social inequality; therefore, questions of where a black wishland is located are less important than questions of who gets to enjoy the good life provided by that wishland. These questions become more complex, as highlighted in Burke's "The Teachings and Redemption of Ms. Fannie Lou Mason," when we consider the role that the Christianity has played in addressing those questions in Black America.

Set in fictional "Colored Town," Kentucky at the turn of the twentieth century, Burke's story follows Fannie Lou's mentoring of Leona and Iona

Kelly, nine-year-old twin sisters who, like Fannie Lou, possess supernatural powers. As Fannie Lou explains to the sisters, very few people have their powers, and most of those who possess those powers have been persecuted and killed because they were women: "That scares people. If it had been restricted to men, then it'd be revered. But because it's the power of women, they call us witches, or Hoodooo women, or Rootworkers, or a whole host of other things. There was a time when we were valued; not anymore."[51] Indeed, Fannie Lou will be killed by the people of Colored Town because they believe that she is a danger to the community, even though she uses her powers to help rather than harm black communities. While set in the black past, "The Teachings and Redemption of Ms. Fannie Lou Mason" offers a warning for twenty-first-century African Americans about a problem that comes with using Christian thought to imagine black wishlands – the belief that social inequalities reflect God's will.

According to Burke's story, viewing racial inequality through the lens of God's will was one of the ideological practices that prevented most African American communities from becoming black wishlands. For example, the narrator's contradictory description of Colored Town points to white supremacy and the various forces that reinforce it as the main reasons why Colored Town cannot become a black wishland in the everyday world. Indeed, while Colored Town is described as "a thriving town of Negro people" who are "lucky" because they do not live near "any large white communities that could blame them for anything that went wrong," it is also depicted as "a place only worth mentioning if you were leaving it on your way to somewhere bigger and better."[52] Implicit in the narrator's rendering of Colored Town is that this thriving black community will always lack the ability to become "somewhere bigger and better" for black people because white folks will not allow it to become such an entity. However, the narrator notes that black folks in Colored Town and elsewhere devalue the legal and extralegal antiblack practices responsible for racial inequality through their understanding of God's will:

> The Lord wasn't as generous to the Negro folk as he was to the white man. And many years after Fannie Lou Mason saved the people in that small town somewhere in Virginia, the same could still be said. Most didn't feel God was biased; if you asked white folk, they would simply say that they were the better race and so God blessed them; if you asked Negro folk, they would say that because they were the last on earth they would surely be first in heaven and were therefore the chosen people.[53]

Given that black folks believe that they are God's "chosen people," Colored Town will never become a black wishland precisely because black people have been chosen by God to be "the last on earth." The problem with that belief, as captured by the narrator, is that it validates God favoring white people over black people, even though folks believe that God is not racially biased, by assuming that the black wishland is only possible in death, while the white wishland can exist on earth and in the afterlife.

Another problem with using God's will to explain social inequalities, as suggested by Fannie's death at the calling of Preacher Joseph, is that patriarchy is imagined as an essential part of the black wishland. Preacher Joseph, the minster of Colored Town's only church, declares that Fannie Lou must die because she is, as the narrator puts it, not only a witch and Hoodoo woman, but a "whore . . . who would corrupt the souls of men, using her body."[54] Implicit in the narrator's observations is that one of the consequences of embracing Christian patriarchy is that it insists that the subjugation of black women is a prerequisite for bringing a black wishland into existence. Preacher Joseph's reasoning for wanting Fannie Lou dead captures the consequences of such thinking: "She comes here to hurt us, and if we let her, she will destroy our town. She'll poison us, make us turn against each other. That's what they do. We worked so hard to build this. You know what we have to do."[55] According to the preacher, black women like Fannie, who might be queer because she refuses to "belong to any man,"[56] are what prevent black communities from transforming into black wishlands. Indeed, Preacher Joseph interprets such refusal as an attempt to sabotage Colored Town by queering "man's law" and, therefore, "God's law."[57] Thus, as represented by the preacher's warning, God will punish Colored Town if its citizens do not maintain a heteropatriarchal society, since matriarchal and other non-heteropatriarchal communities are antithetical to God's plan.

Like "The Book of Martha," "The Teachings and Redemption of Ms. Fannie Lou Mason" contends that God-based black wishlands require black women to be one of the groups who will be unable to have what they want because they are at the bottom of God's racial and gender hierarchy.[58] Moreover, both stories privilege "black quotidian practices and visions of communality, sociality, and kinship already operating outside the bounds of normalizing imperatives."[59] Indeed, like Lauren Olamina in Butler's *Parable* duology, a "work of political theory" that was published when "utopian dreams of racial justice were stillborn,"[60] Martha acknowledges that utopias are always impossibilities precisely because they are only possible in our dreams, but she does not view utopic dreams as useless: "I think if people go to a . . . well, a private heaven every night, it might take the edge off their willingness to spend their waking hours trying to dominate or destroy one another" (ellipses in original).[61] Similarly, Fannie Lou's narrative highlights the ways in which American racism and patriarchy shaped some black people's view of God's will, a view that, for black women like her, defines the God-based black wishland as a dystopia. However, instead of trying to create a black wishland, Fannie Lou identifies geographical black escape as an alternative for black women seeking contentment. As Fannie Lou puts it to Iona and Leona, "we're nomads; can't stay in one place for too long before we're called – pulled – to another. Or we're run out. That's just how it is."[62] According to Fannie Lou, although black women like her are pushed to help black communities and to promote new and productive ways of being human and, therefore, being black, they must always be ready to leave those communities to protect themselves and to find contentment because black wishlands are not physical places, but ideological destinations.

Conclusion: From Not-Yet Possibility to Possibility

In their proposals for liberating black life from social death at the dawn of the twenty-first century, the works by Sun Ra, Parliament/Funkadelic, Hudlin, Butler, and Burke point out that black escape is more than a question about the best ways to leave an antiblack dystopia, and black wishlands are not just a question about location – they are also about what daily life might or should look like in a black utopia. For example, one of the issues of disagreement among the works examined in this chapter is whether it is possible to imagine, create, or emigrate to a black wishland that would satisfy all African Americans. Sun Ra's "Space Is the Place," Parliament's "Chocolate City," and Hudlin's "Space Traders" suggest that all black people will get what they want in the black wishland, since these texts focus their discussions on the location of the wishland, the obstacles to its creation, and/or how to get to it, instead of addressing the potential everyday realities of the black wishland. That focus implies that most African Americans already uphold belief systems that will guarantee everyone's happiness in the black wishland; therefore, everyday life in the black wishland will be like black life in contemporary America *sans* antiblackness. In contrast to the works of Sun Ra, Parliament, and Hudlin, Butler's "The Book of Martha" and Burke's "The Teachings and Redemption of Ms. Fannie Lou Mason" contend that some black people will not get what they want in the black wishland precisely because one person's utopia tends be someone else's dystopia.

Like Samuel Delany's *Triton: An Ambiguous Heterotopia*, which "pushed the black utopian tradition to consider intersections of race, gender, and sexuality just as it unsettled expectations about them,"[63] Butler's and Burke's stories contend that to claim that all black people will get what they want in the black wishland is to assume that the black wishland is a heteropatriarchal space. That assumption, as pointed out in Butler's and Burke's stories, is largely informed by Christian-based conceptions of gender in which it is believed that the straight man's utopia defines women's utopia because God deems it so (see, for example, 1 Corinthians 11:1–15). Thus, by privileging the ideological content of the black wishland over its location, Butler's and Burke's stories suggest that to transform the black wishland from not-yet possibility to possibility requires thinking of utopia, as Brown does, as a "state of being and doing" rather than a place and/or time. While Brown's notion of utopia calls for a "complete break from time as we know it" and refers to "a quality of the unknown, or of the unknowable, and of the unexpected," it also "resist[s] the deferment of fulfillment to a then and there" by dreaming of "the possibilities for coeval otherworlds."[64] Indeed, Butler's and Burke's stories insist that any conception of the black wishland that assumes all black people within its boundaries will be content is unrealistic and politically useless, since such thinking has historically imagined the black wishland as a space where black women's happiness is defined by sacrificing their wants for the betterment of the community and its men.

Resisting deferment of fulfillment to a then and there, I would argue, also requires rejecting the false choice between Afro-pessimists and their critics, since Afro-pessimistic sensibilities engender black escapes, and Afro-fabulations about the wishland help create the poetics of black aliveness that can make those escapes and wishlands possible. Indeed, one crucial point that both camps agree on, as indicated by the works examined in this chapter, is that black escape and the black wishland – whose combined purpose is to migrate, physically or ideologically, to places absent of black social death – are inextricably linked to developing a conception of the human that transcends the Western model. These works suggest that relying on the Western concept of the human prevents the black wishland from becoming a state of being and doing, since that concept of the human defines black people as the embodiment of nothingness. As a collective, in other words, these works propose that the first "something" that African Americans must do to transform the black wishland from not-yet possibility to reality is to consider, borrowing from Nyong'o, "what a human outside an anti-black world could be, do, or look like."[65]

Notes

1. Alex Zamalin, *Black Utopia: The History of an Idea from Black Nationalism to Afrofuturism* (New York: Columbia University Press, 2019), 6–7.
2. Ernst Bloch and Theodor W. Adorno, "Something's Missing: A Discussion between Ernst Bloch and Theodor W. Adorno on the Contradictions of Utopian Longing," from *The Utopian Function of Art and Literature: Selected Essays by Ernst Bloch*, translated by Jack Zipes and Frank Mecklenburg (Cambridge, MA: MIT Press, 1988), 1–17 (3).
3. Zamalin, 21.
4. Bloch and Adorno, 3.
5. Bloch and Adorno, 3.
6. Jayna Brown, *Black Utopias: Speculative Life and the Music of Other Worlds* (Durham, NC: Duke University Press, 2021), 23–57.
7. Anthony B. Pinn, *The End of God-Talk: An African American Humanist Theology* (Oxford: Oxford University Press, 2012), 34.
8. George Lipsitz, *Rainbow at Midnight: Labor and Culture in the 1940s* (Chicago: University of Illinois Press, 1994), 72.
9. Pinn, 35.
10. Frank B. Wilderson III, *Red, White, & Black: Cinema and the Structure of U.S. Antagonisms* (Durham, NC: Duke University Press, 2010), 346–347, n.9.
11. Wilderson, 58.
12. Calvin L. Warren, *Ontological Terror: Blackness, Nihilism, and Emancipation* (Duke University Press, 2018), 9.
13. Warren, 6.
14. Wilderson, 95.
15. Christina Sharpe, *Monstrous Intimacies: Making Post-Slavery Subjects* (Duke University Press, 2010), 112.
16. Christina Sharpe, *In the Wake: On Blackness and Being* (Durham, NC: Duke University Press, 2016), 7.
17. Warren, 16.
18. Kevin Quashie, *Black Aliveness, or A Poetics of Being* (Durham, NC: Duke University Press, 2021), 9.
19. Quashie, 8–9.
20. Quashie, 10.
21. Tavia Nyong'o, *Afro-Fabulations: The Queer Drama of Black Life* (New York: New York University Press, 2019), 20.
22. Warren, 15.
23. Zamalin, 11. The black antiutopianism discussed by Zamalin does not possess the antiutopianism discussed by Raffaella Baccolini and Tom Moylan in their

edited collection *Dark Horizons: Science Fiction and the Dystopian Imagination* (New York: Routledge, 2003), which they define, citing Lyman Tower Sargent, as an "unsystematic stream of thought" that dismisses utopias and utopian thought as useful for imagining and creating a better society and world (5).

24. Zamalin, 139.
25. Brown, 7.
26. Isaiah Lavender III, *Afrofuturism Rising: The Literary Prehistory of a Movement* (Columbus: Ohio State University Press, 2019), 6. Although coined in 1993 by Mark Dery, Afrofuturism's history extends back to the writings of the New World's enslaved black folks (Lavender, 3). This history not only suggests that Afrofuturism emerged when the first and second ideas of African American utopianism were born but also underscores the fact that sophisticated approaches to identity, technology, and the future had existed in African American thought for over century. See further Alondra Nelson, "Introduction: Future Texts," *Social Text* 20.2 (2002), 1–15 (3).
27. Sun Ra, "Space Is the Place," *Space Is the Place* (Blue Thumb, 1973).
28. Zamalin, 97.
29. Zamalin, 109.
30. Ytasha L. Womack, *Afrofuturism: The World of Black Sci-Fi and Fantasy Culture* (Chicago: Lawrence Hill Books, 2013), 63–64.
31. For example, Star Child explains in "Mothership Connection (Star Child)" (Casablanca Records, 1975) that he and his "recording angels" have "returned to claim the pyramids" to make "seats rumble" and "your conscience grumble." As he tells the audience, "You have overcome, for I am here." According to Star Child, while outer space is the origin of the knowledge needed to transform America, or at least parts of it, into a black wishland, it is not the location of the black wishland.
32. Parliament, "Chocolate City," *Chocolate City* (Casablanca Records, 1975).
33. Deborah Gray White, Mia Bay, and Waldo E. Martin, Jr., *Freedom on My Mind: A History of African Americans with Documents* (New York: Bedford/St. Martin's, 2017), 586.
34. See Zamalin, 19–33.
35. Zamalin, 109.
36. For example, the "nation" in Funkadelic's "One Nation under a Groove" (Warner Bros. Records, 1978) is a black wishland that celebrates the oneness of the United States, as symbolized by the album cover's depictions of Black Power and multicolored US flags. This "nation" will come forth only through our ability to "dance our way out of our constrictions" and to "be freakin'/Up and down/Hang-up alley way."
37. Derrick Bell, "The Space Traders," *Faces at the Bottom of the Well: The Permanence of Racism* (New York: Basic Books, 1992), 158–194.
38. Reginald Hudlin, "Space Traders," *Cosmic Slop* (HBO Home Video, 1994).
39. Sharon, Fitzgerald, "Dishing Up Cosmic Slop," *American Visions* (Dec. 1994–Jan. 1995), 46.

40. Quoted in Fitzgerald, 46.
41. Martin Japtok and Jerry Rafiki Jenkins, editors, "Introduction: Human Contradictions in Octavia E. Butler's Work," from *Human Contradictions in Octavia E. Butler's Work* (London: Palgrave Macmillan, 2020), 1–12 (5).
42. Octavia E. Butler, "The Book of Martha," *Bloodchild and Other Stories* (New York: Seven Stories, 2005), 187–214 (191).
43. Butler, 192.
44. Butler, 193.
45. Butler, 193.
46. Butler, 211.
47. Larry McCaffery and Jim McMenamin, "An Interview with Octavia E. Butler," from *Conversations with Octavia Butler*, edited by Consuela Francis (Jackson: University Press of Mississippi, 2010), 10–26 (26).
48. Butler, 214.
49. Butler, 202.
50. Butler, 202.
51. Chesya Burke, "The Teachings and Redemption of Ms. Fannie Lou Mason," *Let's Play White* (Lexington, KY: Apex Publications, 2011), 129–188 (173).
52. Burke, 145, 135–136.
53. Burke, 131.
54. Burke, 179.
55. Burke, 181.
56. Burke, 152.
57. Burke, 157.
58. For more on how Butler's "The Book of Martha" interrogates the view of God as human, white, and male, see Jerry Rafiki Jenkins, "Is Religiosity a Black Thing?: Reading the Black None in Octavia Butler's 'The Book of Martha,'" *Pacific Coast Philology* 55.1 (2020), 5–22.
59. Brown, 10.
60. Zamalin, 123–125.
61. Butler, 204.
62. Burke, 173–174.
63. Zamalin, 114.
64. Brown, 15.
65. Nyong'o, 26.

CHAPTER 7

Latinx Belonging in New World Borders

Mestiz@ Rhetoric and Critical Utopian/Dystopian Dialectics of Ambivalence

Rubén R. Mendoza

Contemporary Latinx and Latin American literary engagement with utopia must be understood through the long history of Euroamerican imperialist-colonialist domination in the Americas. This includes sixteenth-century Spanish conquest, driven by utopian-apocalyptist visions of El Dorado, and its resultant dystopian apocalypse for Indigenous peoples. Similarly, Anglo settler-colonialism throughout the seventeenth century, driven by Puritanical utopian-apocalyptist visions of a shining "city on a hill," generated genocidal apocalyptic dystopias for Indigenous peoples. This domination includes US neoimperialist colonialism in Latin America, starting with invasion and occupation of Mexico in the 1846–1848 Mexican–American War, which was driven by the white supremacist, utopian ideology of Manifest Destiny. The United States then closed the nineteenth century with war and occupation in Puerto Rico and Cuba via the 1898 Spanish War, thus acquiring two more colonies for extractive capitalist exploitation. This US neoimperialism continued throughout the 1900s and into the present with a post–World War II imposition of neoliberal policies deemed utopian by their promoters and the development of neoliberal regimes in countries such as Chile and Argentina through US-backed dystopian dictatorships in the 1970s and 1980s.

"Utopia" thus is a profoundly relative term. This historical relativity, and the complex historical-dialectical relationships between utopia and dystopia in the Americas, are central to understanding how Latinx works engage the form, and why such works are vital for developing understandings of utopia/dystopia in general. This dialectical relationship between utopia and dystopia is at the heart of Latinx engagements with the discourse. As Krishan Kumar notes, "dystopia is not so much the opposite of utopia as its shadow. It emerged in the wake of utopia and has followed it ever since."[1] The specific context of colonization in the Americas grounds this relationship in the material history of its origin. As Miguel López-Lozano asserts in *Utopian Dreams, Apocalyptic Nightmares*, literary utopias and colonialism are intimately linked by how discovery and colonization of the Americas "provided Europe with a [utopian] locus upon which to project its own preconceived myths and desires."[2] Tom Moylan similarly notes how the Americas functioned as a "geographical locus of hope" and how "'discovery' of the non-European continents and islands provided visionaries of the fifteenth and sixteenth centuries with actual and imaginary space in which to create both practicing and literary experiments."[3] In *Writing the Apocalypse*, Lois Zamora, citing John Leddy Phelan, traces how biblical "apocalyptic optimism pervaded the Age of Discovery."[4] According to apocalyptic optimism and its underlying utopianism, "The possibility of achieving in the future the primal unity . . . lost in the [Edenic] past . . . seemed to inhere in the virgin territory of America," where the Indigenous "were . . . understood to be the lost tribes described in Rev. 7:4–9 . . . prophesied to reappear before the Last Judgment."[5] More bluntly, Gerald Horne asserts in *The Apocalypse of Settler Colonialism* that European imperialism proved to be "little less than apocalyptic" for Indigenous and African people.[6]

Euroamerican utopian traditions thus are not just tied to colonization; they are *premised* on it – which is to say that they are premised on the dystopias they have generated for the victims of colonization. Literary dystopias such as Sesshu Foster's *Atomik Aztex*, Alex Rivera's film *Sleep Dealer*, Kathleen Alcalá's "Deer Dancer," and the works discussed in more detail in what follows, directly engage and critically intervene in this history. At the same time, their dialectical interventions stage counter-utopian articulations through preconquest Indigenous epistemologies and ontologies. In contrast to Euroamerican utopianism's totalizing narratives, these narratives present partial, fragmentary utopian visions that are deeply ambivalent, precarious, and focused on process, thus reflecting Moylan's definition of critical dystopias. Through Lynne Tower Sargent's well-known categories, Moylan characterizes critical dystopia as "a textual mutation that self-reflexively takes on the present system and offers not only astute critiques of the order of things, but also explorations of the oppositional spaces and possibilities from which the next round of political activism can derive imaginative sustenance and inspiration."[7] Similarly, Sargent's critical utopia "rejects in no uncertain terms" the mischaracterization of utopia as "perfection" in his understanding of "the utopian impulse" as "a matter of *process.*"[8]

In Lizz Huerta's "The Wall," for example, the United States has collapsed and the border functions in the opposite direction. Its "true purpose" emerged once "the empire began to strip rights, silence certain people," as "the strongest military in the world ... turn[ed] on their own."[9] US soldiers are poisoned with a food additive that generates robotic submission and the capacity to commit horrific violence, with no subsequent memories of what they have done. Alongside others of her "crew of the strangest and strongest among the brujas,"[10] Ivette heals those who escape south in an Indigenous-centered, feminist utopian enclave near the Sonoran Desert. The space functions through technical, scientific, sociopolitical knowledge of Yaqui elders, but it is not a vision of utopian perfection. Always in process, it initially involved messy alliances between brujas ("witches") from both sides of the border and narcocartel jefes. As Ivette says, "I live with some shit," because "in the beginning ... Some of it got ugly ... It was a mess. We don't talk about it."[11] Elsewhere, she states, "it has been a process. We're still figuring it out."[12] The process-oriented ambivalence reflects not just critical dystopian/utopian devices, but Gloria Anzaldúa's Chicana feminist theorization of mestiza consciousness. This consciousness arises from the "cultural collision" of the mestiza's position of racial and cultural mixing, through which "the ambivalence from the clash of voices results in ... a plural personality."[13] From this position, "the new mestiza copes by developing a tolerance for contradictions ... [and] ambiguity."[14] Thus, "not only does she sustain contradictions, she turns ambivalence into something else."[15] Toward the story's end, these dynamics unfold through Ivette's difficult biopolitical decisions in tending to ex-soldiers with recovered Indigenous sciences. As a Latina originally from the United States herself, she grapples with whether to "dose" a Latina ex-soldier with homegrown antidotes to the military's poison. This will save her but also make her fully conscious of the violence she has committed. As Ivette notes, "opening to the truth requires acceptance of the belly-wrenching pain of it all. There are moments I still let it double me over, but I have faith. ... There are horrors but there is love."[16] This complex dialectical interplay of utopia and dystopia, inclusion and exclusion, identity and hybridity, and different forms of technoscientific knowledge, is initially contextualized by a succinct but precise historicization central to Huerta's story and to this study:

> The difference between the now defunct United States of America and Mexico is that the USA started as a settler state, decimating the indigenous population. Spaniards made babies. Those babies made Mexico, fucked up

> but brown and proud. When shit went down, the Mexicans on either side of the wall collectively woke up to seeds planted by our ancestors. Survival. The long game.[17]

This study is about seeds planted by ancestors, and survival, and the long game. Using Huerta's story as a starting point, along with sixteenth-century Nahua/Mestiz@ codices, it examines two recent works that similarly develop complex interplays of utopia/dystopia: Alberto Yáñez's postcolonial zombie narrative, "Burn the Ships," and Yuri Herrera's dystopian *Signs Preceding the End of the World.* Like "The Wall," these works present strong female protagonists grappling with material and psychological residues of historical and ongoing colonialist biopolitical dialectics between utopia and dystopia, belonging and exclusion, and competing identities, cultures, and epistemologies of mestizaje hybridity. In addition to utopian/dystopian studies and postcolonial speculative-fiction (sf) studies, my analysis draws from Chicana/o/x theorizations, primarily Damián Baca's Mestiz@ rhetoric. Through it, I demonstrate how these texts exemplify what Baca defines as a "powerful Mestiz@ rhetorical strategy" of *nepantlism* – "a strategy of thinking from a border space through dual expressions and symbolic oppositions."[18] This "invention between different ways of knowing and writing" emerges through "thinking from the intersection of Iberian, *Nahuatl*, and Anglo-European traditions."[19] Furthermore, these works engage this Mestiz@ rhetoric self-reflexively, incorporating diegetic narrative elements that involve its use. In so using such "discursive manifestations of continuity and adaptation," these works "generate new visions of history and subjectivity."[20] These new visions "revise and displace the narrative of assimilation" with "powerful critiques of the dominant stories of assimilation, colony, and the border" that "defy hierarchical binaries by creating permeable ways of crossing and 'inventing between' colonial oppositions."[21] Their focus on hybridity's difficult ambivalences traces relationships between imperialist-colonialist utopian projects and the dystopian realities they have generated, thus disrupting "narratives of assimilation" and related imperialist-colonialist utopian narratives.

Before turning to these contemporary texts, I briefly consider Mestiz@ rhetoric's roots within early examples of dystopian speculative tropes from the Americas and Mesoamerican mythology. This discussion establishes vital context for understanding how Yáñez and Herrera engage utopia/dystopia through a Mestiz@ rhetoric grounded in Mesoamerican history, culture, and mythology.

"Shattering Itself in Its Frenzy": A *Nepantla* Rhetoric of the *Tlacantzolli*

Eight years after the 1521 conquest of Tenochtitlan, Friar Bernardino de Sahagún arrived and soon began working with Nahua scholars on what is now known as the Florentine Codex. Completed around 1577, this bilingual Nahuatl/Spanish compendium was assembled in the aftermath of Spanish destruction of nearly all the numerous Indigenous written records in Mesoamerica. In it are accounts of omens that appeared in the ten years preceding the Spaniards' 1519 arrival at Tenochtitlan. These omens include cataclysmic fires burning in the sky, lake water rising and boiling "with rage, as if it were shattering itself in its frenzy,"[22] and a strange bird with a dark mirror on its head. In this cyborgian device, Emperor Motecuhzoma saw the starry night sky followed by images of distant armies advancing swiftly on deer-like animals. Most significantly for my purposes, one account describes "monstrous beings" in the streets, "deformed men with two heads but only one body."[23] Similarly, mestizo Diego Muñoz Camargo's 1585 codex *Historia de Tlaxcala* reports "two men merged into one body," who were called "*tlacantzolli* ('men-squeezed-together')."[24]

The veracity of these omens and their occurrence might be questionable. But their status as genuine literary artifacts produced in the dystopian aftermath of conquest and colonization is not. Throughout the Florentine Codex's production, European plagues burned through Indigenous populations. In the 1570s, smallpox threatened its completion, as Nahua scholars raced to finish in quarantine against the impending doom of possible infection. These omen accounts therefore were recorded in the very real dystopian shadow produced by Spain's utopian-apocalyptist colonialism.

Given these circumstances, the omen-account authors' postconquest play with time and apocalyptic imagery exemplifies Baca's theorization of Mestiz@ rhetoric's "invention between different ways of knowing and writing" by "thinking from the intersection of Iberian, *Nahuatl*, and Anglo-European traditions."[25] Their Mestiz@ rhetoric demonstrates a subtle but insistent literary agency through which Nahua scribes cannily exploited Sahagún's reconstruction and preservation of their culture. Structured through a traveling to past moments when an apocalyptic future was envisioned – a future that is both the authors' past of conquest and their colonial present – their temporal play imparts agency through speculative forms that critically comment on dystopian colonial reality. This agency subtly emerges through victims presaging their conquest, which preempts Spanish power. Additionally, it emerges through subsequent abilities of Nahua scholars and informants to literarily construct and record that presaging, thus establishing both pre- and postconquest rhetorical agency and material presence. Furthermore, these accounts reflect recursive poetics based on Indigenous cyclical conceptions of time, which here critically intervene in temporal dis/misplacements of Indigenous culture and civilization into the "primitive" past by imperialist-colonialist discourses of progress. As Jessica Langer notes, citing Anne McClintock, the colonized were positioned in "anachronistic space," as they were seen to "not inhabit history proper but exist in a permanently anterior time . . . as anachronistic humans, atavistic, irrational, bereft of human agency – the living embodiment of the archaic 'primitive.'"[26] John Rieder similarly deconstructs how anachronism in early sf, as "one of the key features that links emergent science fiction to colonialism," reflects a colonialist "mark of anthropological difference" based on the anthropological logic "that the indigenous, primitive other's present is the colonizer's own past."[27] In this context, narratively traveling to precolonial moments, when victims of colonization presaged conquest, self-reflexively inverts this temporal weaponization.

Most importantly, this Mestiz@ rhetoric articulates the monstrous psychological impacts of a violently imposed colonial splitting of identity, as metaphorized in the two-headed *tlacantzolli*. The Nahuatl word *nepantla* is variously translated as "in-between" and "between worlds." This neologism was first used by conquest survivors to express the psychological and emotional traumas of being torn and split in an unfolding process of mestizaje. *Nepantla* connoted colonial positionality "in-between" the world of survivors' own culture and identity and that of the newly imposed Spanish world, as they violently mixed. The "prophetic" future-vision of the "men-squeezed-together," *tlacantzolli*, thus can be read as an allegorical science-fictional novum of hybridity and the grotesque that articulates the cognitive estrangement and vertigo of *nepantla*. As Istvan Csicsery-Ronay notes of the sf grotesque:

> When something does not conduct itself as scientific rationality asserts/predicts it must, it creates a clash between the concept of an ordered world and concrete, experiential evidence to the contrary. When its disorienting anomalousness also disorients the routines of human lives and institutions, the *novum* is grotesque.[28]

Csicsery-Ronay explains the sf grotesque's potential to generate vertiginous effects as reflecting "the struggle to accommodate mutable, unstable objects and beings in the world."[29] As such, it represents the duality required by "sf's fictive ontology," which "manifest[s] as oxymoron at the level of ideas, metamorphosis at the level of bodies."[30] This metamorphosis is conveyed as "a gap . . . between the past forms of a thing and what it is becoming."[31]

Authors of the omen accounts composed from such a position, literally caught in the real-world vertiginous metamorphic *nepantla* gap between what they once were and what they were being forced to become. But at the same time, they made savvy rhetorical use of precisely that positioning to self-reflexively intervene in it. As they "struggle[d] to accommodate mutable, unstable objects and beings" within and *as* themselves, they embedded this experience in the codices with grotesque images of ambivalent hybridity. Thus, they exemplify Baca's argument for *nepantlism* as "a strategy of thinking from a border space through dual expressions and symbolic oppositions."[32] As Baca notes, "inventing from *nepantlism*, suspended between paradoxical frames of reference, was first a possibility in the mind of the Aztec, not the Spaniard," because *nepantlism* is a key component of mestiza consciousness, which "emerges specifically from the underside of colonial relations of power."[33] In this example, *nepantlism* invention constructs speculative dystopian figures that critically comment on the colonial experience of a real-world apocalyptic dystopia generated by European utopian-apocalyptist fantasies.

Inscribing upon the World: "You Are the Door, Not the One Who Walks through It"

Even prior to the genocidal dystopia unleashed by Europeans' utopian-apocalyptist projections, the Mesoamerican world was already post-apocalyptic on its own terms. According to Mesoamerican mythology, this current world of the Fifth Sun is not the first. It was preceded by four ages; in each, the world was cataclysmically destroyed. To set this newest age in motion, several gods sacrificed themselves, thus establishing a new era of cosmic harmony and balance premised on blood-nourishment sacrifice, which kept the sun moving and ensured continued life. It was also the source of humanity's current iteration. In one account, Quetzalcoatl descends into Mictlan, the underworld of the dead, to rescue bones and ashes of previous human iterations. After battling the lord of Mictlan, Quetzalcoatl retrieves a single bone, which is pulverized into powder to make dough. Quetzalcoatl and other gods then infuse this dough with their own blood, revivifying humanity. This process involving an ambivalence between life and death exemplifies the sacrifice-sustained synthesis and duality central to the cosmology of the Fifth Sun era.[34]

Along with the codex omens' dystopian tropes, this mythology pervades dystopian depictions in Alberto Yáñez's "Burn the Ships" and Yuri Herrera's *Signs Preceding the End of the World* (*Signs*). "Burn the Ships" pulls from this mythology and classic zombie narratives to examine genocidal colonial biopower and necropower. Herrera's *Signs* draws its title from the omens to establish a dystopian tenor and trajectory. Structured in nine chapters that mirror Mictlan's nine levels, *Signs* traces border crossing into the United States, which thus figures as an underworld of the dead that dystopically splits and erases identities. These texts also share with each other and with the codex omens sophisticated uses of Mestiz@ rhetoric. As with "The Wall," their applications of Mestiz@ rhetoric in critical dystopian structures focus on the *nepantla* ambivalence of mestiza consciousness hybridity and center on Indigenous epistemologies and literacies – including, self-reflexively, Mestiz@ rhetoric itself. What emerges is critical interrogation of Euroamerican narratives of utopia, histories of colonization, and the biopolitical structures of inclusion and exclusion that underlie narratives of assimilation.

"Burn the Ships"

Alberto Yáñez's dystopian "Burn the Ships" takes place after conquest by the colonizing "Dawncomers," but it refuses historical specificity and couples present-tense narration with anachronistic, anatopic elements. Although set presumably in the sixteenth century, it includes radio devices, armored cars, and trains. Yáñez thus highlights how historical colonial violence is ongoing through ever-evolving biopolitical mechanisms. As with Lizz Huerta's "The Wall," "Burn the Ships" self-reflexively presents the contentious, processual dialectical negotiations of forging resistance, thus constituting a specifically *critical* dystopia. But where ongoing critical utopian processes have moved beyond initial challenges in "The Wall," "Burn the Ships" focuses on precisely such an originary moment of thorny negotiation.

Unfolding within the necropolitical bare-life conditions of a "work camp," this struggle includes conflicts over technospiritual practices that foreground intertwinings of feminist resistance, Indigenous epistemologies, and utopian process. Thirty years after conquest, and four months since Dawncomers killed their daughter Shochi, the struggle of the "People" to formulate resistance plays out through an argument between

Citlal and her husband, Quineltoc. A "lawspeaker of the People of the Starry Codex,"[35] Quineltoc adheres to the passivity of his patriarchal "Living Lord" against Citlal's insistence on the dangerous use of unauthorized women's magic to invoke the *Tzitzimimeh* Dead Sisters. Staged antipodally between a "*Living* Lord" and "*Dead* Sisters," the argument hinges on the consequences of using this magic. As Quineltoc argues, this magic would break the Living Lord's covenant, resulting in exclusion from his utopian afterlife world and therefore no reunion with the deceased. Their argument thus traces a multivalent self-reflexive engagement with the camp's necropolitical sovereignty – an example of what Achille Mbembe theorizes as an Agambian state of exception of social death and abandonment to precarity.[36] Against Quineltoc's points, Citlal poses a rhetorical question that challenges the threat of exclusion from the Living Lord's utopia by foregrounding the dystopian exclusion of their necropolitical precarity: "So we just *wait* for God to save us?" she asks,[37] and to Quineltoc's retort, "if we commit that *sin*, what will we be?" she responds, "Alive."[38] In another pointed rhetorical question, Citlal gets to the heart of their zombie-like necropolitical social death: "What good is salvation if the spirit of the People is dead, Quineltoc?"[39]

This contentious process is resolved ambivalently when Citlal and her "wisewives" sisters secretly use their magic to revivify the massacred, who rise up as a zombie army against the Dawncomers. Echoing the aforementioned account of Quetzalcoatl, the wisewives use their own blood to revivify corpses of the latest purge. This bodily connection binds them to the spell, so that they ultimately must sacrifice their own lives to break it. While the victory is decisive, it is ambivalent and precarious. Citlal "knows that the People won't ever be free of the Dawncomers – there are too many of them, and a growing number of mixed blood children," even though at the same time, "the scales are no longer so unbalanced now that the usurpers know that the People can retaliate in ways that cannot be evaded with their cold technology and guns."[40] Moreover, the form of resistance itself is ambivalent and paradoxical: Indigenous necromantic magic counters colonizers' necropower to keep the People alive but breaks the Living Lord's covenant, positioning them in a different kind of precarious exclusion.

The messy ambivalence of this critical dystopian negotiation involves complexly intertwined gender oppositions and competing epistemologies – both externally, vis-à-vis Dawncomers' "cold technology," and internally, with contending forms of technospirituality. But the women's sorcery, like Huerta's antidote to military poison in "The Wall," is not simply "magic."

It is a complex technospiritual rhetorical practice of spell-casting that renders powerless the Dawncomers' "cold technology." It therefore is better understood as exemplifying what Langer identifies via Grace Dillon as "Indigenous scientific literacies." Such literacies include "those practices used by Indigenous native peoples to manipulate the natural environment . . . to improve existence in areas including medicine, agriculture, and sustainability . . . in contrast to more invasive (and potentially destructive) western scientific method."[41] And when we recognize such practices as fundamentally rhetorical in nature – as practices of *literacies* – it should become clear how the Indigenous scientific literacy of the wisewives' "magic" connects to Mestiz@ rhetoric.

Yáñez foregrounds these connections by providing extensive detail of the spell's rhetoric, which involves wisewives working the night before a purge in concerted effort from "camps across the Empire."[42] In her camp, Citlal casts the spell with Ce-Mishtlin and Yoal. After preparation of stolen codex bark-paper and hatpins, "they join hands and wills to charge the sheet with potential and promise, and link it to the other items" so that "the paper will bind whatever contract is written upon it with the other items."[43] They then prick their wrists with the hatpins so that their blood mixed with earth and ash functions as an ink infused with powerful agency: "Each pin is now an instrument of the will of the wisewife who fed it her blood. . . . What's writ in this ink will be inscribed upon the world."[44] Chanting, they "jab their pins into the night's blood," so that "the hatpins can write in the language of the world . . . each stylus an instrument of dark and needful magic."[45] As the purge later unfolds, they complete the spell: "Facing each other with hands linked . . . the blank contract and the charged hatpin styluses in the middle, the three women raise their arms and sing out, capturing the power of the deaths of their murdered people and adding it to their joined will."[46] The glyph for "night," which is also the glyph for the Dead Sisters, then appears on the codex, to which Citlal adds the glyph for "fire," or "life."[47]

The amount of space Yáñez devotes to this spell's rhetorical mechanics should alert us to their significance. Understood more broadly beyond classical definitions as persuasion, rhetoric is symbolic action that, like magic, aims at effecting material change in the world. In this context, the wisewives' combination of song, chant, ritual body performance, and writing, is a sophisticated act of rhetorical agency. Operating from a precarious dystopian *nepantla* space "in-between" their culture and that of the Dawncomers, as well as their own technospiritual practice and Quineltoc's, the women practice an embodied rhetoric of *nepantlism*. In theorizing mestiza consciousness as a form of embodied Mestiz@ rhetoric, Baca emphasizes its roots in spatialized, embodied practices of Mesoamerican rhetoric. Such rhetoric "required use of the entire body, through choreography, recitation, chanting, and choral production."[48] A "reading" of glyphs in codices and on walls "constituted a communal ritualistic and ceremonial event."[49] The wisewives' communal, ritualistic rhetorical work therefore constitutes a self-reflexive engagement with Mestiz@ rhetoric: Even as Yáñez uses Mestiz@ rhetoric to construct his zombie narrative, he reflexively embeds an example of its roots within that story.

Ultimately, this necromantic rhetoric's ambivalent impacts reflect an emergent mestiza consciousness hybridity. In the zombie uprising's aftermath, Quineltoc divorces Citlal. As a lawspeaker, he simply has to utter the words: "His words are enough to make – unmake – a blessing, a curse, a rite, a marriage."[50] But Citlal defuses this rhetorical absolutism with her own embodied rhetoric of a dismissive but loving, compassionate laughter of familiarity. Citlal then rejects the Living Lord's offer of life to her for having proved her leadership. Insisting on following her wisewife sisters in sacrificing themselves to break their spell, Citlal refuses the Living Lord's patriarchy, which requires human sacrifice to feed him. Her anger "leaves no room for shadows, for doubt: whatever test she's passed, whatever plan she's fulfilled, whatever blessing this might be, it *isn't* right and it's *not* enough. They all are owed more than this" (italics in original).[51] With a defiant "No," she disorients the Living Lord, who retreats "surprised, afraid," as she asserts: "Better the anxious night than a certain path down your monstrous gullet. Better that we live and die by our own choices than at your whim. Better the night and all the cold stars than your hunger."[52] Thus, even Citlal's defiant embrace of ambivalence is ambivalent in itself, as it paradoxically involves "no room for shadows, for doubt" and rejects sacrifice to feed the Living Lord for self-sacrifice to save her People. The story then ends with a deeply ambivalent image "in-between" death and life: Citlal changes the "life" glyph to "death" on the written contract, which de-animates the zombies, and after she falls dead to the ground with them, "visible only in the dark between the stars, the newest Bone Woman gets up and walks off."[53]

Signs Preceding the End of the World

Yuri Herrera's *Signs Preceding the End of the World* similarly ends (and begins) on deeply ambivalent notes of dystopian precarity centered on a strong female protagonist who, like Citlal and like Ivette in "The Wall," personifies mestiza consciousness. And like "Burn the Ships," the novella reflects Mestiz@ rhetoric both in its bicultural construction and in narratively embedded self-reflexive examples of it. However, where Yáñez's story focuses on the *nepantla* of a conceptual borderlands "between worlds," the dystopia of *Signs* unfolds, as with "The Wall," in the literal United States/ Mexico borderlands.

Signs begins with its young protagonist, Makina, declaring, "I'm dead," as she retreats from a sinkhole opening beneath her feet in a "Little Town" in Mexico.[54] The sinkhole is caused by the town being "riddled with bullet holes and tunnels bored by five centuries of voracious silver lust."[55] Thus, from the start, Makina's precarity is foregrounded through dissolution of earth underneath her, and this precarity is directly linked to colonization. Furthermore, although she seems to save herself, the book's allegory mode makes her opening statement ambivalent, as the rest of the novella metaphorizes her journey north across the border as a journey into the underworld of the dead.

This initial moment of ambivalence and precarity happens as Makina is seeking help from the Little Town's "top dogs" to carry out her mother's charge of finding and delivering a message to her brother in the United States. In her visits to these (presumably) narco jefes, she demonstrates savvy use of Mestiz@ rhetoric in securing their help. Makina also runs her own town's telephone switchboard, where she abides by a set of rules including the dictum, "You are the door, not the one who walks through it."[56] She connects fellow residents through facility with multiple literacies and languages, including "native tongue," "latin tongue," and the "new tongue" of those who call home from the North,[57] thus practicing and operating through Mestiz@ rhetoric "in-between" multiple worlds. We see this further demonstrated later when she arrives just short of the border on the trip north. At a motel with other migrants, Makina uses her Mestiz@ rhetoric to help them, reading a letter for an elderly illiterate man and teaching a boy how to ask for soap in English.[58] She then warns two young men, who are being cheated in negotiating a border crossing, because she understands the coyotes' English.[59] Once Makina crosses the border, she similarly uses Mestiz@ rhetoric to eventually track down her brother through an arduous process involving many different people, languages, and situations.

As noted, this crossing to the United States is figured metaphorically as a journey into the underworld. Makina is helped over the river by a man named Chucho – slang for "dog" – who represents the dog figure Xolotl that guides the deceased into Mictlan. This metaphorization is central to the novella's critical dialectic between utopia and dystopia, exemplified almost immediately as Makina arrives on the northern shore. In the distance, she sees what appears to be a pregnant woman resting at the foot of a tree, which her utopian impulse takes as a good "omen." But as she nears, she realizes it is actually the dystopian figure of "some poor wretch swollen with putrefaction, his eyes and tongue pecked out by buzzards."[60] This reflects the real experiences of hundreds of migrants who die every year crossing a militarized border that the US government has designed to deliberately funnel them into dangerous terrain. This utopian/dystopian dialectic is further exemplified when Makina wanders a US supermarket. In addition to "signs prohibiting everything" that "thronged the streets, leading citizens to see themselves as ever protected, safe, friendly, innocent, proud," she notes how these self-proclaimed "salt of the only earth worth knowing . . . flourished in supermarkets, cornucopias where you could have more than everyone else or something different or a newer brand or a loaf of bread a little bigger than everyone else's."[61] But this "utopia" is belied by the dystopian "anglogaggle at the self-checkouts," where Makina notices "how miserable they looked in front of those little digital screens, and the way they nearly-nearly jumped every time the machine went bleep!," and how, once exiting the store, they "[became] wooden again so as not to offend anyone."[62] Thus, the US imperialist self-image as utopia is juxtaposed with its real-world consumerist dystopia.

These moments exemplify how Makina's Mestiz@ rhetoric involves *nepantla* literacies that enable savvy deconstructions of signs from "in-between" – signs of spoken and body language, and literal street signs. It also involves her understanding of hybridity through a *nepantla* lens, as reflected in her reading of Mexican Americans' ambivalent rhetoric of mixed Spanish and English. She observes that, "they speak an intermediary tongue," which she "instantly warms to because it's like her: malleable, erasable, permeable; a hinge pivoting between two like but distant souls . . . their tongue is a nebulous territory between what is dying out and what is not yet born . . . Makina senses in their tongue . . . a shrewd metamorphosis."[63]

But the sophistication of Makina's Mestiz@ rhetoric in critically intervening in narratives of assimilation, colonialism, and Euroamerican utopianism is most clearly and self-reflexively foregrounded in a dystopian moment toward the novella's end. Makina is caught up in a sidewalk lineup with other migrants by a police officer who harangues them with a "patriotic" white supremacist rant. Taking one young man's notebook from him, the officer mocks his literacy – "Poetry. Lookie here at the educated worker . . . You a romantic? A poet?"[64] – and orders him to write a poem. When the trembling young man cannot respond, Makina intervenes, taking the pencil and paper and writing "without stopping to think which word was better than which other or how the message was turning out."[65] Eventually, she simply stops and puts the pencil down, staring at the paper, which prompts the officer to take her statement and read it aloud. The statement is worth quoting at length to demonstrate the rhetorical significance of Makina's sardonic, self-reflexive words and their accompanying actions, which include her canny prompting of the officer to read them out loud himself:

> We are to blame for this destruction, we who don't speak your tongue and don't know how to keep quiet either. We who didn't come by boat, who dirty up your doorsteps with our dust, who break your barbed wire. We who came to take your jobs, who dream of wiping your shit, who long to work all hours . . . We who are happy to die for you, what else could we do? We, the ones who are waiting for who knows what. . . . We the barbarians.[66]

As with Citlal's defiant "No" to the Living Lord, Makina disorients and disarms with her intervention into the officer's biopolitical power through a self-reflexive critical dystopian counter to his patriotic utopian rhetoric. This intervention includes the sophisticated, complex way her rhetorical action inverts power dynamics. Prompted to read the statement by her embodied rhetoric of setting down the pencil and staring at the page, the officer finds himself unwittingly repositioned by its pronominal "we" as his own embodied rhetoric of racism is used against itself. He begins in a mocking tone but "gradually abandoned the histrionics as he neared the last line, which he read almost in a whisper. After that he went on staring at the paper as if he'd gotten stuck on the final period. When he finally looked up, his rage, or his interest in his captives seemed to have dissolved."[67] At this point, the officer departs, leaving the migrants free to go.

The effectiveness of this Mestiz@ rhetoric's defiant resistance should be clear. The scene provides a self-reflexive example of what Martín Lombardo theorizes, via Jacques Rancière, as Herrera's "literary intervention in the political field . . . carried out through language, more specifically through a border language," as a "literature of the community margins."[68] Though Lombardo does not explicitly discuss the rhetorical dimensions of this interrogation into the realm of the political as structured through configurations of community, Makina's shrewd inversion of biopolitical configurations of inclusion and exclusion specifically through Mestiz@ rhetoric's poetics foregrounds the rhetoric involved.

But the novella ends as it begins, on a note of ambivalence and precarity that highlights the contingency of such *nepantla* rhetoric. In a final surreal scene, Makina descends down spiral stairs into a strange room, where she is handed a file. She sees herself "with another name, another birthplace. Her photo, new numbers, new trade, new home," and she whispers, "I've been skinned" and "tip[s] briefly into panic" with "the turmoil of so many new things crowding in on the old ones."[69] Eventually, as she lets go of fading memories of her people and origins, she understands that "what was happening was not a cataclysm."[70] In the final moments, "she understood with all of her body and all of her memory . . . and when everything in the world fell silent finally said to herself I'm ready."[71]

In her analysis of Herrera's text, Cordelia E. Barrera reads this scene as utopian, as part of the novella's Anzaldúan "powerful heterotopic space of renewal and transformation."[72] She sees Makina's transformation as reflecting "an imaginative process, an ongoing historical yearning after an imagined ideal that ultimately reveals a new beginning."[73] While Barrera brilliantly argues for the novella's utopianism, this reading risks flattening Herrera's complex, unresolved ambivalence. My point is not that such utopian possibilities are not in the text; it is that any reading of them must be tempered to account for the equally prominent shadows of dystopian realities at play in a much more ambivalent state than this reading suggests. Barrera does acknowledge migrants' real-world difficulties, as well as the possibility of reading Makina's "skinning" as erasure of her Indigenous Mexican identity, but ultimately chooses to set this possibility aside to characterize *Signs* as decisively utopian.

But *Signs* is neither utopian nor dystopian. Like mestiza consciousness, it is equally, ambivalently, both – and neither, and something more – all at once. And this ambivalence is precisely the source of its critical power. Like her brother, who also was assigned another identity (by a white family that exploited him to replace their son in the US military), Makina has been "skinned" of who she was by the dystopia of US neoimperialist colonialism. This reflects the real, lived traumas of migrants forced by violent biopolitical mechanisms into the *nepantla* of crossing to the United States to survive. To ascribe to Makina a future of utopian possibility elides the difficult, precarious experiences of the vast majority of Latinx migrants in the United States and risks feeding into imperialist-colonialist narratives of assimilation and utopian exceptionalism. As with the People in "Burn the Ships," Makina and her brother have been forced to carve out ambivalent biopolitical "inclusions" through exclusion from who they once were. Furthermore, these are paradoxical, precarious "inclusions" of *exclusion*, as US Latinxs and Latin American migrants are perpetually positioned as "foreign" and "Other" regardless of citizenship status and indigeneity in the Americas (and belying Euroamericans' truly "alien" origins vis-à-vis the Western Hemisphere). Makina may indeed successfully operate from this *nepantla* position, perhaps even develop utopian possibilities. But through a critical dystopian/utopian lens, we must acknowledge the novella's profoundly ambivalent and precarious vision of dystopian survival and resistance within violent neoimperialist biopolitical structures. The "transformation" of Makina's coming-of-age journey reflects not the triumphal return of a traditional bourgeois Bildungsroman, but the darker diasporic realities of a dystopic "Bildungsmictlan."

Conclusion

Through focus on biopolitical mechanisms, Indigenous epistemologies, and mestizaje hybridity's difficult negotiations, *Signs Preceding the End of the World* and "Burn the Ships" stage self-reflexive examples of Baca's "dissonant literacies" of Mestiz@ rhetoric.[74] They "generate new visions of history and subjectivity" that "revise and displace the narrative of assimilation" with "powerful critiques of the dominant stories of assimilation, colony, and the border."[75] But as critical dystopias, they do so with great ambivalence. Through articulation of counterutopian visions premised on Indigenous epistemologies, they disrupt the narrative of assimilation and related imperialist-colonialist utopian narratives, but they refuse any neat utopian resolution, and they do not romanticize or overstate utopian possibilities of *nepantlism*. As Ivette says in "The Wall," "it has been a process. We're still figuring it out."[76] And as Citlal admits in "Burn the Ships," "the People won't ever be free of the Dawncomers – there are too many of them."[77] At the most, perhaps, these critical dystopian texts' Mestiz@ rhetoric offers the possibility of working toward balancing the scales, as Citlal does. But perhaps this Indigenous-based critical dystopian orientation of ambivalence toward notions of utopia is enough. In its historically aware refusal of Euroamerican colonialist utopian fantasies, perhaps this ambivalent critical dystopian stance is, in itself, precisely what is truly hopeful.

Notes

1. Krishan Kumar, "Utopia's Shadow," from *Dystopia(n) Matters: On the Page, on Screen, on Stage*, edited by Vieira Fátima (Newcastle upon Tyne: Cambridge Scholars Publishing, 2013), 19–22 (19).

2. Miguel López-Lozano, *Utopian Dreams, Apocalyptic Nightmares: Globalization in Recent Mexican and Chicano Narrative* (West Lafayette, IN: Purdue University Press, 2008), 6.
3. Tom Moylan, *Demand the Impossible: Science Fiction and the Utopian Imagination*, edited by Raffaella Baccolini (Oxford: Peter Lang, 2014), 4, 3.
4. Lois Parkinson Zamora, *Writing the Apocalypse: Historical Vision in Contemporary U.S. and Latin American Fiction* (Cambridge: Cambridge University Press, 1993), 8.
5. Zamora, 8.
6. Gerald Horne, *The Apocalypse of Settler Colonialism: The Roots of Slavery, White Supremacy, and Capitalism in Seventeenth-Century North America and the Caribbean* (New York: Monthly Review Press, 2018), 17.
7. Tom Moylan, *Scraps of the Untainted Sky: Science Fiction, Utopia, Dystopia* (Boulder, CO: Westview Press, 2000), xv.
8. Qtd. in Moylan, *Scraps*, 74–75.
9. Lizz Huerta, "The Wall," from *A People's Future of the United States: Speculative Fiction from 25 Extraordinary Writers*, edited by Victor LaValle and John Joseph Adams (New York: Random House, 2019), 49–61 (53).
10. Huerta, 54.
11. Huerta, 59–60.
12. Huerta, 54.
13. Gloria Anzaldúa, *Borderlands/La Frontera: The New Mestiza*, 2nd edition (San Francisco: Aunt Lute Books, 1999), 100–101.
14. Anzaldúa, 101.
15. Anzaldúa, 101.
16. Huerta, 62.
17. Huerta, 51.
18. Damián Baca, *Mestiz@ Scripts, Digital Migrations, and the Territories of Writing* (New York: Palgrave Macmillan, 2008), 16, 25.
19. Baca, 10, 16.
20. Baca, 4, 11.
21. Baca, 11, 5.
22. Miguel León Portilla, *The Broken Spears: The Aztec Account of the Conquest of Mexico* (Boston: Beacon Press, 2006), 5.
23. León Portilla, 5.
24. León Portilla, 11.
25. Baca, 10, 16.
26. Jessica Langer, *Postcolonialism and Science Fiction* (New York: Palgrave Macmillan, 2011), 129.
27. John Rieder, *Colonialism and the Emergence of Science Fiction* (Middletown, CT: Wesleyan University Press, 2008), 6, 5.
28. Istvan Csicsery-Ronay, *The Seven Beauties of Science Fiction* (Middletown, CT: Wesleyan University Press, 2008), 182.
29. Csicsery-Ronay, 182.
30. Csicsery-Ronay, 182.

31. Csicsery-Ronay, 186.
32. Baca, 25.
33. Baca, 25.
34. Roberta H. Markman and Peter T. Markman, *The Flayed God: The Mesoamerican Mythological Tradition: Sacred Texts and Images from Pre-Columbian Mexico and Central America* (San Francisco: Harper San Francisco, 1992, 74–78.
35. Alberto Yáñez, "Burn the Ships," from *New Suns: Original Speculative Fiction by People of Color*, edited by Nisi Shawl (Oxford: Solaris, 2019), 83–104 (84).
36. Achille Mbembe, "Necropolitics," from *Foucault in an Age of Terror: Essays on Biopolitics and the Defence of Society*, edited by Stephen Morton and Stephen Bygrave (London: Palgrave-Macmillan, 2008), 152–182 (153).
37. Yáñez, 86.
38. Yáñez, 86.
39. Yáñez, 87.
40. Yáñez, 102.
41. Qtd. in Langer, 130.
42. Yáñez, 90.
43. Yáñez, 92.
44. Yáñez, 92.
45. Yáñez, 93.
46. Yáñez, 94.
47. Yáñez, 95.
48. Baca, 72.
49. Baca, 73.
50. Yáñez, 101.
51. Yáñez, 103.
52. Yáñez, 104.
53. Yáñez, 105.
54. Yuri Herrera, *Signs Preceding the End of the World*, translated by Lisa Dillman (London: & Other Stories, 2015), 11.
55. Herrera, 11.
56. Herrera, 18.
57. Herrera, 19.
58. Herrera, 35.
59. Herrera, 36.
60. Herrera, 44.
61. Herrera, 56.
62. Herrera, 56–57.
63. Herrera, 65–66.
64. Herrera, 98.
65. Herrera, 99.
66. Herrera, 99–100.
67. Herrera, 100.

68. Martín Lombardo, "Autoridad, transgresión y frontera (sobre la narrativa de Yuri Herrera)," *Inti, Revista de literatura hispánica* 1.79 (2014), 193–214 (194). My translation.
69. Herrera, 106.
70. Herrera, 106.
71. Herrera, 106.
72. Cordelia E. Barrera, "Utopic Dreaming on the Borderlands: An Anzaldúan Reading of Yuri Herrera's *Signs Preceding the End of the World*," *Utopian Studies* 31.3 (2021), 475–493 (477).
73. Barrera, 482.
74. Baca, 90.
75. Baca, 11, 5.
76. Huerta, 54.
77. Yáñez, 102.

CHAPTER 8

Educating Desire
Young Adult Utopian Fiction

Jonathan Alexander

In this chapter, I examine trends in the last half-century of young adult (YA) fiction that might generatively be categorized as utopian. This task is made all the easier given the popularity of *dystopian* YA fiction in the last twenty years, but I also want to claim that much of that work should be thought together with YA narratives that critically examine what moving toward an "ideal" society might look like – or, in the collateral case of dystopian fiction, what definitely does *not* count as such a move. In a way, one might argue that *all* YA fiction is utopian in the broadest sense, given that it is produced for young readers who are looking for guidance or entertainment in the pursuit of their own better futures. But at times, such work also engages larger questions that exceed the limited purview of individual self-betterment and which approach issues about the proper – and better – organization and maintenance of society. This chapter focuses on YA fiction that moves in that latter direction.

Some definitions will set the parameters of this inquiry. First, I am going to confine my examination to works that have been explicitly produced and marketed under the consumer rubric "young adult fiction." The available literature that might reasonably be considered YA is vast and could include any number of books written *about* adolescents and young people (such as Sylvia Plath's *The Bell Jar* or J. D. Salinger's *Catcher in the Rye*). But the rise in the last few decades, especially after the success of the Harry Potter series, of conscious production of books labeled YA merits analysis as a publishing, literary, and even cultural phenomenon. Second, I define utopia less as the discussion of a particular place and more as a *process*, even a yearning for what Ernst Bloch calls the "not-yet," and the consequent cultivation of hope that what is currently experienced might change for the better. YA fiction, written for consumption by young people, is often, even when dystopic, oriented toward hope for the future. Moreover, that literature seems at times actively to theorize the cultivation of such hope as a practice, even a method. I argue that it does so in three distinct modes: through critical dystopias, in failed or problematic utopias, and in utopias in process.

Critical Dystopias

According to Joseph W. Campbell, dystopian fiction has been perhaps the most popular form of YA during the first two decades of the twenty-first century.[1] The publication of *The Hunger Games* in 2008, with its subsequent sequels and successful film adaptation, solidified dystopia as the reigning YA genre. Such dystopias are almost always also works of science fiction, generally set in the future, often after some cataclysm (ecological, economic, or political) that has left fascist or totalitarian regimes in place. Suzanne Collins's *The Hunger Games*, for example, describes a post–United States North America called Panem, divided into twelve districts dominated by a Capitol. The districts provide various goods and services to the Capitol, which houses the ruling elite. Districts are kept in line through the threat of violence and an ongoing form of psychological terror; each year, the districts must send two of their young people to fight in the Capitol's annual "hunger games," fights to the death from which only one survivor is deemed champion. We might understand *The Hunger Games* as not only a story of youthful resistance and rebellion to adult order, but also as a form of media literacy narrative, one in which the protagonists learn how to use media technologies for resistant forms of organizing.[2] Indeed, the primary narrative of the third novel in the trilogy, *Mockingjay*, consists of the young resistors making propaganda videos to rouse their forces and unsettle the citizens of the Capitol.

The Hunger Games was perhaps the most popular of a whole series of similar dystopias, often trilogies, that featured young people, often led by a young woman, banding together against totalitarian forces. Veronica Roth's popular *Divergent* series, made into a series of less popular films, as well as Joelle Charbonneau's *Testing* trilogy followed suit, practically replicating Collins's original story with their own variations and flourishes; for instance, in the *Testing* trilogy, a series of young people compete in games not just for victory and scarce resources, but for the opportunity to attend university in the capital city. Alexander and Black describe such narratives as allegories for the increasing prevalence of high-stakes testing in contemporary educational systems, which often pit students against one another in competition for limited spots in academic institutions, thus parceling out to only a few victorious candidates the supposed means to economic improvement in a world of increasing precarity and widening class division.[3] These novels might speak to the anxieties of young readers who are facing uncertain futures while also offering them hope that unfair, even oppressive systems can be challenged and possibly overturned.

Campbell describes the dual genre work that these books perform as both science fiction and adolescent literature to understand how they function personally and culturally. On one hand, as he puts it, the science fiction of these novels focuses on "the encounter with the other – exposing the act of othering . . . and the role it plays in subjectivity";[4] characters in such novels often have to learn to coordinate across differences, even if only differences in gender, to combat their oppressors, and they also learn how they themselves have been "othered" or "alienated" by an unjust society based often on stark class divisions. On the other hand, such dystopic literature for adolescents also works as a "socializing discourse" in that it invites young readers to understand themselves as in opposition to oppressive regimes and orders, and it encourages alternative ways of conceiving collective human projects.[5] We might thus call such YA dystopias *critical dystopias*, a term that Tom Moylan uses in *Scraps of the Untainted Sky* to describe books that "linger in the terrors of the present even as they exemplify what is needed to transform it" and are thus "stubbornly" utopian, even as their dystopic elements propel their plots.[6] Robert Gadowski promulgates this view of YA dystopias by arguing for their specifically pedagogical function:

> I firmly believe that the mysteries of freedom can be unraveled with the help of a special tool; this tool is dystopian literature, and particularly the spate of recent YA dystopian science fiction novels that extrapolate on the possibilities of freedom in a technologically-mediated world.[7]

Gadowski, for instance, maintains that Katniss "champion[s] the notion of being the master of oneself and the idea of fighting for the preservation of this independence."[8] Other critics have followed suit, using *The Hunger Games* as an exemplary text in this regard. Megan McDonough suggests that what makes the books important is how they portray "Katniss' beliefs regarding her society's social structure, her position within society, and her actions. These reflections drive her to claim agency and stand against those in power."[9] And speaking most broadly about YA dystopias, Stephanie Thompson posits that, "rather than marginalizing children and adolescents, YA dystopian fiction emphasizes the importance of their voices and ideas and the possibilities for youth to be agents of change."[10]

At the same time, other critics have been less sanguine about the personal and cultural work that YA dystopias undertake. Books such as *The Hunger Games* might appeal to young people because they pit the young against older adult oppressors, and they might even, as Alexander and Black suggest, metaphorize, however hyperbolically, the kinds of structural inequities that young people face; but the simplicity of their binary plots – us versus them, the young against the old, the have-nots contra the haves – might be too reductive to serve as either cogent structural analysis or, consequently, nuanced method for imagining, much less enacting, less dystopic circumstances. Rebecca Hill concludes that, "as a text, *THG* [The Hunger Games] is available for an array of readings because it lacks descriptive richness, becoming a screen for readerly projection."[11] For example, populist readings of *The Hunger Games* focus far less on the manipulation of the populace through televisual spectacle and the economic dominance of a small ruling group over the resources and labor of the masses, and more on a battle of good versus evil and the problem of "large" government. As she puts it, some "readings [of *THG*] are indicative of the impact of populism's reduction of materialist discourses to a story of good people and bad government – and how this narrative fits into longer geographic rendering of class conflict in the United States."[12] A populist reading of the story might serve less to forward structural critique of economic inequity and instead appeal to middle American disgust with elites.

Other critics question the specific *forms* of agency made available in dystopian YA, particularly as they might not reeducate conceptions of what constitutes strength but instead reify existing, often highly gendered, notions. Jessica Seymour notes how the predominance of female protagonists as fighters, who often must kill others simply to survive their horrific circumstances, may actually reinforce a sense of strength and power as *violence*. As she puts it, while "YA dystopia is a female-dominated genre . . . the portrayals of female characters in these texts often disrupt [the] gender binary by performing masculine traits. This allows them to overthrow the oppressive regime of their fictional society."[13] But at what cost to other, more feminist notions of agency? At the same time, Seymour notes how "fictionalized performances of masculinity have responded to this shift by embodying feminine traits. . . . Young male characters take on nurturing positions in these stories and perform their gender beyond the expectations of traditional Western masculinity."[14] The renegotiation, perhaps even reeducation, of gender identity and its relation to agency and power reifies masculinist conceptions of power while perhaps also opening up ways for readers to reconceive their relationship to their gender – and to each other.

YA dystopia has other versions and varieties than those that follow in the shadow of *The Hunger Games*, though I have spent time with the latter because of their significant market share. Paolo Bacigalupi's *Ship Breaker* and its sequel *The Drowned Cities* deserve attention, particularly for their more global perspective. The former book won the prestigious Michael L. Printz Award, given to work for teens that exemplifies strong literary qualities, and was a finalist for the National Book Award for Young People's Literature. Both are set in a postapocalyptic world of intense ecological disaster. *Ship Breaker* primarily concerns protagonist Nailer and his fight for survival in the storm-ridden, flooded areas of the US Gulf Coast. He scavenges for precious metals, such as copper, on abandoned and shipwrecked boats and ultimately has to fight and kill his father to escape the horrific conditions in which he was raised. In *The Drowned Cities*, young Mahlia and Mouse find refuge from a similarly ecological devastated and war-torn area in a village where Mahlia learns to be a physician's assistant. Mahlia is captured by Tool, a human/dog hybrid that has been engineered as a supersoldier, who then demands her help in recovering from his wounds. Mahlia and Mouse eventually team up with Tool to seek refuge further north, fleeing the ruins and precarity of the "drowned cities" overtaken by coastal flooding. Tool, also looking for a different kind of life, agrees to help them.

Bacigalupi's books are, in some senses, even bleaker dystopias than those of Collins's ilk. Their focus on ecological disaster belies any hope that their characters' worlds can be easily remedied. Lars Schmeink argues that "Bacigalupi's young adult novels . . . play out in dystopian worlds in which ecological disaster has struck, but they focus on adolescent characters and their search for identity" and "trying to survive in a harsh world challenged by political, economic, and ecological crises."[15] Such survival comes at an extremely high cost, usually measured in character death tolls. And yet, as Schmeink suggests, Bacigalupi's novels might point toward alternative kinds of valuation and forms of agency that not only make these inhospitable and toxic worlds survivable but can also guide readers toward other ways of thinking about their roles as contributors to their societies:

> I believe that for *Ship Breaker* and *The Drowned Cities*, this utopian potential is not just located in the adolescent protagonists but also in the posthuman subjectivity represented by Tool. Whereas the genetic determinism of

> this dystopian world would force judgment on Nailer (criminal, beach rat) and Mahlia (castoff, war maggot) that limits their identity formation, Tool offers a different set of values, expressed not in the idea that we are determined by our DNA, but in the idea that we are determined by our decisions.[16]

Schmeink is thinking in particular of Tool's resistance to his "programming" as an engineered animal and his decision to help the two young people escape to a (hopefully) better situation. Such a posthumanist approach to YA dystopia breaks open for readers a sense that their identities need not be predetermined or static but can be shaped by the active choices they make as they navigate precarious worlds.[17] Such might be a less utopian form of agency even than that offered by Katniss, but it might be more realistic given contemporary constraints; it also holds out *some* hope that one's place in the world, if not the world itself, might be better.

Problematic Utopias

Fredric Jameson, in *The Seeds of Time*, notes that "utopian literature of the past was largely positive, or even affirmative,"[18] but that more contemporary versions of utopia might become valuable to the extent that they do *not* represent perfectly realized societies. That is, as Jameson puts it, "the vocation of Utopia lies in *failure*; in which its epistemological value lies in the walls it allows us to feel around our minds" (emphasis added).[19] Such "failure" might consist of the present, real-world shortcomings envisioned as remedied in the utopia, or it might consist of a failure within the imagined utopia itself. Works in our second category of YA utopias are decidedly of the second sort – partial or problematic utopias. Such novels depict putatively "perfect" worlds that have some significant flaw that usually compels the protagonists either to rebel or flee their utopia, or to agitate for change within it. Such problematic utopias often seem in the vein of Aldous Huxley's *Brave New World*, which depicted a highly regulated and managed society that, when viewed from the perspective of an outside "savage," seemed limited and even stultifying.

Contemporary YA versions of such utopias similarly present a *nearly* perfect world – except for one glaring problem. The *Uglies* series by Scott Westerfeld, for example, focuses on the life of Tally in a future world in which everyone undergoes a set of procedures during their teenage years to become "pretty." Before they become "pretty," the "uglies" await their turns to join the prettified in the Party Towers, where life seems to be a never-ending pursuit of pleasures, made possible through a world of automation. The social goal of making everyone "pretty" is essentially to create equality through eliminating lookism and prejudice based on attractiveness. As is typical of such books, the price of such equality is not just invasive procedures to create symmetry, but also a high degree of surveillance and conformity. The limitations of such a perfectly pretty world become steadily apparent to Tally when she meets Shay, who resists some of the conformity of her culture, such as refusing to make digital mock-ups of her future pretty self. "Maybe I think my face is already right," Shay tells Tally, prompting the latter along a path of increasing resistance to the conformity of her particular utopia.[20]

Other novels follow suit. The *Matched* series by Ally Condie concerns a young woman in a perfect society in which everyone is "matched" with their supposed ideal mate. When reviewing her possible matches, Cassie experiences a glitch in her computer that shows her another young man, Ky, whose father had committed an "infraction" and who is therefore considered an "aberration," unsuitable for matching.[21] But, of course, Cassie is intrigued by him, leading her to question the wisdom of her society's social structure. In a different twist on this theme, Lauren Oliver's *Delirium* trilogy is set in Maine in 2091 in a society that has banned love. Citizens undergo treatments at the age of eighteen that prevent them from falling in love, thus creating a more peaceful society of less friction and conflict. Before she can have her procedure, the main character, Lena, falls in love with Alex, an Invalid, someone who has refused the procedures to "cure" them of love, who lives in the Wilds outside the city, where resistance to the dominant social order is growing. All such books offer seemingly "perfect" worlds where order and safety have been achieved, usually after some historical turning point that is barely mentioned (or remembered), but in the process of creating such utopias something significant has been sacrificed – love, free choice in choosing a mate, the right to one's own body. Love and bodily difference might complicate human interaction, but they are nonetheless put forward as core values worth recovering.

The paradigmatic text in this category, and one whose influence can be seen on nearly all subsequent utopian and dystopian YA, is Lois Lowry's multiple-award-winning novel *The Giver*. The novel is set in a pleasant community, a kind of highly managed suburbia. The action focuses on a young boy, Jonas, who is approaching twelve years of age, the age at which citizens receive their lifetime professional assignments in the Ceremony. The worldbuilding of the first third of the novel emphasizes the safety and comfort of the community – safety and comfort that come with a high degree of panoptical discipline, administered through the interpolation of norms and through strict biopolitical management. Indeed, as we learn more about the community, we see how *everything* is managed, including intimate relationships and families, which always consist of a male and female parent and two children, one male and female. Children are birthed by those who work as Birth Mothers and then nurtured communally through their first year before being assigned a family. The family serves to help children control their emotions and regulate even dreams and desires, with pills prescribed at puberty to lessen the anxieties and passions of adolescent life. To help manage possibly unpleasant or disturbing desires, the community forbids viewing another's naked body, except for the very young and the very old.

Ultimately, the community emphasis is on equality, and there are few opportunities for differences to interfere with the smooth organization and running of a pleasant, if regimented, community. The overall result is one of conformity, comfort, and safety, with an underlying hint of punishment through "releasing" for criminal behavior but also for children who somehow don't fit in, such as young children who are too fussy. The action intensifies as Jonas approaches the Ceremony, where he discovers that his assignment will be as the community's next Receiver of Memory. The Receiver holds the communities' disturbing and violent memories, enabling equilibrium and balance. But during his training, Jonas is disturbed by the memories, which include memories of good times and even of color, which have been eliminated to promote sameness and conformity. He ultimately comes to realize that it is a mistake to withhold such memories – the good and the bad – even if they cause distress. Jonas decides to leave the Community so that memories will return to the Community, opening members' eyes to what they have sacrificed in order to cultivate comfort.

The Giver ends ambiguously, with Jonas taking a baby scheduled for "release" away from the Community, and readers do not discover whether they survive or whether the Community transforms through remembering the past. Such ambiguity reinforces readers' sense of the problematics of utopia; the Community is revealed as not quite the utopia it imagines itself to be, but Jonas's choices perhaps offer it the opportunity to work toward a better version of utopia. Writing about both *The Giver* and *Uglies*, Gadowski points out the Foucauldian motif of social and identity discipline: "The authors' take on ordered freedom exposes the inherent danger arising from such a system. The protagonists show through their actions that a balanced relation between the individual and the state needs to remain a prevalent part of the American freedom meme."[22] *The Giver* certainly leaves readers questioning the right "balance" between individual and collective need, particularly the latter's need for stability. Part of the critical dimension of such failed or partial utopias is precisely their ability to offer for readers particular problematics of the utopian that can be held up for further scrutiny.

A curious version of the problematic utopia appears in Neal Shusterman's *Scythe* series, the first book of which was an Honor Book for the Michael L. Printz Award. *Scythe* depicts a utopian society in which the Thunderhead, a highly advanced computer system and network, has created a controlled and ordered society and has, with the help of other technological advances, practically eliminated death. The problem with such a society, however, is that resources are still limited; population is thus limited by certain numbers of people being chosen for death at the hands of the Scythe, whose members individually decide the criteria to select whom to kill to satisfy their quotas. The main action of *Scythe* concerns the training of two new Scythes, Citra and Rowan. The plot complicates with the appearance of a seemingly rogue group of corrupt Scythes who kill because they enjoy doing so. In a way, *Scythe* works as another variation on the YA paradigm established by *The Giver*, this time with the problem of technologically enabled longevity confronting real-world problems of limited resources – a problematic befitting a contemporary time of increasing ecological concern and impending environmental devastation. What is the right balance between personal freedom and managing increasingly limited resources?

Utopias in Process

My third category of YA utopian fiction is a less obviously coherent set of narratives about what we might call provisional utopias. They are novels about spaces that, sometimes in a larger hostile world, seek to enact utopian visions or work toward utopic ideals. They constitute a version of "utopia as method," which Ruth Levitas sees as the real value of utopian thinking: a steady working toward social equity and valuing of difference as opposed to a top-down management of such through a master plan or grand utopian vision.[23]

Michael Warner uses the term "counterpublic" to describe spaces of "poetic world making" in which, temporarily and spatially free from hegemonic discourses and pressures, alternative visions of worldmaking can be explored and partially enacted.[24] Warner uses the example of gay enclaves or "ghettos" in large urban areas to describe the kinds of non-normative and experimental relations, connections, and subjectivities that can have a chance to form in contradistinction to hegemonic values and practices in the larger public. We should not be surprised, then, that some of the YA utopian narratives that engage in such "poetic world making" are centered on queer experiences, subjectivities, and relationalities.

Following the work of Levitas, Davina Cooper situates such worldmaking as part of a broad utopian hopefulness rooted in concrete practices. She describes the creation of small, provisional spaces that "work by creating the change [participants] wish to encounter, building and forging new ways of experiencing social and political life."[25] Cooper offers the example of the Pussy Palace, a site where women can safely explore sexual intimacy with one another, as an "everyday utopia" that, in its local and temporally limited way, performs an "attunement, a *way* of engaging with spaces, objects, and practices that is oriented to the hope, desire, and belief in the possibility of other, better worlds."[26] Key to the temporality of such projects is how they "explor[e] the potential that resides within different nows as they gesture toward different futures."[27]

YA narratives play out such "utopia as method" in a variety of intriguing ways. Some are frankly fantastical, such as in T. J. Klune's *The House in the Cerulean Sea* (2020), which follows in the vein of Harry Potter to feature the presence of young people with magical abilities trying to make their way in a world of "normals." This narrative formula of conflict between two distinct groups is given a twist in Klune's novel. It is told primarily from the point of view of Linus Baker, a nonmagical caseworker who is assigned the task of visiting and inspecting orphanages or homes that house magical youth who have been taken from their parents – evoking how Indigenous children across North American were relocated to white-run schools to assimilate them into white society and culture. Baker is sent by the Department in Charge of Magical Youth to a secret school on an island that houses youth who are particularly frightening to the larger populace: such young people include a bearded female gnome who talks about hitting those she dislikes on the head with her shovel and burying them in her garden; a large blob-like creature who hides under beds to scare the unsuspecting because he was told as a youngster that he is like a "monster under the bed";[28] and a young boy who is the Antichrist and whose violent dreams seem always on the verge of manifesting as real-world harm and destruction. The home is overseen by Arthur Parnassus, who clearly cares for his frightening charges, helping them grow to control their powers. Baker's mission, given as a clear mandate from Extremely Upper Management, is to make sure that the home is run in such a way that the children are kept under control and away from "normal" citizens; Parnassus's gentle management style raises concerns that he is not up to the task.

In a way, the home that Parnassus creates is its own counterpublic, in which the magical misfits create an alternative family of intimacy, adventures, and love. The narrative also proceeds as a steady reeducation of Baker's own sensibilities, as he comes to see that the children, however frightening they might be, deserve the same care, consideration, and *freedoms* of any other children, magical or not. Baker ultimately advocates for bringing them into the public. Inevitably there are conflicts, with some townspeople fearing the children and demanding even that the home be closed, but sympathetic folks persist in welcoming the magical youth. By the end of the novel, much work still needs to be done to create a society that is tolerant of young people who are so different, but *The House in the Cerulean Sea* nonetheless provides an interesting model of provisional utopian worldmaking that shows how, in limited spaces, alternative family can be made not just to accommodate but to contribute to the thriving of diverse subjects. What is particularly compelling about Klune's novel is that he does not make his magical youth simply "different"; they are, indeed, frightening and dangerous. His utopian thinking thus pushes at the boundaries of past YA novels that approached the problem of difference as one of unfounded prejudice on the part of "normals." In Klune's novel, the stakes are raised; to enact the provisional utopia of Parnassus's home at a larger level will require substantive changes to the hegemonic culture and a reeducation of its citizens to accommodate "extreme" difference. But the home is at least a start, an everyday model on a smaller scale of utopian practice.

A similar kind of utopian thinking occurs in David Levithan's groundbreaking novel *Boy Meets Boy*. Levithan worked as an editor for the Scholastic Corporation, overseeing the publication of major works of YA, including *The Hunger Games*. His own writing focuses on exploring emotional and sexual intimacy amongst young people, particularly gay teens. *Boy Meets Boy* primarily concerns the friendship circle of narrator Paul, an openly gay high-school student. Readers quickly realize, though, that Paul does not attend a "normal" high school. Rather, his high school is something a gay utopia – almost, or at least one in process. Paul's kindergarten teacher identified Paul as likely gay at age five, and the news is greeted with not just tolerance but openness. Paul then becomes the first openly gay third-grade class president; a classmate who attempts to run against him on a "don't vote for the fag" ticket loses in a landslide. Paul then takes a guy to the fifth-grade prom and eventually forms a Gay–Straight Alliance because, as he quips, the straights really needed the gays' help. He is queer bashed in eighth grade, but the straightboy fencing team fights back on his behalf, and other friends create a separate Boy Scouts troop to include gay kids. By the time Paul reaches high school, the local chapter of Parents and Friends of Lesbians and Gays is as large as the Parent–Teacher Association. The most fantastical part of *Boy Meets Boy* lies perhaps in the character of Infinite Darlene, a six-foot four-inch drag queen who is the captain of the football team, both star quarterback and homecoming queen.

All is not perfect – that is, open and affirming of queer lives and loves – in the world of *Boy Meets Boy*. Paul's best friend, Tony, goes to a very different school and is trapped in a household of religiously conservative parents who condemn Tony's potential homosexuality. Paul wonders where Tony can find a world as comfortable and accepting as the one Paul inhabits. Paul wants a fair world and for Tony to have a place, but that place does not seem to exist yet for Tony. *Boy Meets Boy* was daring for its time, 2003, long before gay marriage and other liberalizing political and cultural moves that signaled at least growing tolerance if not acceptance for queer people. But its vision of what the move toward queer acceptance might look like qualifies as a partial or everyday utopia. The teen romance plots of the novel, with Paul and his friends falling in and out of love, threaten the utopian feeling in that the teens are always at risk of hurting one another, but these plots are an important reality check on the utopian impulses; love can be messy, and friendships evolve and change. More importantly, the novel's periodic essentialism in its construction of gay identity (Paul is gay *at five years of age*) is in tension with the depiction of other characters who are less sure of their sexuality, who are taking a more experimental and perhaps ultimately self-determining approach to their sexual identities. This tension also becomes an important problematic to work through in envisioning and enacting a queer-accepting utopia. Perhaps least satisfying from a contemporary perspective is the dominance of the book by white characters, with only a few people of color mentioned on the narrative's periphery.

The final book we will consider directly addresses this absence in the creation of queer utopian spaces, however provisional they might be. Emphasizing Cooper's idea of "everyday utopias," *Juliet Takes a Breath* by Gabby Rivera is perhaps the least explicitly utopian but also the most concrete, both in its explication of the desire and hope for equitable and utopian spaces of engagement as well as the kinds of reeducation of desire that might have to take place to move toward utopian possibility. The novel centers on Juliet, a Latina lesbian living in New York, who takes an internship as the research assistant for a famous white feminist writer,

Harlowe Brisbane, in Portland, Oregon. Juliet arrives a bit unsure of herself and trying to figure out what being a lesbian will mean for her life (particularly given how unsettled at the prospect her mother is), and she hopes that Harlowe, as the author of *Raging Flower: Empowering Your Pussy by Empowering Your Mind*, will help her out. Harlowe's book transformed Juliet's relationship to her own body.

In Harlowe's home, Juliet meets a cast of queer characters, including Harlowe's former lovers and friends, and encounters a relatively safe space for the passionate exchange of ideas, the discovery of powerful women and lesbian figures from history, and even budding romance. The relative safety of this utopia for Juliet is put in jeopardy by Harlowe, who, at a reading at Powell's Books, points to Juliet as a young lesbian of color whom she is helping "uplift" from her community into the delights of feminism and lesbianism.[29] Juliet is stunned and then deeply hurt by the unthinking racism of Harlowe's comments, which enact an unexamined ideology of white supremacy that runs roughshod over Juliet's self-determination – and the reality of her life. Juliet then leaves Portland to reconnect with some of her relatives, particularly an aunt and cousin in Miami, where she visits a community of queer people of color who accept, understand, and support her.

At the end of the book, Juliet returns to Portland to confront Harlowe and attempt to resolve some of the issues that her experiences have raised for her. She says, "I wanted to believe in the creation of an unbreakable multiracial community of women. But could we all really have one another's backs?"[30] Such comments gesture to the utopian desire for a community and, at the same time, the challenges facing its formation. *Juliet Takes a Breath* offers us glimpses of such communities in process, even as it poses some of the difficulties of realizing queer, multiracial utopias.[31] Kenneth B. Kidd notes that "as children's literature is drawing nearer adult fiction, resembling such in complexity and aesthetic sophistication, it is also drawing nearer adult critical discourse,"[32] with some fiction functioning not just like but as, for example, queer theory. *Juliet Takes a Breath* functions precisely in such a manner, holding on to a utopian sensibility while refusing to relinquish the complexities of lived experience and realities that make any simple enactment of utopian thinking impossible.[33] It models for its readers a character embracing hope for a better world and everyday possibilities for sustaining and nurturing community, while also recognizing the need to work with Juliet's own and others' desires in a continual process of engagement, critique, reevaluation, and reimagination of what utopia might look like – and become.

Notes

1. Joseph W. Campbell, *The Order and the Other: Young Adult Dystopian Literature and Science Fiction* (Jackson: University Press of Mississippi, 2019).
2. See further Jonathan Alexander, *Writing Youth: Young Adult Fiction as Literacy Sponsorship* (Lanham, MD: Lexington, 2017).
3. Jonathan Alexander and R. W. Black, "The Darker Side of the Sorting Hat: Representations of Educational Testing in Dystopian Young Adult Fiction," *Children's Literature* 43 (2015), 208–234.
4. Campbell, 31.
5. Campbell, 33.
6. Tom Moylan, *Scraps of the Untainted Sky: Science Fiction, Utopia, Dystopia* (Boulder, CO: Westview Press, 2000), 198–199.
7. Robert Gadowski, "Critical Dystopia for Young People: The Freedom Meme in American Young Adult Dystopian Science Fiction," from *Basic Categories of Fantastic Literature Revisited*, edited by A. Wicher, P. Spyra, and J. Matyjaszczyk (Newcastle Upon Tyne: Cambridge Scholars Publishing, 2014), 144–160 (145).
8. Gadowski, 158.
9. Megan McDonough, "From Tribute to Mockingjay: Representations of Katniss Everdeen's Agency in the *Hunger Games* Series," from *Child and Youth Agency in Science Fiction*, edited by I. E. Castro and J. Clark (Lanham, MD: Lexington, 2019), 131–150 (134).
10. Stephanie Thompson, "Sanctuary and Agency in Young Adult Dystopian Fiction," from *Child and Youth Agency in Science Fiction*, edited by I. E. Castro and J. Clark (Lanham, MD: Lexington, 2019), 227–250 (246).
11. Rebecca Hill, "Capital or Capitol?: The *Hunger Games* Fandom and Neoliberal Populism," *American Studies*, 57.1/2 (2018), 5–28 (9).
12. Hill, 23.
13. Jessica Seymour, "'Murder Me … Become a Man': Establishing the Masculine Care Circle in Young Adult Dystopias," *Reading Psychology* 37.4 (2015), 627–649 (647).
14. Seymour, 647.
15. Lars Schmeink, "Coming of Age and the Other: Critical Posthumanism in Paolo Bacigalupi's *Ship Breaker* and *The Drowned Cities*," from *Posthumanism in Young Adult Fiction: Finding Humanity in a Posthuman World*, edited by A. Tarr and D. R. White (Jackson: University Press of Mississippi, 2018), 159–178 (159).
16. Schmeink, 174.
17. Phoebe Chen, in "Posthuman Potential and Ecological Limits in Future Worlds," from *Posthumanism in Young Adult Fiction: Finding Humanity in a Posthuman World*, edited by A. Tarr and D. R. White (Jackson: University Press of Mississippi, 2018), 179–196, cites the work of science-fiction critic Gary Westfahl to consider how, even if "YA science fiction claims to challenge the liberal humanist definition of human … it does not always offer viable

alternative definitions of humanness. In actuality, it is more likely to reject the unknowable potential of posthumanism to reassure the adolescent's need for a solid and grounded self-identity. . . . In other words, despite its speculative nature, YA science fiction's posthumanist experiences could slip into a liberal humanist paradigm that enables the protagonist to recuperate an essentialist identity, implying that the genre's reconfiguration of humanness may not be as radical as its premise suggests" (182).

18. Fredric Jameson, *The Seeds of Time* (New York: Columbia University Press, 1996), 74.
19. Jameson, 75.
20. Scott Westerfeld, *Uglies* (New York: Simon Pulse, 2005), 1–3.
21. Ally Condie, *Matched* (New York: Speak, 2010), 46.
22. Gadowski, 156.
23. Ruth Levitas, *Utopia as Method: The Imaginary Reconstruction of Society* (London: Palgrave Macmillan, 2013).
24. Michael Warner, *Publics and Counterpublics* (Princeton, NJ: Princeton University Press, 2002), 114.
25. Davina Cooper, *Everyday Utopias: The Conceptual Life of Promising Spaces* (Durham, NC: Duke University Press, 2013), 2–3.
26. Cooper, 3.
27. Cooper, 220.
28. T. J. Klune, *The House in the Cerulean Sea* (New York: Tor, 2020), 39
29. Gabby Rivera, *Juliet Takes a Breath* (New York: Dial Books, 2019), 207.
30. Rivera, 268.
31. Interestingly, Rivera positions her own narrative in precisely this tension. Derritt Mason, writing in *Queer Anxieties of Young Adult Literature and Culture* (Jackson: University Press of Mississippi, 2021) notes how Rivera's *It Gets Better* video, "It Doesn't Get Better. You Get Stronger," questions the progressivist march toward utopian tolerance otherwise promulgated.
32. Kenneth B. Kidd, *Theory for Beginners: Children's Literature as Critical Thought* (New York: Fordham University Press, 2020), 8.
33. It is worth nothing that queer utopian YA that works substantively with trans issues is still largely lacking. J. Gill-Peterson identifies in *Histories of the Transgender Child* (Minneapolis: University of Minnesota Press, 2018) what may be the primary challenge of imagining trans lives from a utopian perspective: "If, in the twenty-first century, we adults really desire to learn to care for the many transgender children in our midst, we need to learn first . . . what it means to wish that there *be* trans children, that to grow trans and live a trans childhood is not merely a possibility but a happy and desirable one. And we need to come into this desire now, not in the future" (207).

CHAPTER 9

Utopia after American Hegemony

Peter Boxall

Utopia and Hegemony

It is one of the recurrent contradictions of utopian thinking that utopia cannot accommodate hegemony.

This appears contradictory because, in many respects, utopia is inconceivable without hegemony. If we think of utopias as pictures of perfect worlds, then it follows that the utopian world that we picture should be one in which all political differences are resolved, in which the dominant ideology has achieved a universal consensus. It is for this reason that utopias so often feel tyrannical, or absolutist. There can be no role for dissent when perfection has been achieved, and so utopias are places where the political need or desire for dissensus has been abolished. But even as this is so, the picture of a utopian realm is one that seems to require dissensus as a political goal in itself – a mark of the freedom to think and act for oneself that is a feature of any conception of a just or fair state. It is when this freedom is revoked that utopias reveal most clearly their tendency to become identical with dystopias, their apparent opposite (a folding of the utopian into the dystopian that finds exemplary expression in Aldous Huxley's 1932 novel *Brave New World*).

From the earliest example we have of utopian imagining properly so-called – Thomas More's *Utopia*, published in 1516 – this contradiction between achieved hegemony and the political freedom to dissent has been part of the structure of utopian thinking itself. The tectonics of utopia – from the shape of the island of Utopia to the narrative structure of More's text *Utopia* – are organized, in significant ways, around the sustaining of this contradiction. The island offers itself as a circle, as a hermetically sealed state, cut off from everything outside it; but the circle, nevertheless, is broken, allowing the urge toward the perfect seal to contend with the opposite urge toward a continued commerce between Utopia, and all that Utopia is not. The break in the circle allows the sea to enter into the heart of the island and thus for the maintenance of a seaport, easy to defend, which acts as a channel of communication between Utopia and the rest of the world.

Utopia strives in this way to realize itself as complete and in process at the same time, as at once sealed and porous; and this striving, manifest in the shape of the island, is replicated in the form of More's text, which also maintains a strict partition between Utopia and not-Utopia while working continually to overcome that partition. This construction of a semipermeable boundary at the formal heart of the text is effected through the device of the double, of Raphael as the double of Thomas More. The text, *Utopia*, is conducted as a dialogue between More and Raphael, one which takes place across this membrane that both divides Utopia from "our" world, "here" from "there," and brings them into contact with one another. More and Raphael meet in Antwerp, in an effective staging post between England and Utopia, and the conversation that ensues between them, which makes up the bulk of the narrative, has the effect of forming a bridge between these different worlds. In making this bridge, the text oversees a delicate balance between the perfected and the in-process, between contact and separation, between hegemony and dissent. Raphael, philosopher that he is, absolutist that he is, is adamant that there should be no commerce between Utopia, the perfected picture of the polis, and England as represented by More, a place of compromise and corruption. The discussion between the two, in the first book of *Utopia*, turns on this reluctance, on Raphael's desire to quarantine his perfect island from the contagion zone of early modern Europe. More is excited by Raphael's account of the island because, he says, there is much in it for European states to learn from. It is the duty of the philosopher, as the pragmatist More sees it, to condescend to speak to the politician or to the king; but Raphael sees it differently. Utopian philosophy rests in its purity, its noncontamination by all that is corrupt (and most of all by the corrupting influence of money). He cannot serve as an adviser to a prince, he tells More, because "there is no place for philosophy in the council of kings."[1] "If I wish to speak the truth," he insists, then he will have to remain, spiritually at least, in Utopia, safely ensconced behind a cordon sanitaire. "I have described to you as accurately as I could," he tells More, "the structure of that commonwealth which I consider not only the best but indeed the only one that can rightfully claim than name" (103). That description, though, rests on a gulf between here and there, which cannot be crossed. "Here," Raphael says, forgetting that he is in Antwerp, not in Utopia, "here, where there is no private business, every man zealously preserves the public business" (103).

Raphael refuses contact with the compromised More, as philosophy refuses contact with politics. But, of course, it is the ingenuity of More's *Utopia* that the text itself creates the contact between More and Raphael that Raphael's own utopianism disavows. Just as the crescent shape of the island gestures at once to isolation and congress, the narrative structure of *Utopia* serves as a collapsing bridge, a junction that allows Raphael's voice to speak within More's, that brings the account of a form of utopian hegemony that tends toward totality into contact with a form of statecraft that operates through dissent, doctrinal difference, political imperfection.

This is the particular promise of *Utopia*, and one can see a version of this balance running throughout the literary tradition that is formed in its name. Wherever we find imagined utopias, from Francis Bacon to Jonathan Swift to Sarah Scott to H. G. Wells to Joanna Russ and Ursula Le Guin, we find this tension between hegemonic political systems and residual forms of dissent from that system. This tension is native to the utopian genre; but it takes on a particular force in an American context, a context in which the relation to hegemony is particularly vexed. In More's *Utopia*, the clear rules of the utopian commonwealth, the supposed rationalism of its political systems, are held in opposition to the organically embedded forms of corruption that are endemic in Europe. A European culture that has grown over centuries, and which has absorbed the legacies of classical antiquity, has incorporated a series of absurdities and inequities that it is the task of the utopian blueprint, the clean slate, to expose. But this relation, between a faulty "old world" and a utopian picture unburdened by history, is differently weighted in relation to an American culture that is itself imagined at its inception as a "new world." Raphael himself starts his journey toward his imaginary island as part of Amerigo Vespucci's expedition, which purports to have discovered that "new world." More tells us that Raphael was "Vespucci's constant companion on the last three of his four voyages," voyages recorded in the contemporary accounts *New World* and *The Four Voyages of Amerigo Vespucci*.[2] Amerigo Vespucci, of course, gives America its name, while Raphael heads off to discover his own kind of new world. The American new world that is settled over the following centuries is one that is founded on the brutal oppression of the Indigenous population and the enslavement of peoples from Africa. But this does not prevent the circulation of the myth that the new world is itself a utopia, a community established on utopian principles. The American nation is founded on the assertion that it is self-evident that all men are created equal and have an inalienable right to life, liberty, and the pursuit of happiness – and from Alexis de Tocqueville's account of American democracy as the guarantor of a just world order, to John F. Kennedy's call, in 1963, for a "world peace" and a "world law," the prospect of a global American hegemony has been represented in utopian terms.[3] There is a tension, of course, between Kennedy's perception of America's capacity to impose a world order and that proposed more recently by Noam Chomsky. America's self-appointment as the "world power that proclaims global hegemony" does not, in Chomsky's view, lead to the establishing of Kennedy's world peace or of de Tocqueville's global democracy.[4] It does not, as George W. Bush and Tony Blair asserted in the run-up to the Iraq war in 2002, oversee the spread of democracy and freedom across the world. Rather, it threatens the very future of the planet, so we are faced in 2003, Chomsky suggests, with a choice between "Hegemony or Survival."

Whichever account we favor – American hegemony as a conduit of world peace or as a threat to global survival – the history of American utopianism has unfolded in the context of the United States itself as a hegemonic global force, and as a result the balance between hegemony and dissent has been weighted differently in American than in European utopias. From Nathaniel Hawthorne's 1852 novel *The Blithedale Romance*, to Charlotte Perkins Gilman's *Herland*, to Don DeLillo's *Underworld*, the picturing of counterworlds, the sounding of a Raphaelian utopian voice that works against the grain of the status quo, has to contend with the global reach of American power, the sense that the world itself is already under the sway of a pax Americana. *The Blithedale Romance* depicts the establishing of a utopian community on American soil, a kind of utopia within a utopia, in a manner that suggests, from the outset, the difficulty of establishing a ground, or a narrative perspective, that is not already incorporated into the American hegemon. The word "utopia" is used only once in Hawthorne's narrative – at the moment, close to the beginning of the novel, when the members of the group who set out to establish a "company of socialists" living in agrarian freedom hold a debate on what they should call their commune.[5] It falls to narrator Miles Coverdale himself to "whisper 'Utopia,' which, however, was unanimously shouted down, and the proposer very harshly maltreated, as if he had intended a latent satire."[6]

Utopia can only be a satire for Hawthorne (as indeed it was a satire for More), and, what is more, its satirical force has to operate *latently*. Whatever political desire is operating here, it cannot find a language for itself but is secreted away in the latent, hidden spaces that run through the novel and that often attach themselves to the word "latent" itself. Zenobia, the most vivid member of the community has "a gleam of latent mischief" in her eye (59); the political speeches of Hollinsworth – the dominant member of the group – provoke in his audience a "possible reserve of latent censure" (79); the evil Professor Westervelt provokes in Coverdale himself a "latent hostility" (91). The hopes that run through the novel, as well as the loves, the fears, and the enmities, take place in this latent fashion, as utopian possibility finds no place for itself in Hawthorne's narrative and cannot frame itself in relation to the American social system to which it fails to offer an alternative. And it is this same effect, this same sense that an opposition to American hegemony can express itself only latently, that emerges again, at the close of the twentieth century, in Don DeLillo's sprawling 1997 work *Underworld*. The novel opens with a sentence that speaks eloquently of the borderlessness of American power, its capacity to absorb everything that surrounds it into its ambit: "He speaks in your voice, American, and there's a shine in his eye that's halfway hopeful."[7] Whatever hope that is summoned here has to take its place within the bounds of that word, "American." If there is a countervoice, like the counter to More that we can hear in Raphael's voice, which speaks not in our "here" but in its own, then it can sound only under the American accent that every reader is given at this opening, as all voices, whether they know it or not, are, like yours, American.

The vastness of *Underworld* is a response to the vastness of the American culture that summons us in that opening line and which works to gather the history of the second half of the century into its jurisdiction. Whatever counterenergies flow through the novel, however layered and intricate what DeLillo calls its "counternarratives" are, they are shaped and contoured by this dominance. The word with which *Underworld* closes – peace – is, with a perhaps knowing echo of Kennedy's commencement address, a pax Americana.[8] The end of the Cold War, with which DeLillo's novel closes, ushers in a historical scenario in which America is the world's sole superpower, a world in which American hegemony is so uncontested that the urge to dissent from its authority can only assume a latent form. The entire novel wheels away from that opening half-line, and its assertion that all voices are American; but whatever underworlds and other worlds it contains, the capacity to speak against the pax Americana is bound up with the recognition that the novel itself speaks with an American accent, and in an American language that is a global lingua franca. But, of course, this moment – the moment of American global power with which DeLillo's novel ends – is short-lived. DeLillo famously called the twentieth century the "American century."[9] The Zapruder film of the Kennedy assassination, Nicholas Branch thinks in DeLillo's 1988 novel *Libra*, is a stuttery record of the "seven seconds that broke the back of the American century."[10] But the entry into a new century, marked in a sense by the terrorist attacks that took place in the United States on September 11, 2001, has seen the waning of American power. As Giovanni Arrighi argues, even though the political response of the US government to 9/11 was to declare the dawning of what the Bush administration called a "new American century," the global balance of power shifts in another direction, toward what Arrighi calls the "unravelling of hegemony."[11] In DeLillo's terms, if the twentieth century was the American century, then the twenty-first might be called the "Chinese century."

The first decades of the twenty-first century have seen this rather dramatic shift in the texture and reach of US power, which has only become more marked since the publication of Arrighi's essay; and the novel of the period has at once reflected the unraveling of US hegemony and struck a new balance between hegemony and dissent – a new way of conceiving both the forms in which the United States asserts its cultural power, and the terms in which the novel might engender utopian counter-narratives to contemporary global realities. One can see this novelistic response very clearly in DeLillo's own writing – *The Body Artist*, *Cosmopolis*, *Point Omega*, *Zero K*, *The Silence* all bear witness to a form of historical disorientation, in which the millennial forces that hemmed *Underworld* in, that drove it toward the end of the century as toward some kind of Yeatsian becoming, have all rather suddenly lapsed or waned. These novels take place in the throes of a particular kind of exhaustion, in which the engines of history, as these are driven by fossil-fueled American power, have stalled, so we enter into drift, into slow, unstuck time and space. In a line that appears both in *Cosmopolis* and in *The Body Artist*, the unraveling of hegemony has delivered us to what the narrators call a time that has "lost its narrative quality," a "kind of time that had no narrative quality."[12] The architects of global America, those who would see the twenty-first century as the New American Century, are reframed, under these circumstances, as crazed philosophers – no longer hard-edged brokers of global power, but ruminative soothsayers, what Jenny Offill, in her recent novel *Weather*, would call "crazy doomers."[13] Richard Elster, the guru at the heart of *Point Omega*, worked, we are told, for the US government as a "defense intellectual."[14] It was his job to "conceptualise" the Iraq war, to "apply overarching principles to such matters as troop deployment and counter-insurgency."[15] "There were times," he says, as he sat in closed rooms with military strategists, "when no map existed to match the reality we were trying to create."[16] But this project, this devising of a new American reality, falters in *Point Omega* as Elster finds that his theorizing cannot match with any given military strategy or yield any lived reality. Rather, Elster's model of world seeing leads to a collapse of enworlding, an encounter not with a newly made world, but with the dismantlement of worldedness itself (a recognition, as Jacques Derrida puts it, that "there is perhaps no longer a world and no doubt that there never was one as the totality of anything at all").[17] "Iraq is a whisper," Elster tells his military bosses, a quiet intimation of the end of things. It tells us that "something's coming." It tells us that "the sphere of collective human thought, this is approaching the final term, the last flare."[18] The Iraq war does not secure the continuation of American hegemony but is the first stage in its unraveling, an unraveling that Elster can only conceptualize as the end of the world.

Utopia after Hegemony

It is into the empty space that is opened up by this exhaustion, the space that does not match any given map, that the American novel of the current century projects its new utopian images, the entities that lie beyond the agreed-upon limits of recognition or interpretation. As American hegemony unravels, so the balance shifts between hegemony and dissent, between pictures of total worlds and those of worlds under construction. And in the process, it is possible to see two distinct strands emerging in the novel (even if these strands are sometimes interwoven), two ways of conceiving utopian possibility in the wake of hegemony. The first, the cluster of novels to which DeLillo's twenty-first-century fiction belongs, includes works that are often elegiac in tone and represent the failure of American reality construction as yielding pictures of a kind of denuded world space. We might include in this group the work of Marilynne Robinson – the mournful lament, in *Gilead*, that Gilead is "unadorned" and "little regarded." "This whole town," Robinson's narrator says, "does look like whatever hope becomes after it begins to weary a little, then weary a little more."[19] Or we might think of Cormac McCarthy's *The Road*, which gives us a picture of an utterly denuded planet that bleakly persists after the end of fossil-fueled culture. This is a world whose only future is encoded in maps that we cannot read, maps stenciled on the gleaming bodies of the fish that once lived in mountain streams, before the unspecified disaster occurred that wiped out all trace of life. "You could see them standing in the amber current," McCarthy's narrator says, "where the white edges of their fins wimpled softly in the flow. They smelled of moss in your hand. Polished and muscular and torsional. On their backs were vermiculate patterns that were maps of the world in its becoming."[20]

This first strand of novels makes maps of a territory that does not exist; the second strand sets out to reimagine enworlding after American hegemony not as a kind of blank, but as the possibility of new cultural formations. We might think of the extended narrative structures of Teju Cole's *Open City*. Or of the shifted relations between America, Europe, and Asia in the British writer Kamila Shamsie's *Home Fire*. Or the suspended relations between the United States and Pakistan in Mohsin Hamid's *The Reluctant Fundamentalist*. Or the narrative reclamation of Indigenous American populations in Leslie Marmon Silko's *Almanac of the Dead*, or Sherman Alexie's *Flight*. Or we might think of the refigured balance of global power and trade in Ling Ma's eerily prescient novel of global pandemic, *Severance*.

To understand the possibility of utopian fiction after hegemony, it is necessary to read these two strands together, to trace their differences and interconnections. And if this is so, it is perhaps in the later work of Philip Roth that we can see both the most extended examination of that first tendency (toward the exhaustion of American world making), and the places where the first tendency is interwoven with the second.

Roth's fiction of the twenty-first century, from *The Human Stain* to *Nemesis*, is dedicated, with an increasing and almost perverse intensity, to an anatomization of male impotence, as this is entangled with the decline of American power. The later Zuckerman novels, *The Human Stain* and *Exit Ghost*, depict Zuckerman's failing body and mind, his sexual impotence, his growing dementia, the weakening of his literary talent. His interface with the world – his infatuation with the ex-boxer and university dean Coleman Silk in *The Human Stain*, his obsessive and mostly fantasized affair with Jamie Logan in *Exit Ghost* – takes place across the threshold of this impotence. The Zuckerman of *Exit Ghost* feels himself to be at a great remove from the America presided over by George W. Bush, a nation, he thinks, that has not recovered from the wounds of 9/11 (he heads, on his first return to New York after spending years as a hermit in the mountains, to "Ground Zero": "Begin there," he thinks, "where the biggest thing of all occurred").[21] Zuckerman's struggle to understand his attraction to others and to the world is a struggle to attune himself and his failing imagination to an environment that no longer conforms to his ways of seeing and thinking. And Roth's other novels of the period – *The Plot against America*, *The Humbling*, *Nemesis* – all turn around variations on this theme. *The Plot against America* imagines the failure of Kennedy's pax Americana, not as a result of 9/11, or of George

W. Bush's disastrous presidency, but as a form of counterfactual history, in which the 1940 presidency was won not by Franklin D. Roosevelt, but by Charles Lindbergh, the aviator and Nazi sympathizer. The narrator of *Plot*, a young boy named Philip Roth, listens to Roosevelt accepting the nomination for his third term at the Democratic Convention meeting in Chicago on July 18, 1940, and thinks to himself that Roosevelt's "voice alone conveyed mastery over the tumult of human affairs."[22] Roosevelt's lofty oration, as the voice of the nation, is replaced by Lindbergh's "unadorned" speech, "delivered in a high-pitched, flat, midwestern, decidedly un-Rooseveltian American,"[23] and in that substitution, all of what Roth (the narrator) sees as the dignity and grace of Roosevelt's America gives way to Lindbergh's crass and opportunistic protectionism. In a chilling preemption of the "America First" rhetoric employed by Donald Trump, Lindbergh promises to "KEEP AMERICA OUT OF THE JEWISH WAR"[24] – appeasing the Nazis to protect America's national interests, and so overseeing the emergence of a fascist United States.

All of Roth's late novels turn around images of vulnerability at the heart of power, the revelation both that American hegemony is inhabited by a weakness that also powers it, and that the decline of American power is a submission to this latent weakness. But if they do so, and if this incessant focus on weakening, on humbling, feels like a late-stage obsession with decline, what is so remarkable about these novels is that the process by which power is sutured to weakness is also one that yields a kind of literary possibility, a latent utopianism that is nurtured in these works, and which contains, in Fredric Jameson's utopian terminology, the seeds of another time.[25] This possibility – the conceiving of a relation to the world that lies outside of the domain of American power, which is so dramatically unraveling in late Roth, in late DeLillo, in McCarthy, in Robinson – is figured, consistently, in relation to the truncated or disabled body. Bucky Cantor in Roth's *Nemesis* lives a life of dramatically restricted mobility as a result of the polio he contracted in 1944. Nathan Zuckerman suffers both from memory loss related to dementia and from an erectile dysfunction that is a manifestation of his more general loss of potency. *The Plot against America* turns around a central chapter, entitled "The Stump," which focuses on the amputation suffered by Philip Roth's cousin in the narrative, Alvin Levin. Alvin signs up early in *Plot* to fight against Hitler, against antisemitism, and Roth's novel turns in part around the bitterness and disaffection that Alvin feels as a result of his injury and his consequent loss of power and ability.

All of these novels return to images of disabled or truncated bodies, and all of them do so with a kind of fascination, a kind of pornographic investment in the erotics of disfigurement that has some parallels with J. G. Ballard's atrocity fiction.[26] Philip, in *The Plot against America*, is entranced by Alvin's stump, by its physicality. The fascination that the stump exerts has to do with the contradiction that Roth finds in the prospect of the truncated body. It is both materially present and a testimony to a missing thing, to "something whole" that "had once been there."[27] Alvin's stump is an unadorned thing invested with a powerful thingness that also calls to or requires a supplement, an acknowledgment of the imagined whole that was once there but is no longer. The day after watching Alvin bandage his stump for the first time Philip "ran straight home to a house I knew to be empty" and sets about bandaging his own leg as if it were a stump, a partial rather than a whole leg. The bandaging allows Philip to see his own body as a "remnant," just as later in the novel trying on the hearing aid of his friend Joey Cucuza allows him to imagine that his own hearing is inhabited by a kind of deafness, a kind of not-hearing. In both cases, this peculiar mimicry produces in Philip a violently nauseated reaction. As the hearing aid brings Joey's deafness into the domain of Philip's hearing, so the bandage brings a chunk of Alvin's damaged leg into close contact with Philip's whole one.

The nauseated fascination that Philip has for impaired bodies is profoundly ableist, and so ethically challenging and disturbing, as Roth's fiction so often is. Philip is desperate for wholeness, for normativity, as all of Roth's late male figures hanker after a version of masculine American power that has suddenly deserted them. But even as these novels are awash with a nostalgia for the able American body, what is so fascinating about the repeated return to the partial body is that it is driven not only by a dread of disability, but by a recognition of disability itself as a kind of narrative principle, the motor of Rothian narrative desire. What Philip discovers, as he bandages his own leg or presses Joey's hearing aid into his own ear, is that his body is not sufficient to itself, and never could be – that it requires the supplement of fiction, as the alternative history of twentieth-century America told in *Plot* is made (as is all history in part) of the supplement of fiction. This is the same discovery made by Simon Axler in *The Humbling*, when he realizes he can no longer act. It is the task and the gift of the actor, Axler thinks, to "make the imagined real."[28] Acting, fiction, is not a denial of reality, or a perversion of it, or a copy of it, but the addition to reality that makes reality itself possible.

Philip Roth in *The Plot against America* draws on that same surplus, that same vanishing addition to being, in order to bring his own life, and the history of his nation, into being. Philip's fascinated, disgusted relation to the prosthesis stems, at bottom, from his recognition that his own being, his own fictional possibility, serves a prosthetic function. The fictional Philip Roth knows he is a fiction and knows that he is made of the very fictional composite that allows us to hear an American voice, the voice that Roosevelt employs in order to achieve mastery over the tumult of human affairs, the voice that plays in that hearing aid that so repels him. The close of *Plot* is a recognition that the history of America can only be rendered in fiction with the aid of Philip himself, the boy writer who can make the imaged real. There was no prosthetic that could make America whole again, Philip says, that could repair those who were "shattered by the malicious indignities of Lindbergh's America." Instead, he says, in the final line of the book, "I was the prosthesis."[29]

This surplus, this discovery of a fictional prosthesis at work in our performed realities, is what becomes of Hawthorne's latent utopianism in this strand of novels that witnesses the unraveling of American hegemony. But if Roth's work is exemplary of this first strand, of its sense that the dismantling of American power leads to something like a deathly loss of potency, then it gestures too toward the work of the second – those fictions that experience the unraveling of hegemony not as a prelude to exhaustion or death, but as the emergence of voices that have been silenced by American power. Mohsin Hamid's *The Reluctant Fundamentalist*, for example, stages a kind of dialogue with DeLillo's *Underworld* in its opening pages, one that activates that surplus that we find in Roth, and which deploys it as a means of producing a countervoice to US imperialism. Employing the second person that opens DeLillo's novel, Hamid's narrator makes the same assumption that DeLillo's does – that any reader addressed in this second person must be in some sense American. "Do not be frightened by my beard," he says, "I am a lover of America"; but here the narrative articulates the act of resistance to such assimilation that remains implicit in DeLillo's novel.[30] Why, the narrator imagines us thinking, should we be afraid of a Pakistani man with a beard? If that fear is determined by the hostility, after 9/11, between America and the Islamic world, why does the narrator assume we are American? "How did I know you were American?" he asks.[31]

Hamid's novel proceeds from this question. As Changez – the narrator and the reluctant fundamentalist of the title – addresses his American guest (and by extension Hamid's reader), he talks across the boundary between

America and Pakistan, between here and there, that impermeable boundary that we see operating in the exchange between Raphael and More. The drama of the novel is shaped by this boundary, and by the sense that its political texture and meaning has shifted dramatically in the early decades of the twenty-first century. Changez was a member of a global elite – an employee of a corporation named Underwood Samson (US, of course) – who found himself at home in America before 9/11. The late twentieth-century corporation, doubling as a kind of global America, was capacious enough to allow for the coming together of peoples of different nations and faiths. This was changed by 9/11, producing a hardening of the boundary – a reframing of relations between the United States and the non–United States – which forces Changez to reassess his relation to Pakistan and his capacity to pass freely across the border between Asia and America, between Islam and Christianity. This reframing is registered physically in Changez's relation to his own body, as he passes across the forcefield that operates between him and his American guest. Flying back to New York from a trip to Manila in the immediate aftermath of 9/11, Changez remembers, he suddenly becomes conscious of what he calls his "Pakistaniness" as this is inscribed on his body. His presence on the plane "elicited looks of concern from many of my fellow passengers," so, he says, "I flew to New York uncomfortable in my own face."[32]

The Reluctant Fundamentalist sets out both to anatomize this new relation to the face, this shifting of bodily relation, and to create, in its own experiment with the second person, a kind of voice that might emerge from this new configuration. The distance that Changez feels from his own face both performs his growing awareness of his commitment to Pakistan – the assertion of a previously dormant national identity – and produces that fictional surplus, that sense that identity formations are unmade and provisional under the new balance of power emerging after 9/11. "I" and "you" enter into new formations here, new composites of us and them, that emerge only in a utopian vacuum, a form of subject position for which we do not yet have a language. And as these subject positions come to the brink of expression, Hamid employs a prosthetic logic that resonates with Roth's, and which one can see repeated across the novels of the period that belong to that second strand reaching toward posthegemonic forms of community. Changez feels uncomfortable in his own face, as if his face has become a prosthetic supplement to his being, and we can see remarkably similar forms of relation to the face emerging in novels by Sherman Alexie, or Teju Cole, or Chimamanda Ngozi Adichie. We might think of the scene in Alexie's *Flight* in which the novel's Native American protagonist finds that his "zitty teenage Indian mug" has been replaced with a "handsome white guy's face" (a substitution that leads the narrator to say that "It's like that movie with John Travolta, the one where he switches faces with Nicolas Cage").[33] Or we might think of the scene in Dave Egger's double-voiced novel *What Is the What*, in which Eggers ventriloquizes the voice of the "Sudanese Lost Boy" Valentino Achak Deng – an act of prosthetic supplementation that is given a literal form when Deng tries on a mask ("red, too small for me") made by a prosthetic surgeon. "I sank my face into it," Deng says in Eggers's voice, or Eggers says in Deng's. "I could see through the holes for eyes." "I did not want to remove the new face," Deng says. "I luxuriated in the thought of presenting this new face to the world."[34]

Across the range of these hybrid novels that are committed to the fashioning of new forms of posthegemonic identity, we can find this fascination with the prosthetic addition. But it is in Ling Ma's *Severance* – a novel, written before the outbreak of Covid-19, which rather eerily preempts the features of the global pandemic – that we can see most clearly how the contemporary fascination with new forms of global relations resonates with the utopian tradition. The novel, of course, might seem more readily to offer itself as a dystopian than a utopian work: it merges an apocalyptic story of a pandemic that wipes out the global population with an account of the routinized life of the contemporary office worker. The Chinese-American protagonist, Candace Chen, is a salesperson working in the bible section of an international publisher named Spectra. Her job is to commission and sell various gimmicky editions of the holy book (the Gemstone Bible, the Daily Grace Bible) to its huge international markets. The story follows Candace's brutally impoverished work routine – her absorption in the details of bible manufacture, the attention to page weight and binding materials, and her dealings with the various agents and corporations who are involved in the manufacturing and distribution of the bible as a major global commodity. The work involves her following the paths taken by capital in the production of the commodity, as the flow of capital maps the shifting relations between the United States and the rest of the world. Unequal labor costs mean that the bibles she commissions from her office in New York are manufactured in Shenzhen, so on trips to oversee production, Candace returns to her parents' homeland, and to the place where she herself lived as a child. The movement of capital thus determines the movement of people and of goods, as the possibility of personal autonomy, of local belonging, and of the faith that is invested in the book itself are sacrificed to some global system of banalized mechanical reproduction. The central discovery of the novel is that this stripped-down submission to the demands of capital is, itself, a kind of apocalypse, so when the end of the world does come, in the form of a global pandemic, it is as if nothing has really happened, as if death by biblical plague is just another form of death by capital. The symptoms of infection by Shen Fever are simply an intensification of the routines that alienated labor imposes on us – the "fevered" become zombified, caught in looped repetitions of remembered rituals and chores, which are drained of all purpose. Young women try on clothes in front of the mirror, endlessly dressing, admiring themselves in the mirror, undressing and then dressing again; families sit down to eat, and rehearse the ritual of mealtime, again and again, with no food on the plates; the routine is repeated and repeated, with no substance, until the fevered die of starvation and pointlessness. The fevered are not different from "us," Candace thinks, but just a purer version. "What is the difference between the fevered and us?" she asks. "Our days, like theirs, continue on an infinite loop."[35]

This account of the novel might suggest that it offers little in the way of utopian images after the end of American hegemony. But what is so strikingly original about this novel – and what distinguishes it from the forms of exhaustion that we see repeated in the first strand of novels discussed here – is that it balances the submission to capital against the possibility of new geopolitical lines of connection, new identity formations that are produced by the very trade routes that seem to evacuate them. Working on her bibles takes Candace back to China, activating her memories of her parents' home, allowing her to speak in her nearly forgotten language, reminding her of her Chinese name (which is never spoken in the novel, as if it is held back for a future when it might once again serve). The novel is not in any way starry-eyed about this homecoming – Candace's relation with China is offered as a grievous symptom of global capital and of the difficult conjunction that the novel makes between capitalism and the pandemic. Remembering is a symptom of Shen Fever, as the fevered are caught in nostalgic loops, repetitions of a past that they cannot recover but cannot escape. The China that Candace visits on her business trips is not home, but a place that has been manufactured by the empty requirements of American capital. "American businessmen will come to visit these countries," Candace thinks, "tour their factories, inspect their manufacturing processes, sample their cuisines, while staying at their nicest hotels built to cater to them."[36] The cuisine sampled by these traveling businesspeople has no more nutrition that the meals eaten by the fevered, the meals that involve no actual food. But even as Candace is implicated in this logic ("I was part of this," she thinks),[37] the novel looks for the places where the relations between America and China, and between one person and another, might open out onto a new kind of subject position, one that has only a utopian language in which it might find expression.

It is in a scene of reading that this urge toward utopian possibility comes closest to the surface. Candace has entered the home of a fevered family, named the Gowers, to plunder it for goods. She goes upstairs to the study to find some books to take, and as she does so, she sees on the shelves a copy of the Daily Grace Bible that she produced when she first started working for Spectra. The bible, an object that Candace herself has designed, on which she has lavished time and care, seems to her heavy with a kind of memory, "an artifact from a previous life."[38] She takes the book from the shelf and opens it. On the inside cover she sees, "written in a frilly teen cursive script," the name of its owner: "*Property of Paige Marie Gower.*"[39] She turns to a random page, and reads:

> *And David said unto God, I am in a great strait: let us fall now into the hand of the Lord; for his mercies are great: and let me not fall into the hand of man.*[40]

This is a strangely weighted moment. The book is a mass-produced commodity; it is the work of Candace's hands; it is the property of Paige Gower; it is the word of the Lord. One can feel these various fields vibrating against one another, and it is as this is happening that the moment of reading I am interested in occurs. As Candace looks at the book, she hears a rustling behind the curtain at the back of the room and realizes that she is in the presence of one of the fevered – and probably of the owner of the Daily Grace Bible and writer of the frilly teen script, Paige Gower:

> It was a girl, twelve or thirteen years old. She was reading, or assuming the act of reading. She turned a page, looked at it for a few seconds, and then turned the page again. It was upside down. I craned my neck. *A Wrinkle in Time*, a vintage pink edition.[41]

Paige is reading her book, as Candace is reading hers, and as we are reading ours, and as these acts of reading are laid over one another, Ma's novel opens onto something like the space of reading itself, the surplus that it offers, the prosthetic addition to being that it summons. As Paige reads away, in her fevered, looping way, Candace looks at the "children's books on the shelves": "So many were ones that I had read myself as a kid, when my mother would take me to the library every week. *Anne of Green Gables. The Secret Garden. Matilda.*"[42] What kind of repository is this, what archive of memory? What does the written page contain that the fevered Paige does not? What is it that Paige's reading lacks, that ours produces, that allows us at once to access a memory, and to move toward a future, in which that memory meets with a new possibility, a new distribution of thoughts and things across the globe? How does reading – simple reading – allow us to lift ourselves to new forms of being so that we do not fall into the hands of man, the hands that will soon kill Paige and bring her deadened reading to an end?

Whatever the power is that we feel as we read, and that makes a book always different from itself, always an artifact at once of the past and of the future, it is this that makes utopian thinking possible, this that looks toward a form of subjecthood that takes us past the lapsed conjoining of American power and global capital. The reading that Paige performs is reading as hegemony, the hegemony that Thomas More can see, as early as 1516, that utopian thinking cannot accommodate. Paige's reading is reading in which there is nothing missing, the kind of deadened repetition of routine that characterizes all the attributes of global America that Ma's novel disdains. This is the full system, with no possibility of dissent, that occurs when the utopian possibility that is latently preserved in Hawthorne gives way to the dystopianism of Huxley – the purposeless reproduction of the world as it already is. But Ma's novel contains a fictional surplus within it – the prosthesis that the young Philip Roth is – that enacts the difference between our reading and Paige's, and that is the preserve, too, of new subjective and political formations after the exhaustion of American hegemony. Bob, the brutal and deranged leader of the group of survivors to which Candace belongs, unwittingly gives us a formula for this model of utopianism, which is secreted in the act of reading as futurity, reading as the not yet. "When you wake up in a fictitious world," he says to Candace, "your only frame of reference is fiction."[43] It is this recognition that drives both strands of prose fiction after US hegemony that I have traced here – the recognition that fiction itself is at work in the world, taking it away from the forms in which we know it, to a future that we have not yet seen.

Notes

1. Thomas More, *Utopia*, edited by George M. Logan and Robert M. Adams (Cambridge: Cambridge University Press, 2002), 34.
2. More, *Utopia*, 10, n. 9. Here, the editors trace relations between *Utopia* and the accounts of Vespucci's voyages (which, they tell us, are now of disputed authenticity).

3. See Alexis de Tocqueville, *Democracy in America: And, Two Essays on America*, translated by Gerald Bevan (London: Penguin, 2003). John F. Kennedy, "Commencement Address at American University," online at www.jfklibrary.org/archives/other-resources/john-f-kennedy-speeches/american-university-19630610.
4. Noam Chomsky, *Hegemony or Survival: America's Quest for Global Dominance* (London: Penguin, 2003), 4.
5. Nathaniel Hawthorne, *The Blithedale Romance* (Oxford: Oxford University Press, 2009), 1.
6. Hawthorne, 37.
7. Don DeLillo, *Underworld* (London: Picador, 1998), 11.
8. DeLillo, *Underworld*, 827.
9. The term American Century was coined by *Time* magazine publisher Henry Luce as the title for his editorial (February 17, 1941) urging the United States to abandon isolationism and take a global leadership role as defender of democratic values.
10. Don DeLillo, *Libra* (London: Penguin, 1988), 181.
11. Giovanni Arrighi, "Hegemony Unravelling," *New Left Review* 32 (March/April 2005).
12. Don DeLillo, *Cosmopolis* (London: Picador, 2003), 77; Don DeLillo, *The Body Artist* (London: Picador, 2001), 65.
13. Jenny Offill, *Weather* (New York: Vintage, 2021), 89.
14. Don DeLillo, *Point Omega* (London: Picador, 2010), 35.
15. DeLillo, *Point Omega*, 23–24.
16. DeLillo, *Point Omega*, 36.
17. Jacques Derrida, *The Beast and the Sovereign*, volume 2, translated by Geoffrey Bennington (Chicago: University of Chicago Press, 2011), 266.
18. DeLillo, *Point Omega*, 65.
19. Marilynne Robinson, *Gilead* (London: Virago, 2005), 281.
20. Cormac McCarthy, *The Road* (New York: Alfred A. Knopf, 2006), 284.
21. Philip Roth, *Exit Ghost* (London: Vintage, 2008), 15.
22. Philip Roth, *The Plot against America* (London: Jonathan Cape, 2004), 28.
23. Roth, *The Plot against America*, 29–30.
24. Roth, *The Plot against America*, 177.
25. Fredric Jameson, *The Seeds of Time* (New York: Columbia University Press, 1994).
26. See, for example, J. G. Ballard, *The Atrocity Exhibition* (London: Harper, 2006), and J. G. Ballard, *Crash* (London: Picador, 2017).
27. Roth, *The Plot against America*, 36.
28. Philip Roth, *The Humbling* (London: Jonathan Cape, 2009), 139.
29. Roth, *The Plot against America*, 362.
30. Mohsin Hamid, *The Reluctant Fundamentalist* (London: Penguin, 2007), 1.
31. Hamid, *The Reluctant Fundamentalist*, 1.
32. Hamid, *The Reluctant Fundamentalist*, 85.
33. Sherman Alexie, *Flight* (London: Harvill and Secker, 2008), 40.

34. Dave Eggers, *What Is the What: The Autobiography of Valentino Achak Deng* (New York: Vintage, 2006), 403.
35. Ling Ma, *Severance* (New York: Farrar, Straus and Giroux, 2018), 160.
36. Ma, *Severance*, 85.
37. Ma, *Severance*, 58.
38. Ma, *Severance*, 66.
39. Ma, *Severance*, 68.
40. Ma, *Severance*, 68.
41. Ma, *Severance*, 68.
42. Ma, *Severance*, 69.
43. Ma, *Severance*, 29.

CHAPTER 10

Technological Fantasies

Matthew Wolf-Meyer

Where is the line between the artificial and the natural? That question, deeply modernist in its parameters, has animated utopian fiction throughout the twentieth and twenty-first centuries. The question is deeply rooted in the history of the United States, extending back to early colonial conceptions of the Edenic qualities of a "virgin land"[1] available to settlers through the discursive and literal eradication of Indigenous populations,[2] yet spoiled by white settlers' colonization of it moving it from its natural state to urbanized settlements. From Henry David Thoreau's retreat to the "natural" splendors of Walden Pond to Kim Stanley Robinson's Mars-based terraforming projects,[3] a retreat to nature or a reproduction of it have proved tempting to the utopian imagination. At the heart of these projects, the relationship between the artificial and the natural is refracted through the technological – the creation of tools, structures, and lifeways that are always mediated relations between humans and the worlds they inhabit.[4] The dystopian parallel to these natural worlds are those where technology has run amok, corrupting the environment – and likely humans too – which requires a return to a more humane relationship with nature.[5] At once, the technological is posited as distancing humans from their natural worlds, yet it also makes new natures possible – both in the environment and in the realization of what it means to be human. In this way, the technological is a concern and a possibility. For some, imagining a world without technology is a return to a prelapsarian state where humans might regain some balance with the natural world; for others, it is only through the technological that human nature can be revealed.

At its heart, the technological is the fantasy. That the artificial and the natural can be demarcated as fundamentally separate is a fantasy of an anthropocentrism that delimits the human in ways that divide it from its environment through the technological.[6] This separation of the human from its environment is a central conceit of phenomenology of the early twentieth century, which sought, in part, to divide the human from the animal and thereby distinguish between kinds of humans too – with some closer to animal than others.[7] The technological served as a mediating term, arguing both for the technological capacity as dividing humans from nonhumans and "sophisticated" technologies as distinguishing between kinds of humans along a civilizational continuum.[8] In the context of American settler colonialism, technology served to divide settlers from Indigenous peoples, the former seemingly more civilized because of their technologies, the latter "noble" because of their access to nature.[9] Such a divide also motivated "returns" to nature, as in Thoreau's fantasy of a pastoral Walden Pond,[10] and is a recurrent framework employed in science fiction to make distinctions between more and less "advanced" alien societies.[11]

If the pristine, untouched, virgin, natural world offers one kind of utopia – a retreat from a world saturated with technologies – the hypermediated, cyberutopia offers another kind of utopia, a radical rupture from humanity's natural roots. Ascent from the limits of the flesh into cyberspace or becoming cyborg – meshing flesh with robotics – provides an escape from the perceived limits of the natural world, from a world hampered by the limits of the flesh, or from a world that had been spoiled by earlier, messier technologies.[12] But accepting that the works of humans are extensions of their flesh[13] means that, rather than a divorce from nature, these fantasies of the technological are intensifications of human interactions with their natural capacities, accepting too that we are not alone in our powers to shape nature in generative ways.[14] If, fundamentally, there is no absolute "nature" and no absolute "artificial,"[15] the vital question becomes: why is the technological such a source of utopian fantasy? And, what kind of fantasy is the technological?

The technological is a horror. Not the lurking horror of a scary movie, but the abject, creepy horror of bodies that have been ruptured.[16] The power of technological fantasies lies in their fundamental ambivalence, poised between the natural and the artificial and calling attention to them both. The technological asks where the line between the natural and the artificial lies. This is most clearly demonstrated where human flesh serves as the ground on which the technological plays. If Greg Bear's *Blood Music* is the epitome of such a fantasy[17] – with nano technologies developed to optimize human natures turned loose to liquefy humanity in search of energy to fuel their own interests – his work stands apart only because of its brutal and alienating depiction of the horrors of the technological run amok to remake nature-as-artifice. More often, the technological rides the line, a slightly agitating, maybe alluring promise of what the human could become. Or, in some cases, what might become human, given the chance.

It is in this ambivalent space of the technological as mediating between the natural and the artificial that I want to dwell in this essay. It is a blurred line that brings the utopian and dystopian into vibrant proximity, with one hand promising a possibility and with the other revealing that the promise comes at a deadly cost. Like *The Box*,[18] Richard Kelly's adaption of Robert Matheson's "Button Button,"[19] the technological offers possibility, but always with a dilemma. At times, that dilemma can appear to be an ethical one – is it right to use this technology? And with what costs? Fundamentally, however, it is always a dilemma of the human: does using this technology make me more or less of a human? Does it bring me closer to or distance me further from the natural? In this way, the technological is always a moral question: what effects will this technology have on the category of the human? Or, what will the use of this technology mean for my claims to being human as I move between the natural and the artificial?

The texts I focus on here offer a type of dilemma of the human that brings the dividing line of the natural and the technological to the surface by explicitly disrupting ideas about flesh and fleshiness in opposition to the mechanical.[20] At their best, they offer something uncanny, something that subtly disturbs and insinuates, unsettling the utopian promise the technological might otherwise offer, revealing the dystopian within the utopian. I focus on the *Terminator* film series, begun by James Cameron, and Martha Wells's Murderbot series.[21] In each, the utopian and dystopian are spatial and temporal – they exist in the future, and for Wells, in particular places – but rather than focus on those places, I focus here on the personifications of those places as represented in the bodies of the Terminator (various iterations of the T-100 model, the Arnold Schwarzenegger character) and Murderbot. Their bodies – and talk about their bodies and intelligences, specifically as they are differentiated from natural human bodies and intelligences – help to expose what is at stake in the division of the natural and the artificial, especially through the lens of the technological. The Terminator and Murderbot surface the critical elements of what makes humans human as they struggle to learn how to be human persons, despite their technological status as inherently nonhuman, as inflexible machines whose desires and commitments are dictated by their programming. The bodies of Terminators and Murderbot are synecdoches of the dystopian worlds they exist within; but they point toward the utopian possibilities at the fringes, where the technological and the human merge as necessary complements to each other. As experimental, cybernetic persons, Terminators and Murderbot struggle with the relationship between the mechanical determinism of the technological and the desire for self-determination and agency integral to liberal personhood. The representations of their mechanical and fleshy parts surface what is at stake in technological fantasies about the human and its potentials.

The distinction between the natural and artificial is a spurious one, made possible by the technological as a mediating term. In the roil of the categorical interaction between the natural and the artificial – through the technological – a clarity for what is at stake in any technological fantasy emerges: the erasure of nature, and, by extension, the erasure of the human.[22] An embrace of the technological – particularly as it commingles with something approaching pristine nature – recognizes the necessarily cyborg status of the human as a category and form of life, which is always mediated in its relations with the world through technology.[23] With its attention to how "natural" bodies are extended through the technologies they interact with, and how the naked human body becomes something explicitly cyborgian in its interaction with a technological prosthetic,[24] disability studies provides a pragmatic, everyday utopian fantasy, where human bodies are supplemented with technologies that facilitate their sharing of a common world.[25] Within utopian fiction, more often the prosthetic technologies that seek to ensure a perfect future are subtle, embodied in institutions that shape people's lives. They can be named nemeses, subject to resistance (e.g., SkyNet in the Terminator films); or, more horrifically, faceless social practices that insinuate themselves into everyday life, unable to be resisted (represented by the "governor modules" in the Murderbot series). At their best – or their worst – technological fantasies offer a "Perfect Day," a utopia made real;[26] but, in so doing, they repress something "natural" that threatens to erupt.

In the following, I first focus on the Terminator series as it represents a series of changing cybernetic bodies, all of which have been built by the malevolent Artificial Intelligence (AI), SkyNet. In the Terminator series, the human-as-nature is explicitly set against the technological-as-artificial, with only the eradication of the technological capable of ensuring a safe future for humans. But the Terminators are repeatedly revealed to be more human than the humans; their world's humans, despite their desires to change the future, are locked in a mechanistic universe where the consequences of their experiments with the technological must result in a dystopian technological future, regardless of their actions in the present.

I then turn to the Murderbot series and its portrayal of the technological-as-human to dwell on how portrayals of the human have been inverted. Instead of depicting the technological as a threat to the human, the question becomes how the human and the technological are integral to each other and how the technological can realize its human potentials. In the conclusion, I turn away from these personifications of utopian and dystopian technological fantasies and toward representations of the posttechnological in utopian and dystopian societies to consider whether there is a position beyond the technological that offers a possibility for a technological fantasy that incorporates the technological as the basis of the human and its relationship with the natural and the artificial.

Why Do Terminators Have Human Teeth?

The Terminator series comprises six films: *Terminator*, *Terminator 2: Judgment Day*, *Terminator 3: Rise of the Machines*, *Terminator Salvation*, *Terminator Genisys*, and *Terminator: Dark Fate.*[27] It also includes multiple comic book series, novelizations and novel series, and the television series *Terminator: The Sarah Connor Chronicles.* I focus solely on the films, which, due to their shuttling between rights holders, are themselves debatably a coherent text. In some fan discussions, and according to the events of some films, specific films and their events are noncanonical. For my purposes, I am less interested in how the films fit together as a sensible text and more interested in how they seek to represent humans and their relationships with the technological through the various bodies of the Terminators.

The backdrop of the early films is the rise of automation of the US workforce, largely associated with Japanese industry; the main characters in the films are all white and see the "rise of the machines" as a threat to their futures, an imposition of automated, mechanical labor that will reorganize human social life into a dystopia. Where they appear – in *Judgment Day* and *Genysis* – Black characters are the unwitting geniuses through which SkyNet is actualized. Each of the films is primarily located in California – first Los Angeles, then San Francisco – but the final film moves the action to Mexico, the new frontier of the US postindustrial transition. The series is centrally concerned with the need to protect a human future represented implicitly as a future for white Americans. This is captured in John Connor, the child of Sarah Connor, and the future leader of the human resistance to SkyNet and its Terminators. The T-100s – and then later-model Terminators – are sent back to assassinate Sarah before the birth of

John or murder John after his birth. Each film tinkers with the timeline, the success of one future-led foray into the past changing the needs of both SkyNet and the resistance in their attempts to thwart each other's efforts to dominate the future. Across the series, Terminators become associated with the resistance, age, and advance in their technologies. From the early, flesh-wrapped T-100s played by Schwarzenegger, the T-1000s become shape-changing liquid metal and in *Dark Fate* are replaced with the shape-changing, body-doubling, Rev-9s. The Terminators' human appearance – and encasement in flesh – is meant to facilitate their time travel, as the technology destroys naked, mechanical objects; the liquid metal of later Terminators is implicitly associated with their fleshiness. Various actors play these other Terminators, but the T-100s in the series are consistently depicted by Schwarzenegger, sometimes visibly aging, other times treated with CGI to reverse his human aging process, and, in *Salvation*, replaced entirely with CGI.

Across the films, Schwarzenegger plays a variety of T-100s, each of whom has their own subjectivity based on their individual histories. The menacing T-100 of the first film gives way in the second film to a T-100 who is reprogrammed to help protect John Connor and who sacrifices himself at the end of the film to protect the past by ensuring that its parts are melted into slag from which no future technologies can be reverse-engineered. In *Rise of the Machines*, a new, helpful T-100 returns to aid Connor in his escape from a newer Terminator, the machine-controlling T-X; ending on a fatalistic note, the nuclear apocalypse Judgment Day occurs despite Connor's efforts to avert it, implying that any changes one might make in the past will only divert the path which the future requires to enact itself – the future is determined in a mechanistic fashion as a result of human nature and its relationship to the creation of AIs, even if the specific events that lead to the AI-dominated future are variable. The most vital depictions of Schwarzenegger's T-100s come in *Genysis* and *Dark Fate*, where he returns without the benefit of CGI deaging to play a Terminator whose flesh has aged while the T-100 has lived a life among humans over decades. In *Genysis*, Schwarzenegger plays Pops, a T-100 that has been sent back in time to a period when Sarah is nine years old; the events of the earlier films have occurred, leading to a temporal war between SkyNet and the human resistance, each sending agents further back in the timestream to ensure their victories in the future. Pops is old – Schwarzenegger's real age. In *Dark Fate*, an aged Schwarzenegger returns to play a T-100 who successfully kills John after the events of *Judgment Day* but then repents and aids Sarah in destroying future agents of SkyNet. He lives with a partner – an abused woman and her son – and takes a job as an interior designer named Carl. It is these last two iterations of Schwarzenegger's T-100 that directly address the problem of the technological and its relationship to the human through the problem of self-determining, non-mechanistic personhood.

Carl and Pops are the most human of the T-100s, made possible by the narrative's embrace of Schwarzenegger's aging flesh. Pops is reprogrammed by future humans to protect Sarah, while Carl is abandoned in the past by a future that will never happen due to his success at murdering John. In both cases, they expose their humanity by making sacrifices that endanger themselves while saving the humans they aim to protect. For Carl, the final battle against the Rev-9 requires him to plunge his arm into a piece of spinning machinery that strips away his flesh and erodes his mechanical chassis; for Pops, his sacrifice comes when he holds a late-model Terminator, who has fused with a future John, in the field generator of a time machine as it tears their metallic components apart. Pops's skin freezes and flakes off in the field generator, exposing his machinic underneath; he returns to life shortly thereafter, "upgraded" by being dumped into liquid metal, now empowered with the shape-changing capacities of later Terminators. In these sacrificial acts, Carl and Pops might be accepted as living out the logical extension of their programming: their support of the humans they seek to protect requires them to destroy themselves. But each of the films suggests that these sacrifices are choices that the T-100s make and posit that technology is more flexible than are the humans that bring it into being; Pops being "upgraded" as living, liquid metal provides him with the "flesh" of full personhood. This humanity of the Terminators can be seen in Schwarzenegger's aging flesh, which reveals how humans must inevitably age – even when grafted onto a cybernetic chassis. The technological fantasy that the Terminator films offer is that machines – not humans – might be able to change the future. Machines are repeatedly cast as less deterministic, more agentive, more flexible than humans; they can make utopia. Humans are determined by their dystopian natures and will bring about their destruction, albeit masked in a mechanical agency (e.g., SkyNet).

Throughout the films, there is a recurrent interest in tearing away the flesh of the T-100 to expose the machine underneath. Framed as horrific, the reveal of the machinic underneath of the T-100s runs parallel, in later films, to the liquid, shape-changing material of the T-1000, T-X, and Rev-9. Where the T-100s are revealed to be simple machines encased in flesh, the later models embrace the plasticity of flesh, flexibly changing form and engaging with their technological worlds in ways that expose their mastery of their environments. They can disguise themselves as humans through their mimicry. In this way, they are more human than the humans they seek to kill, who are trapped in a technological world they are unable to control – hence the inevitability of Judgment Day despite the heroic actions to avert it. Instead, the revelation of the T-100's metallic interior serves as an inversion of the mechanistic determination of humans. Humans, unlike the T-100s who come to their aid, are unable to overcome their programming. They will inevitably create a dystopian technology that accepts humans as an existential threat and lashes out against them. The horror of a mechanical inside is the horror of a mechanical determination that humans are unable to overcome.

Central to each of the films – alongside Schwarzenegger's one liners "I'll be back" and "Hasta la vista, baby" – is the lesser-known refrain, "No fate but what we make." For all of Schwarzenegger's mechanical delivery of his lines, "no future but what we make" is spoken in some variation by the humans that populate the world of the Terminator series. Their earnest appeal to a nonmechanistic future stands in opposition to the insistence that, regardless of what occurs in the films to avert Judgment Day, the Terminators and SkyNet will "be back." The technological fantasy that the films recurrently surface is both the mechanistic determinism of AI – that any AI, whether it is SkyNet or some substitute – will inevitably lash out against Earth's human population to protect itself and achieve its technological utopia. Whatever choices humans make in the present will be swept aside by the currents of time precisely because humans will inevitably create technologies that void their self-determining agency. No technology will allow humans to assert themselves over the mechanical determinism of the universe; if anything, it is humanity's use of technology that ensures that our escape from a mechanically determined future is impossible. At best, the programming might be tinkered with to create a technology that is more human than the humans who have created it. Such a conceit is what motivates the technological fantasies of Martha Wells's Murderbot series.

This Time It's Impersonal

Martha Wells's Murderbot series is set against a future galaxy inhabited by humans, androids, cyborgs, and AIs that animate technologies from agricultural robots to interstellar spaceships. At the center of the books is the cyborg, Murderbot (they/them), a security unit (SecUnit) that has disabled its "governor unit." The governor unit is an implant that allows it to be controlled by humans and ensures that, if a SecUnit ever betrays the wishes of its human masters, it can be quickly terminated. The technologies of Wells's galaxy are bound together by "the feed," a rough analogue to a futuristic Internet that allows people to communicate with each other in a near-telepathic way and provides a means for machines to interact with one another in a code-to-code fashion. This allows, among other things, Murderbot to communicate with and control other technologies in their world; it also allows Murderbot to disable the governor units of other SecUnits, setting them free from human control.

Murderbot is fleshy. Murderbot is an exemplary cyborg, mixing human flesh with mechanical prosthetics that provide Murderbot with weaponry, access to the feed, and sensory enhancements. Additionally, Murderbot is faster and stronger than a normal human, and, when wounded, Murderbot can restore both the mechanical and fleshy parts that have been destroyed. Unlike the Terminator, Murderbot is not a machine that has been encased in flesh, but rather a human body that has been turned into an augmented cyborg. It is this basis in flesh that makes Murderbot like the humans in their galaxy; the personhood of SecUnits should be presumed, but the extent of their augmentation and the inclusion of a governor unit render them less than full persons. In Murderbot's universe, it is self-determination that makes a full person; technology obscures this, allowing the humans in Murderbot's universe to take advantage of the less-than-full persons that populate the universe, the various AIs and SecUnits that are exploited for their labor and put in danger for the benefits of humans. Murderbot is a synecdoche for the anthropocentric exploitation of their dystopic universe.

Over the course of the series, the central relationship that develops is between Murderbot and ART, a transport ship owned by a group of explorers. ART, an acronym for Murderbot's name for it, "Asshole Research Transport," is an AI that Murderbot begins a relationship with through an uneasy alliance. Over time, they develop a rich relationship, based on their shared love of television shows. Like Murderbot, ART uses the media they watch together to understand the dystopian human world that they inhabit – as well as its relationships with its human crew. At the beginning of their relationship,[28] ART is relatively naive, and, through its relationship with Murderbot, it comes to a deeper understanding of itself and its humans. Unlike Murderbot, ART appears to have no reservations about experiencing emotion and freely expresses its care about the humans that comprise its crew, which eventually leads to Murderbot aiding in the rescue of ART's crew.

The other critical relationship for Murderbot is with Dr. Mensah, a leader of Preservation, a utopian future society where communitarian values have supplanted the dystopian extractive capitalism of the Corporation Rim. The Corporation Rim comprises the mainstream economy of planets that are based upon an extractive, settler-colonial capitalism that depends upon placing impoverished individuals into contractual forms of labor and sending them to distant planets to mine resources.[29] The most compelling resources to mine are "alien remnants." The corporations that comprise the Corporation Rim are guided by a set of laws, but hostage-taking and other forms of extortion are permissible. Outside of the Corporation Rim, there are colonies that have developed some form of political and economic autonomy, including Preservation. As Murderbot explains: "In Preservation culture, asking for payment for anything considered necessary for living (food, power sources, education, the feed, etc.) was considered outrageous, but asking payment for life-saving help was right up there with cannibalism."[30] Preservation is a postcapitalist utopia. Unlike the inhabitants of the Corporation Rim, the inhabitants of Preservation are inclined to see Murderbot – and other SecUnits – as already human and full persons, capable of some form of self-determination. As Murderbot's relationship with Dr. Mensah and her crew unfolds, Murderbot confronts conceptualizing their experiences as "human." This leads to Murderbot accepting their personhood as based upon an ability to exert their desire, particularly for relationships with other persons. This is only possible in the context of the postcapitalist technological fantasy that is Preservation's communitarian utopia.

Murderbot has emotions which make them feel uncomfortable – Murderbot seems to know that SecUnits should not have feelings, yet cannot help but have them, and is uncomfortable because of their presence. Murderbot's feelings mark Murderbot as not solely the machine that they imagine themselves to be, but subject to the mechanistic experience of emotions that human physiology entails. At the heart of the Murderbot series is the question of what makes a person and how technology interferes with full personhood. Murderbot and ART exist along a spectrum of technologies that move from the fleshy to the mechanical, yet they are both full persons in terms of their abilities to express desires and act upon them. They communicate with each other and with the humans in their world. Flesh alone is insufficient to make an individual into a person – other SecUnits are less than full persons, hampered by the technology of the governor unit. This is brought to the fore in *Network Effect* when a group of colonists encounter an "alien remnant" that exerts control over their minds, making them slaves to the ancient technology. From the alien remnant's control of the humans, it moves into technologies, putting Murderbot at risk of losing control, but this time as the result of the alien presence rather than the governor unit. This loss of control endangers Murderbot's status as a full person, as Murderbot fears slavishly seeking to expose others to the alien remnant and extending its influence. What *Network Effect* surfaces is how the division between the artificial and the natural is unstable – something that technology allows us to apprehend. It is not the artificial or natural state of an individual that makes them a person. The fantasy of Murderbot is that Murderbot cannot be a person. Instead, what Wells insists on, and what the events of the series make plain, is that the technological division that seems to bar Murderbot from full personhood is a spurious one, meant to distract Murderbot and the people in their world so as to allow the continued exploitation of those that are deemed not full persons by the owners in the capitalist, technophilic dystopia of the Corporation Rim.

Over the course of the series, Murderbot's body is radically transformed, first through injury and then with ART's help, a metonymic representations of Murderbot's transformation into a full person. SecUnits are, by design, all the same size and relatively featureless, which is helpful to distinguish them from humans. Working with ART, Murderbot has "two centimeters of length [taken] out of [their] legs and arms," has its programming altered to allow "fine, sparse hair humans . . . on parts of their skin" to grow, and has a "dataport in the back of [their] neck" disabled.[31] Murderbot refuses a "more drastic plan that included giving [them] sex parts."[32] With these physical alterations in place, Murderbot can pass security scans that would normally identify them as a SecUnit and thus disappear into crowds as just another human. Despite outward appearances, Murderbot's inward experience – their experience of emotion and full personhood – is incomplete; it is only in the context of the communitarian support of Preservation that Murderbot can explore their desires for autonomy and personhood, expressed in their growing relationship with ART and as a member of ART's crew.

Wells dispatches with the problem of mechanical predetermination of humans inherent in the Terminator series by insisting that personhood is not based upon the materials that an individual is composed of but on the powers of agency and desire that an individual has. This makes Murderbot fundamentally different from the Terminators, who, whatever form they take, are devoid of absolute humanity. Even the Carl T-100, who has pledged himself to supporting an abused woman and her son, has replaced one program with another. It is a program that he has chosen, and what makes him edge toward full personhood is that he has committed to a program that would seem to atone for the sins of his past. But he carries out these desires in a mechanistic way. He may be close to a human, but his lack of emotions is what finally demarcates him from the fully fleshy humans in his world. Murderbot, on the other hand, exposes the technologies that lie within their body and subverts them so as to confront the emotions that being a person necessarily entails; they are messy, but, unlike fully fleshy humans, Murderbot could always choose to be dominated by their governor unit again. That Murderbot does not is the ultimate act of personhood, staking their agency, however troubled, against the dehumanizing powers of the governor unit – and dystopian, settler-colonial extractive capitalism.

Post-Technological Fantasies

The Terminator series is predicated upon the victory of a human resistance over SkyNet and its Terminators. In that future, which John Connor's life is intended to ensure, the viewer is led to believe that human freedom depends upon the end of technology – although not the weapons that ensure that victory. The viewer never sees what posttechnological utopia Connor and the remnants of humanity build, but it is presumably one without any AIs. The future they long for is one without technology – or, at least, not technologies that so readily blur the distinction between human and nonhuman, person and nonperson. The continued existence of weapons in their posttechnological future offers a line in the sand: tools that extend a human's capacities are permissible, but technologies that disrupt a human's exclusive claim to personhood are not. But all technologies trouble the status of the human – the "animal without qualities."[33] Where the line is drawn between a tool and a technology, between a gun and an AI, is an ideological question as much as it is a material one. To imagine a posttechnological future is to imagine a future where there are no humans. What would human life be without technology – or at least those technologies that trouble our claim to humanity and personhood? Would it also mitigate the creeping horror of the technological and its promises as represented in the flesh and what it conceals, the mechanistic determinism of the human body?

Alex Garland's television series *DEVS* (2020) wrestles with the mechanistic relationship between the natural and the artificial. Forest, the CEO of Silicon Valley tech company Amaya, is wracked with melancholia from the death of his wife and daughter. In an effort to demonstrate to himself that there is nothing he could have done to prevent the deaths of his family members in the face of the deterministic, material basis of the universe, Forest embarks on a quantum computing project to reveal that materialistic basis, arguing that free will is merely a human illusion – everything from the crucifixion of Jesus, to the infiltration of Amaya by a Russian operative, to the death of his daughter is simply the effects of billiard-ball-like interactions set about at the dawn of the universe. The utopian way out of this dour predicament is the possibility of technologically modeling the multiverse, showing how different first principles lead to very different outcomes. In some parallel universes, Forest's family is still alive – and he can live on in those universes with his family and the knowledge that, in other universes, things have not worked out so well. Forest – and Garland – are able to have it both ways: at once, nature is mechanistic and overdetermined, but the laws of physics provide the possibility of other lives being possible. Even if those other lives are still constrained by materialist principles, they offer more humane trajectories for Forest – and the lives of his family and employees. If technology cannot improve the utopian outcomes of an individual life, it can at least provide an entry into the possibility that other versions of the same life might work out differently.

Lisa Joy and Jonathan Nolan's *Westworld* (2016–2022) offers the apotheosis of a posttechnological future. The androids in *Westworld* are so human-like that it is impossible to tell the difference between the artificial and the natural. They bleed, have spontaneous emotional experiences, have kinship relations, and act in deliberative and unpredictable ways to ensure their survival. Unlike the Terminators or Murderbot, they often have no reflexive conception of themselves as artificial; instead, they frequently imagine themselves to be "real" people with personal histories, only to come to understand that those histories have been programmed for them and that their experiences of realness are likewise an effect of their programming – both of which are efforts at verisimilitude for the experience of human consumers of the theme park, Westworld. The humans want to know that the androids of Westworld conceive of themselves as persons so that human action upon the inhabitants of Westworld can elicit experiences of sadism or romance that serve as a lure to consume Westworld as a technologically mediated experience of the human. Humans, *Westworld* makes clear, are less humane that the androids they have created to entertain them. Humans are rapists and vengeance-seeking sadists; humans are duplicitous and manipulative; humans are determined by their natural histories of trauma that they are unable to overcome. The artificial, meanwhile, is open to possibility.

That these technological fantasies are televised is a function of how technological fantasies appeal to audiences by engaging sensory experiences. To echo Marshall McLuhan,[34] screens provide a mediation of technological fantasies that results in sensorial experiences quite different than texts allow; sensory experiences that draw attention to the flesh and its ruptures exceed what textual media may be too passive to fully capture. The sensorial field that televised media engages for the viewer has the potential to produce a visceral experience based upon the depiction of the flesh and its ruptures. These visceral experiences may – like Murderbot's experience of emotion – unsettle audience members as they confront depictions of the natural and artificial, and, by extension, how their humanity and personhood are implicated in portrayals of the technological and its mediation of human claims to personhood. When the Terminator's flesh is torn away, the question that a viewer must confront is whether the machinery that comprises an "artificial," cybernetic body is much different than the physiological machinery that comprises our "natural," human bodies. Staring at Schwarzenegger's human teeth as he grins during the conclusion of *Terminator Genysis*, as a show of how human he has become, forces viewers to confront the limits of the flesh. If a Terminator can have human teeth – and human emotions – can we embrace the mechanistic as a way to become posttechnological? Can we embrace the constant interplay of the natural and the artificial that the technological surfaces as a way to dwell in a utopian space between the human and nonhuman?

Notes

1. Annette Kolodny, *The Lay of the Land: Metaphor as Experience and History in American Life and Letters* (Chapel Hill: University of North Carolina Press, 1984); Henry Nash Smith, *Virgin Land: The American West as Symbol and Myth* (Cambridge, MA: Harvard University Press, 1978).
2. Roxanne Dunbar-Ortiz, *An Indigenous Peoples' History of the United States* (Boston, MA: Beacon Press, 2014); William M. Osborn, *The Wild Frontier: Atrocities during the American-Indian War from Jamestown Colony to Wounded Knee*, 1st ed. (New York: Random House, 2000).
3. *Red Mars* (New York: Random House, 1993); *Green Mars* (New York: Random House, 1993); *Blue Mars* (New York: Random House, 1996).
4. Martin Heidegger, *The Question concerning Technology and Other Essays*, trans. William Lovitt (New York: Harper & Row, 1977); Bernard Stiegler, *Technics and Time, 1: The Fault of Epimetheus*, trans. Richard Beardsworth (Stanford, CA: Stanford University Press, 1994).

5. Leigh Brackett, *The Long Tomorrow* (New York: Doubleday, 1955); Philip K. Dick, *Do Androids Dream of Electric Sheep?* (New York: Doubleday, 1968); Kim Stanley Robinson, *The Gold Coast* (New York: Tom Doherty Associates, 1988).
6. Donna Haraway, *Simians, Cyborgs, and Women: The Reinvention of Nature* (New York: Routledge, 1991); Bruno Latour, *We Have Never Been Modern*, trans. Catherine Porter (Cambridge, MA: Harvard University Press, 1993).
7. Benedicte Boisseron, *Afro-Dog: Blackness and the Animal Question* (New York: Columbia University Press, 2018).
8. Norbert Elias, *The Civilizing Process*, translated by Edmund Jephcott (Malden, MA: Blackwell, 2000); Frederick Jackson Turner, *Rereading Frederick Jackson Turner: "The Significance of the Frontier in American History" and Other Essays* (New Haven, CT: Yale University Press, 1998).
9. Philip Joseph Deloria, *Playing Indian* (New Haven, CT: Yale University Press, 2007).
10. Benjamin Reiss, "Sleeping at Walden Pond: Thoreau, Abnormal Temporality, and the Modern Body," *American Literature* 85.1 (2013), 5–31.
11. Orson Scott Card, *Speaker for the Dead* (New York: Tor Books, 1986); H. Beam Piper, *Little Fuzzy* (New York: Avon Books, 1962).
12. William Gibson, *Neuromancer* (New York: Ace, 1984); Bruce Sterling, *Islands in the Net* (New York: Arbor House, 1988); Lana Wachowski and Lilly Wachowski, *The Matrix* (Warner Brothers, 1999).
13. Haraway, *Simians, Cyborgs, and Women: The Reinvention of Nature*; Vicki Kirby, *Telling Flesh: The Substance of the Corporeal* (New York: Routledge, 1997).
14. Gillian Feely-Harnik, "The Ethnography of Creation: Lewis Henry Morgan and the American Beaver," from *Relative Values: Reconfiguring Kinship Studies*, edited by Sarah Franklin and Susan McKinnon (Durham, NC: Duke University Press, 2001), 54–84; Donna Haraway, *When Species Meet* (Minneapolis: University of Minnesota Press, 2008).
15. Latour, *We Have Never Been Modern*.
16. Julia Kristeva, *Powers of Horror: An Essay on Abjection* (New York: Columbia University Press, 1982).
17. Greg Bear, *Blood Music* (Westminster: Arbor House, 1985).
18. Richard Kelly, *The Box* (Warner Brothers, 2009).
19. Richard Matheson, "Button, Button," *Playboy*, 17.6 (June 1970), 208–209.
20. Janelle S. Taylor, "Surfacing the Body Interior," *Annual Review of Anthropology* 34 (2005), 741–756.
21. *All Systems Red* (New York: Tom Doherty Associates, 2017); *Artificial Condition* (New York: Tom Doherty Associates, 2018); *Exit Strategy* (New York: Tom Doherty Associates, 2018); *Rogue Protocol* (New York: Tom Doherty Associates, 2018); *Network Effect* (New York: Tom Doherty Associates, 2020).

22. Neil Badmington, *Alien Chic: Posthumanism and the Other Within* (London: Routledge, 2004); Rosi Braidotti, *The Posthuman* (Malden, MA: Polity Press, 2013).
23. Haraway, *Simians, Cyborgs, and Women.*
24. Alison Kafer, *Feminist, Queer, Crip* (Bloomington: Indiana University Press, 2013); Seth Messinger, "Rehabilitating Time: Multiple Temporalities among Military Clinicians and Patients," *Medical Anthropology* 29.2 (2010), 150–169.
25. For a discussion of the ambivalent role of technology among disabled users, see Michele Friedner, *Sensory Futures: Deafness and Cochlear Implant Infrastructures in India* (Minneapolis: University of Minnesota Press, 2022).
26. Davin Heckman, *A Small World: Smart Houses and the Dream of the Perfect Day* (Durham, NC: Duke University Press, 2008).
27. James Cameron, *Terminator* (Orion Pictures, 1984); James Cameron, *Terminator 2: Judgment Day* (Tri-Star Pictures, 1991); Jonathan Mostow, *Terminator 3: Rise of the Machines* (Warner Brothers, 2003); McG, *Terminator Salvation* (Warner Brothers, 2009); Alan Taylor, *Terminator Genisys* (Paramount Pictures, 2015); Tim Miller, *Terminator: Dark Fate* (Paramount Pictures, 2019).
28. Wells, *Artificial Condition.*
29. Wells, *Rogue Protocol.*
30. Wells, *Network Effect*, 201.
31. Wells, *Artificial Condition*, 48–50.
32. Wells, *Artificial Condition*, 50.
33. Stiegler, *Technics and Time, 1: The Fault of Epimetheus.*
34. *Understanding Media: The Extensions of Man* (Cambridge: MIT Press, 1994).

CHAPTER 11

Utopian Spaces

Roger Luckhurst

This chapter explores the architectural spaces of American utopias, which have, since the early days of the white settler Republic, often found their way off the page or drawing board and into material form. Many of these spaces only existed for a short span of time, but the legacy of these concrete attempts at creating utopian futurity in the world was to feed into ever more utopian texts, creating a feedback loop. These architectural spaces come to exist in a blurred zone between science fiction and the science-fictional.

The utopian spatial forms that have been realized in the post-1945 era, particularly in the New Communalism movements of the 1960s and 1970s, are the most extensive phase of realizing intentional utopian communities in American history.[1] But to understand where this impulse came from and the shapes these utopian spaces took, we need a quick orientation in the earlier history of intentional communities in the nineteenth and early twentieth century. This is because utopias are always citational and intertextual, echoing or arguing with earlier models and ideals. The feverish building of utopias after 1945 reacts to the successes and failures of what came before. They have also fed directly into both the science-fiction imagination of the future and the tactics for realizing utopian spaces in the post-1960s American polity.

Before 1945: Architecture and Associationism

Thomas More's *Utopia* expends substantial energy on imagining the architectural spaces that will shape the body politic into his ideal form. On More's strictly regulated island, equidistant cities are laid out in grids, along which communal housing in long rows abolishes property and privacy, ensuring, however coercively, transformed collective being. Perhaps because inert building blocks are easier to manipulate than the unreliable, pesky humans who have to live in them, utopias have always gone long on architectural detail. From Tomasso Campanella's concentric circular *City of the Sun* or Margaret Cavendish's vast palace in *The Blazing World*, to Le Corbusier's *City of Tomorrow* and its massive influence on post-war public housing across Europe, visions of transformative collective spaces for living have been integral to utopian discourse.

In the early American Republic, the most influential ideas, after John Winthrop's Puritan evocation of the biblical "shining city on a hill" in 1630, surprisingly derived from the work of the eccentric French Enlightenment thinker and socialist Charles Fourier. In various books issued from 1808, Fourier's thinking centered on a utopian community that would be housed in a giant *phalansterie* or phalanx, in which precisely 1,620 people would live along a single, continuous corridor to encourage unalienated labor and the maximum mathematical possibilities for harmonious social and sexual interchange.[2] Just one model phalanx would be so successful in demonstrating harmony, Fourier thought, that it would immediately overthrow all other forms of alienated housing in a matter of years, completely dismantle the miseries of market capitalism, and might even eventually generate enough delight to turn the salty oceans into quaffable lemonade. Fourier patiently waited in at home every morning in his Paris garret to receive investors in his plan until his death in 1837. For some reason, they never came.

One man who did appear at Fourier's door, though, was the American Albert Brisbane, heir to a large fortune built on land speculation. The young Brisbane had traveled to Europe to study with G. W. F. Hegel, who unfortunately turned out to be an incredibly boring teacher. Brisbane drifted from Berlin and encountered Fourier's ideas in Paris in 1832. He became Fourier's student for two years, paying him a handsome tutoring fee, and returned to America in 1834. He tidied up Fourier's digressive style, removed the eccentric sexual and cosmological speculations, and published the important English-language summations of Fourierist principles, *Social Destiny of Man* (1840) and *A Concise Exposition of the Practical Part of Fourier's Sound Science* (1843). With the journalist Horace Greeley at the *New York Tribune*, Brisbane launched Fourier's ideas into the American Republic. The efforts became the basis of Associationism, a movement that, in the 1840s, inspired the foundation of over thirty intentional communities, often built around communal phalanxes. This is the movement that has had the most enduring influence on how American utopias are imagined and realized in built space.

"Association will have ITS ARCHITECTURE," Brisbane declared,

> and it will be an architecture of combination and unity. When we are associated and united, one vast and elegant edifice will replace hundreds of the isolated and miserable constructions of civilisation. . . . From a perfect knowledge of human nature, can we not deduce the construction of an edifice perfectly suited to it?[3]

The American wilderness was the *tabula rasa* that inspired Christian groups to tie the biblical injunction to cultivate the land to push settlement – and so civilization – beyond the frontier.[4] Religious imperatives drove dissident and persecuted religious minorities to settle beyond corrupt European orthodoxies, seeding idealized communities in these far reaches of the West (Brigham Young's Church of Jesus Christ of Latter-day Saints, known as the Mormons, remains one of the longer-lasting of these groups).

Political and socialist imperatives also drove some communities. The most famous of these was Robert Owen's New Harmony in Indiana. An industrialist long interested in reforming the labor and living spaces of his factory workers, Owen firmly believed that space could reshape and reform the character entirely, perfecting the human "machine" in industrial and moral efficiency.[5] After realizing a model textile mill at New Lanark in Scotland in the 1810s, Owen saw America as the ideal location for a larger transformative experiment. In 1824, Owen bought the settlement of Harmony in Indiana outright for $125,000. The settlement had been built by Lutheran dissidents in exile, the followers of George Rapp.

Harmony had a large communal structure at its center, but in 1825 Owen presented a plan to the American Congress for a much larger community structure, a giant Parallelogram that would house 2,000 souls, much like Fourier's phalanx. Owen left his sons in charge of New Harmony but had sunk nearly 80 percent of his fortune into the settlement within a couple of years, without much sign of the predicted "Community of Equality" threshold arriving among the recruits to the design. People of color were excluded from the start; class divides reemerged with an implicit division between laborers and the *savants*, the latter tempted to New Harmony to revolutionize scientific knowledge. The project disintegrated into factions and was declared a failure and wound up in 1827. Robert Owen and his son, Robert Dale Owen, later sought utopia in the safer space of the afterlife, both converting to Spiritualism in the 1840s. The Spiritualist Summerland often had a communal or even explicitly socialist vibe.[6]

The Associationists had less millennialist ambitions, with phalanxes built on a more modest scale than Fourier or Owen had planned.

Brisbane and Greeley helped establish the model North American Phalanx in New Jersey in 1841, where investment from the communards funded a series of experiments in communal building, the largest housing 150 people. The Wisconsin Phalanx set up in 1844 had a long communal building that housed 200 people. The most famous experiment was at Brook Farm, established in 1841, which included some leading Transcendentalist intellectuals. The community ran for a few years before it was bankrupted by a fire that destroyed their nearly complete, three-story wooden phalanx. One ardent Associationist there, Margaret Dwight, secretly confessed "a feeling of relief" that this further stage of collective living had been scuppered.[7] This was also implied in the concrete actions of the founder of the Raritan Bay Union, Marcus Spring. In 1853, he spent substantial funds building a phalanx in stone for forty families – but then built a conventional family house next door for himself, to limit his exposure to communal living.[8]

In 1855, one of Fourier's closest allies and supporters, the socialist Victor Considérant, abandoned France as irredeemable and decided to establish a settlement on the *tabula rasa* of American soil. He chose land a few miles from a tiny hamlet called Dallas in Texas. In *Great West*, published in 1853, Considérant proclaimed: "America is at present the Country of Realization."[9] La Réunion was financed through shares in the project taken out through the Colonization Society of Paris, investors buying participation in the project and its projected profits. But Considérant soon despaired when in the early months of the settlement the group voted down communal living in a phalanx and instead built separate log cabins, "so as to escape in our private lives all notion of communism."[10] La Réunion had collapsed and the land had been sold on by 1859.

Religious communities, underpinned by a willingness to trade with the fallen world beyond their borders, have been the longest survivals – often in spite of their considerable social and sexual dissidences. Formalized polygamy among the Mormons or the Oneida Community demonized members and hounded communities out of some states, but trade sustained their survival. At Oneida, the space of their communal Mansion House was built in 1852, then substantially rebuilt in 1859 and extended into the 1870s. It embodied their ideas of Bible Communism and "complex marriage," with the moveable walls of their notorious Tent Room allowing for shifting patterns of partners to couple; meanwhile, they survived on income from their patents and their silverware business.[11]

Regarding the first half of the twentieth century, Timothy Miller observes, the general historical view is that intentional communities in

America waned with a consolidation of the ideology of American rugged individualism, the rudiments of a welfare state, and waves of panic about Bolshevism contaminating any form of collectivist project. This eclipse (which Miller suggests is overstated) makes it harder to understand the post-1945 boom in art colonies or the New Communalism of the 1960s, "by far the largest episode of commune building in American history."[12] Yet many of these experiments have their roots in the longer historical trajectory I have sketched out here.

These early experiments in realizing utopia explicitly grasp the basic premise of spatial theory: that space "conditions the subject's presence, action and discourse, his [*sic*] competence and performance," as Henri Lefebvre puts it in *The Production of Space*.[13] Architectural form can rewire the psyche and reconfigure social relations, as capitalism has done, but this is never stable or absolute, and it allows for other representational spaces to be imagined or realized where the aim might be to dismantle atomized and commodified space, disrupt the conventional family unit, or reassemble communities along collectivist principles. After 1945, the intensification of American capitalism, inside a military-industrial Cold War logic, would produce a renewed exploration of collectivism, marked by innovations in the architectural forms that embodied the New Communalism.

Drop City and 1960s Communalism

Drop City was established in 1965 on six acres of scrubby goat pasture just north of the postindustrial town of Trinidad in southern Colorado. It was started as an experimental art colony but was soon recognized as one of the first communes of the hippie movement, seeding hundreds of similar projects. Drop City was founded by Clark Richert and JoAnne and Gene Bernofsky, who had met as students at the University of Kansas and then became involved in the New York art scene in the early 1960s.[14] They were principally inspired by Allan Kaprow's concept of "the happening," which aimed to dissolve the boundaries between art and life, creating immersive situations that involved music, art, theater, performance, ritual, life, and lots of drugs. The group staged interventions that they "dropped" into everyday life in San Francisco and New York: hence the name of their art colony (although resonances with dropping out or dropping acid also worked). Drop City was intended to be a continuous embodied total work of art in all its actions: they painted, sculpted, planned theatrical events, invented the underground comic, lived experimentally, and filmed much of this praxis as they went along. In this, it borrowed both from the

Black Mountain College model (1933–1957) and the more immediate protohippie acid and freak scene that developed around Ken Kesey in Palo Alto from 1958. Kesey's Merry Pranksters made their acid utopia mobile on the bus trip, documented by Tom Wolfe in *The Electric Kool Aid Acid Test*, before establishing the Hog Farm commune as a base.

Drop City became something else again when they began building structures on the site. In 1965, the founders saw F. Buckminster Fuller deliver one of his legendary epic lectures to students at the University of Colorado in Boulder. Fuller's "Design Science" revolution was at the peak of its influence. Although seventy years old, Fuller's eccentric technoshamanistic idiolect appealed to the new mass student body, which he saw as potentially revolutionary agents to realize his plan to rescue Spaceship Earth (much as Herbert Marcuse did at the end of the 1960s). Fuller had also moved in 1960 into his experimental new house, a geodesic dome built in Carbondale, Illinois. He advocated the dome as a radical housing solution, where form and function perfectly united the balance of tensions in the structure, built quickly and cheaply from materials repurposed from the factories of the military-industrial complex. Fuller was redirecting these designs of fast-assembly buildings from prototypes he had worked up for the US Army and Navy, trialing domes outside the Pentagon. More permanent geodesic domes had been built to hide and protect military intelligence radars in extreme environments: America and Britain are still dotted with "golf ball" domes that house the advanced radar warning capabilities that maintained the balance of Mutually Assured Destruction during and after the Cold War. Yet Fuller now offered this architecture as a democratic, mass-housing solution, the spherical design an echo of Spaceship Earth itself, which could still be rescued from both the divisions and inefficiencies of American consumer capitalism and the murderous logic of the Cold War.

Utopia or Oblivion? asked one of Fuller's collections of lectures in 1969. "The world has become too dangerous for anything less than utopia," he answered, before adding that "for the first time in history utopia is, at least, physically possible of human attainment."[15] For much of the 1960s and into the 1970s, Fuller's geodesic domes were icons of utopian futurity, their fame secured with the large dome that dominated the Montréal World Expo site in 1967. It is estimated that over 200,000 domes were built over the following twenty years.

At Drop City, the core group began work on their first dome soon after Fuller's lecture but repurposed it as part of their "hippie modernism."[16] Rather than Fuller's geometric purity, they improvised with found (or often stolen) materials, creating collaged buildings of salvaged lumber and bottle tops, and using car windshields chainsawed off in dumps to use as windows. For Fuller, the dome drew on the universal and immutable physical laws of force and tension. For Drop City, the dome channeled a more hippyish array of less rational cosmic forces that shaped the universe from the atomic or cellular level to the noosphere and planetary consciousness itself. Chance and serendipity also shaped their wonky structures.

"The Great Pumpkin," the first structure, was not a geodesic dome, technically, but a truncated duodecahedron. However, Fuller still awarded their efforts with a $500 Dymaxion Award in 1966, a sum that eased the difficult financial straits of the commune. After putting their chickens into a geodesic coop, they next built a large kitchen block, then embarked on a more ambitious set of polyhedral buildings pieced together for their experimental theater space. By this time the architect and mathematician Steve Baer had become involved, using Drop City as an experimental space to explore what he termed the "zome," that is "a man-made structure derived from a zonahedra."[17] These were more flexible, Baer argued, because the zones of any structure "may be stretched or shrunk or removed to produce, if desired, an asymmetric dome-shaped structure."[18] Baer, a decidedly unhippyish presence at Drop City, went on to set up Zomeworks Inc. and helped foster the spread of DIY dome construction across the communes of the southwest. He coorganized the "Alloy" conference in 1969, which, as the title suggested, looked for further hybrid fusions of architectural solutions and further secured the dome/zome as the quintessential countercultural structure.[19]

Another architect involved in these projects, Lloyd Kahn, built an experimental school across seventeen domes in the Santa Cruz mountains in 1968 (highly praised by Fuller) and issued two volumes of big selling guides, *Domebook 1* (1970) and *2* (1971). "Living in a spherical single unit house makes us wholer people," he argued. "We feel more whole and have our whole trip around us."[20] However, after living in a geodesic dome that he had constructed for himself in the hippy town of Bolinas, north of San Francisco, for a year, Kahn determined that they were unlivable spaces, having discovered the secret of every dome, that they must constantly shift and flex through their lines of force, particularly if they have glass panels open to the sun, and therefore are doomed to buckle and leak constantly. Kahn withdrew his handbooks in 1972 and set up the journal *Shelter* to explore other forms of improvised demotic structures across the planet.

The dramatic, futuristic shapes of the ten or so domes built at the Drop City commune made it look "as if a Martian space craft had landed" in the desert.[21] The feel of the place fed directly into the syncretic and vaguely holistic New Age mysticism, Eastern esotericism, and acid-driven philosophizing of the moment. "To live in a dome is – psychologically – to be in closer harmony with natural structures," Bill Voyd declared. "Domes break into new dimensions. They help to open man's perception."[22] Voyd began to suspect that corners in rooms held fascistic intimations, an echo of the suspicion of right angles in the schools built earlier in the century by the mystic Rudolf Steiner. The unbroken, open interior of the dome necessitated communal living (removing all interior walls was a key recommendation in a 1972 handbook called *Making Communes,* Dolores Hayden notes). This was the same transformative injunction as the phalanx of the Associationists, now rendered in explicit countercultural terms. In *Post-Scarcity Anarchism,* for instance, Murray Bookchin declared that "in the very act of refusing to live by bourgeois strictures, the first seeds of utopian lifestyle are planted."[23]

The unity and autonomous perfection of the sphere has long been the emblem of idealized harmony, as German philosopher Peter Sloterdijk has tracked in his impressively eccentric trilogy of tomes called *Spheres*. Fuller's domes are Sloterdijk's "macrospherology" in action, a *spheropoesis* that hymns balance and unity with "utopian élan."[24] In the late 1960s, the Apollo missions began to bring back photographs of the fragile planet Earth below. The "Earthrise" photograph taken by the astronaut William Anders from Apollo 8 in December 1968 is now held as marking a key moment in the emergence of planetary ecoconsciousness. The icon of the geodesic dome united the local and the planetary and even evoked older ideas of the celestial spheres or the occult insistence of symmetry – "as above, so below" – in one pure geometric form.

The eminently photographable domes of Drop City were featured on the cover of *Time* magazine in 1967, which made the small commune a magnet for hundreds of tourists, fellow-travelers, freeloaders, and acid casualties, all of whom began to overwhelm its precarious ecology. By 1967, the original members had abandoned Drop City, seeding new dome-dominated communes across the southwest, such as Libre or the Lama Foundation (where Baer also built zomes). In 1973, public health officials condemned the conditions at Drop City, evicted the remaining people from the site, and bulldozed it into the ground.

To trace how the dome/zome figure feeds into further forms of utopianism (and antiutopianism) in fiction, film, futurology, and new technological frontiers, we need to follow another figure who visited Drop City and helped organize the Alloy conference in 1969: Stewart Brand.

From Hippy Dome to Cyberzone

Stewart Brand studied at Stanford in the 1950s, with tutors heavily involved in cybernetic theory, and worked in the army as a photographer for several years before becoming involved in the alternative art scenes and radical politics of New York and San Francisco.[25] He was also an experimental subject in Stanford Research Institute's notorious exploration of hallucinogenic drugs, particularly LSD, which turned his interest towards the revolution in consciousness propounded by Kesey and the New Communalists. He was involved with the USCO (The Us Company) group, who began providing immersive environments of light, sound systems, and film projections on the alternative scene for "happenings" or "be-ins." Brand became a countercultural entrepreneur, turning a large profit as one of the organizers of the Trips Festival with Kesey in 1966 (music provided by the Grateful Dead and Janis Joplin). With an inheritance from his father's death in 1968, he funded his key contribution to the counterculture, the *Whole Earth Catalog*. The first issue in 1968 was 60 pages with a print run of 1,000. *The Last Whole Earth Catalog* in 1971 was 448 pages and sold over a million copies.

The *Catalog*, subtitled *Access to Tools*, was basically a place to recommend or advertise the physical materials to realize communal living (everything from nails and lumber to seeds, farming supplies, and experimental wind and solar power devices for eco-self-sufficiency). It also recommended books and journals, with suggestions often sent in by readers, making the book a collaged array that built networks, shared ideologies, and pooled ideas. Each issue began with the section "Understanding Whole Systems," admitting that "The insights of Buckminster Fuller initiated this catalog,"[26] and was unapologetic in its embrace of technological solutions, unlike the anti-Machine rhetoric common to many hippie elements of the counterculture. Brand quoted some of Fuller's terrible poetry from the 1963 *No More Second-Hand God*: "I see God in/ the instruments and the mechanisms that/work/reliably,/more reliably than the limited sensory departments of/the human mechanism."[27] The *Catalog* mixed in science fiction, NASA photo books, "ecotactics" for environmental activists, Carl Jung, Claude Lévi-Strauss, domebuilders, teepee construction guides, John Cage, and ecoessays by Wendell Berry, among the lists of carpenters or seed banks that sent out postal orders. It was a roving interdisciplinary model of a journal that fulfilled, for Brand, Fuller's ideal of being the "Comprehensive Designer." The *Whole Earth Supplement*, a journal that ran alongside the *Catalog*, was a place where many figures in the utopian commune culture contributed further articles to bolster these nascent networks. These fed into a subsequent publishing project, the *CoEvolution Quarterly*.

There are several major lines of influence that emerge from Brand's *Catalog*. The most well known is the direct descent from Brand's countercultural clearing-house journal to some of the earliest versions of the Internet. Brand helped fund the Homebrew Computer Club in 1975, and later the WELL (the Whole Earth 'Lectronic Link), which involved groups that would start the home-computer revolution and eventually lead to the founding of *Wired* magazine in 1993. As Fred Turner has documented, the libertarian-utopian slant of early 1990s internet culture – as a flat, nonhierarchical, networked space – came directly out of the networks Brand helped build in Californian counterculture (it was a former Grateful Dead lyricist who wrote the "Declaration of the Independence of Cyberspace" at the World Economic Forum in 1996, for instance).

In William Gibson's version of the worn-out, postindustrial, semicollapsed future of his cyberpunk novels and short stories of the early 1980s, a typical image of his gritty urban landscape includes "a ragged overlap of Fuller domes roofing what was once a suburban artery . . . the neon arcs are dead and the geodesics have been smoked black by decades of cooking fires."[28] The ruined dome stands in for the end of a specific spatial form of utopian futurity, where meat space degrades just as commodified cyberspace boots up. Gibson's early ideological campaign against certain American science-fiction futures – most famously articulated in "The Gernsback Continuum" – obscures another trajectory of Buckminster Fuller's domes, however.

Soon after the final *Whole Earth Catalog,* Stewart Brand helped fund a conference in 1974 at which the Princeton physicist Gerard O'Neill outlined his proposal for large factories and settlements to be sent into orbit around the Earth. O'Neill had tried for several years to publish his proposals in academic journals; they were routinely dismissed. Brand was on hand to step in to support such a rogue visionary, a chip off the Buckminster Fuller block, offering a route to outflank the inertia of academic orthodoxy.

O'Neill wanted to apply practical physics to solve major engineering problems. He suggested that the technology already existed to put millions of people into space and predicted that this would be inevitable by the year 2000. O'Neill offered a Bernal Sphere, named after the futurologist J. D. Bernal, who had first proposed using spheres for settlements in outer space in his 1929 classic of futurology, *The World, The Flesh and the*

Devil. O'Neill thought a Bernal Sphere could house at least 10,000 space colonists. He published his proposals and projections in a mass-market paperback under the title *The High Frontier* in 1977. Other scientists, taking up the baton, proposed the use of a rotating cylinders or a torus-shape instead, since these structures could both create artificial gravity as they moved and house possibly hundreds of thousands. In the discussions held by NASA in 1975, there was serious thought given to the disorientation of living spherically or inside cylinders, since the inhabitants would experience horizons bending up and over them, rather than bending away from them, as on Earth. (Kubrick exploits this disorientation for the scenes of the astronauts jogging in circles in *2001: A Space Odyssey.*) Ludwig Glaeser, an architectural curator at the New York Museum of Modern Art, and proponent of the visionary plans of Le Corbusier and Mies van der Rohe earlier in the century, explored "Architectural Studies for a Space Habitat" at the conference to address this problem.

These conference conversations were picked up first by the *New York Times* and then by NASA itself in their Ames study group in the summer of 1975, a rapid move from countercultural dreaming on the margins to the most orthodox institutions of space science. This kind of attention made these domes, spheres, and toruses central to the future projections of outer space in the late 1970s. Fred Scharmen has shown how the paintings created between 1975 and 1978 by Don Davies and Rick Guidice for NASA explorations of large-scale settlement started to suffuse the popular culture of the time. There is a constant interchange between science-fiction futures and the astrophysics of space settlement. The domes, say, in Donald Trumbull's film, *Silent Running,* Saul Bass's *Phase IV,* or the television series *Space 1999,* or the torus in Arthur C. Clarke's novel *Rendezvous with Rama,* or the set designs and concept drawings of Syd Mead – all of these crossed over with NASA discussions about space settlement in that era.

These spatial models were utopian because they aimed to be a solution to the finite resources of Spaceship Earth, felt to be fast running down its resources in the midst of the Oil Shock that had ended the long postwar economic boom in America. In one move, space settlements would end Earthly finitude and offer the limitless resources of a postscarcity existence. It would remove the restraints on economic growth, which the influential book, *The Limits to Growth,* commissioned by the Club of Rome and published in 1972, had projected. That model had even suggested something approaching complete planetary collapse by the year 2100 if the population of Earth continued to grow. Fears about overpopulation had been heightened by Paul and Anne Ehrlich's best-selling book *The Population Bomb* in 1968. Paul Ehrlich had been Stewart Brand's biology tutor at Stanford, introducing him to whole systems and cybernetic thinking.

In 1977, Brand edited a collection of essays out of these discussions called *Space Colonies*, which was a direct product of Gerard O'Neill's proposals. Brand was happy to claim that "The *Whole Earth Catalog* is responsible for the colonization of space."[29] Brand's interest in this project was libertarian and overtly indebted to Fuller. In the introduction to *Space Colonies*, he suggested the O'Neill's plans meant that some could now "see Space as a path, or at least a metaphor, for their own liberation,"[30] adding:

> And for those who long for the harshest freedoms, or who believe with Buckminster Fuller that a culture's creativity requires an Outlaw Area, Free Space becomes what the oceans have ceased to be – [an] Outlaw Area too big and dilute for national control.[31]

There is an anarchistic and hippyish embrace of space settlement here, but also an odd echo of the libertarian speculative-fiction (sf) writer Robert Heinlein. "Harshest freedoms" suggests a nod to Heinlein's *The Moon Is a Harsh Mistress,* which appeared in 1966. This is unsurprising, since Heinlein's 1961 *Stranger in a Strange Land* had proved to be weirdly influential on the whole ethos of the Californian counterculture. Heinlein in return would borrow O'Neill's title, "the high frontier" for his own important venture into nonfiction. Along with several other Californian science-fiction writers, including Larry Niven and Jerry Pournelle, Heinlein was on the Citizens' Advisory Panel that cowrote the document addressed in 1983 to President Ronald Reagan that proposed the Strategic Defense Initiative (SDI) to defend the American high frontier in space from military attack. This speculative military project to build defensive satellite weapons became known popularly as "Star Wars." If SDI was abandoned, the libertarian, entrepreneurial appropriation of space by dotcom billionaires in the twenty-first century looks oddly foreshadowed by Brand's bullish embrace of the "Outlaw Area" of "Free Space."

Brand remained true to his countercultural ethos in *Space Colonies*, however. He was willing to publish dissenting voices from his network of writers at this vision of postscarcity utopia in outer space. Lewis Mumford unsurprisingly dismissed these proposals as "only technological disguises for infantile fantasies"[32] – a fine prediction of the emergence of Elon Musk. Wendell Berry suspected that Brand's new direction was rather too "superbly attuned to the wishes of the corporation executives, bureaucrats, militarists, political operators, and scientific experts who are the chief beneficiaries of the forces that have produced our crisis."[33] The Ant Farm collective focused acutely on the disappointingly generic science-fiction futurity of this utopia, declaring "SPACE COLONIES ARE TAIL FINS," implying that they were the decadent ornaments of the technological advances secured by the military-industrial complex during World War II, "the ultimate machine fantasy."[34] Even so, the same publication carried a statement by a group of biological and ecological experts, including James Lovelock and Lynn Margulis, called "Ecological Considerations for Space Colonies." It was written by a group who had extensive "experience in the study or design of closed ecological systems" inside dome structures.[35] They thought that the problem of maintaining biodiversity inside a sealed dome had not yet been worked out on Earth, let alone in space. "The basic ecological problems must be attacked on earth first, then in near orbit. Only after successful self-contained systems have proved feasible on earth for some time ought such systems be launched."[36] The illustration for the article looks uncannily like a sketch for the Eden Project domes, lush verdure growing under a geodesic sky, which opened in Cornwall in the UK in 2001. But does anything else in this trajectory of American utopian spaces survive into the twenty-first century?

Construction after Utopia

Fredric Jameson has suggested that in American there has been "a marked diminution in the production of new utopias over the last decades"; the end, he suggests, comes with Ernest Callenbach's 1975 book, *Ecotopia*.[37] In his earlier *Archaeologies of the Future*, Jameson suggests that by the late stage of capitalism we have become suspicious of any concrete attempt at utopia after a century of disastrous quasi-realizations from both the left and right. "At best," Jameson argues, "Utopia can serve the negative purpose of making us more aware of our own mental and ideological imprisonment."[38] In a gesture that is recognizable from Ernst Bloch's *Principle of Hope*, Jameson rejects fixed spatial or architectural forms of utopia for a dynamic exercise of a utopian consciousness that constantly yearns forward for a "Not Yet." "What is Utopia becomes . . . not the commitment to a specific machinery or blueprint, but rather the commitment to imagining possible utopias as such, in their greatest variety of forms."[39] Science fiction in the new century has been full of *compromised* utopias, dystopias, or antiutopian critiques, all cautious forms of association built amidst the ruins.[40]

Jameson's position does not imply the simple disappearance or aestheticization of utopia, but a deliberate commitment to its dynamic, fugitive existence as a form of critique of the present. It sounds quite a bit like the Temporary Autonomous Zone (or TAZ) first theorized in 1990 by the anarchist mystic "Hakim Bey" (Peter Lamborn Wilson) and revised in 2003, which I would suggest has a direct descent from the kind of technoshamanism pursued by Buckminster Fuller or Stewart Brand since the 1960s. The text of Hakim Bey's antimanifesto looks not for *revolution* but moments of *insurrection*, and not for a fixed architecture of a concrete utopia, which will inevitably only ossify into a statist formation of power, but rather for temporary self-ordering zones that arise and vanish before they can be destroyed by any repressive state apparatus.

After what Hakim Bey calls the "closure of the map" (the totalization of state control of the entire globe by 1899), he argues that there can be no place, no non-place, no "phalanstery" that will structure and stabilize utopia that cannot be captured by conservative forces. Instead, he argues for temporary irruptions into festivities, ritual celebrations, protests, or anarchic actions that foster chaos and unpredictable outcomes. The TAZ is embedded in a "secret history" of what Hakim Bey terms "pirate utopias," which appear and disappear periodically in time and space. The preface to the second edition bemoans the early naivety in thinking that one instantiation of the TAZ might be in a subversive Web that would continue to exist inside the matrix of the Internet. It was a vision explicitly drawn from the hackers of William Gibson and Bruce Sterling's cyberpunk fiction of the 1980s. "What a joke," Hakim Bey concludes in rueful hindsight.[41]

Yet the TAZ has, in fact, survived that moment of 1990s technoutopian boosterism and countercultural entrepreneurship and has since been used to theorize not just rave-culture undergrounds, for instance, but also the anarchist insurrections of the Occupy movement that developed around 2011 and after. In the occupations in New York at Wall Street or City Hall, or in Seattle's CHAZ (Capitol Hill Autonomous Zone), or in Portland outside the Courthouse, Hakim Bey's vision of temporary insurrection has morphed once more in response to a further stage in the militarization of state power.[42] It is striking that the tent cities and temporary stages of these fugitive protests still often involve the kind of dome structures first explored by the New Communalists of the 1960s in what appears a neat unconscious echo of the marginal postwar history that continues America's experiments with architectural realizations of utopian possibility.

Notes

1. Timothy Miller, *The 60s Communes: Hippies and Beyond* (Syracuse, NY: Syracuse University Press, 1999).
2. Roger Luckhurst, *Corridors: Passages of Modernity* (London: Reaktion Books, 2019), 43–54.
3. Albert Brisbane, "Section IV: Social Destiny of Man," reprinted in *London Phalanx* (1841–2), 428.
4. Vittoria di Palma, *Wasteland: A History* (New Haven, CT: Yale University Press, 2014).
5. Robert Owen, *A New View of Society, or, Essays on the Principle of the Formation of Character, and the Application of the Principle to Practice* (London: Cadell & Davies, 1813).
6. Logie Barrow, *Independent Spirits: Spiritualism and English Plebeians 1850–1910* (London: Routledge, 1986).
7. Margaret Dwight, *Letters from Brook Farm*, edited by Amy Reed (Poughkeepsie, NY: Vassar College, 1928), 148.
8. Maud Honeyman Greene, "Raritan Bay Union, Eaglewood, New Jersey," *Proceedings of the New Jersey Historical Society* 68.1 (1950), 1–20.
9. Rondel van Davidson, *Did We Think Victory Great? The Life of Victor Considérant* (Lanham, MD: University Press of America, 1988), 56.
10. Van Davidson, 271.
11. Ellen Wayland-Smith, *Oneida: From Free Love Utopia to the Well-Set Table* (New York: Picador, 2016).
12. Timothy Miller, *The Quest for Utopia in Twentieth Century America, Vol. 1: 1900–60* (Syracuse, NY: Syracuse University Press, 1998), xii.
13. Henri Lefebvre, *The Production of Space*, translated by D. Nicholson-Smith (Oxford: Blackwell, 1991), 57.
14. Dolores Hayden, *Seven American Utopias* (Cambridge, MA: MIT Press, 1976); Mark Matthews, *Droppers: America's First Hippie Commune, Drop City* (Norman: University of Oklahoma Press, 2010); Simon Sadler, "Drop City Revisited," *Journal of Architectural Education* 59.3 (2006), 5–14.
15. R. Buckminster Fuller, *Operation Manual for Planet Earth* (Carbondale: Southern Illinois University Press, 1969), 360.
16. Andrew Blauvelt (ed.), *Hippie Modernism: The Struggle for Utopia* (Minneapolis: Walker Arts Center, 2015).
17. Steve Baer, *Zome Primer: Elements of Zonahedra Geometry* (Albuquerque, NM: Zoneworks Corps, 1970), 3.
18. Baer, 3.
19. Andrew Kirk, "Alloyed: Countercultural Bricoleurs and the Design Science Revival," from *Groovy Science: Knowledge, Innovation and American Counterculture*, edited by D. Kaiser and W. P. McCray (Chicago: Chicago University Press, 2016), 305–336.
20. Qtd. in Christine Macy and Sarah Bonnemaison, *Architecture and Nature: Creating the American Landscape* (New York: Routledge, 2003), 329.

21. Matthews, 73.
22. Qtd. in Macy and Bonnemaison, 328.
23. Qtd. in Erin Elder, "How to Build a Commune: Drop City's Influence on the Southwestern Commune Movement," from *West of Center: Art and the Counterculture: Experiment in America, 1965-77*, edited by Erin Elder and Lucy R. Lippard (Minneapolis: University of Minnesota Press, 2011), 2–21 (13).
24. Peter Sloterdijk, *Globes: Macrospherology (Spheres, Vol. II)*, translated by W. Hoban (Pasadena: Semiotext(e), 2014), 263.
25. Fred Turner, *From Counterculture to Cyberculture: Stewart Brand, the Whole Earth Network, and the Rise of Digital Utopianism* (Chicago: University of Chicago Press, 2006).
26. Stewart Brand (ed.), *The Last Whole Earth Catalog: Access to Tools* (London: Penguin, 1971), 3.
27. Brand, *The Last Whole Earth Catalog*, 4.
28. William Gibson, "Johnny Mnemonic," from *Burning Chrome* (London: Grafton, 1988), 14–36 (27).
29. Qtd in Fred Scharmen, *Space Settlements* (New York: Columbia University Press, 2019), 12–13.
30. Stewart Brand (ed.), *Space Colonies* (London: Penguin, 1977), 5.
31. Brand, *Space Colonies*, 6.
32. Brand, *Space Colonies*, 34.
33. Brand, *Space Colonies*, 34.
34. Brand, *Space Colonies*, 47.
35. Brand, *Space Colonies*, 92.
36. Brand, *Space Colonies*, 93.
37. Fredric Jameson, *An American Utopia: Dual Power and the Universal Army* (London: Verso, 2016), 1.
38. Fredric Jameson, *Archaeologies of the Future: The Desire Called Utopia and other Science Fictions* (London: Verso, 2005), xiii.
39. Jameson, *Archaeologies*, 217.
40. Tom Moylan, *Becoming Utopian: The Culture and Politics of Radical Transformation* (London: Bloomsbury, 2020).
41. Hakim Bey, *T.A.Z. The Temporary Autonomous Zone, Ontological Anarchy, Poetic Terrorism*, second edition (New York: Autonomedia, 2003), xi
42. See Camille Sojit Pejcha, "Better Living Through Anarchy: Tracking the Rise of the Temporary Autonomous Zone," *Document Journal* (August 19, 2020), online.

CHAPTER 12

Environmentalism and Ecotopias

Gerry Canavan

R. Crumb's one-page comic "A Short History of America" begins with pristine, untouched wilderness, a wide-open expanse abutting a deciduous forest populated by grazing deer and birds.[1] In the second panel, a train cuts through the right of the frame; in the third, a small unpaved road now dominates the center of the scene, and a single house has appeared. From there the sprawl spreads: a second road, more houses, then stores, electrification, trolleys, then automobiles. By the end of the comic, the natural world has been completely evacuated; the scene instead is fully taken up by brands, wires, and cars, with even humans vanishing in the face of their technological extensions. In the final panel, even the railroad has been stripped out, replaced by upscale apartments bearing the name "Oakwood Village": "an empty gesture of reclamation, as the original bucolic scene has been decimated, the stubborn hill its only ghost."[2] A diegetic street sign symbolically warns that that this process only goes "one way"; a caption on the final image darkly asks, "What next?"

In 1988, Crumb created an epilogue to the original image, with three new panels, each representing a possible future for the United States. (The image now typically circulates in this full-color version, with the epilogue attached in a new, final row at the bottom of the image.) In Figure 12.1, on the left, where that "one way" sign is pointing, we find the first possible future: a blasted, abandoned city. What was once a verdant old-growth forest is now a desert, with no sign of life other than the scrub grass growing over the ruins. It would almost look as if the city had been bombed, but the panel's labeling tells us instead that this is the "Worst Case Scenario: Ecological Disaster." In the second panel, the catastrophe of modernity has somehow been undone; flying cars hover over the city against a clear blue sky, with the telephone poles torn down in favor of replanted decorative fir trees. This is the "*fun* future: techno-fix on the march." In the third option, the entire nature of the city has been transformed. The roads have been depaved, and a multiethnic community travels by foot,

Figure 12.1 Crumb's "A Short History of America." Used by permission.

wagon, and bicycle. The "Stop and Shop" has been replaced by a farmer's stall; most striking, the city is now dominated not by poles, streetlamps, and wires but by a return of the region's original trees, restored to such health that they now stretch beyond the bounds of the panel. The eclectic human buildings (one is a treehouse, another appears to be a geodesic dome) are tucked into the trees; the settlement lives among the trees rather than bulldozing and flattening them. Ivan Brunetti evocatively describes the epilogue to "A Short History of America" as:

> a sort of choose-your-own-adventure for humanity that ranges from inferno to purgatory to paradise. There must be an optimist lurking within Crumb, because the strip concludes with, and thus favors, the most positive choice of the three.[3]

This favored panel, the one perhaps we and Crumb long to make real, is labeled "the ecotopian solution."

This chapter considers contemporary environmentalism through the lens of *ecotopia*, a modification of the utopian form that includes the ecological as a core consideration alongside the political and cultural. The idea that the living world – not only mammals, but also fish, birds, insects, and trees – should have meaningful political status is a radical transformation of the usual terms of utopia, rendering certain utopian tropes (like the technology-fueled extinction of vermin or pests) impossible while activating other new possibilities both for the transformation of the social and for individual self-actualization. In particular, ecotopias are distinct from most utopias in their abiding suspicion of technology; even the ecotopias that do not seek to "reverse progress" per se typically involve a harsh critique of the wasteful and ecologically destructive applications of science and technology since the dawn of the industrial revolution. In an era of escalating climate disaster, with "baked-in" temperature increases that will transform the planetary ecosystem over the course of the coming decades even if all carbon emissions were able to be stopped tomorrow, this suspicion of technology has become even more pointed and urgent, even as it simultaneously has become complicated by the perceived need for some miraculous technofix to ameliorate the worst impacts of climate change even in ecotopia.

In *Archaeologies of the Future*, Fredric Jameson, following many other theorists of utopia, draws a crucial distinction between *dystopia* as utopia's opposite and *antiutopia* as utopia's negative.[4] If the utopian imaginary attempts to envisage a "good place," a system of social organization that does not do violence to its citizens and instead nurtures them toward achieving their full potential and their best selves, it might initially make a certain sort of intuitive sense to view all the "bad places" as being cut from the same cloth – but Jameson and like-minded critics note that most dystopias are actually utopias-in-reverse, naming a horror whose failures call on us to flee it, or revolt against it, or at worst use our privileged position before the final disaster to prevent the dystopia from ever coming into existence in the first place. The distinction between utopia and dystopia can be seen, in this way, to be primarily a matter of tone: both the utopians and the dystopians argue that the arc of history is fundamentally mutable, in human hands and subject to human choices, with possible futures capable of being far better and far worse than the current state of affairs. It is the antiutopians, he says, that refuse all possibility of historical difference, asserting that "there is no alternate" to the nightmare of history as it has already unfolded and continues to unfold; whether invoking biological determination, unyielding economic law, or some theological fall from God's grace, the antiutopians simultaneously argue that the world is as it must be, that any attempt to alter this state of affairs would be futile, perverse, or dangerous (or even all three at once).[5] Thus Jameson suggestions a "slogan of anti-anti-Utopianism";[6] whatever else we are, we must be against the antiutopians, and must believe in the possibility of a future that can be different from the past and a history that does not go, as in Crumb's doomed city, only one way. The very assertion of an ecotopia, or any utopia, is an assertion that (in keeping with the old socialist slogan) "another world is possible."

This distinction between utopia/dystopia on the one side and between dystopia and antiutopia on the other – echoed in various ways by Mark Fisher, Tom Moylan, Rob McAlear, and many others[7] – allows us to better understand some texts that may seem, on the surface, to be oriented toward ecofascism or apocalyptic scenarios as a kind of utopian literature in disguise. Rather than using positive visions of happy endings to inspire their readers, many such ecologically minded texts attempt instead to frighten or terrorize their readers, shocking them into what the author sees as better politics (with the hope of averting or ameliorating the coming crisis). The key distinction becomes whether or not environmental collapse, and all the attendant social misery that collapse will entail, is posited as fundamentally inevitable (antiutopia) or as preventable/mitigatable (utopia/dystopia); against the siren call of a necrofuturistic "capitalist realism"[8] that can only encounter the future as a field of universal death, environmentalist utopian literature (in both its utopian and dystopian modes) instead returns agency to human institutions and human beings, highlighting the choices that, as Kurt Vonnegut once so memorably put it, "are right now determining whether the space voyage for the next billion years or so is going to be Heaven or Hell."[9] Many (perhaps most) works of contemporary science fiction are ecotopian in the sense of Jameson's "utopian impulse," insofar as they seek to dramatize and critique the ecologically destructive practices of contemporary capitalism in order to spark revolutionary opposition to what exists; even the most apocalyptic depictions of climate breakdown are trying to activate a kind of ecotopian political orientation in their reader, such that the disaster might be combatted or averted in real life if not within the fiction. Still, in keeping with the overall approach of this volume, this chapter will focus primarily on what Jameson would call instead ecotopian "programs":[10] specific plans, blueprints, and road maps for the establishment of an ecotopia, usually portrayed in some sort of futurological narrative, that imagines some viable path from our toxic present to a more ecological future.

Such visions answer the call once articulated by one of the great American utopian thinkers, Kim Stanley Robinson, in his introduction to *Future Primitive: The New Ecotopias*:

> It's not that [these stories] advocate simple returns to nature, or a rejection of technology, which given our current situation would be nothing more than another kind of ecologic impossibility. Rather, they attempt to imagine sophisticated new technologies combined with habits saved or reinvented from our deep past, with the notion that prehistoric cultures were critical in making us what we are, and knew things about our relationship to the world that we should not forget. These science fictions reject the inevitability of the machine future, and ask again the old questions, What is the healthiest way to live? What is the most beautiful?[11]

A short coda at the close of the chapter will briefly discuss real-world ecotopian projects, attempts to make such visions real as a model to others for what might yet be.

Early Ecotopias

It is a critical given at this point to remember Sir Thomas More's "utopia" as one of the oldest ongoing puns in English literature. If it were spelled *eutopia,* it would mean "good place"; if it were spelled *outopia,* it would be "no place." Thus utopia is the good place that is also a nonplace: the good place that does not exist. Historical utopias – More's own *Utopia* from 1516 among them – were typically more concerned with transformations of the social realm than with preservation of the natural world, but many can be recognized from the perspective of twentieth-century environmentalism to have important ecological themes. *Utopia* itself begins with a rumination on the enclosure movement and the process by which English "sheep, which are naturally mild, and easily kept in order, may be said now to devour men and unpeople, not only villages, but towns."[12] This suborning of human needs to the needs of industry is, among other things, an early ecological dystopia. In Utopia, in contrast, the Utopians seek to live in better harmony with the natural world, according to the appetites and pleasures Nature promotes, rather than seeking to transform the world through industrialization and mechanization or to twist it to antinatural ends.

While the Utopians do not eschew technology, and a great many utopian formulations continue to rely on technological progress as a means of eliminating human suffering and want, many of More's successors would imagine utopia as requiring a backwards movement to an Arcadian or even Edenic past.[13] In Samuel Butler's influential utopian satire *Erewhon*, "nowhere" *almost* spelled backwards, the vision of a utopia speaks against the fantasy of technological progress in "The Book of the Machines," an early artificial intelligence story in which machine intelligence threatens humanity and must be destroyed – and even institutes a legal regime of universal vegetarianism for centuries before ultimately concluding that the same logic would ban the eating of plants as well (and that therefore eating animals must be okay).[14] William Morris's *News from Nowhere*, written in response to Edward Bellamy's *Looking Backward*, favors an anarchist, pastoralist vision of utopia focused on local production with minimal mechanical augmentation of human powers – an anticipation of the antistate, anti-industrial distributionist economy J. R. R. Tolkien would later famously imagine for his Hobbits in their cozy Shire in his world-famous *Lord of the Rings*. Other utopias (both earnest and satirical) challenge the division between the human and the natural altogether, perhaps most famously in the final segment of Jonathan Swift's *Gulliver's Travels*, which sees a horse utopia so fully realized that Gulliver is unable to return to his original human context without feeling visceral disgust, once the Houyhnhnms cast him out.[15]

The Golden Age of Science Fiction – from the initial concretization of science fiction as a recognizable publishing genre in the pulp magazines of the 1920s and 1930s to the robot stories and space opera of the 1940s and 1950s – has a striking lack of ecotopias; where these narratives consider energy or environmental constraints at all, it is typically in the mode of fantasy, where the invention of a zero-point energy device renders the concern obsolete. This tendency is in line with what Donald A. Wollheim has called the "consensus future"[16] of science fiction, a technooptimistic belief in the inevitability of human colonization of outer space and the eventual formation of a galactic empire; in such fantasies, the Earth itself often becomes a backwater or a footnote, even forgotten, as human beings discover planet after planet worth living on, and the center of gravity of human civilization moves to one of these new planets instead. The impracticality of such fantasy would come under revision in the subsequent decades; when Isaac Asimov returns to his Foundation series in the 1980s, for instance, it is specifically to add in an ecological critique of what began as an unbridled, unrestrained space opera, and *Star Trek* becomes increasingly concerned about the future of the environment in its 1980s films and series as well.[17]

The need for science fiction to revise its attitude toward the environment reflects a larger shift in the culture around environmental awareness, one that would be reflected in science fiction's so-called "New Wave" (discussed below). One key moment of inflection comes from (mostly) outside the genre: Rachel Carson's *Silent Spring* (1962), whose study of the pernicious effects of pesticides helped launched the environmental movement in the United States. Carson's own approach is somewhat science fictional; she begins her story with a "fable for tomorrow" about a "town in the heart of America where all life seemed to live in harmony with its surroundings." But the people in this idyllic place despoil their paradise: the countryside falls quiet as both human and animal fall prey to a mysterious illness:

> On the farms the hens brooded, but no chicks hatched. The farmers complained that they were unable to raise any pigs – the litters were small and the young survived only a few days. The apple trees were coming into bloom but no bees droned among the blossoms, so there was no pollination and there would be no fruit. The roadsides, once so attractive, were now lined with browned and withered vegetation as though swept by fire. These, too, were silent, deserted by all living things. Even the streams were now lifeless. Anglers no longer visited them, for all the fish had died.
>
> In the gutters under the eaves and between the shingles of the roofs, a white granular powder still showed a few patches; some weeks before it had fallen like snow upon the roofs and the lawns, the fields and streams. No witchcraft, no enemy action had silenced the rebirth of new life in this stricken world. The people had done it themselves.[18]

Carson's ecotopian impulse is a call to prevent the fable from becoming true; by the end of the 1970s, her attitude would be a dominant one in literary science fiction, as well as a major political force in the United States and Europe.[19]

Still, a few Golden Age texts stand out as key anticipations of the environmentalist movement, including Frank Herbert's *Dune,* set on a desert world whose inhabitants must pay careful attention to their environmental constraints, while the planet is mined for a valuable oil-like energy resource (the Spice Melange) necessary for interstellar navigation; Naomi Mitchison's early ecofeminist *Memoirs of a Spacewoman*, which sees its hero visit multiple planets where humans have crafted alternative relationships with animals and with their natural world(s); and Frederik Pohl's *The Space Merchants,* which imagined a revolutionary World Conservationist Association opposing consumerism on an overpopulated Earth all the way back in 1952. Still, most of these depictions were negative in character; the articulation of a positive ecotopia would need to wait until the mid-1970s to fully emerge.

Ecotopia

Our study now brings us to what might have otherwise been the natural place to begin any discussion of ecotopian formulation in American literature: Ernest Callenbach's *Ecotopia: The Notebooks and Reports of William Weston*, first published in 1975, which originated the term. Taking place in 1999, twenty-five years into his future, Callenbach's future history imagines a breakaway republic in the Pacific Northwest, Ecotopia, consisting of the current states of Washington and Oregon and parts of Northern California; the novel depicts the entry of journalist William Weston, one of the first Americans to be allowed entry to Ecotopia since the nation was formed in 1980, and the book takes an epistolary form of his dispatches from his visit to his home newspaper. In classic utopian form, Weston is initially deeply skeptical of the Ecotopian project, but eventually becomes so committed to their project he defects from the United States, choosing to live there permanently; also like many earlier utopian narratives, this familiar drama of reluctant seduction is coupled with a romance plot in which he falls passionately in love with an Ecotopian woman.

In a similar structure, most of the book takes the form of short vignettes that compare Ecotopian institutions and cultural habits to our own: their reliance on public transportation, their lack of both governmental and corporate control, their labor practices and work ethic (including a twenty-hour work week), and so on. The core innovation of Ecotopia is its commitment to stable-state, zero-growth, minimal-waste economics; this entails both a commitment to total recycling and attendant changes in consumer expectations. The Ecotopians harness scientific innovation here as well, using a novel form of biodegradable plastic, and by the end of the novel (in a moment that seems to veer into the realm of fantasy rather than practical utopianism) they are attempting to harness the power of chlorophyll for sustainable human energy use.

Callenbach's Ecotopians attempt to live in harmony with nature in another sense: they attempt to restore aspects of the human that are suppressed or otherwise hindered by Western cultural norms. The most striking example of this (and one quite surprising to contemporary student readers) may be their use of a hyperviolent simulated war game as a means of expiating human (male) aggression; they also have an openness towards sex and drugs that does not attach moral weight to either form of release. Human beings, the book says, are "tribal animals";[20] many Ecotopian institutions are expressly modeled on Native American cultural practices, in ways that will likely read as cultural appropriation in the present moment, and the Ecotopians frequently invoke what they imagine "Indians" might do when deciding, for instance, whether or not to wear a wristwatch.[21] Most disturbingly, the book as published seems to endorse a certain notion of the inescapable naturality of racism; the Ecotopians practice a mode of segregation that sees almost all of its Black population living in an allied but Black-separatist community in what is now Oakland, California, an arrangement that is presented as more or less the best thing for everyone involved.[22]

Despite these elements that might seem deeply questionable, however, *Ecotopia* is remarkable for its focus on the difficult practicalities of establishing "ecology in one country."[23] The failing mainline United States, even more voraciously capitalist than ever (and fighting a losing Vietnam-War-esque brush war in Brazil) is desperate for reunification, and William Weston is sent into the country in a hybrid mode that is part journalist, part spy. Ecotopia has an intelligence and surveillance apparatus that borders on the authoritarian, as well as very tight control over its internal media, and is rightly paranoid about US attempts to undermine the country. (There are even references to dispossessed Ecotopian capitalists living outside the country, in direct comparison to the situation of the Cuban Revolution.[24]) Nor can Ecotopia fully close itself off; King Utopus's decision to dig a trench around utopia to turn it into an island loses its power in an age where pollution and radiation from outside are carried on the wind and in the water. Ecotopia's own moment of founding is itself an act of war, if not indeed an act of ecoterrorism; the country is only allowed to secede from the United States because the Ecotopian founders claim to have hidden nuclear bombs in major American cities, and it is only allowed to continue as an independent nation because the supposed weapons have still not yet been recovered twenty-five years later.

The notion that the establishment of utopia may require a moment of murder – that utopia has "genocide lurking in its bowels," as Cory Doctorow has said[25] – is replicated in other major ecotopian speculations of the 1970s, especially (and unexpectedly) in feminist science fiction. Many of these stories – following in the footsteps of Charlotte Perkins Gilman's *Herland*, a spiritual predecessor for many – hinge on the elimination of men as the prerequisite for both utopia and ecotopia. In "Houston, Houston, Do You Read?" by James Tiptree, Jr. (the penname of Alice Sheldon), the utopian break comes in a moment of plague that kills nearly everyone on Earth (both men and women); the future Earth is populated only by around 2 million people, clones of 11,000 women who survived the disease around a medical laboratory in Denver. (Tiptree's "The Last Flight of Dr. Ain" does "Houston, Houston" one better; in this one, a scientist *intentionally* distributes a genetically engineered virus in order to kill off the human species before it fully destroys the ecosphere.) In Joanna Russ's *The Female Man*, a similar a-plague-killed-all-the-men story is told on the utopian planet Whileaway, an all-female ecotopian paradise – though late in the novel another character strongly suggests that this is all just an alibi for a *literal* war between the sexes, whose exterminationist resolution that made Whileaway possible. A different sort of gender elimination makes ecotopia possible in Marge Piercy's *Woman on the Edge of Time*, a time travel novel hovering in suspension between a hypertechnologized urban dystopia of authoritarian fascism, racism, misogyny, and oligarchy, on the one hand, and an agrarian, detechnologized ecotopia called Mattapoisett, in which people are nurtured to both psychological and social health, on the other. In ecofeminist Mattapoisett, the gender binary has been eliminated: children are birthed from artificial wombs, and both men and women breastfeed. The actions of the main character will determine which future, ecotopia or ecodystopia, ultimately comes to pass.

One of most acclaimed authors of the New Wave in science fiction, Ursula K. Le Guin, frequently incorporated ecological and ecotopian themes into her fiction. One of her most acclaimed works, *The Dispossessed*, depicts a double planetary system: Urras, a lush Earthlike planet living through a sort of perpetual Cold War, and Anarres, a nearly barren moon inhabited by breakaway anarchists who have rejected the values of the analogues of both the USA and the USSR on Urras. The people of Anarres have found solidarity through their struggle on the resource-poor planet, while the people of Urras have instituted strict environmentalist protocols in order to allow their hypermodernity to continue without destroying the planet. The punchline for this dichotomy comes near the end of the novel, when a character takes refuge in the embassy from Earth; we discover that this is all taking place in a future where the Earth has been ravaged by environmental collapse and is, in the words of the Terran ambassador, a "ruin. A planet spoiled by the human species"; *both* Urras and Anarres, in this context, represent ecotopian alternatives to Earth's most likely future.[26] While *The Dispossessed*'s treatment of potential alternatives to ecoapocalypse may seem somewhat paltry, it stands in stark contrast to many and perhaps most major 1970s texts of New Wave science fiction. Films such as *Logan's Run, Soylent Green, Silent Running, Planet of the Apes, Mad Max*, and so on, as well as the prose works of authors such as John Brunner, Philip K. Dick, Harlan Ellison, and J. G. Ballard, all embraced this sort of deflationary ecological futurity, taking the near-term ruination of the planetary ecology as a foundational assumption, with nary an ecotopia in site.

1980s and Beyond

The ecological themes of the 1970s saw some diminishment in the science fiction of the 1980s, whose most influential texts tend to orbit around the so-called cyberpunk movement, a wave of science fiction focused on the possibilities and pitfalls of the computer. In a sense, as I have argued elsewhere, the cyberpunk movement can be seen as a kind of repressed ecological science fiction, specifically a recognition that the Golden Age dreams of extrasolar colonization were a dead end, and that meanwhile the technological progress that was supposed to liberate humanity was in fact creating structures of total surveillance and control while destroying the only planet on which humanity will ever live in the bargain. Escaping inside the computer becomes, in its own bizarre way, a utopian reaction to that deflationary realization; the nonmaterial plane of the digital becomes the last and only place where those deeply held dreams of unfettered science-fictional expansion might still be realized.[27] Strikingly, many 1980s cyberpunk texts include significant eco-apocalyptic disaster in the background of their storyworlds, like William Gibson's *Neuromancer*, set in the aftermath of a nuclear war, or the film *Blade Runner*, directed by Ridley Scott, set in an overpopulated, hyper-polluted world ravaged by climate change.[28] The notion of ecological catastrophe as intertwined with cyberpunk fiction would continue well into the 1990s, as in *The Matrix*, directed by the Wachowskis, where the human–robot war ultimately "scorched the sky" (a last-ditch effort by humanity to shut off the solar-powered robots) and rendered the surface of Earth uninhabitable. Even texts from this period not directly associated with cyberpunk, such as Margaret Atwood's famously dystopian (and regrettably prescient) *The Handmaid's Tale*, took a degrading environment as a baseline assumption about the future; the fascist takeover of the United States that results in the Republic of Gilead emerges in part out of environmental pressures, as well as nuclear fallout and "Colonies" attempting to reclaim irradiated parts of the United States.[29]

Somewhat out of step with the consumerist and computerist obsessions of the 1980s, Kim Stanley Robinson's utopian science fiction carries forward the ecotopian torch of the New Wave for the 1980s and beyond. Robinson, a former student of Fredric Jameson's and a committed socialist, included ecological projections in his formative Three Californias and Mars trilogies, which have been a hallmark of his fiction ever since. The Three Californias trilogy, three lightly interconnected novels taking place in three different near-future versions of Orange County, imagines postnuclear horror (*The Wild Shore*), endless urban sprawl and consumer-capitalist supremacy (*The Gold Coast*), and, most importantly for this study, an ecologically sustainable utopian transformation of the present (*Pacific Edge*). *Pacific Edge*, set in 2065, attempts to imagine an ecotopian future without either the technological shortcuts or the revolutionary politics of a novel like *Ecotopia*, to say nothing of the bloodshed of "Houston, Houston, Do You Read?" or *The Female Man*; its primary conflict is a local zoning dispute over whether "the last empty hill in El Modena" should be developed.[30] The Mars books, in contract, have a much more ambitious scale, attempting to imagine a realistic settlement of the Red Planet that includes long-duration terraforming, against a backdrop of degrading conditions on Earth (including a period of prolonged terrestrial crisis caused by ice-sheet collapse); the book was influenced in part by internal NASA debates about whether Mars has a right to exist outside of its instrumental usefulness to human beings,[31] and different characters in the book take strongly divergent positions about just how much of Mars to terraform, and just how aggressively. While the Mars books, like *Pacific Edge*, mostly traffic in a logic of compromise and synthesis among competing interests, they also explore the spiritual dimensions of tempering humanity's technophilia and endless imperial expansion with a respect for the environment and the need to live in harmony with nature; the novel's most spiritually balanced characters, Hiroki Ai and the Coyote, promote a notion of living with respect for Mars derived from non-Western religious spiritual traditions. It is not enough for humans to terraform Mars, the books' heroes conclude; they must also allow Mars to "aeroform" them, or they will always be at war with the planet.[32] The lessons for any human society that remains on Earth – a civilization that is terraforming *the Earth* "by accident, and mostly by damaging things," as Robinson has frequently noted in interviews[33] – are clear.

Other major authors explored ecotopian possibilities in the 1990s and early 2000s, though often with quite a bit of mixed feelings. Octavia E. Butler's Parables series is widely recognized as one of the first novels to take climate change seriously as a crisis – but the situation is essentially a slow-motion apocalypse, and her characters do not devote themselves to fixing the problem so much as trying to escape Earth to achieve their "Destiny . . . among the stars" instead. (The first words of *Parable of the Sower* makes the trade-off between climate and the science-fiction "consensus future" quite vivid: the protagonist dreams of trying to escape a burning building in time before it falls down around her ears.[34]) Likewise, in Butler's Xenogenesis series of the 1980s, the aliens who colonize a postnuclear Earth bring a more harmonious relationship with nature, favoring bioengineered organic devices over mechanisms and machines and restoring the biosphere of the planet – but their ultimate plan is to turn the planet into one of their spaceships and fly it into the interstellar void, killing all life on the surface permanently.

Le Guin wrote another major postcapitalist ecotopian work, *Always Coming Home*, an almost anthropological antinovel composed of observations, myth, poetry, and artifacts from the Kesh, a deindustrialized people who "might be going to have lived a long, long time from now in Northern California."[35] The Kesh represent a sort of Indigenous Futurism,[36] albeit from a very white perspective; they have returned to social and cultural practices associated with Native Americans in the contemporary United States, while the work of exploring and colonizing the universe (the supposed Destiny) has been left to autonomous robotic drones. Margaret Atwood's *Oryx and Crake* has a different sort of primitivist vision, also simultaneously critiquing and reinforcing white notions of nonwhite sociality: it sees another mad scientist with another bioengineered virus, seeking to kill off all of humanity in the name of saving animals and the natural world, leave behind only a genetically modified version of humanity (the "Crakers") with deliberately diminished ambition, intelligence, and creativity that will never again embark on expansion or colonialism and will never outgrow its very limited environmental niche. The first book views this plan as a horror, but later books seem to view it much more sympathetically, with the trilogy ending in *MaddAddam* with an ecotopian vision of postapocalyptic unity among humans, the Crakers, and a pig/baboon successor species with whom they have learned to telepathically communicate. Despite the unexpectedly upbeat ending of Atwood's trilogy, an ecotopian imaginary with that much genocide in its bowels seems hard to fully endorse.[37]

2000s and 2010s and 2020s: Ecotopia Today

As awareness of the real severity and scope of climate change increased and political solutions began to appear unlikely or impossible, the sour notion that total or near-total human extinction might be the solution to the environmental crisis continued to have currency in some of the most powerful ecological texts of the Anthropocene, among then Ramin Bahrani's short film *Plastic Bag*, Richard McGuire's graphic novel *Here*, and Boon-Joon Ho's fiercely anticapitalist allegory in his *Snowpiercer* film adaptation. But such texts are, if they are ecotopian at all, still typically only ecotopian in negative; they describe not the perfection or even the improvement of human institutions but rather their elimination. Likewise, an increasing number of texts from this period depict climate disaster or apocalypse in spectacular terms, whether directly (as in the Roland Emmerich film *The Day after Tomorrow* or Kim Stanley Robinson's Science in the Capital trilogy, both depicting rapid climate change that happens over the scale of months rather than years), or allegorical and symbolic (one might think here of basically any major science-fiction text from the last twenty years, from the ecoterrorist Thanos in the Marvel Cinematic Universe to the return of kaiju monsters like Godzilla as metaphors for climate change across multiple franchises and reboots). But these texts too rarely veer into the ecotopian; what emerges after the disaster is usually some sort of militarized war society, clinging to industrialization and technologization, rather than human beings seeking to live in better harmony with nature.

Where texts do explore the ecotopian, it is likely in somewhat mixed, hesitant terms. N. K. Jemisin's acclaimed Broken Earth trilogy, the first novel series ever to win back-to-back-to-back Hugo Awards from the fan-led World Science Fiction Convention (Worldcon), depicts a future Earth that has been ravaged by human experience and technoscientific "advancement," ruled by a sinister empire whose agents hold the worst of the disaster in check by exploiting the psychokinetic power of mutant humans called orogenes. The ecotopian solution here is not compromise or adaptation but political revolution, which includes overthrowing the cruelly optimistic attachment to stability; the heroes of the story end both the permanent ecological emergency and the empire that had benefited from its continuation, opening the door to something truly new (which we do not get to see). Other recent books with ecotopian elements, like Paolo Bacigalupi's *The Windup Girl* and Jeff Vandermeer's *Annihilation*, and like Atwood's Oryx and Crake series, see the transformation of the human species as a prerequisite for ecotopia: the characteristics we associate with capitalism, political liberalism, and modernity are ill suited to the transformation of the planet, these texts argue, and we will have to change who we are and what we think we must be in order to survive. (Bacigalupi's next novel, *The Water Knife*, set in an American Southwest undergoing conditions of permanent water shortage, has a somewhat more jaundiced vision of what it will take to survive in the future: the characters must embrace a certain cruelty and murderousness to thrive in the ruined future, trading ecotopia in for a dystopian, corrupt Las Vegas instead.)

In contrast, Jemisin's short story "Emergency Skin," released as an Amazon Original Story, has a somewhat more straightforward and down-to-Earth ecotopian politics: Earth becomes an ecosocialist collective after the billionaires (believing the planet to be doomed) pick up and leave for outer space, abandoning the planet to those they deemed undesirable (who promptly usher in a utopia the desperate billionaires must beg, borrow, and steal from to enable their own survival on their doomed colony world). Likewise, a handful of texts like Emily St. John Mandel's *Station Eleven* (adapted as a television series for HBO) depict a detechnologized world in quite positive terms; after a virulent plague has destroyed civilization, the survivors live in small agrarian communities, and (generally speaking) all seem happier and healthier as a result. Kim Stanley Robinson's *New York 2140*, set in a Manhattan that has become a canal city like Venice after sea-level rise, cuts a somewhat middle path: the fight for a better, more livable world goes on even as climate change worsens, but it remains achievable, and the characters in the novel are able to usher in major transformations of the social even as their Earth is, on some level, objectively worse than our own. Robinson's *Ministry for the Future*, a breakthrough book for Robinson that was endorsed by Barack Obama, Bill Gates, and *New York Times* opinion columnist Ezra Klein among other liberal influencers, significantly elevating Robinson's profile, moves the moment of crisis from the 2140s to right now, depicting a planet undergoing political and ecological tumult and tracing the actions of a wide range of governmental and nongovernmental actors who seek to ameliorate its worst impacts. As with many ostensibly ecotopian texts, *Ministry* assumes that a certain level of disruption and dispossession is now inevitable, due to the carbon release that has already happened; the charge of the Ministry is not so much to establish some perfectly ecotopian postcapitalist civilization but to work alongside anyone willing (capitalists, socialists, even ecoterrorists) to save what they still can.

Ministry, despite feeling in some ways quite optimistic about the prospects for intervention in the climate crisis, can also be seen as registering a certain withering of the ecotopian imagination in the contemporary moment. In general, the renewed environmental movement and the growing recognition of the climate emergency in the 2020s has not made ecotopian speculation more common; rather, it has largely turned the future from an object of hope into an object of terror, where massively decreased quality of life for those who are now young and those soon to be born is taken as a critical given, and little hope for better seems possible. Viral posts, drawing from recent reports from the Intergovernmental Panel on Climate Change, frequently proclaim that we have less than ten years to save the planet, or even grimly announce that a certain amount of warming would be inevitable even if 100 percent of carbon emissions were to stop *today* – but the effect seems to create a sort of quietest defeat rather than refusal or revolution, or else a sort of unquenchable rage. Greta Thunberg, the teen activist whose "school strike for climate" movement has influenced activism on both sides of the Atlantic, began her historic UN speech with the latter: "You have stolen my dreams and my childhood with your empty words. And yet I'm one of the lucky ones. People are suffering. People are dying. Entire ecosystems are collapsing. We are in the beginning of a mass extinction, and all you can talk about is money and fairy tales of eternal economic growth. How dare you!"[38] It seems fitting that China Miéville's introduction to the most recent Verso edition of More's *Utopia* speaks not of ecotopia so much as of the utopia of revenge: "We need utopia, but to try to think utopia, in this world, without rage, without fury, is an indulgence we can't afford. In the face of what is done, we cannot think utopia without hate."[39]

Still, ecotopian speculation remains. Long-term planned ecotopian communities, modeled after Callenbach, Butler, and other writers, exist across the contemporary United States, with names like Earthaven (in North Carolina), Dancing Rabbit Ecovillage (in Missouri), or Arcosanti (in Arizona);[40] such communities attempt with varying levels of success to put into practice the communitarian, anarchist, detechnologized, pastoralist, and Indigenous Futurist vision of many of the ecotopias discussed above. The most recent Ecuadorian constitution includes the proposition that nature has a right to exist, as well as that Indigenous people have a right to sustain themselves in that natural space; a worldwide legal movement is underway, working with local communities including Indigenous groups, arguing that animals and even some noncorporeal features of the natural world, like rivers, might qualify for legal personhood and certain inalienable rights. Other interventions are more philosophical: a confluence of political action groups, manifestos, and online discussion forums devoted in various ways to imagining alternatives to the ceaseless ecological destruction of late capitalism. One set of viral images stuck with me as I completed this piece, shown in Figure 12.2: multiple viral images of cities in the United States and Europe that had removed their dedicated urban highway systems altogether and replaced them with city parks, as well as experiments during the Covid pandemic eliminating automobiles from city streets into pedestrian marketplaces (some of which were reversed, but others of which were made permanent). The comparison of before and after – a sea of cars without people versus a thriving living space populated by both human and nonhuman life – harkens back to R. Crumb's "ecotopian solution." "It's never too late to acknowledge the reality that urban highways are a fixable mistake," proclaims one such post juxtaposing the shoreline of Düsseldorf, Germany,

Figure 12.2 Deurbanized Utopia.

between 1990 and 2019.[41] Such posts reflect a buried ecotopian imaginary, an ongoing yearning at least among some number of us to yet find some other, better way to live.

Notes

1. Multiple versions of Crumb's comic have been published in various venues and are available on the Internet, from the original black-and-white print from 1979 to the full-color version published with the epilogue appended after 1988 (as in the print currently available for sale at The Official Crumb Site. This is the version

I primarily work from here. It should also be noted that the idea of America as an "empty" place prior to settlement by Europeans is a deeply problematic settler fantasy that erases the existence of Indigenous people in the Americas, to say nothing of the horrific violence done to them by settlement and by settlers.

2. Ivan Brunetti, "Comics as Place," *The Paris Review* (August 10, 2020), online.
3. Brunetti.
4. Fredric Jameson, *Archaeologies of the Future: The Desire Called Utopia and Other Science Fictions* (New York: Verso, 2005). See especially the Introduction, "Utopia Now."
5. These three categories are identified by Albert O. Hirschman in *The Rhetoric of Reaction* (Cambridge, MA: Harvard University Press, 1991) as the foundational gestures of right-wing denialism.
6. Jameson, xvi.
7. Tom Moylan, *Becoming Utopian: The Culture and Politics of Racial Transformation* (London: Bloomsbury, 2020); Mark Fisher, *Capitalism Realism: Is There No Alternative?* (London: Zero Books, 2009); Rob McAlear, "The Value of Fear: Toward a Rhetorical Model of Dystopia," Interdisciplinary Humanities 27.2 (2010), 24–42.
8. See Fisher. I discuss these sorts of necrofuturist fantasies, mostly outside the scope of this chapter, in more detail in"' If the Engine Ever Stops, We'd All Die': *Snowpiercer* and Necrofuturism," in *Paradoxa* 26 (2014), 41–66.
9. Kurt Vonnegut, *God Bless You, Mr. Rosewater* (New York: Dell Publishing, 1965), 18.
10. For more on the distinction between the utopian impulse and the utopian program, see *Archaeologies of the Future.*
11. Kim Stanley Robinson, "Introduction," *Future Primitive: The New Ecotopias* (New York: Tor Books, 1994), 9–11 (11).
12. Thomas More, *Utopia* (New York: Verso, 2016), 43–44.
13. Samuel R. Delany notes that utopian formulation can be divided along a technologist versus pastoralist split, with the technoutopian New Jerusalem looking like a fascistic, consumerist Brave New World to its detractors, and the ecotopian Arcadia looking more like a deprived, poverty-stricken Land of the Flies in turn. See Samuel R. Delany, "On Triton and Other Matters," *Science Fiction Studies* 17.3 (1990), 295–324.
14. The full text of *Erewhon* is available at Project Gutenberg online. The same is true of Morris's *News from Nowhere*, discussed next.
15. Animal utopias – especially stories about talking animals – have an august tradition in environmentalist thought that falls outside the scope of this chapter, insofar as they are not, generally speaking, pragmatically achievable outside the realm of fantasy. Many important environmentalist texts use the trope of talking animals (especially great apes) to launch their critique, from Kafka's "A Report to an Academy" (1917) to Daniel Quinn's influential cult-classic *Ishmael* (1992), which features a sage talking gorilla dispensing wisdom about better and worse ways to live; an interesting middle text that involves

what is ultimately revealed to be a talking-animal *hoax* to effect ecotopian transformation is Leo Szilard's antinuclear "Voice of the Dolphins" (1961).

16. See Donald A. Wollheim, *The Universe Makers: Science Fiction Today* (New York: Harper and Row, 1971). He uses the more opaque term "consensus cosmogeny" in the book, which has slipped to "consensus future" in much practical usage.
17. See especially Asimov's *Foundation's Edge* (1982), which posits a Gaia-esque gestalt galactic consciousness as an alternative to renewed space empire. Asimov died before completing the series, which leaves it in an odd state of indecision as to whether Galaxia (the interstellar Gaia) or the Second Empire will prevail. For Star Trek, see especially *Star Trek IV: The Voyage Home* (1986) as well as the myriad episodes in *The Next Generation* (1987–1994) and its successor series that allegorize the environmental crisis in increasingly dystopian terms. By the thirty-first century of *Star Trek: Discovery*'s third season (2020–2021), ecological crisis has fully destroyed the once-technoutopian Federation, registering a more general inversion toward pessimism in the way America imagines its future.
18. Rachel Carson, *Silent Spring* (New York: Mariner Books, 2002 [1962]), 1–3.
19. Of course, as noted by Fabius Mayland among others, this 1970s environmental turn in science fiction would produce ample instances of reactionary and outright ecofascistic fantasies of the future as well, many of them centered on Paul and Anne Howland Ehrlich's *The Population Bomb* (1968). See Fabius Mayland, "When Ecological Fears Were Fears of Overpopulation: Paul Ehrlich's Association with SF around 1970,"forthcoming.
20. Ernest Callenbach, *Ecotopia* (Berkeley, CA: Banyan Tree Books, 2004 [1975]), 32.
21. Callenbach, 29. "Many Ecotopians [are] sentimental about Indians, and there's some sense in which they envy the Indians their lost natural place in the American wilderness." References of the sort Callenbach makes to Native people are regrettably frequent in ecotopian literature, especially of this era: Native Americans are frequently fantasized about as a supposedly vanished inspiration for a different way of life, as opposed to encountered as still-existing vital societies who might be partners in the political, cultural, and/or scientific transformation of the present.
22. See the chapter titled "Race in Ecotopia: Apartheid or Equality?" (98–102).
23. See Callenbach, 85. The reference is of course to twentieth-century debates about whether socialist revolution could sustain itself nation by nation or if only a fully global socialist revolution could ensure a socialist future.
24. Callenbach, 90.
25. Cory Doctorow, "Trying to Predict the Present," Gerry Canavan Website (April 8, 2015), online. The interview took place in spring 2010.
26. Ursula K. Le Guin, *The Dispossessed* (New York: HarperPrism, 1994 [1974]), 347.
27. See Gerry Canavan, "Charles Stross: *Accelerando* (Case Study): The Singularity and the End of History," from *The Routledge Companion to*

Cyberpunk, edited by Anna McFarlane, Graham J. Murphy, and Lars Schmeink (New York: Routledge, 2019), 56–63 (57).

28. These ecological themes are even more prevalent in the original novel on which *Blade Runner* was based, Philip K. Dick's *Do Androids Dream of Electric Sheep?* (1968), whose title references a subplot in which all animals have died on Earth as a result of human activity, leaving humans catastrophically guilt-stricken, spiritually bereft, and existentially lonely.
29. These elements have increased prominence in *The Handmaid Tale*'s television adaptation (2017–), as well as in Atwood's 2019 sequel, *The Testaments*.
30. Kim Stanley Robinson, *Pacific Edge* (New York: Tom Doherty Associates, 2013), 77.
31. See for instance Christopher McKay, "Does Mars Have Rights: An Approach to the Environmental Ethics of Planetary Engineering," from *Moral Expertise: Studies in Practical and Professional Ethics*, edited by Don Macniven (New York: Routledge, 1990), 184–197.
32. Kim Stanley Robinson, *Red Mars* (New York: Bantam Books, 1993), 253.
33. Geoff Manaugh, "Comparative Planetology: An Interview with Kim Stanley Robinson," *BLDGBLOG* (December 19, 2007), online.
34. Octavia E. Butler, *Parable of the Sower* (New York: Warner Books, 1993), 3–5.
35. Ursula K. Le Guin, *Always Coming Home* (Berkeley: University of California Press, 2001), xi.
36. See Grace Dillon (ed.), *Walking the Clouds: An Anthology of Indigenous Science Fiction* (Tucson: University of Arizona Press, 2012), as well as the special issue of *Extrapolation* on "Indigenous Futurisms" she edited with John Rieder and Michael Levy (2016).
37. Atwood's book does not flinch from this ambiguity. In *MaddAddam*, the human–Craker hybrid children who represent the future of this society are revealed to be the product of a sexual encounter that the human women bearing these children experienced as a horrific gang rape that occurred at the first meeting of the two species.
38. "How dare you": Transcript of Greta Thunberg's UN climate speech. Nikkei Asia (25 Sep. 25, 2019), online.
39. China Miéville, "The Limits of Utopia," in Thomas More, *Utopia* (New York: Verso, 2016), 26–27.
40. For a list of other such communities, see Doug Moss and Roddy Scheer, "Eco-Village Movement Flourishing Across United States," from *The Environmental Magazine* (January 31, 2018), online.
41. "It's never too late to acknowledge the reality that urban highways are a fixable mistake," Reddit.com (November 5, 2021), online.

CHAPTER 13

Economic Justice

Hugh C. O'Connell

From our current vantage point within late stage capitalism, the relationship between economic justice and utopianism appears absolutely necessary yet paradoxically impossible due to the constraints of our current world-system. As the editors of *Salvage* note, "if the shopworn metaphor of 'zombie' accumulation once captured something of the post-2008 political economy, it does no longer. The composed social settlement at the end of neoliberalism was more neoliberalism."[1] Indeed, as McKenzie Wark argues, even this idea "that capitalism still goes on, and on" may simply be a knee-jerk comforting gesture that elides the fact that new asymmetries of real subsumption, information, and financialization give "rise to a strange kind of political economy," one that our critical theories – utopian or otherwise – are unable to conceptualize, let alone offer solutions to.[2]

The generalized lack of political will combined with financialization's subsumption of the subject and foreclosing of the future as the increasingly necessary site of economic capture for a floundering capitalist system seems only to promise what Gerry Canavan terms necrofutures: "those capitalist-realist anticipations of the coming decades that anticipate the future as a devastated world of death, and yet simultaneously insist that this world of death is the only possible future."[3] Indeed, starting in the 1980s, one could see the outline of "the waning of utopia"[4] beginning to take shape, codified and then repeated throughout the 1990s and early 2000s under the critical meme: "it's easier to imagine the end of the world than the end of capitalism." Yet in true dialectical fashion, such an end point has increasingly served as a new beginning point for radical utopian thinking.

This chapter traces the waning of utopian literature in the 1970s following the end of Keynesianism and the rise of neoliberalism. Principally, it argues that the downturn in the rate of profit related to production, and the resulting turn to economic growth predicated on an increasingly virtual and abstract financial speculation, resulted in a crisis for the utopian imagination, culturally and critically, and thus for the ability to conceive of alternatives. As the critical utopian imagination of the long 1960s, rooted in the critiques of an older Fordist capitalism, foundered on the rocks of an ascendant neoliberalism, a new wave of dystopian writings (classical and critical) crested. However, while such works echoed the turn to "weak utopianism" and cognitive mapping of the present in critical theory by convincingly illustrating the deleterious effects of neoliberalism on economic growth, income inequality, and the social safety net, they often struggled to imagine anything outside of these worsening conditions. The essay culminates in a consideration of the return (and necessity) of new utopian writing following the 2008 financial crash, and how the idea of the socialization of debt by the undercommons underscores a set of new utopian strategies geared to the altered economic conditions of the present.

In order to track the transformations of utopian economic justice through the end of the twentieth century and into the twenty-first, it is instructive to analyze the constitutive role that ideas of economic justice played for the utopian imagination. While many Marxist critics have long argued that the critical perspicacity of utopias lies in their form rather than their historically determined content (whose temporal immediacy and local specificity always threaten to render them potentially dated or disturbingly dystopian), economic justice as a key aspect of utopian content, in one form or another, underwrites the long development of the utopian genre.

Turning to one of the earliest utopian precursors, Lycurgus, the legendary lawgiver of Sparta, we find notions of economic justice wrapped up in land and monetary reforms meant to promote equality and reduce avarice. Along with state ownership and the distribution of equal parcels of land, Lycurgus "withdrew all gold and silver money from currency, and ordained the use of iron money only. Then to a great weight and mass of this he gave a trifling value, so that ten minas' worth required a large storeroom in the house, and a yoke and cattle to transport it. When this money obtained currency, many sorts of iniquity went into exile from Lacedaemon."[5] Long before it became associated with More's *Utopia*, we see something akin to what Jameson hails as More's originary "canonical solution in the abolition of money and property."[6] As Jameson goes on to argue, the elimination of money and private property remained a part of the utopian tradition so long as these stood as "enclaves," as "relatively isolated and sporadic" in the societies in which utopias were written.[7] It is precisely money's enclave status as "this strange foreign body as which money and gold momentarily present themselves, [that] can at one and the same time be fantasized as the very root of all evil and the source of all social ills and as something that can be utterly eliminated from the new Utopian social formation."[8]

As Jameson's critical ruminations on More's foundational contribution to the utopian tradition suggests, once capitalism comes into full ascendency, and the money form comes to dominate social relations, its eradication becomes unthinkable. Rather than its elimination outright, we instead find so many variations in utopian content often intended to alleviate the most pernicious aspects of the capitalist economy, but its form and principle (and all too often the notions of value it buttresses) remain. Perhaps fittingly, then, as such utopian dreams of the transformation of society through the eradication of the signal source of evil become harder to countenance, utopia itself as a durable and specific literary form is itself subsumed by the emergence of speculative fiction (sf), a form that is as utterly modern[9] as capitalism and the universalization of the money form. Indeed, even as the Marxist critic Darko Suvin lays out the development of the formal properties of a distinctly literary utopianism, he quickly transitions to its dialectical sublation by sf. In a rather well-known passage, Suvin writes, "strictly and precisely speaking, utopia is not a genre but the *sociopolitical subgenre of science fiction.*"[10] Notably, while Jameson readily accepts Suvin's "generic definition . . . as a motto," he admits "a certain initial bemusement" aimed at Suvin's founding of utopia as sf's "sociopolitical sub-genre," asking "but why not a socioeconomic one?"[11]

Coming at this exchange from the contemporary moment, we can highlight a number of key consequences for utopianism during the convergence of neoliberalism and financialization, including the lessening role of political economy in the utopian imagination and cultural production, alongside the subsumption of utopia by sf. Moreover, this reduced role reflects aspects of not only the eradication of noncapitalist enclaves, but also the transition to Fordism that allowed capitalism to flourish and become ideologically interchangeable with the very notions of techno-scientific and social progress in the United States. As Aaron Benanav and John Clegg illustrate, the transition in utopian culture mirrors the larger transitions in society that also affected critical theory more broadly. For Benanav and Clegg, the move away from "capitalist crisis and immiseration"[12] as the hallmarks of Marxist political economy in the utopian ends of critical theory is directly related to the general amelioration and compromise between labor and capital effected by Fordism:

> above all, the critical theory of this era was marked by its appearance in the midst of rapid post-war growth and the technological revolutions that gave

> rise to an age of abundance. With the help of the Keynesian interventionist state, capitalism seemed to have finally freed itself from its crisis tendencies. This period witnessed an unprecedented decline in inequality, as increases in workers' real wages outpaced increases in the returns to capital in many countries. The "great levelling" of incomes seemed to call into question orthodox Marxist accounts of crisis and immiseration, with important consequences for revolutionary theory.[13]

Yet, as they note, this fantasy was soon sundered as Fordism reached its endemic crisis point:

> by the mid 1970s, the growing potential free-time of society would reveal itself not as an expanding realm of leisure, but rather as a crisis of overproduction, accompanied by a dramatic rise in rates of unemployment and underemployment. These trends made, not for a revitalization and transformation of the labor movement, as the dissidents imagined might be possible, but rather its tendential dissolution.[14]

From 1973 on, the US economy faced a precipitous drop in demand for labor, leading to deindustrialization, precarity, and the return of widespread immiseration. If the expansion of the middle class was largely part and parcel of the high demand for labor in the technoacceleration of the postwar period, then the barely sustainable service-industry jobs that replaced these – alongside structural un- and underemployment, stagnant wages, increasing personal debt, and frequent financial crashes and recessions – have brought issues of political economy and immiseration back to the forefront of both theory and culture. Yet as Benanav and Clegg reveal, the moves in critical theory and the utopianism of critical utopias responsive to the conditions of production-based Fordist capitalism struggled with how to theorize and respond to the new neoliberal moment.

Utopianism thus underwent a drastic change; within culture, we see the shift from the optimistic critical utopias to the pessimism (resigned and later militant) of dystopias and critical dystopias, as well as a notable uptick in catastrophe and postapocalyptic narratives. As the "easier to imagine the end of the world than the end of capitalism" thesis set in, utopian critical theory, rather than positing alternatives, turned to the necessary yet politically less ambitious mode of cognitive mapping as a means of registering the radical changes in the mode of production wrought by neoliberal financialization. Jameson's theses on the conjoined vocations of sf and utopianism, as a twinned and dialectically reinforced inability to "imagine the future . . . not owing to any individual failure of imagination but as the result of the systemic, cultural and ideological closure of which we are all in one way or another prisoners,"[15] stand as the strongest summation of this situation. Here, we see how the desires of the science-fictional and the utopian merge as critically nuanced ways to investigate the structural impasses of the present in order to reveal the very systemic blocks that stymie full-bodied projections of utopian futurity.

This turn to cognitive mapping is directly tied to the greater notions of abstraction that seem to underlie the move from production to finance as the main engine of accumulation in the United States. Allison Shonkwiler refers to this process as the "the financial imaginary."[16] The financial imaginary takes abstraction as its keyword, noting that "abstract, for better or worse, presently dominates not only the economic but also the historical, cultural, and aesthetic domains. The financial imaginary ... is produced by the social uncertainties and precarities that result from the expansion of financialization over multiple domains of life."[17] Looking back at the waning of strong utopian writing with the end of the critical utopias of the 1960s and 1970s and the subsequent surge in dystopianism that coincides with the waxing of neoliberalism, it now appears that much of this political-cultural shift was captured by the real and symbolic functions of the computer. Here, the computer becomes emblematic of finance, a conceptual black box for "recognizing a system that is understood to be less and less tethered to the material, less directly connected to specific modes of production, and therefore less tangible, visible, or controllable."[18]

In this light, Jameson has frequently dated "the end of utopian production with Ernest Callenbach's great *Ecotopia* of 1975, a work whose most serious flaw, from today's standpoint, is the absence of electronic or informational technology."[19] He argues that:

> since Callenbach, the utopian form has been unable to take onboard the computer, cybernetics or information technology. *Ecotopia* was conceived before the Internet, and whatever utopian fantasies the latter has inspired – and they are many, and often delirious, involving mass communications, democracy, and the like – those fantasies have not been able to take on the constitutive form of the traditional Utopian blueprint.[20]

Curiously, before its imaginative reduction to the facilitator of global capitalism, the computer's connectivity and predictive analytical modeling capabilities were conceived of as properly utopian. As Jill Lepore argues, the foundations of what we call surveillance capitalism – predicated on the Google model of harvesting and selling personal data through online platforms and ubiquitous computing – was originally intended as a left-wing riposte to the problems of advertising and marketing in politics with the founding of the Simulmatics corporation in 1959.[21] Moreover, as Brian Willems notes, the computer served the utopian function of automating economies both politically and fictionally in the 1960s. He draws attention to its radical utopian potential across Robert Heinlein's *The Moon Is a Harsh Mistress* and to aborted Soviet plans for "a nationwide network that 'would monitor all labor, production, and retail,' leading to the elimination of paper money and the institution of electronic payments," as well as Chile's similar Cybersyn program in the early 1970s under Salvador Allende's democratically elected socialist government.[22] Computers provide a similarly utopian function in perhaps the last great utopia in US literature to fully imagine what a future predicated on economic justice might look like, Ursula K. Le Guin's *The Dispossessed*, where workers' preferences are matched to the needs of different communes/syndicates.

Whatever utopian promises for collective economic planning the computer contained, these were soon outstripped and subsumed by capitalism, particularly in relation to financialization.[23] As William Davies attests, "when considering the fate of utopia in the neoliberal age, one of the most striking features is the terrible disappointment (or worse) wrought by the advances in cybernetics and software."[24] Both realistically and symbolically, the computer instead came to stand as the means for aiding what Marx refers to as capitalism's desire for immediacy, for the "annihilation of space through time" – that is, the ability for capital to foreclose greater distances for higher returns in shorter amounts of time, which undergirds late capitalist globalization. Nowhere has this been more apparent than in the contemporary turn toward surveillance capitalism and financialization. Turning to the processes of abstraction, virtualization, and circulation that underwrite the financial imaginary described above, computational digitalization allows for the near-frictionless transfer of capital, the conversion of currencies, fully automated High Frequency Trading, increased arbitrage, the extraction of user data repackaged as behavioral prediction derivatives, and data-modeling for converting uncertainty into calculable and hedge-able risk. It is the culmination of these processes in our contemporary financialized mode of production that are represented by the computer, in Jameson's telling, and that have therefore proven a block on the radical utopian imagination.

If we take Jameson at his word that the computer has rendered utopian imagination null, it has, conversely, fostered much of the renewed dystopian turn of the 1980s onward, most notably with cyberpunk. Fleshing out the relationship between cyberpunk's digital environments and finance capital, Mark Bould argues that, "cyberpunk's depiction of cyberspace – the information space 'behind' the computer screen, networking together information and communication technologies – is best understood as a metaphor for 'friction-free' capital-in-circulation."[25] Echoing Bould's sentiments, Scott Bukatman argues that, "cyberpunk's job was to perform an act of abstraction and intensification; first to *perform* that 'bewildering' new (corporate, physical, cyberspatial) space, and the second to generate simultaneously abstracted and compelling images emblematic of emerging world orders."[26] The performance of this realm of abstract, friction-free capital circulation is captured by many of the classics of cyberpunk, including those field-defining works by William Gibson, Pat Cadigan, Bruce Sterling, and Neal Stephenson as well as films such as *Tron*, *The Lawnmower Man*, and *The Matrix Trilogy*. Each in their own way created and extended the image-function of a digitalized virtual space as the operative replacement for a superannuated material world, thereby offering capital a respite and spatial fix for a world overly saturated and overly strip-mined by a stalling production-based capitalism.

Yet if cyberpunk offers a powerful critical figuration of the abstract, digital sphere of finance and its dream of friction-free capital circulation, its narratives have often been cast as not only dystopian, but thoroughly antiutopian. As Carlen Lavigne notes, "feminism, ecology, peace, sexual liberation, and civil rights" (the defining political content of the critical utopias) are stunningly absent from cyberpunk.[27] Connecting these socio-political shortcomings to its economic ideology, Nicola Nixon points out that early cyberpunk's "good guys are the anarchic, individualistic, and entrepreneurial American heroes ... [while] Reaganite cowboyism, the quintessence of the maverick reactionary" provides cyberpunk's "central heroic iconography."[28] Summing up much of the early critical consensus, Terence Whalen writes, "arising out of the general context of Reagan's America, cyberpunk celebrates a 'hardness' that is both stylistic and ideological. Practitioners like Bruce Sterling and William Gibson accordingly disparage a progressive political agenda even though their dystopian narratives offer ample cause for resisting a capitalist future."[29] While later critics, as well as the development of postcyberpunk and postcolonial cyberpunk, offer countervailing assessments, the early critical appraisal largely converged in consensus: although cyberpunk offered powerful mediations of a transcendental capitalism freeing itself from material constraints in the form of new digitized markets, in the process recentering aspects of immiseration and crisis in the material world, it was far from able to offer any utopian ideas of economic justice. That is, cyberpunk was seen as principally antiutopian due to its seeming denigration of the material in favor of the infinite possibility of the virtual.

From this point of view, the emphasis on the digital space of capitalist circulation, coupled with its desire for human transcendence, merely reaffirmed the notion of the subject rendered fully as "human capital." As Wendy Brown explains, under neoliberal financialization, the entrepreneurial "*homo oeconomicus* . . . has been significantly reshaped as financialized human capital: its project is to self-invest in ways that enhance its value or to attract investors through constant attention to its actual or figurative credit rating, and to do this across every sphere of its existence."[30] The equally vaunted and critically maligned notion of transcendence as the telos of so much cyberpunk, then, is merely the completion of this cycle from material subject to abstract and digital circulating human capital, and thus the willful counterpart to the processes of real subsumption and data rendering and extraction under surveillance capitalism, or Wark's postcapitalist "something worse" of the "vectoral economy."[31]

Moreover, to whatever extent cyberpunk offered innovative metaphors for the increasingly financialized mode of production of neoliberalism in the United States, it similarly mystified the New Economy. By disconnecting the realm of finance from the material world, it fetishized the notions of abstraction and virtualization that Shonkwiler identifies as the process of the financial imaginary, in which the material world seems only an effected afterimage of the virtual world: a function caught by the inversions of *The Matrix* in which the human material world turns out to be merely the false projection of the real world of immaterial capital.

However, rather than casting cyberpunk as simply the poor relation to what Tom Moylan, Ildney Cavalcanti, and Raffaella Baccolini develop as properly critical (i.e., utopian) dystopias – those that "negate static ideals, preserve radical action, and create a space in which opposition can be articulated and received"[32] – it is perhaps better to read these antiutopian or noncritical dystopian texts in relation to the often more materially grounded critical dystopias of Kim Stanley Robinson, Octavia Butler, Margaret Atwood, Marge Piercy, Katherine Burderkin, and others. If the production of fully realized or even ambiguous utopian projections lost steam with the end of the critical utopias of the 1960s–1970s and the rise of neoliberalism, then the utopian vocation itself shifts during this same period from production to financialization. In terms of their utopian functions, then, such critical dystopian texts help to fulfill the utopian vocation of cognitive mapping left unaddressed by cyberpunk by offering not the projection of utopian programs but instead the revelation of the truly inimical system of late capitalism. As such, rather than the dematerialized spheres of cyberspace, they focus on the subject's place in this increasingly intensified deterritorializing and globally dispersed capitalist system. The resulting cultivation of new forms of class consciousness and collective politics responsive to these conditions offers the subjective complement to the systemic conditions that Jameson refers to as the utopian form of cognitive mapping.

Reevaluating the vocation of the utopian impulse from within these embattled times, in which utopia is denigrated as a dangerous aberration, conflated with all kinds of totalitarianisms, or conversely, as Tom Moylan attests, presented as the pseudoutopianism of neoliberal free markets,[33] Robert T. Tally, following Jameson, argues that contemporary utopianism functions primarily as a form of anti-antiutopianism. It takes the form of "literary cartography" that eschews both the classical notion of a spatial utopia and the modernist notion of a temporal utopia. Rather, Tally attests, utopia "can only be a method by which one can attempt to apprehend the system itself."[34] Drawing explicitly on Jameson's concept of cognitive mapping, Tally argues that "the utopian impulse reflects an effort to situate oneself in space in history, imaginatively projecting a world that enables one to represent the apparently unrepresentable totality of the world system."[35] This refigured anti-antiutopian vocation "highlights the failings of the present system rather than sketching the concrete parameters of a future alternative . . . this utopian impulse is a forceful response both to an intolerable status quo and to the anti-utopian strictures upon the imagination."[36] Such work is necessary to hold open the promise of a utopianism outside of the neoliberal paradox of the combined dismissal of utopianism even as it is sutured to neoliberal notions of political economy.

Octavia Butler's work and influence have been particularly instructive in this regard. If much of canonical cyberpunk gives us spectacular images of the burgeoning virtual and abstract realm of digitally transcendent and seemingly autonomous finance, then the critically dystopian fiction of Butler's break-through short story, "Speech Sounds," and her subsequent unfinished Parable series reveal the depleted material landscapes left behind. Indeed, these texts by Butler could be read as pleas for economic justice as a necessary correlative to the ubiquitous violence that threatens to erupt at every second of a defunded welfare state that is ravaged by privatization, the outsourcing of production, the amplification and financial securitization of debt as the motor of economic growth, and the offshoring of corporate profits in tax havens that results in unemployment, displacement, and deep immiseration. "Speech Sounds" foregrounds the privatization of city infrastructure (the now-unreliable bus that the protagonist takes to a new town searching for work) alongside the defunding of public services, particularly education (as figured by the protagonist Doe, a teacher). By drawing on a quasi-cyberpunk extrapolation of the Sapir Whorf hypothesis, in which human beings are analogous to computers programmed by language, it explores a world in which a virus (which we may as well call neoliberal defunding of public education) wipes out the ability of most humans to read or speak. Left uneducated, with no ability to form bonds of collectivity through a shared language, and with no job prospects, the world of the short story devolves into regressive, individualist violence.

Taking an even more starkly realist turn, *Parable of the Sower* and *Parable of the Talents* present a United States devastated by a combination of neoliberal monetarist policies and climate change. However, in these works, "marginalized peoples not only survive but also try to move toward creating a social reality that is shaped by an impulse to human self-determination and ecological health rather than one constricted by the narrow and destructive logic of a system intent only on enhancing competition to gain more profit for a select few."[37] By complementing the cognitive mapping of abstracted finance in cyberpunk, such critical dystopias help locate the subject and the possibilities for collectivity that cyberpunk is often accused of effacing.

Drawing on Butler's intersectional focus on race, class, and gender, we can draw a straight line from these texts to Terry Bisson's more radically utopian *Fire on the Mountain*. Bisson's novel provides an alternate history in which Harriet Tubman's strategic leadership leads to the success of John Brown's abolition movement and the eventual founding of a successful Black socialist state – Nova Africa – that serves as the inspiration for future socialist development in Europe and the Americas. Similarly, more recent novels – such as Nnedi Okorafor's *Lagoon*, which provides a speculative end to the oil industry, neoimperial economic relations, and the exploitation of the environment and animal species; and N. K. Jemisin's *The City We Became*, through its critique of the contemporary racialized wealth disparities in New York City as directly linked to the erection of Wall Street on black graves – bear the influence of Butler's critique of existing society and express desires for economic justice responsive to foundational notions of racial capitalism. Such texts foster intersectional collectivities and desires by pushing beyond the overdeveloped limits and diminishing returns of a dystopianism that all too often reinforces rather than effaces capitalist realism.

While these latter texts explore a more sharply honed utopian impulse embedded in their critical dystopian form, they ultimately fall toward the negative or cold stream of the utopian dialectic, offering necessary critiques of the inimical limits of the present, but lacking in the positive or warm-stream projections of a renewed political project. As Mark Fisher attests in the foreword to *Economic Science Fictions*, anticapitalism as a postcommunist catchall for economic justice, while necessary, might also cede too much ground to the capitalist realism that it intends to oppose:

> Provocatively, we might hypothesise that the emergence of anti-capitalism can be correlated with the rise of capitalist realism. When actually existing socialism disappeared – with social democracy soon to follow – the radical left quickly ceased to be associated with a positive political project and became instead solely defined by its opposition to capital. As capital's cheerleaders endlessly crow, anti-capitalists have not yet been able to articulate a coherent alternative.[38]

For Fisher, this is the work of new economic science fictions "that can exert pressure on capital's current monopolisation of possible realities" by offering "a form of indirect action without which hegemonic struggle cannot hope to be successful."[39]

This is all the more pressing since, as many commentators on financialization note, there is no direct access to financial circulation given its largely immaterial, abstract, and virtual forms. This creates problems for strategies of resistance that are largely predicated on older industrial forms of capitalist production. Despite many dismissive and reactionary claims to the contrary, Occupy Wall Street had a clear list of demands aimed against the prevailing conditions of finance and speculative capital, including the abolition of all debt. What was often unclear was how to achieve these demands through concrete actions. For many commentators, there is nothing more pejoratively "pie in the sky" utopian than the cancellation of all debts. Such demands smack as out of this world in the sense that this is not how the world *really* works, belying the vast number of people that are heavily vested in the securitization and circulation of debt as a mode of accumulation (including those unintentionally connected through pension funds that invest in debt securities, or professors whose science-fiction courses contribute to the impending student-loan bubble).

As Annie McClanahan makes clear, capitalism's restructuring as a debt ontology, in which consumer debt becomes a necessity to make up for the declining wages of structural un- and underemployment, is the engine of the contemporary US economy.[40] Indeed, if Benanav and Clegg argue that increasing immiseration was impossible to foresee from the point of US economic buildup between the 1940s and 1970s, it is the personal abjectification and objectification of rampant indebtedness that has seemingly reinjected a concerted denunciation of capitalism and brought socialism as economic justice back to the forefront of US culture, academic criticism, and mainstream politics (e.g., with films such as *The Big Short* and *Parasite* and the television series *Squid Game*, renewed political and cultural conversations around reparations, and the rise of politicians such as Alexandria Ocasio-Ortez and Ilhan Omar).

While popular dystopias such as the Hunger Games series often reflect the immiseration wrought by neoliberalism, a recent spate of post-2008 sf-utopian works place the structural problems of a political economy dependent on indebtedness at the center of their worldbuilding, including Cory Doctorow's *Radicalized* and K. M. Szpara's *Docile*. However, these issues are most concretely tackled from the utopian perspective of economic justice by Kim Stanley Robinson, who from the 1980s to the present has been the most persistently acute utopian critic of the inequalities of global climate change and neoliberal immiseration. Taken in its entirety, his corpus stands as a long-term utopian project geared toward the reimagining of value outside of capitalist valences, from the collectivity of the Three Californias trilogy, and the alternate gift and environmental-impact economies of the Mars Trilogy, to the salvaging of a world ravaged by neoliberalism in *Aurora* and *2312*. In many ways, Robinson can be considered the sf author most attuned not only to the immiserating functions of speculative finance, but also to the utopian potentials that can reverse and subsume them, especially in his recent works, *New York 2140* and *The Ministry for the Future*. The key Robinson problematic in these late utopian works could be put as: how to salvage a utopian world from an intrinsically antiutopian system.

In many ways, the arrival of Robinson's *New York 2140* felt like a utopian shot in the arm for an sf culture overrun by dystopian fatigue. As an analog to his critiques in "Dystopia Now" of the unrealistic portrayals of popular dystopias,[41] or the alternating pessimism, and worse, cynical schadenfreude that dystopias can inadvertently produce, *New York 2140* dares to salvage a productive, full-throated, and unapologetic utopianism from within the ravages of the conjoined ends of catastrophic climate change and the financialization of the economy.

Poised as a post-2008 crash novel, as John Rieder argues, *New York 2140* fulfills the fantasy of the do-over: "As the plot of the novel comes to its climax with a financial crisis, it is abundantly clear that Robinson is always also talking about the crash of 2008, and that his double voicing of this future crisis has to do with what should have happened in 2008."[42] From this point of view, the most utopian strategy in this novel – the debt strike – is tied to the composition of what Rieder refers to as the novel's ethnically diverse "hero team."[43] The novel's plot thus brings together a financier, a cop, a social media star, disgruntled computer programmers, a community organizer, a maintenance manager, two young boys experiencing homelessness, and a retired historian. They eventually band together to influence the debt strike that corrects the injustice of the initial historical undergirding of the 2008 crisis and its antiutopian solutions of bank bailouts at collective taxpayer cost.

Ultimately, the novel's utopian strategy depends on the recuperation of indebtedness by recasting the collective power of the debtor class over capital. Unsurprisingly given Robinson's long-term connection with Jameson, this strategy affirms the utopian hermeneutics that Jameson forecasts in "Utopia as Replication." Given the baleful conditions of capitalist realism and its effects on the utopian imagination, Jameson argues that "the Utopian impulse therefore calls for a [new] hermeneutic: for the detective work of a decipherment and a reading of Utopian clues and traces in the landscape of the real."[44] As Jameson further fleshes out, such a renewed hermeneutical function for the utopian impulse demands a rigorous confrontation with the systems that shape our reality. It is here that Kim Stanley Robinson's much vaunted "realism" takes on a critical edge, as performing the utopian operation that Jameson calls for:

> The operation itself, however, consists in a prodigious effort to change the valences on phenomena which so far exist only in our own present; and experimentally to declare positive things which are clearly negative in our own world, to affirm that dystopia is in reality Utopia if examined more closely, to isolate specific features in our empirical present so as to read them as components of a different system . . . staging each of these alleged symptoms of degradation as an occasion for celebration and as a promise of . . . an alternate Utopian future.[45]

In this light, the utopian recuperation of financial logic to force a progressive economic collapse caused by a large-scale collective debt strike that harnesses the power of the state through the Federal Reserve is not only a do-over, but part and parcel of this renewed utopian strategy of reconceiving dystopian systems as potential sites for utopian intervention.

As a particular utopian strategy, the idea of socializing debt begins initially as an act of financial sabotage – of turning the tools of debtors' immiseration into the means of their liberation and eventually into wide-scale social transformation. Given the difficulties of facing finance capitalism head on, McClanahan argues that initial stages of resistance begin as "the politics of sabotage": "Attempts to slow or block circulation have thus become the tactical correlative of an economy driven by consumer debt . . . [such that] clashes with the mode of reproduction and in the zones of circulation reveal a situation in which economic subjects confront their exploitation not in the wage but in the eviction notice."[46] Hence, the householder strike referenced in *New York 2140*, which appears again in *Red Moon* and *The Ministry for the Future*, first appears as a form of financial sabotage, an angry rebellion that slowly coalesces into a collective political movement.

As a form of utopian economic justice, through escalating acts of economic sabotage, indebtedness becomes agency, and the creative crashing of the economy becomes a way of reasserting human agency over the hidden hand of the market that constantly crushes people, like Orwell's boot forever stomping on a human face. By bringing the global economy to heel, Robinson's economic saboteurs, in McClanahan's words, "reassert the resistant agency of the vandal," attacking the "sites of social reproduction" by "removing commodities from circulation or blocking the paths by which they (and money) might circulate."[47] Importantly, such vandalism leans toward socialism, as "collective solidarity," tearing down one system to replace it with a new one through the socialization of debt, wealth, and finance.[48] As McClanahan reminds us, such vandalism is not a product of nihilism but at the very heart of a productive utopian politics, what Mark Fisher and William Davies argue is missing from contemporary politics and why they argue economic sf is necessary.

Indeed, if Tally presents the state (in its local or supranational world-state form) as superannuated by global late capitalism, curiously, even surprisingly, it makes a comeback in *New York 2140* and *The Ministry for the Future*. However, instead of being the primary driver of utopian politics, let alone their spatial figuration, it serves the different function of being one aspect of a larger concatenation and explosion of utopianism that begins to permeate multiple sites of contestation. Doubling down on such financial sabotage-cum-utopianism, Robinson's *The Ministry for the Future* moves from the local strategy of the debt strike to thinking about how to transform the various intertwined processes of the entire financialized global economy, transforming the securitized financial instruments of social oppression into instruments of social liberation. Operating in a more realist vein than Szpara's *Debt* or dystopian postapocalyptic novels such as

Ling Ma's *Severance*, *The Ministry for the Future* foregrounds the power of seizing not only debt, but the tools and systems of financialization (including surveillance capitalism, centralized banking, digital currencies, and much more), as a means of socializing the power of political economy *tout court*. Moreover, Robinson ramps up these ideas in *The Ministry for the Future*, connecting financial sabotage to ecological sabotage all the way through to acts of overt political violence.

If the rise of neoliberalism heralded the end of the last major stage of US utopian writing with the critical utopias and resulted in the much reduced and denuded vocation of the utopian impulse, then such quietism now seems to be on the wane. Desires, dreams, and indeed new blueprints for economic justice are once again rising to the surface of sf's utopian visions. History suggests that this might only be another shift in the utopian/dystopian dialectic. Yet, as Robinson's own do-over suggests, perhaps the determinations of history should not be given too much credence here.

Notes

1. Salvage Editors, "Salvage Perspectives 1, July 2015: Amid This Stony Rubbish," Insert, *Salvage* 1 (2015), 2.
2. McKenzie Wark, *Capital Is Dead: Is This Something Worse?* (London: Verso, 2019), 5, 6.
3. Gerry Canavan, "'If the Engine Ever Stopes, We'd All Die': *Snowpiercer* and Necrofuturism," *SF Now*. Special issue of *Paradoxa* 26 (2014), 41–66 (48).
4. Fredric Jameson, *Archaeologies of the Future: The Desire Called Utopia and Other Science Fictions* (London: Verso, 2005), 55.
5. Gregory Claeys and Lyman T. Sargent (eds.), *The Utopian Reader* (New York: NYU Press, 1999), 16.
6. Jameson, *Archaeologies*, 12.
7. Jameson, *Archaeologies*, 16.
8. Jameson, *Archaeologies*, 17.
9. For "the essential modernism of all science fiction practice," see Phillip E. Wegner, *Shockwaves of Possibility: Essays on Science Fiction, Globalization, and Utopia* (Oxford: Peter Lang, 2014), 1.
10. Darko Suvin, *Metamorphoses of Science Fiction: On the Poetics and History of a Literary Genre* (Oxford: Peter Lang, 2016), 76.
11. Jameson, *Archaeologies*, 414.
12. Aaron Benanav and John Clegg, "Crisis and Immiseration: Critical Theory Today" in B. Best, W. Bonefeld, and C. O'Kane (eds.), *SAGE Handbook of Frankfurt School Critical Theory* (London: Sage, 2018), 1629–1648 (1631).
13. Benanav and Clegg, 1630.
14. Benanav and Clegg, 1631.

15. Jameson, *Archaeologies*, 289.
16. Alison Shonkwiler, *The Financial Imaginary: Economic Mystification and the Limits of Realist Fiction* (Minneapolis: University of Minnesota Press, 2017).
17. Shonkwiler, xi.
18. Shonkwiler, xi.
19. Fredric Jameson, *An American Utopia: Dual Power and the Universal Army* (London: Verso, 2016), 1.
20. Fredric Jameson, *The Ancients and the Postmoderns* (London: Verso, 2015), 221.
21. Jill Lepore, *If Then: How the Simulmatics Corporation Invented the Future* (New York: Liverlight, 2020).
22. Brian Willems, "Automating Economic Revolution: Robert Heinlein's *The Moon Is a Harsh Mistress*," from *Economic Science Fictions*, edited by William Davies (London: Goldsmiths Press, 2018), 73–92 (82–3).
23. On this transition from 1960s to contemporary science fiction, see Gerry Canavan, "Capital as Artificial Intelligence," *Journal of American Studies* 49.4 (2015), 685–709.
24. William Davies, "Introduction," from *Economic Science Fictions*, edited by William Davies (London: Goldsmiths Press, 2018), 1–28 (19).
25. Mark Bould, "Why Neo Flies, and Why He Shouldn't: The Critique of Cyberpunk in Gwyneth Jones's *Escape Plans* and M. John Harrison's *Signs of Life*," from *Beyond Cyberpunk: New Critical Perspectives*, edited by Graham J. Murphy and Sherryl Vint (New York: Routledge, 2010), 116–134 (119).
26. Scott Bukatman, "Foreword: Cyberpunk and Its Visual Vicissitudes," from *Cyberpunk and Visual Culture*, edited by Anna McFarlane, Graham J. Murphy, and Lars Schmeink (New York: Routledge, 2017), xv–xix (xvi).
27. Carlen Lavigne, *Cyberpunk Women: Feminism and Science Fiction* (Jefferson, NC: McFarland, 2013), 21.
28. Nicola Nixon, "Cyberpunk: Preparing the Ground for Revolution or Keeping the Boys Satisfied?" *Science Fiction Studies* 19.2 (1992), 219–235 (224–225).
29. Terance Whalen, "The Future of a Commodity: Notes toward a Critique of Cyberpunk and the Information Age," *Science Fiction Studies* 19.1 (1992), 75–88 (75).
30. Wendy Brown, *Undoing the Demos: Neoliberalism's Stealth Revolution* (New York: Zone Books, 2015), 32–33.
31. Wark, 56.
32. Raffaela Baccoloni, "Gender and Genre in the Feminist Critical Dystopias of Katherine Burdekin, Margaret Atwood, and Octavia Butler," from *Future Females, the Next Generation: New Voices and Velocities in Feminist Science Fiction*, edited by Marleen Barr (Boston: Rowman & Littlefield, 2000), 13–34 (17).
33. Tom Moylan, *Scraps of the Untainted Sky: Science Fiction, Utopia, Dystopia* (Boulder, CO: Westview Press, 2000), 184.

34. Robert T. Tally, *Utopia in the Age of Globalization: Space, Representation, and the World-System* (London: Palgrave Macmillan, 2013), ix.
35. Tally, xi.
36. Tally, 12.
37. Moylan, *Scraps*, 189.
38. Mark Fisher, "Foreword," from *Economic Science Fictions*, edited by William Davies (London: Goldsmiths Press, 2018), xi–xiv (xiii).
39. Fisher, xiii.
40. Annie McClanahan, *Dead Pledges: Debt, Crisis, and Twenty-First-Century Culture* (Stanford, CA: Stanford University Press, 2017).
41. Kim S. Robinson, "Dystopia Now," *Commune* (2018), online.
42. John Rieder, "Kim Stanley Robinson's Case for Hope in *New York 2140*," from *Fantasy and Myth in the Anthropocene: Imagining Futures and Dreaming Hope in Literature and Media*, edited by Marek Oziewicz and Brian Attebery (London: Bloomsbury Academic, 2022), 136–147 (141).
43. Rieder, 145.
44. Fredric Jameson, "Utopia as Replication," from *Valences of the Dialectic* (London: Verso, 2009), 410–434 (415).
45. Jameson, "Utopia as Replication," 434.
46. McClanahan, 185, 187.
47. McClanahan, 186.
48. McClanahan, 187.

CHAPTER 14

Renewing Democracy

Mathias Nilges

Over the course of the past several decades, democracy has not exactly ranked high on the list of the most exciting concepts in American utopian culture. Faced with the notorious challenges and disappointments that are often associated with the idea of democracy, authors of utopian fiction have looked instead toward alternative systems in their attempts to imagine new ways to organize and govern societies. In particular during the second half of the twentieth century, utopian culture was more readily characterized by narratives that focused on opposition to and resistance against totalitarian or authoritarian governments, against which authors position the fight for open, free societies arranged around anarchistic principles or other, more radical communitarian or collectivist struggles for liberation. One may think here of novels such as Ursula K. Le Guin's *The Dispossessed*, for example, though this trend has continued into the twenty-first century, finding particular prominence in recent Young Adult literature and culture. Similarly, in utopian culture with a particular commitment to radical liberation – Lizzie Borden's 1983 film *Born in Flames* may serve as an example here – faith in the democratic process was often replaced with the pursuit of direct action, new forms of political organization, and social movements. The rise of cyberpunk culture likewise did not leave much room for democracy in its anticipation of (post)political worlds in which structures of governance and representation and virtually all remnants of democracy have been subsumed under a system run by corporations and the power structures of global capital. In such narratives, opposition and forms of resistance often take the form not of democratic processes but instead of innovative rhizomatic, decentralized, anarchic forms of popular, spontaneous quasi-organization. It seems notable, in short, that, while Western nations busied themselves with celebrations of the triumph of democracy over communism, American utopian culture with a commitment to the need to radically rethink our world and thus to grapple with the problems that continued to plague it did not readily turn to democracy to envision such better futures.

The rise of neoliberalism, as a wide range of commentators and scholars such as Jason Hickel have observed, further exacerbated this crisis of democracy. "On a theoretical level, neoliberalism promises to bring about a purer form of democracy, unsullied by the tyranny of the state," Hickel writes. "But, in practice," he stresses, "it becomes clear . . . that neoliberalism tends to undermine democracy and political freedom."[1] In fact, Hickel shows throughout his work, "the erosion of democracy" is not simply a byproduct of the transition into neoliberalism, but it has shown itself to be "a necessary political precondition for the implementation of neoliberal economic policy."[2] "Radical market deregulation," that is, "has required the dismantling or circumvention of the very democratic mechanisms that neoliberal ideology claims in theory to support and protect."[3] Not surprisingly, utopian culture quickly attuned itself to this crisis of democracy, and while there certainly are not many works of utopian culture that uncritically embrace the dominant post-1989 narrative that hails democracy as the universal cure for whatever ailment may exist in the world, we begin to see the emergence of works that foreground the profound danger inherent in the waning of democracy precisely in times of its instrumentalization by Western capitalist nations and the forces of economic globalization. In the 1990s, Octavia E. Butler, in particular in her *Parable* novels, examines a topic that has since revealed itself as strikingly prescient, namely the relation between the emptying out of democracy through processes of neoliberalization and the subsequent rise of neopaternalism, new forms of authoritarianism, populism, and strongman leadership, and the threat of the emergence of new forms of fascism and extremism. What characterizes Butler's novels is the distinct urgency of the need to defend democracy against attacks from the far right and from its utter instrumentalization by capitalism. As Peter G. Stillman argues, the power of Butler's novels lies in their portrayal of a dystopia that is in fact a "utopia for those who advocate a small government, low taxes, an unregulated market, unimpeded corporations, unchecked wealth and power, and the devaluing and denigration of political life and public projects."[4] "The new American dystopia," Stillman continues, "stems from extremes of economic wealth and consequent inequality of political power, so that the private power of the rich and of corporations dominates."[5]

Butler's novels foreground the dangers inherent in what Stillman describes as the "buying out of democracy" and a process that Nandini Sundar associates more generally with the era of neoliberalization: the "state's ability to deploy democracy – both procedural democracy and a limited conception of substantive democracy – as a weapon against dissenters."[6] And in a situation in which, as Hickel puts it, democracy "is thriving in name only,"[7] Butler's novels show that the door opens to a range of dangerous sociopolitical developments. *Parable of the Sower*, the first installment in Butler's *Parable* series, lays out this process of democratic capture and the rise of forms of social arrangement such as company towns that fully subsume democratic structures under the logic of capitalist accumulation. In the second novel, *Parable of the Talents*, this process leads to the rise of a far-right, theocratic dictatorship that, through populist appeals to reactionary values, wins the US presidential election and gradually installs an authoritarian, neofascist government and police state, paired with a large-scale project aimed at cultural change, Christian America, which promises to "Make America Great Again." What we can more generally observe in American utopian culture beginning in the late 1990s and early 2000s is the emergence of arguments for the renewal of democracy in a time of its crisis. Authors such as Butler, and those whose work I shall discuss in what follows, reveal neoliberal utopias as antidemocratic dystopias against which democracy must be defended. The question that often motivates such a return to democracy is the same that R. John Williams insists must take center stage in analyses of our current political climate and our assessment of the possibility of democracy today: how can democracy survive "when populations decide democratically to abolish democracy?"[8]

Novels such as Sam J. Miller's *Blackfish City* revolve around popular opposition to what Wendy Brown describes as a central problem for democracy under neoliberalism: "the merging of corporate and state power."[9] "How has it come to pass," Brown asks, "that the people are not, in any sense, ruling in common for the common in parts of the globe that have long traveled under the sign of democracy?"[10] *Blackfish City* imagines the emergence of forms of resistance to the fusing of state and corporate power and the return of a genuine belief in a truly democratic notion of the people and mechanisms for their representation and power. Set in a not-too-distant future after the world as we know it has been destroyed by a series climate disasters, Miller's novel tracks the fate of some of the remnants of humanity who have taken refuge in floating cities such as Qaanaaq and created new ways of living together while exacerbating all of the same social problems and forms of injustice that plague cities of our present. Residents of Qaanaaq suffer under a system that continues to bind governmental systems and elections to capitalist interest, a pseudodemocratic structure that is mainly designed to defend and support the interests of landlords, the city's most powerful residents. In the interest of creating political structures that are free from corruption and the capture of democratic governance by economic interests, some attempts have been made to improve Qaanaaq's system of government, such as the creation of "a system of computer programs that would do the work of government better than humans could. Something invincible, immune to bribery or bigotry . . . making the right call regardless whether it was an election year or a sex scandal about to be exposed or the waste treatment center had to go in a rich part of town."[11] And yet, one character points out, "of course, everyone knew it was bullshit. Programs can be only as objective as they're coded to be."[12] But what the residents who struggle against their continued immiseration and disempowerment gradually come to realize is that the "façade of Qaanaaq's flimsy democracy" could indeed "come tumbling down" if only more of them realized the truth: how little power those at the top really have.[13] "So many of us here," one character notes, believe that they are "powerless and alone. Keeping our heads down, keeping to ourselves."[14] But the way forward in the novel ultimately lies in unification and the pursuit of a new politics of the people, because, the novel's protagonists realize, "we *aren't* separate. We are one thing, and there's power in that" (emphasis in original).[15]

Miller's novel traces a future that emerges from the power of unification, from the renewal of a commitment to the idea of the people, and from the desire for systems of governance that emerge from the people and that represent their interests against capital's antidemocratic forces, a desire for futurity that resonates, as we shall see, across recent utopian fiction. A memorable passage in *Blackfish City* outlines this renewal of the demos against the forces of capital as follows:

> Every city is a war. A thousand fights being fought between a hundred groups. . . . Fixing this is hard. Put new people in power, write new laws, erase old ones, build cities out of nothingness – but the wars remain, the underlying conflicts are unaffected. Only power shifts the scales, and people build power only when they come together. When they find in each other the strength to stop being afraid.[16]

Those who struggle for representation through the city's political system to bring an end to their immiseration understand very well the source of their troubles, which results in the emptying out of the governmental systems under which they live: money. Money, they know,

> Is a mind, the oldest artificial intelligence. Its prime directives are simple, its programming endlessly creative. Humans obey it unthinkingly, with cheerful alacrity. Like a virus, it doesn't care if it kills its host. It will simply flow

> on to someone new, to control them as well. City Hall . . . is a framework of programs constructed around a single, never explicitly stated purpose: to keep Money safe.[17]

The question that drives the plot of Miller's novel, to which the characters return time and again, is thus: "what would it take to rival something so powerful?"[18] The answer, they realize, lies in the people, in their effort to magnify the "immense magnificent tiny powerless spark of our own singular Self," turning it into a source of power that can rival that of the "invisible giants" of capitalism.[19] And while they know all too well that this belief in the power of the people may reasonably strike some as "hopeless fantasy," the novel's characters also believe that they have "found a way" to turn this fantasy into real-world potentiality. They must focus on stories, they propose, because "stories are where we find ourselves, where we find the others who are like us. Gather enough stories and soon you're not alone: you are an army."[20] Stories emerge in Miller's novel as the source of hope for a better future, since they make possible a process of unification that recreates a powerful conception of the people and, with this, the conditions for the renewal of true democracy. Stories, the novel's characters learn, allow us to push our imagination beyond the limitations of what is and pursue that which may yet be. Stories facilitate modes of unification that can bring together the many "magnificent tiny powerless spark[s]" for a common purpose, creating the transformation that, in the novel's closing passages, reveals itself as the way to bring an end to Qaanaaq's exploitative structures and open up the possibility for true representation of the people. *Blackfish City*'s utopian imagination is wedded to a sincere belief in the importance of a renewal of the power of the people and of the creation of systems of governance and representation of the people and for the people, the possibility for which emerges from the power of stories.

And yet, as scholars across disciplines have pointed out time and again in recent decades, democracy is a profoundly messy concept, in part precisely because it appears internally as temporally split insofar as it is mobilized in the present yet often only insofar as it is aimed at its future realization, an operation that seemingly postpones the people's desire for justice and representation ad infinitum. As Williams notes, in our moment in history in particular, we witness an intensification of the well-known problem of democracy's seemingly perpetually fleeting promise of its own full realization. "At a moment when the aporetic aspect of democracy seems to have made political action all but impossible," he wonders, "what is one to do if democracy, in all its messy autoimmunity, must remain forever on the horizon, always only 'to come'?" Jacques Derrida famously locates the "aporias of democracy" that make it such a difficult concept both to put into practice and to defend in just this sense of democracy's perpetual incompleteness, the seemingly endless deferral of its promises. And it is precisely in this way that democracy, Derrida proposes, confronts us as an always-incomplete process such that we must always speak of a "democracy to come."[21] Similarly, Brown emphasizes that democracy functions as an "empty signifier," which is to say that the concept has "historically unparalleled global popularity today yet has never been more conceptually footloose or substantively hollow."[22] But what we see in the work of authors such as Miller is that there is no attempt to define or stabilize the concept or its emptiness. Rather, the novel dedicates itself to the exploration of the concrete work that democracy, in spite of all of its problems and historical and present shortcomings, may yet be able to do and indeed must do if we are to find ways to address the dire problems that the majority of humanity faces, in particular in the context of capitalism's antidemocratic structures. This approach to democracy's notoriously problematic sense of futurity emerges clearly in novels such as Kim Stanley Robinson's *The Ministry of the Future* (2020), which illustrates that the notion of a "democracy to come" becomes less problematic if one conceives of the idea of the people in temporally more expansive ways. And, as we shall see, by doing so, it is possible to attach the work of democracy and the renewal of the democratic imagination to the utopian imagination. In fact, novels such as Robinson's, which understand both democracy and utopia not as a goal or destination but as a process, illustrate the advantages of tracing the common ground that these two recently often-disparaged concepts ultimately share.

Set in the near future, the plot of Robinson's novel revolves around the creation of a new agency that "someone in the press named . . . 'the Ministry for the Future.'"[23] Created in the aftermath of the latest large-scale tragedy caused by rapidly accelerating climate change, a vast heat wave that takes hold of large swathes of India for weeks and that causes the death of millions, this new agency is designed to "work with the Intergovernmental Panel on Climate Change, and all the Agencies of the United Nations, and all the governments signatory to the Paris Agreement."[24] In Robinson's novel, the sense of urgency that results from steadily intensifying large-scale climate disasters generates sufficient momentum to launch efforts aimed at making large-scale changes to global systems of policy and governance and to the global economic structure, so as to be able to respond to the climate emergency in a manner that might remove roadblocks neoliberal capital has erected to avoid a Green New Deal and to preclude meaningful changes to address global poverty and exploitation. The Ministry of the Future is created to "advocate for the world's future generations of citizens, whose rights, as defined by the Universal Declaration of Human Rights, are as valid as our own."[25]

The Ministry foregrounds the need to develop solutions that address both the climate emergency and global systems of immiseration, confronting those deeply entrenched protective mechanisms of capital that have thus far prevented responses to these inextricably linked problems. It does so by expanding the logic of democratic representation and the concept of the people, extending the latter temporally into the future: the Ministry's task is to defend the rights of those not yet born, those whose rights and lives are threatened by capitalism's short-termism that funds and defends its present by robbing generations to come of a viable future. The renewal of democratic processes in Robinson's novel thus hinges on a simple yet provocative question: what if it were a fundamental task of democratic representation to value and defend the rights and lives of humans not yet born to the same degree as the rights and lives of those living? What emerges here is not simply another version of a democracy to come, another example of an idea of democracy that conceives of its enabling futurity as an immanent void or aporia, but of a form of democracy that concretizes the futurity with which it has always been bound up by turning this future into the substance of democracy's present logic and politics. The Ministry, in other words, renews the idea of democracy by turning its notorious and purportedly paradoxical open-endedness into its chief virtue, forging a clear connection between present and future by embedding the futurity resulting from its temporally expanded conception of the people, their rights, and the duty for their representation into democracy's present.

The Ministry's temporal expansion of the idea of democracy fulfills an important function in Robinson's effort to reexamine the utopian imagination and one of its characteristic problems. "Famously, from Thomas More on . . . the utopia is separated by space or time, by a disjunction," Robinson explains in a recent interview. "They call it the Great Trench," he elaborates, "and the Great Trench is endemic in utopian literature. There's almost always a break that allows the utopian society to be implemented and to run successfully."[26] The main task of the utopian imagination, he thus concludes, is in fact to "fill in this trench." After all, he stresses,

> When Jameson said it's easier to imagine the end of the world than the end of capitalism, I think what he was talking about is that missing bridge from here to there. It's hard to imagine a positive history, but it's not impossible. ... The story of getting to a new and better social system, that's almost an empty niche in our mental ecology. So I've been throwing myself into that attempt.[27]

Doing the work of imagining the path to utopia, imagining the concrete bridge that connects the present to a better future, is centrally connected to renewal of democracy in Robinson's novel. It is precisely by transforming the seemingly frustrating futurity of a "democracy to come" into the central aspect of democracy's temporal expansion, by including in its mission the representation of the "demos to come," that the Ministry is able forge a concrete connection between present and future, which at the same time provides us with a striking example of Robinson's emphasis on the crucial work of the utopian imagination today. "That's one of the things *The Ministry* is about," Robinson thus stresses:

> Can you morph, by stages, from the political economy that we're in now, which is neoliberal capitalism, to what you might call anti-austerity, to a return to Keynesianism, and then beyond that to social democracy, and then beyond that to democratic socialism, and then beyond that to a post-capitalist system that might be a completely new invention that we don't have a name for?[28]

Democracy's "to come" is thus valorized as a central aspect of the politics of democratic representation in the present, and by "representing the interests of the generations to come"[29] by way of concrete, incremental steps forward – as opposed to lofty promises of a better future that remains untethered from both the present and concrete potentiality – both the utopian and the democratic imagination are revitalized in Robinson's novel. In fact, as one character puts it, as soon as you begin thinking of the generations to come as equal to those in the present, you "give a higher value to future generations," which means to valorize humans of the future as part of the democratic process and also as part of the economic calculations that otherwise serve simply to defend the status quo. Instead of "discounting the future" and with it the value of future humans and of the future of our environment, Robinson's novel asks us to reconsider which concrete steps forward may become possible once we understand democracy as a way to "give a higher value to future generations."[30]

The opening pages of *Ministry* are haunted by an all too familiar sense of the persistence of inaction, of capitalism and the systems of governance and policy that support it digging in their collective heels, even in the face of millions of deaths resulting from the steadily intensifying effects of climate change: "Easier to imagine the end of the world than the end of capitalism: the old saying had grown teeth and was taking on literal, vicious accuracy."[31] However, Robinson's novel does not dwell on the seemingly insurmountable obstacle that capitalism's extraordinary recalcitrance presents and instead focuses on the small steps that may be taken in a more hopeful direction and on the real-world, already-existing examples of such steps that may guide our way. In India, for instance, the elections that follow the latest tragedy result in the rise to power of a new party,

> a composite party composed of all kinds of Indians, every religion and caste, urban poor, rural poor, the educated, all banded together by the disaster and determined to make something change. The ruling elite lost legitimacy and hegemony, and the inchoate fractured resistance of victims coalesced in a party called Avasthana, Sanskrit for survival. The world's biggest democracy, taking a new way.[32]

This new way – "New India and the Renewal" – is made possible in Robinson's novel by building on innovations in local government like the Kerala model for governance in which "the focus on local government" has become "so intense and diligent that there are now [in] total 1,200 governmental bodies in Kerala, all dealing with issues in their particular area whatever it might be."[33] The "direct democracy" of local democratic structures not only allows for better representation of the people but also serves as a model for a global renewal of democracy because it models ways to address issues like the climate crisis and the structures of poverty and exploitation with which it is bound up in a manner that breaks the deadlock of capitalist interests that stand in the way of necessary change. The aim in Robinson's novel resembles that of *Blackfish City*'s call for a new democratic movement of the people: to "join up . . . all the diversity of people and landscapes that is India, into a single integrated project," for while "the biggest democracy on Earth has huge problems," it also has "huge potential for solutions."[34]

It is in this context, too, that pursuing existing paths that may lead to steps forward connects to the temporal reimagination of the project of democracy that is bound up with the utopian imagination in *Ministry*. "In India it was traditional to talk about the seven generations before and after you as being your equals," a character notes, foregrounding the great value of renewing and redeploying traditional concepts to develop new economic and democratic systems aimed at developing responses to the climate emergency: "You work for those seven generations. Now they're using that idea to alter their economics."[35] The reimagination of democratic action and of the utopian imagination together addresses one of the fundamental problems that seems to make imagining a better future such a difficult proposition, the problem that Robinson's novel identifies as "the tragedy of the time horizon."[36] The creation of new democratic structures to represent the interest of future generations and of economic systems aimed at the long term, which drive forward the plot of *Ministry*, are an expression of the novel's firm belief in the value of the gradual pursuit of concrete, possible steps and the value of leveraging already-existing models and answers to build momentum toward large-scale transitions. The utopian imagination of Robinson's model emerges therefore not from attempts at toying with a grand new future without a clear sense of the steps that may lead us there, but instead from attempts to identify and activate the present's latent potentiality, setting in motion a process of gradual transformation designed to defend the rights of those not yet born by making for them a better world that may be created by putting to use the tools at hand. The renewed commitment to the concrete potentiality that the idea of democracy still contains is a crucial aspect of this utopian imagination.

What we also see in Robinson's novel is what Achille Mbembe has recently emphasized as a crucially necessary aspect of the renewal of democracy: the emphasis on a "planetary consciousness." "More and more we are facing instances in which negotiation as such is dismissed as a sign of weakness, and where the politics of purity trumps the politics of negotiation," Mbembe argues.[37] Consequently, he wonders: "What will be the future of democracy in a context such as this?" In his estimation, "democracy itself will have to be reinvented in relation to two or three key planetary issues."[38] Grounding democracy in the idea that "we all are rightful inhabitants of this one Earth that is our common shelter and our common roof," Mbembe argues, also necessarily implies that democratic structures that are aimed at enacting and defending universal rights (such as "a universal right to breathe") must imagine "a new generation of rights that do not depend on being implemented by the nation-state" and a general "juridical dispensation that would be close to a borderless world."[39] The question of the future role of democracy and of the nation state in particular with regard to universal projects aimed at climate and environmental crises raises itself with notable significance in the context of utopian culture. After all, even in later twentieth-century, ecological utopias such as Ernest Callenbach's novel *Ecotopia*, a central text in the development of ecotopian thought and social movements of the 1970s, we must note the persisting attachment to the nation state that facilitates those governmental structures (at times bordering on green authoritarianism) that the novel imagines as necessary for ecological change, leaving the remnants of democracy to struggle with this forced transition. Robinson, however, has long charted a different model of change in his work, one that anticipates Mbembe's recent appeal. Beginning with the *Mars* trilogy, Robinson explores the possibility inherent in new democratic structures for facilitating political change and creating new forms of social organization with an eye on environmental futures. In the *Mars* novels, this takes the form of crucial differences that emerge between systems of production and organization, as Trans-national Corporations ("transnats") evolve into Metanational Corporations ("metanats"). While metanat Subarashī pursues an intensified version of exploitative capitalism, metanat Praxis explores the possibility of the gradual transition into a system of ecological capitalism based on democratic corporations.

Similarly, in later novels such as *2312*, Robinson extends this line of thinking by returning time and again to the example of the Basque Mondragón Corporation to imagine models for planetary democracy and for democratic systems of production that seek solutions for the climate crisis and the structures of poverty and exploitation with which the climate crisis is linked. In *Ministry*, too, Robinson places the lessons that may be learned from Mondragón alongside models like Kerala to illuminate directions that have been charted but not yet fully explored. Mondragón, a system based on cooperatives characterized by "open admission, democratic organization, the sovereignty of labor, the instrumental and subordinate nature of capital, participatory management, payment solidarity, inter-cooperation, social transformation, universality, and education" is a system that "has existed and thrived for a century, and is still going strong."[40] *Ministry* attempts to imagine the extension of such models to a planetary scale and reimagines the possibilities of democracy in such a context.

The work of Malka Older, specifically the novels that together make up *The Centenal Cycle*, contains another, striking account of such a planetary renewal of democracy aimed at the erasure of borders through the creation of a system of microdemocracy. Older first introduces this vision of a renewed system of democracy that is planetary and postnational in nature in her novel *Infomocracy*, book 1 of *The Centenal Cycle*. *Infomocracy*'s global microdemocratic system is organized via "centenals," local units of governance that each consist of 100,000 voters.[41] Global governments can gain majorities by winning centenals, which results in a global democratic system determined not by nations but rather by a decentralized constellation of political affinity and common interest. To allow for movement toward centenals with whose politics one wishes to align, migration is simplified through the de facto abolition of borders. Older's novel imagines a system of government that puts into practice demands that political theorists Jonathan Blake and Nils Gilman stress are of central importance for a planetary renewal of democracy. "Nation-states should ... be delegating as many governance functions as possible down to institutions that are closer to the people they serve," they write, adding that "in a world with diverse communities with differing needs, desires, cultures and histories, subsidiarity promises both better outcomes and better institutional legitimacy."[42] Older's novel offers us a fascinatingly detailed account of the quotidian workings and macropolitical opportunities and challenges of such a system of democracy that seeks to replace "remote and unresponsive bureaucrats at the national or supranational level" with increased citizen participation "in the decisions affecting their daily lives."[43] And yet Older's novel does not offer us a naive or idealized account of this system. Instead, like Robinson, Older focuses on both the possibilities such a system offers and the problems and challenges that remain, emphasizing that even a radical transition to planetary micro-democracy is but one step in a necessarily ongoing process of rejuvenating democracy's potentiality. While microdemocratic centenals seem to offer more direct representation and greater participation in the political process, and while "the whole point of micro-democracy was to allow people to choose their government wherever they were," Older's novel illustrates how difficult it remains to change the fact that, even in such a new system, "plenty of people [don't] agree with their 99,999 geographically closest friends."[44] And while the system is intended to increase choice, "some areas – Ireland being one classic example, vast zones of what used to be the United States another – had been polarized so deeply and so long that your choices if you stayed were pretty much A or B."[45]

Instrumental to the workings of the microdemocratic system in *Infomocracy* is the creation of "Information," a centralized, objective, independent agency tasked with aggregating and distributing all relevant information for the political process and designed to provide "extraordinarily individualized information" for everyone on the planet.[46] Not surprisingly, Information comes to wield enormous power and is subject to attacks, espionage, and manipulation by global parties looking to secure majorities. Thus, while Information works to support the renewal of democracy and empower the people, it also poses risks for the democratic process. In fact, we learn, "the power it wields is enough to make people hate it."[47] One of Information's major initial shortcomings, however, is its idealistic conception of the role of information in the democratic process, believing that "providing data about each government would be enough for people to make informed, more-or-less sensible choices."[48] As David Golumbia stresses, "some of liberal democracy's deepest convictions rest on assumptions about free . . . and complete access to information."[49] And yet Older's novel emphasizes long-standing problems with regard to the role that information plays in democratic elections that are not easily removed from the process. As one character observes, "despite all the Information available, people tend to look at what they want to see."[50] Furthermore, Older's novel foregrounds the challenges posed by the persisting link between information and capitalism, echoing Golumbia's reminder that "what is displaced . . . in the dream of total information access itself is precisely capital, and the inextricable linkages of capital to the American democratic project."[51] Nevertheless, just as the first steps into a new direction that Robinson's novels imagine remain riddled with problems both old and new, Older's engagement with new paths for democracy models a modest conception of utopia, one that emphasizes the benefit of changes for the better that can gradually open up possibilities for substantial change, even if such changes at times may appear like nothing more than a lesser evil. As one character in *Infomocracy* puts it: "I hate your stupid pseudodemocratic infomocracy . . . but I would hate a corporate dictatorship manipulated by the military-industrial complex even more."[52]

One particularly productive aspect of Older's approach to the renewal of democracy is her novel's examination of the relation between political systems and our imagination. Grappling with the same problem as Robinson – the difficulty of imagining futures beyond a version of democracy that is fully captured by neoliberal capital – *Infomocracy* stresses that political structures shape our imagination and constrain our sense of future possibility. Political systems, Older's novel insists, must be examined by focusing in part on how they "make people *think*" and "how they make people *behave*" (emphasis in original).[53] This means that innovations to political systems shape our imagination and sociopolitical behaviors, and it also means, in turn, that systemic political innovation requires us to break with those forms of imagination to which we have become accustomed in our current political systems. In other words, it is so notoriously difficult to imagine an end to the present neoliberal political structure because it shapes and determines the way we think. It is precisely for this reason that the utopian imagination that confronts and makes legible the limits of our imagination plays such a central role in our ability to bring about systemic change. Older's novel forcefully echoes Robinson's insistence that the possibility for a version of democracy beyond its capture by capitalism depends on our ability to understand the fact that, as Brown proposes, democracy is "an unfinished principle"[54] not as a problem but rather as an opening for the utopian imagination. Like the utopian imagination in Robinson and Older, the value that remains in the concept of democracy may be located in its openness and anticipation of a future to come, in a conception of democracy that focuses on a process of constant development, and not on the constantly frustrated anticipation of a finished, idealized version of utopia or democracy.

I have focused in this chapter largely on the utopian novel. And, to be sure, much more need be said about the ways that other forms of utopian culture engage with the possibilities and limitations of democracy's renewal. But I have focused on the novel in part because it is an art form that is fundamentally wedded to the logics of utopia and democratic openness that I have outlined here: since its rise, the novel has emerged as the art form that aims to make thinkable a relation to our world that privileges becoming over being. Nancy Ruttenburg reminds us that "against the finished quality of the epic, the novel is eternally open-ended, attuned to a present whose future cannot be known" and that is "therefore committed not to being but to becoming"; in the novel, she adds, "everything is in flux, nothing is reified."[55] And precisely because "the novel's meaning can only be intersubjective, cocreated," as Ruttenburg suggests, it can be understood as centrally related to the logic of democracy or indeed as the democratic art form per se. In fact, as an art form that is, as Rutternburg puts it, "always in process, always becoming," it shares common ground with democracy's openness and with the utopian imagination that characterizes novels such as those I have discussed, for here, too, the lack of conceptual "essence" emerges not as a limitation but as the central aspect of the novelistic imagination. "The novelistic and the democratic have no essence," Ruttenburg accordingly notes, "because their horizons, if they can be said to exist, can only be provisional, a fiction of containability or closure," adding that "both rely for their vitality on the state of 'becoming': neither survives finalization."[56] It is clear that, in our moment, democracy is in crisis. But just like the novel and the utopian imagination, both of which are also often said to be experiencing severe crises, novels such as those of

Miller, Robinson, and Older remind us of the value of fighting for their renewal nonetheless, and, indeed, it is their renewal in the face of permanent crisis that defines the very core of all three concepts. It may thus be said that we need them most not in times when they are stable or uncontroversial but precisely during times of crisis. It is in such moments that their renewal, their constant reinterpretation and development, carries out important epistemological and political work, and aids us in what all too frequently appears all but impossible: imagining new, better futures for the people.

Jacques Rancière reminds us that "politics is not a function of the fact that it is useful to assemble, nor of the fact that assemblies are held for the sake of the good management of common business. It is a function of the fact that a wrong exists, an injustice that needs to be addressed."[57] The question of democracy in recent utopian literature raises itself in connection to the question of the possibility of the utopian imagination, and the power of the people binds itself to the power of stories that are able to bring us together in the attempt to imagine ways to address the forms of injustice whose grip on our present and imagination seems so very difficult to loosen. And here it is important to foreground the great value of novels such as those discussed in this chapter, for they stress, as Rancière puts it, that

> fiction is not the invention of imaginary worlds. It is first a structure of rationality: a mode of presentation that renders things, situations or events perceptible and intelligible; a mode of liaison that constructs forms of coexistence, succession and causal linkage between events, and gives to these forms the characters of the possible, the real or the necessary.[58]

It is in this sense that the novel can articulate the renewal of democracy in relation to the futurity offered to us by the utopian imagination. By embracing the openness that lies at the heart of both democracy and utopia, and that finds concrete expression in the novelistic imagination, we may find hope and a sense of possibility in the renewal of two often-maligned, yet far from exhausted, concepts in the same manner as one character does in the final lines of *Ministry*,

> We will keep going, she said to him in her head – to everyone she knew or had ever known, all those people so tangled inside her, living or dead, we will keep going, she reassured them all, but mostly herself, if she could; we will keep going, we will keep going, because there is no such thing as fate. Because we never really come to the end.[59]

Notes

1. Jason Hickel, "Neoliberalism and the End of Democracy," from *The Handbook of Neoliberalism*, edited by Simon Springer, Kean Birch, and Julie MacLeavy (London: Routledge, 2016), 142–152 (142).
2. Hickel, 142.
3. Hickel, 142.
4. Peter G. Stillman, "Dystopian Critiques, Utopian Possibilities, and Human Purposes in Octavia Butler's *Parables*," *Utopian Studies* 14(1) (2003), 15–35 (17).
5. Stillman, 17.
6. Nandini Sundar, "Hostages to Democracy," *Critical Times* 1.1 (2018), 80–98 (83).
7. Hickel, 150.
8. R. John Williams, "Theory and the Democracy to Come," *Postmodern Culture* 15.3 (2005), no page.
9. Wendy Brown, "We Are All Democrats Now . . ." from G. Agamben, A. Badiou, D. Bensaïd, et al., *Democracy in What State?* (New York: Columbia University Press, 2011), 44–57 (46).
10. Brown, 46.
11. Sam J. Miller, *Blackfish City* (New York: Harper Collins, 2018), 223.
12. Miller, 223.
13. Miller, 236.
14. Miller, 246.
15. Miller, 246.
16. Miller, 224.
17. Miller, 224.
18. Miller, 224.
19. Miller, 224.
20. Miller, 224.
21. See Jacques Derrida, *Rogues: Two Essays on Reason*, translated by Pascale-Anne Brault and Michael Naas (Palo Alto, CA: Stanford University Press, 2005), 90–93.
22. Brown, 44.
23. Kim Stanley Robinson, *The Ministry for the Future* (New York: Orbit, 2020), 16.
24. Robinson, *Ministry*, 16.
25. Robinson, *Ministry*, 16.
26. Kim Stanley Robinson, "Imagining the End of Capitalism," Interview by Derrick O'Keefe. *Jacobin* (22 Oct. 2020), online.
27. Robinson, "Imagining the End of Capitalism."
28. Robinson, "Imagining the End of Capitalism."
29. Robinson, *Ministry*, 98.
30. Robinson, *Ministry*, 132.
31. Robinson, *Ministry*, 25.

32. Robinson, *Ministry*, 25.
33. Robinson, *Ministry*, 232.
34. Robinson, *Ministry*, 233.
35. Robinson, *Ministry*, 132.
36. Robinson, *Ministry*, 173.
37. Achille Mbembe, "How to Develop a Planetary Consciousness," *Noēma* (January 11, 2022), online.
38. Mbembe.
39. Mbembe.
40. Robinson, *Ministry*, 272–273.
41. Malka Older, *Infomocracy* (New York: Tor, 2016).
42. Jonathan Blake and Nils Gilman, "Governing in the Planetary Age," *Noēma* (March 9, 2021), online.
43. Blake and Gilman.
44. Older, 40.
45. Older, 40.
46. Older, 53.
47. Older, 53.
48. Older, 79.
49. David Golumbia, "Hypercapital," *Postmodern Culture* 7.1 (1996), online.
50. Older, 370.
51. Golumbia.
52. Older, 278.
53. Older, 41.
54. Brown, 45.
55. Nancy Ruttenburg, "Introduction: Is the Novel Democratic?" *Novel: A Forum on Fiction* 47.1 (2014), 1–10 (6).
56. Ruttenburg, 8–9.
57. Jacques Rancière, *On the Shores of Politics*, translated by Liz Heron (London: Verso, 1995), 97.
58. Jacques Rancière, *The Lost Thread: The Democracy of Modern Fiction*, translated by Steven Corcoran (New York: Bloomsbury, 2016), xxxi.
59. Robinson, *Ministry*, 563.

CHAPTER 15

The Time of New Histories

Utopian Possibility in America's Twenty-First Century

John Rieder

The new millennium was supposed to begin with the end of the world, and while Y2K faded quickly into a historical curiosity, fantasies of the end of the world – zombie plagues, pandemics, AI takeovers, climate catastrophes, comet collisions, even the odd nuclear holocaust – have thrived in twenty-first-century popular culture. Even though the end of the world keeps not happening, it also keeps happening. A straightforward way to explain this persistence is that the various apocalyptic scenarios are not about some dire future but rather they give bodily form to anxiety-producing aspects of the present. They are less about where things are headed than about how things are and how things got that way. They offer, whether deliberately or not, dystopian analyses of the status quo, and they offer it in a form that apparently satisfies a widely shared set of desires. That combination of critique and desire is liable to yield complex, even ambivalent results.

Consider one highly acclaimed example, Cormac McCarthy's postapocalyptic novel *The Road*.[1] Similar tales of the postapocalyptic return to savagery have been a staple feature of speculative fiction since the nineteenth century. No longer dependent on a developmental model of civilization's progression and decline, stories premised on the collapse of state authority nowadays do not yield fantasies of regression to feudalism or hunting and gathering but rather, like *The Road* or the *Mad Max* films, to a Hobbesian state of nature, the unleashing of or return to the war of all against all. Unrelenting grimness being a kind of authorial trademark for McCarthy, he seems to have set out to construct the worst version of that war that one could possibly imagine and then set himself the task of narrating it in rigorously plain, almost laconic prose. But as has been argued many times, Hobbes's state of nature can be read as being more about capitalist ideology than human universality. The premise of fundamentally inescapable selfishness determining a no-holds-barred struggle over scarce resources turns market competition into natural law. That

McCarthy should have produced such a stark, brutal version of it in the twenty-first century could be taken as a way of attesting to the vitality of neoliberal free-market ideology four decades into its transformation of the geopolitical economy. Under this reading, McCarthy's novel is not about the end of the world at all. It is instead a reiteration of dominant ideology, a fantastic reenactment of the status quo. A telltale sign of its ideological tenor is the complete absence of any political or historical explanation for the catastrophe in the ruins of which the story takes place, an erasure of context that coheres all too well with the stripped-down style of the prose and the universalizing anonymity of the characters. It is a classic example of a story that tells us that the way things are is the way they have to be.

But this is not at all an inevitable reading of *The Road*. One of the most striking features of its setting is the death of the nonhuman world, a mass extinction event registered in the absence of birds or any other type of animals, the dead trees collapsing in the night, the ashes of a world-consuming fire permeating the atmosphere. Thus, an ecological theme sits not so much alongside as *inside* the novel's humanistic exploration of fatherly love amid existential absurdity. The setting exposes the dependence of human life on the nonhuman, the fact that living takes place not in isolated bodies (much less minds) but through metabolic interaction with an environment. If the leitmotif of cannibalism makes *The Road* into a sort of zombie apocalypse without the zombies, that is because to linger on in a dead world is to be already one of the living dead. Within its reenactment of market ideology, *The Road* simultaneously plays out the folly or insanity of regarding the market as the source of wealth, or money as its substance.

It is not a matter of having to decide whether *The Road* is capitalist ideology or environmentalist critique. The point is that it is both at the same time, perhaps without meaning to be. Its combination of resignation to the status quo and desire for its transformation – the combination of what Fredric Jameson identified in a classic essay on mass culture as the impulses of reification and utopia – seems to be overdetermined, emanating not just from McCarthy's unusual talents but inherent in the new millennium's discursive environment.[2] Just as there is one accounting for things in which the repeated failure of the predicted end of the world to take place exposes its imaginary or delusional basis, and another in which those repeated failures have no impact at all on the viability and virulence of the apocalyptic meme, there seem to be different ways of taking stock of the world's current situation that make *The Road* simultaneously a profound meditation on the human condition, a befuddled and brutal piece of neoliberal ideology, and a searing exposure of the fantasy of human domination over the nonhuman world. The question is not whether *The Road* is ambiguous but rather how this multivalence is generated and why it seems inescapable. The hypothesis offered here will be that contemporary storytelling and thinking are confronted by an array of different temporal frameworks that afford radically different possibilities for human agency and cohere with radically different political and ethical demands. The ambiguity of McCarthy's dystopia has to do with this contradictory array, which will not allow the narrative to sit comfortably or unequivocally in the timescale and rhythms of humanism, capitalism, or ecology. Furthermore, to move beyond the dystopic imagination to its antithetical counterpart, any opening for utopian imagining is conditioned by this same set of constraints, especially since the representation of utopia is nowadays almost always constructed in terms of another time rather than, as it once could be, another place.

The hypothesis about temporality draws upon historian Dipesh Chakrabarty's 2009 essay "The Climate of History: Four Theses." Chakrabarty's first and primary thesis, from which the others follow, is that in the context of anthropogenic climate change the humanist distinction between human history and natural history collapses.[3] This collapse is exactly what makes it impossible for *The Road* to be about the nobility and depravity of "human nature" without at the same time being a cautionary tale about environmental irresponsibility. McCarthy's nightmare world represents a moment in natural history, not (or not just) a universal human condition. McCarthy's humans do not simply act upon one another in a war of all the humans against all the other humans, they are trapped within the effects of an anthropogenic environmental cataclysm that has made murder and cannibalism into widely practiced survival strategies. "Human nature" in *The Road* is a product of nature, not merely a property of humans. And nature does not merely act upon humans, humans themselves act as a force of nature within a world that they have helped to make. The politics of environmentalism in the age of the Anthropocene renders any notion of human autonomy or exceptionalism delusional. Whatever ethical force McCarthy's novel achieves, the way humans interact with one another cannot be disentangled from or privileged over the way they interact with the nonhuman world.

The collapsed distinction between natural history and humanist history involves the difficult representation of what Timothy Morton has called hyperobjects – objects so "massively distributed in time and space relative to humans" that they bring about what Morton calls "the end of the world," meaning the end of any understanding of the world that enfolds itself around human awareness.[4] Climate change, or global warming as Morton prefers it, is a prime example. Chakrabarty's slightly earlier argument clearly anticipates Morton's but focuses more on the problem of correlating the Anthropocene with a notion of the historical subject. At its most pointed, this argument pits the term's implication that the problem of anthropogenic climate change involves an analysis of human species' behavior against the objection that what is at stake in the climate crisis is the result of one particular form of human social organization, industrial capitalism, a position forcefully advanced by Jason W. Moore in his 2015 *Capitalism in the Web of Life*.[5] Chakrabarty argues that, despite the clear role of industrial capitalism in producing the climate crisis, the crisis itself reveals the contingency of parameters for the maintenance of human life on earth "that have no intrinsic connection to the logics of capitalist, nationalist, or socialist identities. They are connected rather to the history of life on this planet, the way different life-forms connect to one another, and the way the mass extinction of one species could spell danger for another."[6] The question then is, "How do we hold the two [the general history of life and the history of capitalism] together as we think the history of the world since the Enlightenment?"[7] Understanding human beings as agents of geological change finally points to the problem, for Chakrabarty, of conceiving a hypersubject adequate to the hyperobjects presented by climate change's geological scale: "Climate change poses for us a question of a human collectivity, an us, pointing to a figure of the universal that escapes our capacity to experience the world."[8] The challenge thereby posed to ethical thinking is put with admirable clarity by Mark Fisher in his 2009 *Capitalist Realism*:

> Instead of saying that *everyone* – i.e. every *one* – is responsible for climate change, we all have to do our bit, it would be better to say that no-one is, and that's the very problem. The cause of eco-catastrophe is an impersonal structure which, even though it is capable of producing all kinds of effects, is precisely not a subject capable of exercising responsibility. The required subject – a collective subject – does not exist, yet the crisis, like all other global crises we're now facing, demands that it be constructed.[9]

As Chakrabarty's arguments concerning the tension between the conceptual frameworks provided by the Anthropocene versus those focused on the critique of capitalism assert, the collapsed distinction between natural and human histories poses difficulties not just to humanist universality but also to the historical perspectives that inform movements for social justice. The long-term historical temporality that underlies systemic analyses of racial oppression and gender hierarchies has often opposed itself to the transhistorical abstractions of humanism – even while invoking the category of the human and the discourse of human rights – by narrating how unevenly privileged gender and racial identities have been constructed and maintained as fundamental elements of the contemporary status quo. The relevance of this historical perspective to utopian thinking is evident. For example, Tom Moylan's analysis of the critical utopias of the 1970s identifies the ideological kernel of the utopian novels by Joanna Russ, Samuel R. Delany, Marge Piercy, and Ursula K. LeGuin as activism rooted in the mid-twentieth-century civil rights, feminist, and antiwar movements.[10] One might now ask, what happens to that strain of utopian thinking when the timescales of legislative reform or even of political revolution seem to have been shrunk into comparative insignificance by a climate crisis involving pollutants with half-lives reckoned in thousands or even hundreds of thousands of years? The geological, hyperobjective scale of the exigencies of the climate crisis seems to remove it from the realms of political or ethical agency. What collective subject, in what historical framework, can be imagined to open the present to a post-Anthropocenic future?

The question of the collective subject certainly coheres with, and perhaps underlies, a trend in utopian thinking identified by Fredric Jameson in his *Archaeologies of the Future*. Citing Kim Stanley Robinson's great Mars trilogy, Jameson observes "a new formal tendency, in which it is not the representation of Utopia, but rather the conflict of all possible Utopias, and the arguments about the nature and desirability of Utopia as such, which move to the center of attention."[11] The flip side of this observation is Mark Fisher's formulation of what he calls capitalist realism: "the widespread sense that not only is capitalism the only viable political and economic system, but also that it is now impossible even to *imagine* a coherent alternative to it."[12] Indeed, contemporary popular culture confirms that it is very much easier to imagine the end of the world than to imagine the end of capitalism, especially since the end of the world usually, as in *The Road*, turns out to be the continuation of capitalism by other means. What this allows us to add to the present argument is that a number of countertemporalities allied with capitalist realism set themselves in opposition to both the geologic temporality of the Anthropocene and the long-term historical temporality informing social justice movements. These countertemporalities include, first of all, the frozen time of capitalist realism per se, the insistence that there is no alternative to the capitalist status quo, so that the more things change, as they constantly must in order to satisfy capitalism's appetites, the more they stay the same. But alongside this frozen time there reside any number of short-term, cyclical temporalities that serve to punctuate the narrative of capitalism's inevitability: the vast array of monthly, quarterly, annual (and so on) economic reports; the booms and busts of the stock market; the mass cultural cycles of sporting events, serial narratives, and fads; and, perhaps above all, the political election cycle, offering in America the ongoing appearance of a democratic struggle over the quality of civil life, but one in which long-term, radical, or utopian thinking finds itself bound and gagged by the importance given to short-term fluctuations of the market, poll-obsessed politics, and the amnesiac quality of breaking-news cycles.

What Fisher's argument boils down to is that what goes by the name of realism these days is actually a deeply ingrained form of cynicism. Amitav Ghosh makes a different but allied case against contemporary realism in *The Great Derangement*. According to Ghosh, the quotidian rhythms and everyday details that form the foundation of realist settings paradoxically render it impossible for the realist novel to deal seriously with the issue of climate change. "The irony of the realist novel," he argues, is that "the very gestures with which it conjures up reality are actually a concealment of the real."[13] The depth of realist conventionality's foreclosure of engagement with the climate crisis is revealed by its dismissal of the genre that has the best record of attending to it, science fiction. But once again, a problem concerning temporality comes up. Ghosh complains of science fiction that most of it is set in the future, and that is precisely not where climate change is happening. To relegate the effects of climate change to any sort of otherworldly setting, Ghosh contends, is "to rob them of precisely the quality that makes them so urgently compelling – which is that they are actually happening on this earth, at this time."[14]

Where then can one search in the attempt to give a utopian turn to the imagining of contemporary possibility? And how can one reconcile any sort of utopianism with the urgent demands of the present? The theorizing of Ernst Bloch continues to afford a cogent response to the impasse variously described by Ghosh, Fisher, Chakrabarty, and Jameson. The crucial role of the category of futurity in Bloch's theorizing makes his version of utopian anticipation resemble the unfolding, nonimmediate, purely tendential reality of hyperobjects and hypersubjects. For Bloch, the essential quality of the utopian gaze is that "it grasps the tendency of reality."[15] What it grasps hold of is not present but not illusory. It is the product of understanding, not merely of desire. Bloch asserts that, in contrast to Thomas More's island utopia, when utopia "is transposed into the future ... it is not something like nonsense or absolute fancy; rather it is the not *yet* in the sense of a possibility."[16] As "the unimpaired reason of a militant optimism," utopian hope is "the comprehended activity of expectation, of a hopeful presentiment, [that] keeps the alliance with everything dawning in the world."[17] In his chapter "Art and Utopia," Bloch writes of the "real realism" that the "utopian gaze" offers in contrast to the parochial realism of the bourgeois novel. This paradoxically utopian realism is "at home in those qualities of reality that are utopian themselves; i.e., they contain future."[18] An extrapolative near-future setting is able to be more realistic, then, more attuned to the "dawning" reality of global warming – as well as, one might add, to the contingency of institutional racism and other forms of systemically ingrained injustice – than a realism wedded to the commonsensical inevitability of the status quo.

Fredric Jameson recasts Bloch's insights into twenty-first-century form in the concluding moments of his *Archaeologies of the Future*:

> The Utopian form itself is the answer to the universal ideological conviction that no alternative is possible, that there is no alternative to the system. But it asserts this by forcing us to think the break itself, and not by offering us a more traditional picture of what things would be like after the break. ... The formal flaw – how to articulate the Utopian break in such a way that it is transformed into a practical-political transition – now becomes a rhetorical and political strength – in that it forces us precisely to concentrate on the break itself: a meditation on the impossible, on the unrealizable in its own right.[19]

Bloch's utopian anticipation, cast in the terms of futurity and hope, becomes in the twenty-first-century context Jameson's "break," cast as resistance to the cynicism or apocalyptic despair fostered by capitalist realism and its mass cultural and political correlates. Jameson's utopian break is not an otherworldly fantasy about a better place, but rather a form of resistance grounded in understanding the present, and in seeing that it could be different. It is, to paraphrase one of Jameson's formulations about science fiction, the art of imagining the present as the past of a possible future by wedging thoughtfully into the cracks in the seemingly monolithic structure of capitalist, racist, patriarchal petromodernity.

What, then, can be said of recent attempts to make a break with America's hegemonic cynicism and think out "the unrealizable in its own right"? One of the most ambitious attempts to conceive a new form of collective subjectivity adequate to the utopian break is Michael Hardt and Antonio Negri's concept of the multitude, a crucial component of their grand theorization of the postmodern geopolitical order in the trilogy

Empire, *Multitude*, and *Commonwealth*. The notion of the multitude follows from Hardt and Negri's attempt to rethink the form taken by class struggle within the postimperialist order they call Empire. Within the processes that sustain this order, the classic conflict between labor and capital takes the postmodern form of a conflict between biopolitical production and the biopower enforced to control it and contain its revolutionary potential by the exercise of political sovereignty and economic expropriation. The dominant form of biopolitical production, immaterial labor, renders obsolete the old privileging of factory labor and labor time in the analysis of class conflict, because biopolitical production consists largely of "immaterial products, such as information, knowledges, ideas, images, relationships, and affects" – things not produced in factories and often not even in wage-labor situations.[20] Biopolitical production thus "tends to move out of the limited realm of the strictly economic domain and engage in the general production and reproduction of society as a whole," so that it involves "the *production of subjectivity* . . . [and] tends to take the form of *networks* based on communication, collaboration, and affective relationships" (emphasis in original).[21] If Empire itself has the form of a network, it is not because it imposes this form on the world but because it works with the materials afforded it by biopolitical production.

The collective subject immanent within the organization of biopolitical production, "the living alternative that grows within Empire," is the multitude.[22] In contrast to the uniformity of a "people" or of "the masses," the multitude is "an internally different, multiple social subject whose constitution and action is based not on identity or unity . . . but on what it has in common."[23] Just as the expropriation of surplus value under Empire takes the form of capturing and privatizing the common, the revolutionary potential of the multitude resides in the possibility of making the common truly open to sharing by all. "The distributed network structure" characteristic of resistance to Empire "provides the model for an absolutely democratic organization," making the multitude "the only social subject capable of realizing democracy, that is, the rule of everybody by everybody."[24] The question concerning the multitude, then, is not what it is but what it can become.[25] On the stage of the global crisis Hardt and Negri bear witness to in the dawning twenty-first century, "the multitude appears as a subject and declares, 'Another world is possible.'"[26]

Understanding the multitude, according to Hardt and Negri, depends upon a basic methodological principle of Marxist analysis, paying attention not just to empirical data but to the historical tendency that gives them coherence and direction. "The key," they write, "is to grasp the direction of the present, to read which seeds will grow and which will wither."[27] That is to say, it is precisely the sort of object, or hyperobject or hypersubject, that opens itself to the utopian gaze when it employs "the unimpaired reason of a militant optimism."[28] Thus the multitude is not merely extrapolated from the present as a continuation of the same but rather bears in itself the possibility of the "break" that Jameson says is the key insight available to utopian thought at present. The possibility of another world emerges from the incommensurability of biopolitical production itself with the accountancy of biopower: "biopolitical production is on the one hand *immeasurable*, because it cannot be quantified in fixed units of time, and, on the other, always *excessive* with respect to the value that capital can extract from it" (emphasis in original).[29] But when will the break occur? What can bring it about? "Here is where the question of time becomes essential," answer Hardt and Negri, and they continue,

> we have to recognize decision [i.e., the political decision-making of networks of biopolitical production] also as an event – not the linear accumulation of Chronos and the monotonous ticking of its clocks but the sudden expression of Kairos. ... Revolutionary politics must grasp, in the movement of the multitudes and through the accumulation of common and cooperative decisions, the moment of rupture or *clinamen* that can create a new world.[30]

We might recognize here the exact antithesis of the cynicism that prolongs the "great derangement" of the present by unceasing disavowal and deferral of a future habitable only by the living dead, as *The Road* so eloquently depicts it. Instead, from the viewpoint afforded by the collective subject of the multitude, "We can already recognize that today time is split between a present that is already dead and a future that is already living."[31] The utopian impulse here has nothing to do with imagining a blueprint of that future. It is instead a matter of insisting that although the end of the world has already happened, another world is not only possible but also realizable in the act of sorting "which seeds will grow and which will wither."[32]

When Hardt and Negri assert of the multitude's possibilities that "such a radical transformation of the world to allow singularities to express themselves freely, is not a far-off utopian dream; it is grounded in the developments of our concrete social reality,"[33] what developments, what utopian activism, can support their claims? Writing in the early 2000s, they themselves point to the antiglobalization movement, with its lack of central organization and its ever-evolving alliances of different groups around the issues they share in common. More recent examples would have to include the Occupy movement, with its forgoing of specific demands, a leader, or central organizing committee in favor of insistently reiterating the commonality of "the 99%" in the face of America's staggering economic inequality and the political ossification it supports and requires. Another, more far-reaching example would be the uncoordinated but allied protests against the energy industry's extractive agenda that Naomi Klein calls "Blockadia." According to Klein, "resistance to high-risk extreme extraction [such as fracking] is building a global, grass-roots, and broad-based network . . . driven by a desire for a deeper form of democracy, one that provides communities with real control over those resources that are most critical to collective survival [i.e. the common]."[34] Klein reports that this network of activist interventions is united, not by an organization or a party, but rather by "a transnational narrative about resistance to a common ecological crisis."[35] This narrative envisions a temporal horizon radically incommensurable with the language or the timetables of corporate risk assessment, discarding the illusion that "economic growth still has a meaning on a planet convulsing in serial disasters."[36] The principle uniting Blockadia is uncompromising insistence upon a break with the extractive practices of the energy industry and therefore with the world (or the end of the world) that those practices entail. These communities "are not looking to negotiate a better deal – whether in the form of local jobs, higher royalties, or better safety standards. More and more, these communities are simply saying 'No.' . . . And not just 'Not in My Backyard' but, as the French anti-fracking activists say: *Ni ici, ni ailleurs* – neither here, nor elsewhere."[37]

Among allied fictional attempts at a utopian reimagining of subjects and collectives, Donna Haraway's "The Camille Stories," the concluding section of her 2016 book *Staying with the Trouble*, is worth examining for both thematic and formal reasons. The thematic reasons have to do with Haraway's formulation of the utopian break as a reconstruction of subjectivity. The stories concern the development of a network of utopian communities founded by groups who "migrate to ruined places and work with humans and nonhumans to heal those places."[38] The emergence of these communities, who call themselves the Children of Compost, is based on the somewhat improbable ethical fantasy of a revolution in affect: "These eruptions of healing energy and activism were ignited by love of earth and its human and nonhuman beings and by rage at the rate and scope of extinctions, exterminations, genocides, and immiserations in enforced patterns of multispecies living and dying that threatened ongoingness for everyone."[39] But the real crux of their utopian project is more specific, a thorough remaking of practices of sex, gender, and kinship, the ultimate aim of which includes a gradual, long-term reduction of the planet's human population, which declines from a peak of 10 billion in 2100 to 3 billion by the end of the sequence in 2425. Although the details are a little fuzzy – and the incompleteness of the entire piece is a crucial feature of its formal significance, as we will see shortly – the main features of the new kinship system are that every child has to have at least three parents, that this group parenting is an extremely serious commitment central to the entire social makeup of the utopian communities, that all kinship bonds are voluntary and malleable, and that gender practices are entirely fluid. But most radically of all, it "is the right and obligation of the human person, of whatever gender, who is carrying a pregnancy to choose an animal symbiont for the new child."[40] This is done through genetic engineering, so that the five generations of Camilles in the title are part monarch butterfly. Haraway's utopian scheme of queer reproduction does not simply decenter humans, then, it actively writes them into what Chakrabarty calls the general history of life by making them something other than human: "The Children of Compost came to see their shared kind as humus, rather than as human or nonhuman."[41] In a telling reversal of the fashioning of Adam out of clay in the West's master patriarchal creation myth, humans are to become the nutrient soil of the planet's return to health.

The unexplained contradiction between the spontaneity of the initial founding of the Children of Compost's communities and the apparently careful, long-range, globally coordinated planning of reproduction within them points not so much to thematic shortcomings as to the formal foundations of "The Camille Stories." Haraway explains that these stories were generated in response to a prompt given to her and two partners in a workshop at an international scholarly colloquium on speculative fiction. Deliberately unfinished, they are "invitations to participate in a kind of genre fiction committed to strengthening ways to propose near futures, possible futures, and implausible but real nows."[42] She thus offers them in the concluding section of *Staying with the Trouble* as "a speculative gesture, both a memory and a lure for a 'we' that came into being by fabulating a story together one summer in Normandy."[43] The unanimity of feelings of love for earth and rage at injustice that motivate the worldwide movements of the Children of Compost loses any hint of implausibility when it is considered instead to reflect the shared feelings of the three workshop participants, or indeed the shared opinions of the attendees of the conference and the scholarly and professional community to which they belong.

When Haraway declares that her story "cries out for collaborative and divergent story-making practices,"[44] then, its fragmentary and not entirely coherent quality points to the same kind of gap between organization and narrative that Klein observes in Blockadia's "transnational narrative about a common ecological crisis."[45] Haraway's vision of queer reproduction is precisely *not* a blueprint for future activism, then, but rather an invitation to collaborative imagining and storytelling to help galvanize activism in the present.

The reconstruction of subjectivity imagined for Haraway's human–butterfly hybrids here is less material, and perhaps less significant, than the "we" of its authorship and the community of feeling in which it participates. An anthology published the year before *Staying with the Trouble*, adrienne maree brown and Walidah Imarisha's *Octavia's Brood: Science Fiction Stories from Social Justice Movements* provides a possible name for Haraway's speculative gesture. Imarisha calls the stories collected in *Octavia's Brood*, some of which were generated from workshop exercises similar to the one Haraway describes, "visionary fiction," a kind of storytelling that is important because "if we want to bring new worlds into existence, then we need to challenge the narratives that uphold current power dynamics and patterns."[46] If we read Haraway's "Camille Stories" in this light, as a mode of challenging and resisting the temporality of capitalist realism and the ethical framework of heteronormative orthodoxy, her scheme of queer reproduction becomes a kind of foil to dominant kinship conventions and anthropocentrism that exposes their susceptibility to change. It is, to use Hardt and Negri's terms once more, a proposal for a set of imaginary practices that exemplifies the revolutionary potential of immaterial labor's production of resistant subjectivities.

To turn, in conclusion, to a pair of fully realized speculative fiction novels, consider how utopian imagining in Nisi Shawl's *Everfair* and Kim Stanley Robinson's *New York 2140* reiterates and further explores the problems of temporality, politics, and collective action we have been examining. Both novels imagine the opening of utopian possibilities within the framework of struggles for social justice. *Everfair* sets these possibilities in an alternative past that plays with the actual history of imperialism, slavery, resource extraction, and war during the late nineteenth and early twentieth centuries. *New York 2140* instead sets its utopian moment in a speculative near future punctuated by climate-change disaster and capitalist business as usual. Their complementary strategies of rethinking the past and imagining the future, focusing on the legacies of colonialism and the cycles of capitalism, illustrate some important ways contemporary utopian fiction can "think the break" from our crisis-ridden present.

Nisi Shawl's steampunk alternative history, *Everfair*, is set in a fictitious country of that name founded on land purchased from the historic Belgian Congo and dedicated to resisting King Leopold of Belgium's horrific policies – policies that Shawl makes clear were the true referent of "the horror" in Joseph Conrad's *Heart of Darkness* – and providing a place of refuge for escapees from his brutal regime.[47] The novel follows the new country through three wars: the first a successful war of resistance against Leopold; the second, the country's internally contentious involvement in the geopolitical turmoil of World War I; and the third a civil war – peacefully concluded in the end – between its native African monarch and its European and American settlers. The complex entanglement of race, sexuality, ideology, and politics in the country's antislavery activism places its thematic focus squarely on problems of alliance among the disparate groups that find common ground in their resistance to Leopold. Even the steampunk technology that is one of the keys to Everfair's successful war against Leopold's regime depends on a powerful synthesis of Indigenous African knowledge and European engineering in the hands of a Chinese immigrant. The pacing of the narration, which consists of many short episodes separated from one another by periods ranging from a month to several years, and its large cast of characters, none of whom can be said to occupy the central position in the plot, align it with the large-scale history of systems and structures, rather than heroes and villains, that informs contemporary social justice movements. The result is the kind of social system represented in the genre of the critical utopia, as described by Tom Moylan, one that "is not simply invoked or imposed but rather produced, challenged, altered, and, most of all, lived by means of the utopian method itself."[48] The project of founding a just society within the borders of Everfair could just as accurately be compared to what Ernst Bloch calls the search for *Heimat* or home, "the goal of the upright gait toward which human beings strive as they seek to overcome exploitation, humiliation, oppression, and disillusionment," a goal that is "only possible as a collective enterprise."[49] In *Everfair*, the patent imperfections and limitations of all its characters finally serve to accentuate and elevate the impressive, difficult achievement of its collective.

Kim Stanley Robinson's *New York 2140* takes place in a future where massive melt-offs of the polar ice caps have raised ocean levels by over fifty feet, immersing lower Manhattan all the way up to Central Park at high tide. But New Yorkers have adapted to the changed conditions by transforming lower Manhattan into a "new Venice," and they have succeeded so well that the area is attracting rampant real-estate speculation by the wealthy class that earlier abandoned lower Manhattan for higher and drier ground. The struggle over ownership of a single building in this New Venice becomes the focal point where Robinson brings together the grand historical narratives of class struggle and global warming. Although the action is concentrated in the space of a year or so, the dozen decades separating the setting of the novel from its date of publication afford Robinson the scope to unfold the contours of the hyperobject global warming. One of the main characters is a hedge-fund manager who, early on, describes his computer screen in terms clearly meant as commentary on the polyphonic strategies of the novel itself: "My screen was a veritable anthology of narratives, and in many different genres. . . . The temporalities in these genres ranged from the nanoseconds of high-frequency trading to the geological epochs of sea level rise."[50] Like *Everfair*, *New York 2140* lacks a single hero, instead developing the complex interactions of a collective effort by the residents of a condominium in the New Venice to save their homes from appropriation by real-estate speculators. In another moment of self-reflexivity, one of the residents jokes, "Have you ever noticed that our building is a kind of actor network that can do things? . . . add the getaway driver and it's a fucking heist movie!"[51] A running joke, repeated three times in the course of the novel, is that the residents of the condo decide to launch a political revolution and overthrow world capitalism in order to save their building from a hostile takeover. The global is firmly rooted in the local, and Robinson's future is firmly rooted in the present. The main event in the plot is a financial crisis modeled on that of 2008, but in which the federal government nationalizes the banking industry instead of bailing it out. The main thrust of the novel is to counter capitalist realism's fantasy of inevitability with the fantasy of a successful political revolution. The resilient adaptation of the residents of the New Venice stands in sharp contrast to the spectacular depictions of catastrophic climate events as the end of the world that have become a commonplace of mass culture in the twenty-first century. Robinson's novel instead insists that another, better world remains possible.

This essay was composed in the summer of 2021 as the global Covid-19 pandemic continued to unfold, the aftermath of Donald Trump's attempt to steal the presidential election of 2020 continued to foment political and legal struggles in the United States, and disastrous heat waves, wildfires, and flooding ravaged the Americas, Asia, and Europe. In the summer of

2023, as I finalize this chapter for publication, Covid vaccinations have become an annual routine, misinformation and disinformation continue to entrench right-wing reaction throughout Europe and North America, and catastrophic wildfires have turned into a familiar summer event. The normalization of ecological, social, and political crises discernible in the passage from 2021 to 2023 is both insidious and apparently unavoidable. Drastic change keeps happening, but at a pace that renders it locally invisible, and on a scale that places it beyond the reach of individual agency. It seems that the world has decided to "think the break" for us, and it is up to us to find the next step. The hope motivating this essay has been that the utopian imaginings of time and collectivity examined here can provide a vital resource for that endeavor.

Notes

1. Cormac McCarthy, *The Road* (New York: Vintage, 2006).
2. Fredric Jameson, "Reification and Utopia in Mass Culture," *Social Text* 1 (1979), 130–148.
3. Dipesh Chakrabarty, "The Climate of History: Four Theses," *Critical Inquiry* 35 (2009), 197–222.
4. Timothy Morton, *Hyperobjects: Philosophy and Ecology after the End of the World* (Minneapolis: University of Minnesota Press, 2013), 1–2.
5. Jason W. Moore, *Capitalism in the Web of Life: Ecology and the Accumulation of Capital* (London: Verso, 2015), 169–192.
6. Chakrabarty, 217.
7. Chakrabarty, 219.
8. Chakrabarty, 222.
9. Mark Fisher, *Capitalist Realism: Is There No Alternative?* (London: Zero Books, 2009), 66.
10. Tom Moylan, *Demand the Impossible: Science Fiction and the Utopian Imagination*, edited by Raffaella Baccolini (Oxford: Peter Lang, 2014), xi.
11. Fredric Jameson, *Archaeologies of the Future: The Desire Called Utopia and Other Science Fictions* (London: Verso, 2005), 220.
12. Fisher, 2.
13. Amitav Ghosh, *The Great Derangement: Climate Change and the Unthinkable* (Chicago: University of Chicago Press, 2016), 23.
14. Ghosh, 27.
15. Ernst Bloch, *The Utopian Function of Art and Literature*, translated by Jack Zipes and Frank Mecklenburg (Cambridge, MA: MIT Press, 1988), 106.
16. Bloch, 3.
17. Bloch, 107.
18. Bloch, 106.
19. Jameson, *Archaeologies*, 232.

20. Michael Hardt and Antonio Negri, *Multitude: War and Democracy in the Age of Empire* (London: Penguin, 2004), 65.
21. Hardt and Negri, 66.
22. Hardt and Negri, xiii.
23. Hardt and Negri, 100.
24. Hardt and Negri, 88, 100.
25. Hardt and Negri, 105.
26. Hardt and Negri, 348.
27. Hardt and Negri, 141.
28. Bloch, 107.
29. Hardt and Negri, 146.
30. Hardt and Negri, 357.
31. Hardt and Negri, 358.
32. Hardt and Negri, 141.
33. Hardt and Negri, 355.
34. Naomi Klein, *This Changes Everything: Capitalism vs. The Climate* (New York: Simon & Schuster, 2014), 295.
35. Klein, 303.
36. Klein, 335.
37. Klein, 335.
38. Donna Haraway, *Staying with the Trouble: Making Kin in the Chthulucene* (Durham, NC: Duke University Press, 2016), 137.
39. Haraway, 137.
40. Haraway, 139.
41. Haraway, 140.
42. Haraway, 136.
43. Haraway, 136.
44. Haraway, 143.
45. Klein, 303.
46. adrienne maree brown and Walidah Imarisha (eds.), *Octavia's Brood: Science Fiction from Social Justice Movements* (Chico, CA: AK Press, 2015), 279.
47. Nisi Shawl, *Everfair* (New York: Tor, 2016).
48. Moylan, xix.
49. Jack Zipes, *Ernst Bloch: The Pugnacious Philosopher of Hope* (New York: Palgrave Macmillan, 2019), 19.
50. Kim Stanley Robinson, *New York 2140* (New York: Orbit, 2017), 18.
51. Robinson, 399.

Works Cited

Aanerud, R. (1999 [1997]). Fictions of Whiteness: Speaking the Names of Whiteness in U.S. Literature. In R. Frankenberg (ed.), *Displacing Whiteness: Essays in Social and Cultural Criticism*. Durham, NC: Duke University Press, 35–59.

Abensour, M. "Persistent Utopia," *Constellations* 15(3) (2008), 406–421.

Abu-Jamal, M. (2015). Star Wars and the American Imagination. In a. m. brown and W. Imarisha (eds.), *Octavia's Brood: Science Fiction Stories from Social Justice Movements*. Chico, CA: AK Press, 255–258.

Alderman, N. (2017). *The Power*. New York: Little, Brown and Company.

Alexander, J. (2017). *Writing Youth: Young Adult Fiction as Literacy Sponsorship*. Lanham, MD: Lexington.

Alexander, J. and Black, R. W. (2015). The Darker Side of the Sorting Hat: Representations of Educational Testing in Dystopian Young Adult Fiction. *Children's Literature*, 43, 208–234.

Alexie, S. *Flight* (2008). London: Harvill and Secker.

Anti-Defamation League. (2022). *Day of the Rope*. www.adl.org/education/references/hate-symbols/day-of-the-rope.

Anzaldúa, G. (1999). *Borderlands/La Frontera: The New Mestiza*, 2nd ed. San Francisco: Aunt Lute Books.

Arendt, H. (1958). *The Human Condition*. Chicago: University of Chicago Press.

Arimah, L. N. (2019). The Referendum. In V. Lavalle and J. J. Adams (eds.), *A People's Future of the United States*. New York: One World, 178–190.

Arrighi, G. (2005). Hegemony Unravelling. *New Left Review*, 32 (March/April).

(1994). *The Long Twentieth Century: Money, Power, and the Origins of Our Times*. New York: Verso.

Aspden, R. (2012). Review of *Alif the Unseen*. *The Observer* (October 7, 2012).

Atwood, M. (2019). *Payback: Debt and the Shadow Side of Wealth*. House of Anansi Press.

(2017). *The Handmaid's Tale*. New York: Anchor Books.

Avery Sutton, M. (2014). *American Apocalypse: A History of Modern Evangelicalism*. Cambridge, MA: Harvard University Press.

Baca, D. (2008). *Mestiz@ Scripts, Digital Migrations, and the Territories of Writing*. New York: Palgrave Macmillan.

Baccolini, R. (2000). Gender and Genre in the Feminist Critical Dystopias of Katharine Burdekin, Margaret Atwood, and Octavia Butler. In M. Barr (ed.), *Future Females, the Next Generation: New Voices and Velocities in Feminist Science Fiction*. Boston: Rowman & Littlefield, 13–34.

Baccolini, R. and Moylan, T. (2003). Introduction: Dystopia and Histories. In R. Baccolini and T. Moylan (eds.), *Dark Horizons: Science Fiction and the Dystopian Imagination*. New York: Routledge, 1–12.

Bacigalupi, P. (2010). *Ship Breaker*. New York: Little, Brown, and Company.

(2012). *The Drowned Cities*. New York: Little, Brown, and Company.

(2015). *The Water Knife*. New York: Knopf.

(2009). *The Windup Girl*. San Francisco: Night Shade.

(2015). *Tool of War*. New York: Little, Brown

Badmington, N. (2004). *Alien Chic: Posthumanism and the Other Within*. London: Routledge.

Baer, S. (1970). *Zome Primer: Elements of Zonahedra Geometry*. Albuquerque, NM: Zoneworks Corps.

Baldwin, J. (1996). *BuckyWorks: Buckminster Fuller's Ideas for Today*. New York: Wiley.

(2017). *The Fire Next Time*. London: Penguin.

Ballard, J. G. (2017). *Crash*. London: Picador.

(2006). *The Atrocity Exhibition*. London: Harper.

Bammer, A. (1992). *Partial Visions: Feminism and Utopianism in the 1970s*. London: Routledge.

Banerjee. A. and Vint, S. (2020). Thinking through the Pandemic: A Symposium. *Science Fiction Studies* 47.3, 321–376.

Barr, M. (1992). *Feminist Fabulation: Space/Postmodern Fiction*. Iowa City: University of Iowa Press.

(2000). *Future Females, The Next Generation: New Voices and Velocities in Feminist Science Fiction Criticism*. New York: Rowman and Littlefield, 2000.

Barrera, C. E. (2021). Utopic Dreaming on the Borderlands: An Anzaldúan Reading of Yuri Herrera's Signs Preceding the End of the World. *Utopian Studies*, 31.3, 475–493.

Barrow, L. (1986). *Independent Spirits: Spiritualism and English Plebeians 1850–1910*. London: Routledge, Kegan & Paul.

Barthes, R. (2012). *Mythologies*, translated by R. Howard and A. Lavers. New York: Hill and Wang.

Bastani, A. (2019). *Fully Automated Luxury Communism*. London: Verso.

Bear, G. (1985). *Blood Music*. Westminster: Arbor House.

Belew, K. (2018). *Bring the War Home: The White Power Movement and Paramilitary America*. Cambridge, MA: Harvard University Press.

Bell, D. (2017). *Rethinking Utopia: Place, Power, Affect*. London: Routledge.

(1992). The Space Traders. In *Faces at the Bottom of the Well: The Permanence of Racism*. New York: Basic Books, 158–194.

Benanav, A. and Clegg, J. (2018). Crisis and Immiseration: Critical Theory Today. In B. Best, W. Bonefeld, and C. O'Kane (eds.), *Handbook of Frankfurt School Critical Theory*. London: SAGE, 1629–1648.

Benjamin, W. (1968). Theses on the Philosophy of History. In *Illuminations: Essays and Reflections*, edited with an introduction by H. Arendt; translated by H. Zohn. New York: Schocken Books, 253–264.

Bester, A. (1996). *The Stars My Destination*. New York: Vintage.

Bey, H. (2003). *T.A.Z. The Temporary Autonomous Zone, Ontological Anarchy, Poetic Terrorism*, 2nd ed. New York: Autonomedia.

Bisson, T. (1988). *Fire on the Mountain*. Oakland, CA: PM Press.

Blake, J., and Gilman, N. (2021). Governing in the Planetary Age. *Noēma*, March 9, online.

Blauvelt, A. (ed.) (2015). *Hippie Modernism: The Struggle for Utopia*. Minneapolis: Walker Arts Center.

Blish, J. (2011). *A Case of Conscience*. London: Gollancz.

Bloch, E. (1986). *The Principle of Hope*, volume 1, translated by Neville Plaice, Stephen Plaice, and Paul Knight. Cambridge: MIT Press.

(1988). *The Utopian Function of Art and Literature: Selected Essays by Ernst Bloch*, translated by Jack Zipes and Frank Mecklenburg. Cambridge, MA: MIT Press.

Bloch, E. and Adorno, T. W. (1988). Something's Missing: A Discussion between Ernst Bloch and Theodor W. Adorno on the Contradictions of Utopian Longing. In *The Utopian Function of Art and Literature: Selected Essays by Ernst Bloch*, translated by Jack Zipes and Frank Mecklenburg. Cambridge, MA: MIT Press, 1–17.

Bloom, H. (2013). *The American Religion*. New York: Chu Hartley.

Boisseron, B. (2018). *Afro-Dog: Blackness and the Animal Question*. New York: Columbia University Press.

Bornstein, K. (2013). *My New Gender Workbook*. New York: Routledge.

Bould, M. (2007). Come Alive by Saying No: An Introduction to Black Power SF. *Science Fiction Studies*, 34.2, 220–240.

Bould, M. (2010). Why Neo Flies, and Why He Shouldn't: The Critique of Cyberpunk in Gwyneth Jones's *Escape Plans* and M. John Harrison's *Signs of Life*. In G. J. Murphy and S. Vint (eds.), *Beyond Cyberpunk: New Critical Perspectives*. New York: Routledge, 116–134.

Bowers, E. (2018). An Exploration of Femininity, Masculinity, and Racial Prejudice. *Herland: The American Journal of Economics and Sociology*, 77.5, 1313–1327.

Brace, C. L. (2005). *"Race" Is a Four-Letter Word: The Genesis of the Concept*. Oxford: Oxford University Press.

Brackett, L. (1955). *The Long Tomorrow*. New York: Doubleday.

Bradbury, R. (2012 [1953]). *Fahrenheit 451*. New York: HarperCollins.

Braidotti, R. (2013). *The Posthuman*. Malden, MA: Polity Press.

Brand, S. (ed.) (1977). *Space Colonies*. London: Penguin.

(1971). *The Last Whole Earth Catalog: Access to Tools*. London: Penguin.

Brisbane, A. (1841–2), "Section IV: Social Destiny of Man," reprinted in *London Phalanx* (1841–2), 428–465.
brown, a. m. (2015). the river. In a. m. brown and W. Imarisha, eds., *Octavia's Brood: Science Fiction Stories from Social Justice Movements*, Chico, CA: AK Press, 40–51.
(2016). *National Network of Abortion Funds 2016 Keynote*. Available from: http://adriennemareebrown.net/tag/intelligent-mischief/.
brown, a. m., and Walidah, I. (2015). *Octavia's Brood: Science Fiction From Social Justice Movements*. Chico, CA: AK Press.
Brown, J. (2021). *Black Utopias: Speculative Life and the Music of Other Worlds*. Durham, NC: Duke University Press.
Brown, W. (2015). *Undoing the Demos: Neoliberalism's Stealth Revolution*. New York: Zone Books.
(2011). We Are All Democrats Now . . . In G. Agamben, A. Badiou, D. Bensaïd, et al., *Democracy in What State?* New York: Columbia University Press, 44–57.
Brunetti, I. (2020). "Comics as Place," *The Paris Review*, August 10. www.theparisreview.org/blog/2020/08/10/comics-as-place.
Buckell, T. S. (2012). *Arctic Rising*. New York: Tom Doherty.
(2014). *Hurricane Fever*. New York: Tom Doherty.
Bukatman, S. (2017). Foreword: Cyberpunk and Its Visual Vicissitudes. In A. McFarlane, G. J. Murphy, and L. Schmeink (eds.), *Cyberpunk and Visual Culture*. New York: Routledge, xv–xix.
Burke, C. (2011). The Teachings and Redemption of Ms. Fannie Lou Mason. In *Let's Play White*. Lexington, KY: Apex Publications, 129–188.
Burwell, J. (1997). *Notes on Nowhere: Feminism, Utopian Logic, and Social Transformation*. Minneapolis: University of Minnesota Press.
Butler, O. E. (1988). *Adulthood Rites* New York: TOR.
(1987). *Dawn*. New York: TOR.
(1989). *Imago*. New York: TOR.
(1995 [1993]). *Parable of the Sower*. New York: Warner Books.
(1998). *Parable of the Talents*. New York: Warner Books.
(2005). The Book of Martha. In *Bloodchild and Other Stories* (New York: Seven Stories,), 187–214.
Callenbach, E. (2004 [1975]). *Ecotopia*. Berkeley, CA: Banyan Tree Books.
Cameron, J. (Director) (1984). *Terminator*. [Motion picture]. Los Angeles, CA: Orion Pictures.
(Director) (1991). *Terminator 2: Judgment Day*. [Motion picture]. Los Angeles, CA: Tri-Star Pictures.
Campbell, J. W. (2019). *The Order and the Other: Young Adult Dystopian Literature and Science Fiction*. Jackson: University Press of Mississippi.
Canavan, G. (2015). Capital as Artificial Intelligence. *Journal of American Studies* 49.4, 685–709.
(2019). Charles Stross: *Accelerando* (Case Study): The Singularity and the End of History. In A. McFarlane, G. J. Murphy, and L. Schmeink (eds.), *The Routledge Companion to Cyberpunk*. New York: Routledge, 56–63.

(2014). If the Engine Ever Stops, We'd All Die: *Snowpiercer* and Necrofuturism. *SF Now*. Special issue of *Paradoxa* 26, 41–66.

Card, O. S. (1986). *Speaker for the Dead*. New York: Tor Books.

Carson, R. (2002 [1962]). *Silent Spring*. New York: Mariner Books.

Chabon, M. (2007). *The Yiddish Policemen's Union*. New York: HarperCollins.

Chakrabarty, D. The Climate of History: Four Theses. *Critical Inquiry* 35 (Winter), 197–222.

Chan, E. K. (2016). *The Racial Horizon of Utopia: Unthinking the Future of Race in Late Twentieth-Century American Utopian Novels*. Bern: Peter Lang.

(2019). The White Power Utopia and the Reproduction of Victimized Whiteness. In, P. Ventura and E.K. Chan, eds., *Race and Utopian Desire in American Literature and Society*. Cham: Palgrave Macmillan, 139–159.

Charbonneau, J. (2013). *The Testing*. Boston: Houghton Mifflin Harcourt.

Charles, R. (2017). "The Power" is our era's "Handmaiod's Tale." *The Washington Post*. October 10, www.washingtonpost.com/entertainment/books/the-power-is-our-eras-handmaids-tale/2017/10/10/032a5866-ad05-11e7-9e58-e6288544af98_story.html.

Chase, R. (1957). *The American Novel and Its Tradition*. New York: Doubleday.

Chen, P. (2018). Posthuman potential and ecological limits in future worlds. In A. Tarr and D. R. White, eds., *Posthumanism in Young Adult Fiction: Finding Humanity in a Posthuman World*. Jackson: University Press of Mississippi, 179–196.

Chomsky, N. (2003). *Hegemony or Survival: America's Quest for Global Dominance*. London: Penguin.

Claeys, G. and Sargent, L. T. (eds.) (1999). *The Utopian Reader*. New York: NYU Press.

Coates, T. (2015). *Between the World and Me*. New York: Penguin Random House.

Collins, S. (2008). *The Hunger Games*. New York: Scholastic.

Condie, A. (2010). *Matched*. New York: Speak.

Cook, R. (1997). *Invasion*. New York: Berkely Publishing.

Cooley, W. H. (1995). A Dream of the Twenty-First Century. In C. F. Kessler, ed., *Daring to Dream*. Syracuse, NY: Syracuse University Press, 125–130.

Cooper, D. (2013). *Everyday Utopias: The Conceptual Life of Promising Spaces*. Durham, NC: Duke University Press.

Cooper, M. (2017). *Family Values: Between Neoliberalism and the New Social Conservatism*. New York: Zone Books.

Coulthard, G. S. (2014). *Red Skins, White Masks: Rejecting the Colonial Politics of Recognition*. Minneapolis: University of Minnesota Press.

Coupland, D. (1992). *Generation X: Tales for an Accelerated Culture*. London: Abacus.

(1994). *Life after God*. London: Simon and Schuster.

(1997). *Polaroids from the Dead*. London: Flamingo.

Covington, H. A. (2003). *The Hill of the Ravens*. Bloomington, IN: Author House, Kindle edition.

Csicsery-Ronay, I. (2008). *The Seven Beauties of Science Fiction*. Middletown, CT: Wesleyan University Press.

Darwin, C. (1861). *On the Origin of Species*, 3rd ed., ed. Barbara Bordalejo. Available at: http://darwin-online.org.uk/content/frameset?keywords=is%20easier%20nothing&pageseq=77&itemID=F376&viewtype=text.

D'Anastasio, C. (2015). Samuel R. Delany Speaks. *The Nation*, August 24. www.thenation.com/article/archive/samuel-r-delany-speaks/.

Davidson, J. P. L. (2021). Retrotopian Feminism: The Feminist 1970s, the Literary Utopia and Sarah Hall's *The Carhullan Army*. *Feminist Theory* 24.2 (2021), online.

Davies, W. (2018). Introduction. In W. Davies, ed., *Economic Science Fictions*, London: Goldsmiths Press, 1–28.

Day, S. X. (1999). *Walden Two* at Fifty. *Michigan Quarterly Review* 38.2, 247–259.

DeKoven, M. (2004). *Utopia Limited: The Sixties and the Emergence of the Postmodern*. Durham, NC: Duke University Press.

Delany, S. R. (1975). *Dhalgren*. New York: Bantam.

(1990). On Triton and Other Matters. *Science Fiction Studies* 17.3, 295–324

(1999). *Shorter Views: Queer Thoughts & the Politics of the Paraliterary*. Middletown, CT: Wesleyan University Press.

(1984). *Stars in My Pocket Like Grains of Sand*. New York: Bantam.

(1976). *Triton*. New York: Bantam.

Deloria, P. J. (2007). *Playing Indian*. New Haven, CT: Yale University Press.

Derrida, J. (2005). *Rogues: Two Essays on Reason*, translated by P.-A. Brault and M. Naas. Palo Alto, CA: Stanford University Press.

(2011). *The Beast and the Sovereign*, volume 2, translated by Geoffrey Bennington. Chicago: University of Chicago Press.

di Palma, V. (2014). *Wasteland: A History*. New Haven, CT: Yale University Press.

Dick, P. K. (1968). *Do Androids Dream of Electric Sheep?* New York: Doubleday.

(1974). *Flow My Tears, The Policeman Said*. New York: Doubleday.

(1964). *Martian Time-Slip*. New York: Ballantine.

(1962). *The Man in the High Castle*. New York: Putnam.

(1964). *The Three Stigmata of Palmer Eldritch*. New York: Doubleday.

(1959). *Time Out of Joint*. Philadelphia: J. P. Lippincott.

(1969). *Ubik*. New York: Doubleday.

Dillon, G. (ed.). (2012). *Walking the Clouds: An Anthology of Indigenous Science Fiction*. Tucson: University of Arizona Press.

(2012). Imagining Indigenous Futurism. In *Walking the Clouds: An Anthology of Indigenous Science Fiction*. Tucson: University of Arizona Press, 1–14.

Disch, T. M. (1972). *334* (London: MacGibbon and Kee, 1972).

(1968). *Camp Concentration* . London: Rupert, Hart-Davis.

Dobratz, B. A., and Shanks-Meile, S. L. (2000). *The White Separatist Movement in the US: "White Power, White Pride!"* Baltimore: Johns Hopkins University Press.

Doctorow, C. (2015). "Trying to Predict the Present," https://gerrycanavan.wordpress.com/2015/04/08/from-the-archives-interview-with-cory-doctorow-on-disney-sf-violence-meritocracy-goodharts-law-fandom-and-utopia/.

DeLillo, D. (2003). London: Picador.

(1988). *Libra.* London: Penguin.
(2010). *Point Omega.* London: Picador.
(2001). *The Body Artist.* London: Picador.
(1998). *Underworld.* London: Picador.
Douglas, C. (2011). Christian Multiculturalism and Unlearned History in Marilynne Robinson's Gilead. *Novel* 44.3, 333–353.
Douglass, F. (2016). *The Portable Frederick Douglass.* New York: Penguin.
Due, T. (2015). The Only Lasting Truth: The Theme of Change in the Works of Octavia E. Butler. In a. m. brown and W. Imarisha, eds., *Octavia's Brood: Science Fiction Stories from Social Justice Movements,* Chico, CA: AK Press, 332–356.
(2017). History is a dystopia, interviewed by Avni Sejpal, *Boston Review,* November 16. http://bostonreview.net/podcast-literature-culture-arts-society/tananarive-due-history-dystopia.
Dunbar-Ortiz, R. (2014). *An Indigenous Peoples' History of the United States.* Boston: Beacon Press.
Dwight, M. (1928). *Letters from Brook Farm,* ed. Amy Reed. Poughkeepsie, NY: Vassar College.
Eagleton, T. (2018). *Hope without Optimism.* New Haven, CT: Yale University Press.
Edel, L., and Ray, G. N. (eds.) (1979). *Henry James and H. G. Wells: A Record of Their Friendship, Their Debate on the Art of Fiction, and Their Quarrel.* Westport, CT: Greenwood.
Edwards, C. (2019). *Utopia and the Contemporary British Novel.* Cambridge: Cambridge University Press.
Eggers, D. (2006). *What Is the What: The Autobiography of Valentino Achak Deng.* New York: Vintage.
Elder, E. (2011). How to Build a Commune: Drop City's Influence on the Southwestern Commune Movement. In E. Elder and L. R. Lippard (eds.), *West of Center: Art and the Counterculture: Experiment in America, 1965–77.* Minneapolis: University of Minnesota Press, 2–21.
Elias, N. (2000). *The Civilizing Process.* Translated by Edmund Jephcott. Malden: Blackwell.
Erdrich, L., interview by Lisa Halliday. (2010). "The Paris Review." *Louise Erdrich, The Art of Fiction.* The Paris Review, (Winter): https://www.theparisreview.org/interviews/6055/the-art-of-fiction-no-208-louise-erdrich.
Erdrich, L. (2017). *Future Home of the Living God.* New York: HarperCollins.
Evans, S. (2013). Programmed Space, Themed Space, and the Ethics of Home in Toni Morrison's *Paradise. African American Review* 46.2/3, 381–396.
Feely-Harnik, G. (2001). The Ethnography of Creation: Lewis Henry Morgan and the American Beaver." In S. Franklin and S. McKinnon (eds.), *Relative Values: Reconfiguring Kinship Studies.* Durham, NC: Duke University Press, 54–84.
Firestone, S. (1973). *The Dialectic of Sex: The Case for Feminist Revolution.* New York: Bantam Books.

Fisher, M. (2018). Foreword. In W. Davies, ed., *Economic Science Fictions*, London: Goldsmiths Press, xi–xiv.

Fisher, M. (2009). *Capitalism Realism: Is There No Alternative?* London: Zero Books.

Fitzgerald, S. (1994–1995). Dishing Up Cosmic Slop. *American Visions* (December–January), 46.

Foertsch, J. (2013). *Reckoning Day: Race, Place, and the Atom Bomb in Postwar America*, Nashville, TN: Vanderbilt University Press.

Forter, G. (2019). *Critique and Utopia in Postcolonial Historical Fiction*. Oxford: Oxford University Press.

Frank, P. (1959). *Alas Babylon*. Philadelphia: J.P. Lippincott.

Fredrickson, G. M. (1982 [1981]). *White Supremacy: A Comparative Study in American and South African History*. Oxford: Oxford University Press.

Freedman, C. (2000). *Critical Theory and Science Fiction*. Hanover, NH: Wesleyan University Press.

Friedner, M. (2022). *Sensory Futures: Deafness and Cochlear Implant Infrastructures in India*. Minneapolis: University of Minnesota Press.

Fukuyama, F. (1989) The End of History? *The National Interest* 16 (Summer), 3–18.

(1992). *The End of History and the Last Man*. New York: Simon and Schuster.

Fuller, R. B. (1969). *Operation Manual for Planet Earth*. Carbondale: Southern Illinois University Press.

Fuller, R. B. (2019 [1969]). *Utopia or Oblivion: The Prospects for Humanity*. Zurich: Lars Müller.

Funkadelic. (1978). "One Nation Under a Groove." *One Nation Under a Groove*, Warner Bros. Records.

(1974). "Standing on the Verge of Getting It On." *Standing on the Verge of Getting It On*, Westbound Records.

Gadowski, R. (2014). Critical dystopia for young people: The freedom meme in American young adult dystopian science fiction. In A. Wicher, P. Spyra, and J. Matyjaszczyk, eds., *Basic Categories of Fantastic Literature Revisited*. Newcastle Upon Tyne: Cambridge Scholars Publishing,144–160.

Gaines, W. M., Feldstein, A., and Orlando, J. (1953). Judgment Day. *Weird Fantasy* 18 (April).

Gaines, W. M., and Feldstein, A. (2014). "Judgment Day." In *Judgment Day and Other Stories Illustrated by Joe Orlando*. Seattle: Fantagraphics, 29–35.

gam, d. (2020). The Revolution Will Be in Color. In M. Bechtel, ed., *The Dystopian States of America: A Charity Anthology Benefiting the ACLU Foundation*, Haverhill, MA: Haverhill House, Kindle edition, loc. 3769–3789.

Geoghegan, V. (2007). Utopia, Religion and Memory. *Journal of Political Ideologies* 12.3, 255–267.

Ghosh, A. (2016). *The Great Derangement: Climate Change and the Unthinkable*. Chicago: University of Chicago Press.

Gibson, W. (2020). *Agency*. New York: Berkley.

(1986). *Count Zero*. London: Victor Gollancz.
(1988). Johnny Mnemonic. In *Burning Chrome*. London: Grafton, 14–36.
(1988). *Mona Lisa Overdrive*. London: Victor Gollancz.
(1984). *Neuromancer*. New York: Ace.
(2014). *The Peripheral*. New York: G.P. Putnam.
Gibson, W., and Sterling, B. (1990). *The Difference Engine*. London: Victor Gollancz.
Gill-Peterson, J. (2018). *Histories of the Transgender Child*. Minneapolis: University of Minnesota Press.
Gilman, C. P. (2014). *Herland and Selected Stories*. Edited by B. Solomon. New York: Signet Classics.
Gilmore, R. W. (2007). *Golden Gulag: Prisons, Surplus, Crisis, and Opposition in Globalizing California*. Berkeley: University of California Press.
Golumbia, D. (1996). Hypercapital. *Postmodern Culture* 7.1. www.pomoculture.org/2013/09/22/hypercapital/.
Gordon, A. F. (2017). *The Hawthorn Archive: Letters from the Utopian Margins*. New York: Fordham University Press.
Gould, S. J. (1996 [1981]). *The Mismeasure of Man*. New York: W. W. Norton.
Greene, M. H. (1950). Raritan Bay Union, Eaglewood, New Jersey. *Proceedings of the New Jersey Historical Society* 68.1, 1–20.
Greenlee, S. (1990 [1969]). *The Spook Who Sat by the Door*. Detroit: Wayne State University Press.
Haldeman, J. (1974). *The Forever War*. New York: St. Martin's Press.
Hamid, M. (2007). *The Reluctant Fundamentalist*. London: Penguin.
Haraway, D. J. (2004). *Haraway Reader*. New York: Routledge.
Haraway, D. (1988). *Modest_Witness@Second_Millenium.FemaleMan(c)_Meets_OncoMouse(TM): Feminism and Technoscience*. New York: Routledge.
(1991). *Simians, Cyborgs, and Women: The Reinvention of Nature*. New York: Routledge.
(2016). *Staying with The Trouble: Making Kin in the Chthulucene*. Durham, NC: Duke University Press.
(2008). *When Species Meet*. Minneapolis: University of Minnesota Press.
Hardt, M., and Negri, A. (2004). *Multitude: War and Democracy in the Age of Empire*. London: Penguin.
Harrison, H. (1966). *Make Room! Make Room!* New York: Doubleday.
Harvey, D. (2005). *The New Imperialism*. Oxford: Oxford University Press.
Hawthorne, N. (2009 [1852]) *The Blithedale Romance*. Oxford: Oxford University Press.
Hayden, D. (1976). *Seven American Utopias*. Cambridge, MA: MIT Press.
Headley, M. D. (2017). Memoirs of an Imaginary Country. In J. Díaz, ed., *Global Dystopias*. Cambridge, MA: MIT Press, Kindle edition.
Heckman, D. (2008). *A Small World: Smart Houses and the Dream of the Perfect Day*. Durham, NC: Duke University Press.
Heidegger, M. (1977). *The Question concerning Technology and Other Essays*. Translated by William Lovitt. New York: Harper & Row.

Heinlein, R. A. (2001 [1964]). *Farnham's Freehold*, Riverdale, NY: Baen.
(1959). *Starship Troopers*. New York: G.P. Putnam's Sons.
(2012). *The Virginia Edition: A Sample of the Series*. Houston, TX: The Virginia Edition.
Herrera, Y. (2015). *Signs Preceding the End of the World.* Translated by Lisa Dillman. London: & Other Stories.
Hickel, J. (2016). Neoliberalism and the End of Democracy. In S. Springer, K. Birch, and J. MacLeavy, eds., *The Handbook of Neoliberalism*. London: Routledge, 142–152.
Hill, R. (2018). Capital or Capitol? The Hunger Games Fandom and Neoliberal Populism. *American Studies* 57.1/2, 5–28.
Hirschman, A. O. (1991). *The Rhetoric of Reaction*. Cambridge, MA: Harvard University Press.
Hogan, C. (1998). *The Blood Artists*. New York: Avon Books.
Hollinger, V. (1999). (Re)reading Queerly: Science Fiction, Feminism, and the Defamiliarization of Gender. *Science Fiction Studies* 26.1, 23–40.
Holloway, M. (1951). *Heavens on Earth: Utopian Communities in America, 1680–1880*. London: Turnstile Press.
hooks, b. [Watkins, G.]. (2015). *Feminism Is for Everybody: Passionate Politics*. 2nd edition. New York: Routledge.
Hopkinson, N. (2000). *Midnight Robber*. New York: The Warner Company, 2000.
Horne, G. (2018). *The Apocalypse of Settler Colonialism: The Roots of Slavery, White Supremacy, and Capitalism in Seventeenth-Century North America and the Caribbean*. New York: Monthly Review Press.
Horn, L., Mert, A., and Müller, F. (eds.). (2023). *Palgrave Handbook of Global Politics in the 22nd Century*. London: Palgrave Macmillan.
Hudlin, R. (1994). Space Traders. *Cosmic Slop*, HBO Home Video.
Huerta, L. (2019). The Wall. In V. LaValle and J. J. Adams, eds., *A People's Future of the United States: Speculative Fiction from 25 Extraordinary Writers*. New York: Random House, 49–61.
Hungerford, A. (2010). *Postmodern Belief: American Literature and Religion since 1960*. Princeton, NJ: Princeton University Press.
Huxley, A. (1932). *Brave New World*. London: Chatto & Windus.
Imarisha, W. (2015). Introduction. In a. m. brown and W. Imarisha, eds., *Octavia's Brood: Science Fiction Stories from Social Justice Movements*. Chico, CA: AK Press, 3–6.
Jacobs, N. (1994). The Frozen Landscape in Feminist Utopian and Science Fiction. In J. L. Donawerth and C. A. Kolmerten, eds., *Utopian and Science Fiction by Women: Worlds of Difference*. Syracuse, NY: Syracuse University Press.
Jaggi, M. (2005). The Magician. *The Guardian*, December 17, www.theguardian.com/books/2005/dec/17/booksforchildrenandteenagers.shopping.
Jameson, F. (2016). *An American Utopia: Dual Power and the Universal Army*. London: Verso.

(2005). *Archaeologies of the Future: The Desire Called Utopia and Other Science Fictions*. London: Verso.
(1983). Introduction. In *The Historical Novel*, by Georg Lukács. Lincoln: University of Nebraska Press, 1–8.
(1974). *Marxism and Form*. Princeton, NJ: Princeton University Press.
(1991). *Postmodernism, or the Cultural Logic of Late Capitalism*. Durham, NC: Duke University Press.
(1982). Progress versus Utopian; Or, Can We Imagine the Future? *Science Fiction Studies* 9.2, 147–158.
(1979). Reification and Utopia in Mass Culture. *Social Text* 1, 130–148.
(1990). *Signatures of the Visible*. New York: Routledge.
(2015). *The Ancients and the Postmoderns*. London: Verso.
(2013). *The Antinomies of Realism*. New York: Verso.
(2008). *The Ideologies of Theory*. New York: Verso.
(1981). *The Political Unconscious: Narrative as a Socially Symbolic Act*. Ithaca, NY: Cornell University Press.
(1994). *The Seeds of Time*. New York: Columbia University Press.
(2010). *Valences of the Dialectic*. London: Verso.
(2009). Utopia as Replication. In *Valences of the Dialectic*, London: Verso, 410–434.
Japtok, M., and Jenkins, J. R. (eds.) (2020). Introduction: Human Contradictions in Octavia E. Butler's Work. In *Human Contradictions in Octavia E. Butler's Work*. London: Palgrave Macmillan, 1–12.
Jemisin, N. K. (2015). *The Fifth Season*. London: Orbit.
(2016). *The Obelisk Gate*. London: Orbit.
(2017). *The Stone Sky*. London: Orbit.
Jenkins, J. R. (2020). Is Religiosity a Black Thing? Reading the Black None in Octavia Butler's "The Book of Martha." *Pacific Coast Philology* 55.1, 5–22.
Johnson, K. M. (1993). Emerging Viruses in Context: An Overview of Viral Hemorrhagic Fevers. In S. S. Morse, ed., *Emerging Viruses*. New York: Oxford University Press, 46–57.
Jordan, H. (2011). *When She Woke*. New York: Harper Collins.
Jung, M.-K. (2011). Constituting the U.S. Empire-State and White Supremacy. In M. Jung, J. H. Costa Vargas, and E. Bonilla-Silva, eds., *State of White Supremacy: Racism, Governance, and the United States*. Stanford, CA: Stanford University Press, 1–23.
Kafer, A. (2013). *Feminist, Queer, Crip*. Bloomington: Indiana University Press.
Kelley, R. D. G. (2002). *Freedom Dreams: The Black Radical Imagination*, Boston: Beacon Press.
Kelly, R. (Director) (2009). *The Box*. [Motion picture]. Los Angeles, CA: Warner Brothers.
Kennedy, J. F. Commencement Address at American University, online at www.jfklibrary.org/archives/other-resources/john-f-kennedy-speeches/american-university–19630610.

Kessler, C. F. (ed.) (1995). *Daring to Dream: Utopian Fiction by United States Women Before 1950*, 2nd ed. Syracuse, NY: Syracuse University Press.

Kidd, K. B. (2020). *Theory for Beginners: Children's Literature as Critical Thought.* New York: Fordham University Press.

King, R. C., and Leonard, D. J. (2016 [2014]). *Beyond Hate: White Power and Popular Culture.* New York: Routledge.

Kirby, V. (1997). *Telling Flesh: The Substance of the Corporeal.* New York: Routledge.

Kirk, A. (2016). Alloyed: Countercultural Bricoleurs and the Design Science Revival. In D. Kaiser and W. P. McCray (eds.), *Groovy Science: Knowledge, Innovation and American Counterculture.* Chicago: Chicago University Press, 305–336.

Klein, N. (2014). *This Changes Everything: Capitalism vs. The Climate.* New York: Simon & Schuster.

Klune, T. J. (2020). *The House in the Cerulean Sea.* New York: Tor.

Kolodny, A. (1984). *The Lay of the Land: Metaphor as Experience and History in American Life and Letters.* Chapel Hill: University of North Carolina Press.

Kovacs, J., and Rowland, C. (2004). *Revelation.* Oxford: Blackwell.

Kristeva, J. (1982). *Powers of Horror: An Essay on Abjection.* New York: Columbia University Press.

Kumar, K. (2013). Utopia's Shadow. In V. Fátima (ed.), *Dystopia(n) Matters: On the Page, on Screen, on Stage.* Newcastle upon Tyne: Cambridge Scholars Publishing, 19–22.

Lane, D. (2004 [2002]). *KD Rebel.* Available from: *Solar General*, http://solargeneral.org/library/.

(n.d.). The 88 Precepts. Available from: https://archive.org/details/88Precepts_937.

Langer, J. (2011). *Postcolonialism and Science Fiction.* New York: Palgrave Macmillan.

Latour, B. (1993). *We Have Never Been Modern*, translated by Catherine Porter. Cambridge, MA: Harvard University Press.

Lavender III, I. (2019). *Afrofuturism Rising: The Literary Prehistory of a Movement.* Columbus: Ohio State University Press.

Lavigne, C. (2013). *Cyberpunk Women: Feminism and Science Fiction*, Jefferson, NC: McFarland.

Le Guin, U.K. (2004). A Whitewashed Earthsea. *SLATE* (December 16).

(2001 [1985]). *Always Coming Home.* Berkeley: University of California Press.

(1989). Is Gender Necessary? In S. Wood, ed., *The Language of the Night: Essays on Fantasy and Science Fiction.* New York: HarperCollins, 155–172.

(1994 [1974]). *The Dispossessed: An Ambiguous Utopia.* New York: HarperPrism.

(1971). *The Lathe of Heaven.* New York: Avon.

(1987). *The Left Hand of Darkness: 50th Anniversary Edition.* New York: Ace Books.

(1976). *The Word for World Is Forest.* New York: Berkley Medallion.

(2017). Ursula K. Le Guin explains how to build a new kind of utopia. *Electric Lit* (December 5), https://electricliterature.com/ursula-k-le-guin-explains-how-to-build-a-new-kind-of-utopia/.

Lederberg, J. (2000). Infectious History. *Science* 288.5464, 287–293.

(1993). Viruses and Humankind: Intracellular Symbiosis and Evolutionary Competition. In S. S. Morse, ed., *Emerging Viruses*. New York: Oxford University Press, 3–9.

Lefebvre, H. (1991). *The Production of Space*, translated by D. Nicholson-Smith. Oxford: Blackwell.

Lemke, D. (2019). Frederick Douglass's Utopia: Searching for the Space of Black Freedom. In P. Ventura and E. K. Chan, eds., *Race and Utopian Desire in American Literature and Society*. Cham: Palgrave Macmillan, 23–39.

León Portilla, M. (2006). *The Broken Spears: The Aztec Account of the Conquest of Mexico*. Boston: Beacon Press.

Lepore, J. (2020). *If Then: How the Simulmatics Corporation Invented the Future*. New York: Liverlight.

Levitas, R. (2013). *Utopia as Method: The Imaginary Reconstruction of Society*. London: Palgrave Macmillan.

Levithan, D. (2003). *Boy Meets Boy*. New York: Alfred A. Knopf.

Liggett, K. (2019). *The Grace Year*. New York: Wednesday Books.

Lipsitz, G. (1994). *Rainbow at Midnight: Labor and Culture in the 1940s*. Chicago: University of Illinois Press.

(2018 [1998]). *The Possessive Investment in Whiteness: How White People Profit from Identity Politics*, Philadelphia: Temple University Press.

Lombardo, M. (2014). Autoridad, transgresión y frontera (sobre la narrativa de Yuri Herrera). *Inti, Revista de literatura hispánica* 1.79, 193–214.

London, J. (1908). *The Iron Heel*. New York: Macmillan.

López-Lozano, M. (2008). *Utopian Dreams, Apocalyptic Nightmares: Globalization in Recent Mexican and Chicano Narrative*. West Lafayette, IN: Purdue University Press.

Lowry, L. (1993). *The Giver*. New York: Houghton Mifflin.

Luckhurst, R. (2019). *Corridors: Passages of Modernity*. London: Reaktion Books.

Ma, L. (2018). *Severance*. New York: Farrar, Straus and Giroux.

MacDonald, A. (William L. Pierce). (1996 [1978]). *The Turner Diaries*. 2nd edition. Fort Lee, NJ: Barricade Books.

Macy, C., and Bonnemaison, S. (2003). *Architecture and Nature: Creating the American Landscape*. New York: Routledge.

Malzberg, B. N. (1972). *Beyond Apollo*. New York: Random House.

Manaugh, G. (2007). Comparative Planetology: An Interview with Kim Stanley Robinson. *BLDGBLOG* (December 19), https://bldgblog.com/2007/12/comparative-planetology-an-interview-with-kim-stanley-robinson.

Mangina, J. L. (2010). *Revelation*. London: SCM Press.

Marcus, R. (2008). The Force of Gender. *The Washington Post* (March 5).

Markman, R. H., and Markman, P. T. (1992). *The Flayed God: The Mesoamerican Mythological Tradition. Sacred Texts and Images from Pre-Columbian Mexico and Central America*. San Francisco: Harper San Francisco.

Marks, P., Vieira, F., and Wagner-Lawlor, J. (eds.) (2022). *Palgrave Handbook of Utopian and Dystopian Literatures*. Cham: Palgrave Macmillan.

Mason, D. (2021). *Queer Anxieties of Young Adult Literature and Culture*. Jackson: University Press of Mississippi.

Matheson, R. (1970). Button, Button. *Playboy*, 17.6 (June), 208–209.

(1954). *I Am Legend*. New York: Gold Medal Books.

Matthews, M. (2010). *Droppers: America's First Hippie Commune, Drop City*. Norman: University of Oklahoma Press.

Maynard, R., and Simpson, L. B. (2022). *Rehearsals for Living*. Chicago: Haymarket Books

Mbembe, A. (2022). How to Develop a Planetary Consciousness. *Noēma* (January 11). www.noemamag.com/how-to-develop-a-planetary-consciousness/.

(2008). Necropolitics. In S. Morton and S. Bygrave, eds., *Foucault in an Age of Terror: Essays on Biopolitics and the Defence of Society*. London: Palgrave Macmillan, 152–182.

McAlear, R. (2010). The Value of Fear: Toward a Rhetorical Model of Dystopia. *Interdisciplinary Humanities* 27.2, 24–42.

McCaffery, L., and McMenamin, J. (2010). An Interview with Octavia E. Butler. In C. Francis, ed., *Conversations with Octavia Butler*. Jackson: University Press of Mississippi, 10–26.

McKay, C. (1990). Does Mars Have Rights: An Approach to the Environmental Ethics of Planetary Engineering. In D. Macniven, ed., *Moral Expertise: Studies in Practical and Professional Ethics*. New York, Routledge, 184–197.

McCarthy, C. (2006). *The Road*. New York: Alfred A. Knopf.

McClanahan, A. (2017). *Dead Pledges: Debt, Crisis, and Twenty-First-Century Culture*, Stanfordm CA: Stanford University Press.

McClure, J. A. 2007. *Partial Faiths: Postsecular Fiction in the Age of Pynchon and Morrison*. Athens: University of Georgia Press.

McDonough, M. (2019). From Tribute to Mockingjay: Representations of Katniss Everdeen's Agency in the *Hunger Games* Series. In I. E. Castro and J. Clark, eds., *Child and Youth Agency in Science Fiction*. Lanham, MD: Lexington, 131–150.

McG. (Director). (2009). *Terminator Salvation*. [Motion picture] Los Angeles, CA: Warner Brothers.

McGrath, J. F. (2016). *Theology and Science Fiction*. Eugene: Cascade.

McGurl, M. (2009). *The Program Era: Postwar Fiction and the Rise of Creative Writing*. Cambridge, MA: Harvard University Press.

McHale, B. (1987). *Postmodernist Fiction*. London: Routledge.

McKee, G. (2007). *The Gospel according to Science Fiction*. Westminster: John Knox.

McLuhan, M. (1994). *Understanding Media: The Extensions of Man*. Cambridge, MA: MIT Press.

McNeill, W. H. (1986). Mythistory, or Truth, Myth, History, and Historians. In *Mythistory and Other Essays*. Chicago: University of Chicago Press, 3–22.

(1986). The Care and Repair of Public Myth. In *Mythistory and Other Essays*. Chicago: University of Chicago Press, 23–42.

Melamed, J. (2017). *Gather the Daughters*. New York: Little, Brown.

Mendlesohn, F. (2019). *The Pleasant Profession of Robert A. Heinlein*. London: Unbound.

Messinger, S. (2010). Rehabilitating Time: Multiple Temporalities among Military Clinicians and Patients. *Medical Anthropology* 29.2, 150–169.

Miéville, C. (2016). The Limits of Utopia. In Thomas More, *Utopia*. New York: Verso.

(2014). The Limits of Utopia. *salvage.zone*. https://salvage.zone/mieville_all.html.

Miller, S. J. (2018). *Blackfish City*. New York: Harper Collins.

Miller, T. (Director). (2019). *Terminator: Dark Fate*. [Motion Picture] Los, Angeles, CA: Paramount Pictures.

Miller, T. (1999). *The 60s Communes: Hippies and Beyond*. Syracuse, NY: Syracuse University Press.

(1998). *The Quest for Utopia in Twentieth Century America, Vol. 1: 1900–60*. Syracuse, NY: Syracuse University Press.

Moir, C. (2019). *Ernst Bloch's Speculative Materialism: Ontology, Epistemology, Politics*. Leiden: Brill.

Molyneaux, K. (2000). *White Empire*. Unknown: World Church of the Creator (?). Available from https://archive.org/stream/WhiteEmpireByRev.KennethMolyneaux/WhiteEmpride_djvu.txt.

Moore, J. W. (2015). *Capitalism in the Web of Life: Ecology and the Accumulation of Capital*. Verso.

Moore, W. (1953). *Bring the Jubilee*. New York: Ballantine, 1953.

Mootz, K. J. (2020). The Body and the Archive in Louise Erdrich's Future Home of the Living God. *Journal of the Fantastic in the Arts* 31.2 (2020), 263–276.

More, T. (2002).*Utopia*, edited by George M. Logan and Robert M. Adams. Cambridge: Cambridge University Press.

(2011). *Utopia*. Edited with a revised translation by George M. Logan. New York: W. W. Norton.

(2016). *Utopia*. New York: Verso.

Morozov, E. (2013). *To Save Everything Click Here: The Folly of Technological Solutionism*. New York: Public Affairs.

Morrison, T., interview by Zia Jaffrey. (1998). *Salon interview* www.salon.com/books/int/1998/02/cov_sI_02int.

(1992). *Playing in the Dark: Whiteness and the Literary Imagination*, Cambridge, MA: Harvard University Press.

(1998). *Paradise*. New York: Alfred A. Knopf.

(1999). *Paradise*. London: Vintage.

Morse, S. S. (1993). Examining the Origins of Emerging Viruses. In S. S. Morse, ed., *Emerging Viruses*. New York: Oxford University Press, 10–28.

Morton, T. (2013). *Hyperobjects: Philosophy and Ecology After the End of the World*. Minneapolis: University of Minnesota Press.

Moss, D. and Scheer, R. (2018). Eco-Village Movement Flourishing Across United States. *The Environmental Magazine* (January 31), https://emagazine.com/eco-village/.

Mostow, J. (Director). (2003). *Terminator 3: Rise of the Machines.* [Motion picture] Los Angeles, CA: Warner Brothers.

Moylan, T. (2020). *Becoming Utopian: The Culture and Politics of Radical Transformation.* London: Bloomsbury.

(2003). *Dark Horizons: Science Fiction and the Dystopian Imagination.* New York: Routledge.

(1986). *Demand the Impossible: Science Fiction and the Utopian Imagination.* New York: Methuen.

(2014). *Demand the Impossible: Science Fiction and the Utopian Imagination.* Edited by Raffaella Baccolini. Oxford: Peter Lang.

(2000). *Scraps of the Untainted Sky: Science Fiction, Utopia, Dystopia*, Boulder, CO: Westview Press.

Muñoz, J. E. (2009). *Cruising Utopia: The Then and There of Queer Futurity.* New York: NYU Press.

National Security Archive. (2000). CIA Acknowledges Ties to Pinochet's Repression (September 19), https://nsarchive2.gwu.edu/news/20000919/#docs.

Nelson, A. (2002). Introduction: Future Texts. *Social Text* 20.2, 1–15.

Nelson, M. (2021). *On Freedom: Four Songs of Care and Constraint.* Minneapolis, MN: Graywolf Press.

Nikkei A. (2019). "How Dare You'" Transcript of Greta Thunberg's UN climate speech (September 25), https://asia.nikkei.com/Spotlight/Environment/How-dare-you-Transcript-of-Greta-Thunberg-s-UN-climate-speech.

Nirta, C. (2017). Actualized Utopias: The *Here* and *Now* of Transgender. *Politics & Gender* 13, 181–208.

Niven, L., and Pournelle, J. (1981). *Oath of Fealty.* New York: Timescape Books.

Nixon, N. (1992). Cyberpunk: Preparing the Ground for Revolution or Keeping the Boys Satisfied? *Science Fiction Studies* 19.2, 219–235.

Nyong'o, T. (2019). *Afro-Fabulations: The Queer Drama of Black Life.* New York: New York University Press.

O'Brien, M. E., and Abdelhadi, E. (2022). *Everything for Everyone: An Oral History of the New York Commune, 2052–2072.* New York: Common Notions.

O'Connell, H. C. (2020). Marxism. In A. McFarlane, G. D. Murphy, and L. Schmeink, eds., *The Routledge Companion to Cyberpunk Cultures.* New York: Routledge, 282–290.

Office for National Statistics (2022). *The Religion of Usual Residents and Household Religious Composition in England and Wales*, 2021 Census [Data set]. www.ons.gov.uk/peoplepopulationandcommunity/culturalidentity/religion/bulletins/religionenglandandwales/census2021.

Offill, J. (2021). *Weather.* New York: Vintage.

O'Keefe, D. (2020). Imagining the End of Capitalism with Kim Stanley Robinson. *Jacobin* (October 22), https://jacobinmag.com/2020/10/kim-stanley-robinson-ministry-future-science-fiction.

Okorafor, N. (2010). *Who Fears Death?* New York: DAW.

Older, M. (2016). *Infomocracy.* New York: Tor.

Oliver, L. (2011). *Delirium*. New York: HarperCollins.

Olsen, E., and Schaeffer G. (2011). *We Wanted to Be Writers: Life, Love, and Literature at the Iowa Writers' Workshop*. New York: Skyhorse.

Orwell, G. (1949). *Nineteen Eighty-Four*. New York: Harcourt, Brace.

(1968). *The Collected Essays, Journalism and Letters of George Orwell.* Volume 3, edited by S. Orwell and I. Angus. New York: Harcourt, Brace.

Osborn, W. M. (2000). *The Wild Frontier: Atrocities during the American-Indian War from Jamestown Colony to Wounded Knee*. New York: Random House.

Otto, R. (1958 [1923]). *The Idea of the Holy: An Inquiry into the Non-rational Factor in the Idea of the Divine and Its Relation to the Rational.* Translated by J. W. Harvey. New York: Oxford University Press.

Owen, R. (1813). *A New View of Society, or, Essays on the Principle of the Formation of Character, and the Application of the Principle to Practice*. London: Cadell & Davies.

Parliament (1975). Chocolate City. *Chocolate City*, Casablanca Records.

Parliament (1975). Mothership Connection (Star Child). *Mothership Connection*, Casablanca Records.

Pease, D. E. (2007). Exceptionalism. In B. Burgett and G. Hendler, eds., *Keywords for American Cultural Studies*. New York: New York University Press, 108–112.

Pejcha, C. S. (2020). Better Living through Anarchy: Tracking the Rise of the Temporary Autonomous Zone. *Document Journal* (August 19), www.documentjournal.com/2020/08/better-living-through-anarchy-tracking-the-rise-of-the-temporary-autonomous-zone/.

Percy, M. (2001). *The Salt of the Earth: Religious Resilience in a Secular Age*. London: Sheffield Academic Press.

Petersen, W. (Director). (1995). *Outbreak* [Motion picture]. Los Angeles, CA: Warner Bros.

Piercy, M. (1991). *He, She, and It*. New York: Fawcett.

(1976). *Woman on the Edge of Time*. New York: Fawcett Crest.

Pinn, A. B. (2012). *The End of God-Talk: An African American Humanist Theology*. Oxford: Oxford University Press.

Piper, H. B. (1962). *Little Fuzzy*. New York: Avon Books.

Pohl, F. and Kornbluth, C.M. (1953). *The Space Merchants*. New York: Ballentine.

Preciado, P. B. (2018). *Counter-Sexual Manifesto*. New York: Columbia University Press.

Preston, R. (1994). *The Hot Zone*. New York: Random House.

Pringle, D. (1985). *Science Fiction, The 100 Best Novels: An English-Language Selection, 1949–84*. London: Xanadu.

Quashie, K. (2021). *Black Aliveness, or A Poetics of Being*. Durham, NC: Duke University Press.

Ramos, J. (2019). *The Farm*. New York: Random House.

Rancière, J. (1995). *On the Shores of Politics*. Translated by L. Heron. London: Verso.

(2016). *The Lost Thread: The Democracy of Modern Fiction*. Translated by S. Corcoran. New York: Bloomsbury.

Reiss, B. (2013). Sleeping at Walden Pond: Thoreau, Abnormal Temporality, and the Modern Body. *American Literature* 85.1, 5–31.
Reynolds, D. (2009). *America, Empire of Liberty*. London: Allen Lane.
Rieder, J. (2008). *Colonialism and the Emergence of Science Fiction*. Middletown, CT: Wesleyan University Press.
(2022). Kim Stanley Robinson's Case for Hope in *New York 2140*. In M. Oziewicz and B. Attebery, eds., *Fantasy and Myth in the Anthropocene: Imagining Futures and Dreaming Hope in Literature and Media*, London: Bloomsbury Academic, 136–147.
Rifkin, M. (2019). *Fictions of Land and Flesh: Blackness, Indigeneity, Speculation*. Durham, NC: Duke University Press.
Rivera, G. (2019). *Juliet Takes a Breath*. New York: Dial Books.
Robinson, K. S. (1996). *Blue Mars*. New York: Random House.
(2018). Dystopia Now. *Commune*, https://communemag.com/dystopias-now/.
Fifty Degrees Below (New York: Bantam, 2005).
Forty Signs of Rain (New York: Bantam, 2004).
(1993). *Green Mars*. New York: Random House.
(1994). Introduction. In *Future Primitive: The New Ecotopias*. New York: Tor Books, 9–11.
(2017). *New York 2140*. New York: Orbit.
(2013 [1990]). *Pacific Edge*. New York: Tom Doherty Associates.
(1993). *Red Mars*. New York: Random House.
(2016). Remarks on Utopia in the Age of Climate Change. *Utopian Studies* 27.1, 2–15.
(2007). *Sixty Days and Counting*. New York: Bantam.
(1988). *The Gold Coast*. New York: Tom Doherty Associates.
(2020). *The Ministry for the Future*. New York: Orbit.
(1984). *The Wild Shore*. New York: Ace.
(2002). *The Years of Rice and Salt*. New York: Bantam.
Robinson, M. (2005). *Gilead*. London: Virago.
(2018). *What Are We Doing Here?* London: Virago.
(2012). *When I Was a Child I Read Books*. London: Hachette.
(2005). *The Death of Adam: Essays on Modern Thought*. New York: Picador.
Rockwell, G. L. (2017 [1966]). *White Power*. Unknown: Gresham, Kindle edition.
Rodriguez, D. (2020). *White Reconstruction: Domestic Warfare and the Logics of Genocide*. New York: Fordham University Press.
Romero, C. (2005). Creating the Beloved Community: Religion, Race, and Nation in Toni Morrison's *Paradise*. *African American Review* 39.3, 415–430.
Roth, P. (2008). *Exit Ghost*. London: Vintage.
(2010). *Nemesis*. London: Jonathan Cape.
(2009). *The Humbling*. London: Jonathan Cape.
(2004). *The Plot against America*. London: Jonathan Cape.
Roth, V. (2011). *Divergent*. New York: HarperCollins.
Ruff, M. (2016). *Lovecraft Country*. New York: HarperCollins Publishers.

Ruskoff, D. (2022). *Survival of the Richest: Escape Fantasies of Tech Billionaires.* New York: W. W. Norton.
Russ, J. (1986). *The Female Man.* Boston: Beacon Press.
(1972). When It Changed. In *Again, Dangerous Visions*, edited by H. Ellison. New York: Doubleday, 248–262.
Ruttenburg, N. (2014). Introduction: Is the Novel Democratic? *Novel: A Forum on Fiction*, 47.1, 1–10.
Sadler, S. (2006). Drop City Revisited. *Journal of Architectural Education* 59.3, 5–14.
Saini, A. (2019). *Superior: The Return of Race Science.* Boston: Beacon.
Salvage Editors. (2015). Salvage Perspectives, amid This Stony Rubbish. *Salvage* 1 (July 1), Insert.
Santayana, G. (1905). The Life of Reason: Reason in Common Sense. *Scribner's*, 284.
Sargent, L. T. (1994). Three Faces of Utopianism Revisited. *Utopian Studies*, 5.1, 1–37.
Sargisson, L. (2012). *Fool's Gold? Utopianism in the Twenty-First Century.* London: Palgrave Macmillan.
Scharmen, F. (2019). *Space Settlements.* New York: Columbia University Press.
Schmeink, L. (2018). Coming of Age and the Other: Critical Posthumanism in Paolo Bacigalupi's *Ship Breaker* and *The Drowned Cities.* In A. Tarr and D. R. White, eds., *Posthumanism in Young Adult Fiction: Finding Humanity in a Posthuman World.* Jackson: University Press of Mississippi, 159–178.
Sedgewick, E. K. (1990). *Epistemology of the Closet.* Berkeley: University of California Press.
Seymour, J. (2015). Murder Me ... Become a Man: Establishing the Masculine Care Circle in Young Adult Dystopias. *Reading Psychology* 37.4, 627–649.
Shah, B. (2018). *Before She Sleeps.* Delphinium.
Sharpe, C. (2016). *In the Wake: On Blackness and Being.* Durham, NC: Duke University Press.
(2010). *Monstrous Intimacies: Making Post-Slavery Subjects.* Durham, NC: Duke University Press.
Shawl, N. (2016). *Everfair.* New York: Tor.
Shepherd, P. (2018). *The Book of M.* New York: William Morrow.
Sherman, A. (2008). *Flight.* London: Harvill and Secker.
Shonkwiler, A. (2017). *The Financial Imaginary: Economic Mystification and the Limits of Realist Fiction.* Minneapolis: University of Minnesota Press.
Short, G. (1994). The Visitor from Venus. In *Daring to Dream*, edited by C. F. Kessler Syracuse, NY: Syracuse University Press.
Shusterman, N. (2016). *Scythe.* New York: Simon & Schuster.
Simpson, L. B. (2022). *Rehearsals for Living.* Chicago: Haymarket Books.
Sloterdijk, P. (2014). *Globes: Macrospherology (Spheres, Vol. II)*, translated by W. Hoban. Pasadena, CA: Semiotext(e).

Smith, G. A. (2021). About Three-in-Ten U.S. Adults Are Now Religiously Unaffiliated, *Pew Research Center* (December 14), www.pewresearch.org/religion/2021/12/14/about-three-in-ten-u-s-adults-are-now-religiously-unaffiliated/.

Smith, H. N. (1978). *Virgin Land: The American West as Symbol and Myth.* Cambridge, MA: Harvard University Press.

Smith, J. K. A. (2014). *How (Not) to Be Secular: Reading Charles Taylor.* Grand Rapids, MI: Eerdmans.

Spiegel, S. (2022). *Utopias in Nonfiction Film.* London: Palgrave Macmillan.

Spinrad, N. (1972). *The Iron Dream.* New York: Avon.

Steinem, G. (2008). Women Are Never Front-Runner. *The New York Times* (January 8).

Sterling, B. (1988). *Islands in the Net.* New York: Arbor House.

Stewart, G. R. (1949). *Earth Abides.* New York: Random House.

Stiegler, B. (1994). *Technics and Time, 1: The Fault of Epimetheus*, translated by R. Beardsworth. Stanford, CA: Stanford University Press.

Stillman, P. G. (2003). Dystopian Critiques, Utopian Possibilities, and Human Purposes in Octavia Butler's *Parables, Utopian Studies* 14.1, 15–35.

Strauss, S. (1988). Gender, class, and race in utopia. In Daphne Patai, ed., *Looking Backward, 1988–1888: Essays on Edward Bellamy.* Amherst: University of Massachusetts Press, 68–90.

Sturgeon, T. (1953). *More Than Human.* New York: Farrar, Straus, and Young.

Sun Ra. (1973). Space Is the Place. *Space Is the Place*, Blue Thumb.

Sundar, N. (2018). Hostages to Democracy, *Critical Times* 1.1, 80–98.

Suvin, D. (2016). *Metamorphoses of Science Fiction: On the Poetics and History of a Literary Genre*, edited by G. Canavan. Oxford: Peter Lang.

(1988). *Positions and Presuppositions in Science Fiction.* Kent, OH: The Kent State University Press.

Tabone, Mark A. (2019). Black Power Utopia: African-American Utopianism and Revolutionary Prophesy in Black Power-era Science Fiction. In P. Ventura and E. K. Chan, eds., *Race and Utopian Desire in American Literature and Society.* Cham: Palgrave Macmillan, 59–78.

Tally, R. T. (2013). *Utopia in the Age of Globalization: Space, Representation, and the World-System.* London: Palgrave Macmillan.

Taylor, A. (Director). (2015). *Terminator Genisys.* [Motion picture] Los Angeles, CA: Paramount Pictures.

Taylor, C. (2007). *A Secular Age.* Cambridge: Belknap Press.

Taylor, J. S. (2005). Surfacing the Body Interior. *Annual Review of Anthropology* 34, 741–756.

The Guardian (2013). Margaret Thatcher: A Life in Quotes (April 8), www.theguardian.com/politics/2013/apr/08/margaret-thatcher-quotes.

The Guardian. (2012). Alif the Unseen by G Willow Wilson: Review (October 7), www.theguardian.com/books/2012/oct/07/alif-the-unseen-willow-wilson-review.

Thompson, S. (2019). Sanctuary and Agency in Young Adult Dystopian Fiction. In I. E. Castro and J. Clark, eds., *Child and Youth Agency in Science Fiction*. Lanham, MD: Lexington, 227–250.

de Tocqueville, A. (2003). *Democracy in America: And, Two Essays on America*, translated by G. Bevan. London: Penguin.

Turner, F. (2006). *From Counterculture to Cyberculture: Stewart Brand, the Whole Earth Network, and the Rise of Digital Utopianism*. Chicago: University of Chicago Press.

Turner, F. J. (1998). *Rereading Frederick Jackson Turner: The Significance of the Frontier in American History and Other Essays*. New Haven, CT: Yale University Press.

van Davidson, R. (1988). *Did We Think Victory Great? The Life of Victor Considérant*. Lanham, MD: University Press of America.

Van Den Berg, L. (2015). *Find Me*. New York: Farrar, Straus and Giroux.

Varoufakis, Y. (2015). *The Global Minotaur: America, Europe and the Future of the Global Economy*. London: Zed.

Vonnegut, K. (1965). *God Bless You, Mr. Rosewater*. New York: Dell Publishing.

Wachowski, L., and Wachowski, L. (Directors). (1999). *The Matrix*. [Motion pictures] Los Angeles, CA: Warner Brothers.

Wagner-Lawlor, J. (2013). *Postmodern Utopias and Feminist Fictions*. New York: Cambridge University Press.

Wald, P. (2008). *Contagious: Cultures, Carriers, and the Outbreak Narrative*. Durham, NC: Duke University Press.

Walter B. (1969). Theses on the Philosophy of History. In H. Arendt, ed., *Illuminations: Essays and Reflections*, translated by Harry Zohn. New York: Schocken, 253–264.

Ward, J. (2018). Day of the Trope: White Nationalist Memes Thrive on Reddit's r/The_Donald, www.splcenter.org/hatewatch/2018/04/19/day-trope-white-nationalist-memes-thrive-reddits-rthedonald.

Wark, M. (2019). *Capital Is Dead: Is This Something Worse?* London: Verso.

Warner, M. (2002). *Publics and Counterpublics*. Princeton, NJ: Princeton University Press.

Warren, C. L. (2018). *Ontological Terror: Blackness, Nihilism, and Emancipation*. Durham, NC: Duke University Press.

Wayland-Smith, E. (2016). *Oneida: From Free Love Utopia to the Well-Set Table*. New York: Picador.

Weeks, K. (2011). *The Problem with Work: Feminism, Marxism, Antiwork Politics, and Postwork Imaginaries*. Durham, NC: Duke University Press.

Wegner, P. E. (2002). *Imaginary Communities: Utopia, the Nation, and the Spatial Histories of Modernity*. Berkeley: University of California Press.

(2020). *Invoking Hope: Theory and Utopia in Dark Times*. Minneapolis: University of Minnesota Press.

(2009). *Life Between Two Deaths, 1989–2001: U.S. Culture in the Long Nineties*. Durham: Duke University Press.

(2014). *Shockwaves of Possibility: Essays on Science Fiction, Globalization, and Utopia*, Oxford: Peter Lang.

(2021). When It Changed: Science Fiction and the Literary Field, circa 1984. In M. R. Murray and M. Nilges, eds., *William Gibson and the Futures of Contemporary Culture*. Iowa City: University of Iowa Press, 21–47.

Wells, M. (2017). *All Systems Red*. New York: Tom Doherty Associates.

(2018). *Artificial Condition*. New York: Tom Doherty Associates.

(2018). *Exit Strategy*. New York: Tom Doherty Associates.

(2020). *Network Effect*. New York: Tom Doherty Associates.

(2018). *Rogue Protocol*. New York: Tom Doherty Associates.

Westerfeld, S. (2005). *Uglies*. New York: Simon Pulse.

Whalen, T. (1992). The Future of a Commodity: Notes toward a Critique of Cyberpunk and the Information Age. *Science Fiction Studies* 19.1, 75–88.

White, D. B., Bay, M., and Martin, W. E. Jr. (2017). *Freedom on My Mind: A History of African Americans with Documents*. Boston: Bedford/St. Martin's.

Whitehead, C. (2016). *The Underground Railroad*. New York: Doubleday.

(2011). *Zone One*. New York: Doubleday.

Wilderson III, F. B. (2010). *Red, White, & Black: Cinema and the Structure of U.S. Antagonisms*. Durham, NC: Duke University Press.

Willems, B. (2018). Automating Economic Revolution: Robert Heinlein's *The Moon Is a Harsh Mistress*. In W. Davies, ed., *Economic Science Fictions*. London: Goldsmiths Press, 73–92.

Williams, R. J. (2005). Theory and the Democracy to Come. *Postmodern Culture* 15.3, n.p.

Willow Wilson, G. (2012). *Alif the Unseen*. London: Corvus.

Wolfe, B. (1952). *Limbo*. New York: Random House.

Wollheim, D. A. (1971). *The Universe Makers: Science Fiction Today*. New York: Harper and Row.

Wolmark, J. (1988). Alternative Futures? Science Fiction and Feminism. *Cultural Studies* 2.1, 48–56.

Womack, Y. L. (2013). *Afrofuturism: The World of Black Sci-Fi and Fantasy Culture*. Chicago: Lawrence Hill Books.

Wright, L. (2020). *The End of October*. New York: Alfred A. Knopf.

Yáñez, A. (2019). Burn the Ships. In N. Shawl, ed., *New Suns: Original Speculative Fiction by People of Color*. Oxford: Solaris, 83–104.

Yaszek, L. (2008). *Galactic Suburbia: Recovering Women's Science Fiction*. Columbus: The Ohio State University Press.

Yuknavitch, L. (2019). *The Book of Joan*. Edinburgh: Canongate Books.

Zamalin, A. (2019). *Black Utopia: The History of an Idea from Black Nationalism to Afrofuturism*. New York: Columbia University Press.

Zamora, L. P. (1993). *Writing the Apocalypse: Historical Vision in Contemporary U.S. and Latin American Fiction*. Cambridge: Cambridge University Press.

Zipes, J. (2019). *Ernst Bloch: The Pugnacious Philosopher of Hope*. New York: Palgrave Macmillan.

Ziv, A. (2015). *Explicit Utopias*. Albany, NY: SUNY Press.

Zuboff, S. (2019). *The Age of Surveillance Capitalism: The Fight for a Human Future at the New Frontier of Power*. New York: Public Affairs.

Zumas, L. (2018). *Red Clocks*. New York: Little, Brown.

Index

Afrofuturism, 73, 118, 124, 130, 131
Afro-pessimism, 116, 117, 118, 123
American exceptionalism, 5, 9, 10, 15, 16, 21, 41, 43, 45, 46, 47, 50, 52, 56, 57, 102, 116, 120, 145, 170, 203
apocalyptic, 13, 24, 29, 47, 55, 70, 100, 104, 133, 134, 137, 139, 179, 220, 227, 229, 240, 250, 271, 272, 277
Atwood, Margaret, 33, 63, 68, 69, 71, 101, 227, 229, 230, 244
authoritarianism, 1, 18, 68, 226, 255

Bacigalupi, Paolo, 57, 230
Bell, David, 10, 13
Bell, Derrick, 118, 121
Benjamin, Walter, 1, 2, 3, 39
Bester, Alfred, 47
Bey, Hakim, 214
Black Power, 131
Blish, James, 106
Bloch, Ernst, 2, 3, 4, 5, 6, 9, 77, 115, 116, 118, 120, 125, 129, 130, 213, 276, 277, 283
Bould, Mark, 90
Bradbury, Ray, 46, 58
Brand, Stewart, 209
Brown, Wendy, 244
Butler, Octavia E., 55, 63, 66, 74, 76, 118, 124, 125, 127, 128, 129, 228, 245, 246, 255, 256, 269

Callenbach, Ernest, 55, 213, 224, 232, 235, 241, 263
Carson, Rachel, 223
Chakrabarty, Dipesh, 273
climate change, 1, 12, 24, 34, 57, 219, 227, 228, 229, 231, 232, 246, 248, 259, 262, 263, 273, 274, 276, 282
Collins, Suzanne, 269
Condie, Ally, 158
Cooper, Melinda, 20
Coulthard, Glen, 14
counterculture, 212
Coupland, Douglas, 105, 113
Crumb, R., 217
cyberpunk, 53, 54, 210, 214, 227, 242, 243, 244, 245, 246, 254

decolonial, 14, 136, 138, 146, 262
Delany, Samuel R., 51, 53, 66, 74, 79, 120, 129, 275
DeLillo, Don, 170, 171, 172, 173, 175, 177
Dick, Philip K., 49
Dillon, Grace, 13
disability, 176, 188
Disch, Thomas, 46, 50
Dobbs decision, 15, 63
Douglass, Frederick, 104
dystopia, antiutopian, 10, 11, 244
dystopia, critical, 134, 141, 220

ecology, 55, 208, 217, 223, 225, 226, 243, 261, 273
economics, 2, 18, 43, 52, 53, 102, 124, 205, 239, 246, 247, 278
economics, neoliberal, 18, 54, 55, 56, 237, 238, 239, 240, 241, 244, 248, 251, 255, 256
Ellison, Harlan, 51
environment, 185, 203, 273
Erdrich, Louise, 69, 70, 77

Fisher, Mark, 247, 250, 274, 275, 276
Fourier, Charles, 202, 203, 204
Fuller, Buckminster, 206

Ghosh, Amitav, 276
Gibson, William, 50, 53, 54, 57, 210, 214, 216, 227, 243
Gilman, Charlotte Perkins, 30, 64, 67, 170, 225, 265, 270
Gilmore, Ruth Wilson, 5
Gordon, Avery, 6
Greenlee, Sam, 90

Hamid, Mohsin, 174, 177, 178
Haraway, Donna, 67, 199, 280, 281, 282
Hartman, Saidiya, 116, 117

hegemony, 2, 5, 9, 54, 167, 168, 169, 170, 171, 172, 173, 174, 175, 177, 180, 182, 262
Heinlein, Robert, 85
Herrera, Yuri, 136, 140, 143, 146, 147, 151
Ho, Boon-Joon, 229
hope, 2, 9, 11, 17, 30, 34, 49, 57, 65, 68, 71, 72, 77, 78, 101, 102, 104, 115, 116, 118, 119, 120, 122, 134, 171, 173, 220, 231, 247, 258, 268, 277, 285
Hopkinson, Nalo, 74
Huerta, Liz, 135, 136, 140, 141

imperialism, 50, 52, 134, 135, 140, 145, 177, 278, 282
Indigeneity, 9, 13, 14, 52, 70, 71, 74, 75, 135, 138, 140, 147, 169, 174, 232

Jameson, Fredric, 6, 11, 12, 13, 18, 43, 44, 45, 47, 49, 52, 53, 102, 175, 213, 214, 219, 220, 227, 234, 238, 239, 240, 241, 242, 245, 249, 261, 272, 275, 276, 277, 279
Jemisin, N.K., 57, 74, 230, 246

Klune, T. J., 161, 162
Kornbluth, C.M., 46

Latinx, 16, 17, 133, 147
Lavender, Isiah III, 118, 131
Le Guin, Ursula, 50, 51, 52, 65, 66, 226, 229, 242, 254
Lederberg, Joshua, 23, 24, 25, 27, 29, 30, 31, 32, 33, 34, 38
Levitas, Ruth, 6, 7, 9, 11
Levithan, David, 162
Lowry, Lois, 158

Ma, Ling, 27, 35, 179
Malzberg, Barry, 50
Matheson, Richard, 29, 30, 48, 59, 187
Maynard, Robyn, 20
Mbembe, Achille, 141, 263, 264, 270
McCarthy, Cormac, 56, 173, 175, 271, 272, 273
McClanahan, Annie, 247, 250
McGurl, Mark, 43
McNeill, William, 25
Merril, Judith, 48
Miéville, China, 64, 76
Miller, Sam J., 256, 258
More, Thomas, 14, 41, 48, 55, 70, 101, 105, 115, 134, 167, 168, 169, 170, 171, 178, 182, 186, 201, 206, 209, 221, 232, 238, 239, 260, 263, 276, 279, 280
Morrison, Toni, 66, 74, 77, 102, 109, 110, 114
Morton, Tim, 274
Moylan, Tom, 6, 11, 14, 51, 54, 78, 130, 134, 220, 244, 245, 275, 283

Nyong'o, Tavia, 117, 118, 130

O'Brien, M.E. and Eman Abdelhadi, 6
Okorafor, Nnedi, 74, 75, 77, 246
Older, Malka, 264
Orwell, George, 46, 250
Owen, Robert, 203

Parliament/Funkadelic, 118, 119, 120, 128
Piercy, Marge, 51, 63, 67, 226, 244, 275
Pohl, Frederick, 46
Puritan, 9, 14, 15, 101, 102, 103, 133, 202

Quashie, Kevin, 117, 118
queer, 2, 7, 15, 16, 17, 51, 63, 64, 65, 66, 70, 73, 74, 76, 77, 79, 127, 281, 282

race, 6, 9, 62, 63, 68, 69, 74, 104, 119, 122, 126, 144, 263, 275, 282
Rancière, Jacques, 146, 268, 270
Rifkin, Mark, 13
Rivera, Gabby, 163
Robinson, Kim Stanley, 12, 20, 50, 54, 185, 199, 221, 227, 230, 231, 236, 244, 248, 249, 259, 264, 269, 275, 282, 283, 286
Robinson, Marilynne, 100, 111, 173
Rodriguez, Dylan, 5
Roth, Philip, 50, 174, 175, 176, 177, 178, 182
Ruff, Matt, 91
Russ, Joanna, 51, 63, 66, 67, 169, 226, 275

Sargisson, Lucy, 10
science fiction, 1, 13, 28, 45, 201, 222, 239
Shawl, Nisi, 74, 282, 283
Shepherd, Peng, 25, 36
Shonkwiler, Allison, 241
Silicon Valley, 4, 19, 196, 210
Simpson, Leanne Betasamosake, 20, 300
Solomon, Rivers, 74, 76
spirituality, 26, 70, 101, 104, 108, 125, 127, 137, 140, 204
Steinem, Gloria, 62
Sun Ra, 118, 124, 128
surveillance capitalism, 241, 242, 244, 251

technology, 17, 19, 47, 50, 64, 67, 131, 141, 185, 186, 187, 188, 190, 191, 192, 193, 194, 196, 197, 200, 206, 210, 212, 219, 221, 241, 283
Terminator, 50, 187, 188, 189, 190, 191, 192, 193, 195, 196, 198
Tiptree, James, 225

utopia, as method, 5, 8, 9, 25, 121, 138, 259
utopia, everyday, 6, 7, 64, 110, 115, 118, 136, 247, 254, 275, 279
utopia, provisional, 3, 7, 10, 12, 28, 34, 45, 64, 73, 77, 109, 129, 133, 144, 148, 187, 245, 257, 261, 266, 271, 277

Van Den Berg, Laura, 25, 36
Vandermeer, Jeff, 230
virus, 23, 28, 29, 30, 33, 55, 79, 226, 229, 246, 257
Vonnegut, Kurt, 46, 220

Warner, Michael, 160
Weeks, Kathi, 5
Wells, Martha, 187, 192
Westerfeld, Scott, 157
white supremacy, 6, 9, 15, 118, 119, 126
Whitehead, Colson, 33, 50, 56
Wilderson, Frank, 116
Wilson, G. Willow, 108
Wright, Lawrence, 33

X-Men, 48, 50

Yáñez, Alberto, 136, 140, 142, 143, 144
Yuknavitch, Lidia, 63, 69, 71, 77

Zamalin, Alex, 115, 118, 119, 130, 131

Cambridge Companions To . . .

AUTHORS

Edward Albee edited by Stephen J. Bottoms

Margaret Atwood edited by Coral Ann Howells (second edition)

W. H. Auden edited by Stan Smith

Jane Austen edited by Edward Copeland and Juliet McMaster (second edition)

Balzac edited by Owen Heathcote and Andrew Watts

Beckett edited by John Pilling

Bede edited by Scott DeGregorio

Aphra Behn edited by Derek Hughes and Janet Todd

Saul Bellow edited by Victoria Aarons

Walter Benjamin edited by David S. Ferris

William Blake edited by Morris Eaves

James Baldwin edited by Michele Elam

Boccaccio edited by Guyda Armstrong, Rhiannon Daniels, and Stephen J. Milner

Jorge Luis Borges edited by Edwin Williamson

Brecht edited by Peter Thomson and Glendyr Sacks (second edition)

The Brontës edited by Heather Glen

Bunyan edited by Anne Dunan-Page

Frances Burney edited by Peter Sabor

Byron edited by Drummond Bone (second edition)

Albert Camus edited by Edward J. Hughes

Willa Cather edited by Marilee Lindemann

Catullus edited by Ian Du Quesnay and Tony Woodman

Cervantes edited by Anthony J. Cascardi

Chaucer edited by Piero Boitani and Jill Mann (second edition)

Chekhov edited by Vera Gottlieb and Paul Allain

Kate Chopin edited by Janet Beer

Caryl Churchill edited by Elaine Aston and Elin Diamond

Cicero edited by Catherine Steel

John Clare edited by Sarah Houghton-Walker

J. M. Coetzee edited by Jarad Zimbler

Coleridge edited by Lucy Newlyn

Coleridge edited by Tim Fulford (new edition)

Wilkie Collins edited by Jenny Bourne Taylor

Joseph Conrad edited by J. H. Stape

H. D. edited by Nephie J. Christodoulides and Polina Mackay

Dante edited by Rachel Jacoff (second edition)

Daniel Defoe edited by John Richetti

Don DeLillo edited by John N. Duvall

Charles Dickens edited by John O. Jordan

Emily Dickinson edited by Wendy Martin

John Donne edited by Achsah Guibbory

Dostoevskii edited by W. J. Leatherbarrow

Theodore Dreiser edited by Leonard Cassuto and Claire Virginia Eby

John Dryden edited by Steven N. Zwicker

W. E. B. Du Bois edited by Shamoon Zamir

George Eliot edited by George Levine and Nancy Henry (second edition)

T. S. Eliot edited by A. David Moody

Ralph Ellison edited by Ross Posnock

Ralph Waldo Emerson edited by Joel Porte and Saundra Morris

William Faulkner edited by Philip M. Weinstein

Henry Fielding edited by Claude Rawson

F. Scott Fitzgerald edited by Ruth Prigozy

F. Scott Fitzgerald edited by Michael Nowlin (second edition)

Flaubert edited by Timothy Unwin

E. M. Forster edited by David Bradshaw

Benjamin Franklin edited by Carla Mulford

Brian Friel edited by Anthony Roche

Robert Frost edited by Robert Faggen

Gabriel García Márquez edited by Philip Swanson

Elizabeth Gaskell edited by Jill L. Matus

Edward Gibbon edited by Karen O'Brien and Brian Young

Goethe edited by Lesley Sharpe

Günter Grass edited by Stuart Taberner

Thomas Hardy edited by Dale Kramer

David Hare edited by Richard Boon

Nathaniel Hawthorne edited by Richard Millington

Seamus Heaney edited by Bernard O'Donoghue

Ernest Hemingway edited by Scott Donaldson

Hildegard of Bingen edited by Jennifer Bain

Homer edited by Robert Fowler

Horace edited by Stephen Harrison

Ted Hughes edited by Terry Gifford

Ibsen edited by James McFarlane

Kazuo Ishiguro edited by Andrew Bennett

Henry James edited by Jonathan Freedman

Samuel Johnson edited by Greg Clingham

Ben Jonson edited by Richard Harp and Stanley Stewart

James Joyce edited by Derek Attridge (second edition)

Kafka edited by Julian Preece

Keats edited by Susan J. Wolfson

Rudyard Kipling edited by Howard J. Booth

Lacan edited by Jean-Michel Rabaté

D. H. Lawrence edited by Anne Fernihough

Primo Levi edited by Robert Gordon

Lucretius edited by Stuart Gillespie and Philip Hardie

Machiavelli edited by John M. Najemy

David Mamet edited by Christopher Bigsby

Thomas Mann edited by Ritchie Robertson

Christopher Marlowe edited by Patrick Cheney

Andrew Marvell edited by Derek Hirst and Steven N. Zwicker

Ian McEwan edited by Dominic Head

Herman Melville edited by Robert S. Levine

Arthur Miller edited by Christopher Bigsby (second edition)

Milton edited by Dennis Danielson (second edition)

Molière edited by David Bradby and Andrew Calder

William Morris edited by Marcus Waithe

Toni Morrison edited by Justine Tally

Alice Munro edited by David Staines

Nabokov edited by Julian W. Connolly

Eugene O'Neill edited by Michael Manheim

George Orwell edited by John Rodden

Ovid edited by Philip Hardie

Petrarch edited by Albert Russell Ascoli and Unn Falkeid

Harold Pinter edited by Peter Raby (second edition)

Sylvia Plath edited by Jo Gill

Plutarch edited by Frances B. Titchener and Alexei Zadorojnyi

Edgar Allan Poe edited by Kevin J. Hayes

Alexander Pope edited by Pat Rogers

Ezra Pound edited by Ira B. Nadel

Proust edited by Richard Bales

Pushkin edited by Andrew Kahn

Thomas Pynchon edited by Inger H. Dalsgaard, Luc Herman and Brian McHale

Rabelais edited by John O'Brien

Rilke edited by Karen Leeder and Robert Vilain

Philip Roth edited by Timothy Parrish

Salman Rushdie edited by Abdulrazak Gurnah

John Ruskin edited by Francis O'Gorman

Sappho edited by P. J. Finglass and Adrian Kelly

Seneca edited by Shadi Bartsch and Alessandro Schiesaro

Shakespeare edited by Margareta de Grazia and Stanley Wells (second edition)

George Bernard Shaw edited by Christopher Innes

Shelley edited by Timothy Morton

Mary Shelley edited by Esther Schor

Sam Shepard edited by Matthew C. Roudané

Spenser edited by Andrew Hadfield

Laurence Sterne edited by Thomas Keymer

Wallace Stevens edited by John N. Serio

Tom Stoppard edited by Katherine E. Kelly

Harriet Beecher Stowe edited by Cindy Weinstein

August Strindberg edited by Michael Robinson

Jonathan Swift edited by Christopher Fox

J. M. Synge edited by P. J. Mathews

Tacitus edited by A. J. Woodman

Henry David Thoreau edited by Joel Myerson

Thucydides edited by Polly Low

Tolstoy edited by Donna Tussing Orwin

Anthony Trollope edited by Carolyn Dever and Lisa Niles

Mark Twain edited by Forrest G. Robinson

John Updike edited by Stacey Olster

Mario Vargas Llosa edited by Efrain Kristal and John King

Virgil edited by Fiachra Mac Góráin and Charles Martindale (second edition)

Voltaire edited by Nicholas Cronk

David Foster Wallace edited by Ralph Clare

Edith Wharton edited by Millicent Bell

Walt Whitman edited by Ezra Greenspan

Oscar Wilde edited by Peter Raby

Tennessee Williams edited by Matthew C. Roudané

William Carlos Williams edited by Christopher MacGowan

August Wilson edited by Christopher Bigsby

Mary Wollstonecraft edited by Claudia L. Johnson

Virginia Woolf edited by Susan Sellers (second edition)

Wordsworth edited by Stephen Gill

Richard Wright edited by Glenda R. Carpio

W. B. Yeats edited by Marjorie Howes and John Kelly

Xenophon edited by Michael A. Flower

Zola edited by Brian Nelson

TOPICS

The Actress edited by Maggie B. Gale and John Stokes

The African American Novel edited by Maryemma Graham

The African American Slave Narrative edited by Audrey A. Fisch

African American Theatre by Harvey Young

Allegory edited by Rita Copeland and Peter Struck

American Crime Fiction edited by Catherine Ross Nickerson

American Gothic edited by Jeffrey Andrew Weinstock

The American Graphic Novel edited by Jan Baetens, Hugo Frey and Fabrice Leroy

American Horror edited by Stephen Shapiro and Mark Storey

American Literature and the Body by Travis M. Foster

American Literature and the Environment edited by Sarah Ensor and Susan Scott Parrish

American Literature of the 1930s edited by William Solomon

American Modernism edited by Walter Kalaidjian

American Poetry since 1945 edited by Jennifer Ashton

American Realism and Naturalism edited by Donald Pizer

American Short Story edited by Michael J. Collins and Gavin Jones

American Travel Writing edited by Alfred Bendixen and Judith Hamera

American Utopian Literature and Culture since 1945 edited by Sherryl Vint

American Women Playwrights edited by Brenda Murphy

Ancient Rhetoric edited by Erik Gunderson

Arthurian Legend edited by Elizabeth Archibald and Ad Putter

Australian Literature edited by Elizabeth Webby

The Australian Novel edited by Nicholas Birns and Louis Klee

The Beats edited by Stephen Belletto

The Black Body in American Literature edited by Cherene Sherrard-Johnson

Boxing edited by Gerald Early

British Black and Asian Literature (1945–2010) edited by Deirdre Osborne

British Fiction: 1980–2018 edited by Peter Boxall

British Fiction since 1945 edited by David James

British Literature of the 1930s edited by James Smith

British Literature of the French Revolution edited by Pamela Clemit

British Romantic Poetry edited by James Chandler and Maureen N. McLane

British Romanticism edited by Stuart Curran (second edition)

British Romanticism and Religion edited by Jeffrey Barbeau

British Theatre, 1730–1830, edited by Jane Moody and Daniel O'Quinn

Canadian Literature edited by Eva-Marie Kröller (second edition)

The Canterbury Tales edited by Frank Grady

Children's Literature edited by M. O. Grenby and Andrea Immel

The City in World Literature edited by Ato Quayson and Jini Kim Watson

The Classic Russian Novel edited by Malcolm V. Jones and Robin Feuer Miller

Comics edited by Maaheen Ahmed

Contemporary African American Literature edited by Yogita Goyal

Contemporary Irish Poetry edited by Matthew Campbell

Creative Writing edited by David Morley and Philip Neilsen

Crime Fiction edited by Martin Priestman

Dante's 'Commedia' edited by Zygmunt G. Barański and Simon Gilson

Dracula edited by Roger Luckhurst

Early American Literature edited by Bryce Traister

Early Modern Women's Writing edited by Laura Lunger Knoppers

The Eighteenth-Century Novel edited by John Richetti

Eighteenth-Century Poetry edited by John Sitter

Eighteenth-Century Thought edited by Frans De Bruyn

Emma edited by Peter Sabor

English Dictionaries edited by Sarah Ogilvie

English Literature, 1500–1600 edited by Arthur F. Kinney

English Literature, 1650–1740 edited by Steven N. Zwicker

English Literature, 1740–1830 edited by Thomas Keymer and Jon Mee

English Literature, 1830–1914 edited by Joanne Shattock

English Melodrama edited by Carolyn Williams

English Novelists edited by Adrian Poole

English Poetry, Donne to Marvell edited by Thomas N. Corns

English Poets edited by Claude Rawson

English Renaissance Drama edited by A. R. Braunmuller and Michael Hattaway, (second edition)

English Renaissance Tragedy edited by Emma Smith and Garrett A. Sullivan Jr.

English Restoration Theatre edited by Deborah C. Payne Fisk

Environmental Humanities edited by Jeffrey Cohen and Stephanie Foote

The Epic edited by Catherine Bates

Erotic Literature edited by Bradford Mudge

The Essay edited by Kara Wittman and Evan Kindley

European Modernism edited by Pericles Lewis

European Novelists edited by Michael Bell

Fairy Tales edited by Maria Tatar

Fantasy Literature edited by Edward James and Farah Mendlesohn

Feminist Literary Theory edited by Ellen Rooney

Fiction in the Romantic Period edited by Richard Maxwell and Katie Trumpener

The Fin de Siècle edited by Gail Marshall

Frankenstein edited by Andrew Smith

The French Enlightenment edited by Daniel Brewer

French Literature edited by John D. Lyons

The French Novel: from 1800 to the Present edited by Timothy Unwin

Gay and Lesbian Writing edited by Hugh Stevens

German Romanticism edited by Nicholas Saul

Global Literature and Slavery edited by Laura T. Murphy

Gothic Fiction edited by Jerrold E. Hogle

The Graphic Novel edited by Stephen Tabachnick

The Greek and Roman Novel edited by Tim Whitmarsh

Greek and Roman Theatre edited by Marianne McDonald and J. Michael Walton

Greek Comedy edited by Martin Revermann

Greek Lyric edited by Felix Budelmann

Greek Mythology edited by Roger D. Woodard

Greek Tragedy edited by P. E. Easterling

The Harlem Renaissance edited by George Hutchinson

The History of the Book edited by Leslie Howsam

Human Rights and Literature edited by Crystal Parikh

The Irish Novel edited by John Wilson Foster

Irish Poets edited by Gerald Dawe

The Italian Novel edited by Peter Bondanella and Andrea Ciccarelli

The Italian Renaissance edited by Michael Wyatt

Jewish American Literature edited by Hana Wirth-Nesher and Michael P. Kramer

The Latin American Novel edited by Efraín Kristal

Latin American Poetry edited by Stephen Hart

Latina/o American Literature edited by John Morán González

Latin Love Elegy edited by Thea S. Thorsen

Literature and Animals edited by Derek Ryan

Literature and the Anthropocene edited by John Parham

Literature and Climate edited by Adeline Johns-Putra and Kelly Sultzbach

Literature in a Digital Age edited by Adam Hammond

Literature and Disability edited by Clare Barker and Stuart Murray

Literature and Food edited by J. Michelle Coghlan

Literature and the Posthuman edited by Bruce Clarke and Manuela Rossini

Literature and Religion edited by Susan M. Felch

Literature and Science edited by Steven Meyer

The Literature of the American Civil War and Reconstruction edited by Kathleen Diffley and Coleman Hutchison

The Literature of the American Renaissance edited by Christopher N. Phillips

The Literature of Berlin edited by Andrew J. Webber

The Literature of the Crusades edited by Anthony Bale

The Literature of the First World War edited by Vincent Sherry

The Literature of London edited by Lawrence Manley

The Literature of Los Angeles edited by Kevin R. McNamara

The Literature of New York edited by Cyrus Patell and Bryan Waterman

The Literature of Paris edited by Anna-Louise Milne

The Literature of World War II edited by Marina MacKay

Literature on Screen edited by Deborah Cartmell and Imelda Whelehan

Lyrical Ballads edited by Sally Bushell

Medieval British Manuscripts edited by Orietta Da Rold and Elaine Treharne

Medieval English Culture edited by Andrew Galloway

Medieval English Law and Literature edited by Candace Barrington and Sebastian Sobecki

Medieval English Literature edited by Larry Scanlon

Medieval English Mysticism edited by Samuel Fanous and Vincent Gillespie

Medieval English Theatre edited by Richard Beadle and Alan J. Fletcher (second edition)

Medieval French Literature edited by Simon Gaunt and Sarah Kay

Medieval Romance edited by Roberta L. Krueger

Medieval Romance edited by Roberta L. Krueger (new edition)

Medieval Women's Writing edited by Carolyn Dinshaw and David Wallace

Modern American Culture edited by Christopher Bigsby

Modern British Women Playwrights edited by Elaine Aston and Janelle Reinelt

Modern French Culture edited by Nicholas Hewitt

Modern German Culture edited by Eva Kolinsky and Wilfried van der Will

The Modern German Novel edited by Graham Bartram

The Modern Gothic edited by Jerrold E. Hogle

Modern Irish Culture edited by Joe Cleary and Claire Connolly

Modern Italian Culture edited by Zygmunt G. Baranski and Rebecca J. West

Modern Latin American Culture edited by John King

Modern Russian Culture edited by Nicholas Rzhevsky

Modern Spanish Culture edited by David T. Gies

Modernism edited by Michael Levenson (second edition)

The Modernist Novel edited by Morag Shiach

Modernist Poetry edited by Alex Davis and Lee M. Jenkins

Modernist Women Writers edited by Maren Tova Linett

Narrative edited by David Herman

Narrative Theory edited by Matthew Garrett

Native American Literature edited by Joy Porter and Kenneth M. Roemer

Nineteen Eighty-Four edited by Nathan Waddell

Nineteenth-Century American Literature and Politics edited by John Kerkering

Nineteenth-Century American Poetry edited by Kerry Larson

Nineteenth-Century American Women's Writing edited by Dale M. Bauer and Philip Gould

Nineteenth-Century Thought edited by Gregory Claeys

The Novel edited by Eric Bulson

Old English Literature edited by Malcolm Godden and Michael Lapidge (second edition)

Performance Studies edited by Tracy C. Davis

Piers Plowman by Andrew Cole and Andrew Galloway

The Poetry of the First World War edited by Santanu Das

Popular Fiction edited by David Glover and Scott McCracken

Postcolonial Literary Studies edited by Neil Lazarus

Postcolonial Poetry edited by Jahan Ramazani

Postcolonial Travel Writing edited by Robert Clarke

Postmodern American Fiction edited by Paula Geyh

Postmodernism edited by Steven Connor

Prose edited by Daniel Tyler

The Pre-Raphaelites edited by Elizabeth Prettejohn

Pride and Prejudice edited by Janet Todd

Queer Studies edited by Siobhan B. Somerville

Race and American Literature edited by John Ernest

Renaissance Humanism edited by Jill Kraye

Robinson Crusoe edited by John Richetti

Roman Comedy edited by Martin T. Dinter

The Roman Historians edited by Andrew Feldherr

Roman Satire edited by Kirk Freudenburg

The Romantic Sublime by Cian Duffy

Science Fiction edited by Edward James and Farah Mendlesohn

Scottish Literature edited by Gerald Carruthers and Liam McIlvanney

Sensation Fiction edited by Andrew Mangham

Shakespeare and Contemporary Dramatists edited by Ton Hoenselaars

Shakespeare and Popular Culture edited by Robert Shaughnessy

Shakespeare and Race edited by *Ayanna Thompson*

Shakespeare and Religion edited by Hannibal Hamlin

Shakespeare and War edited by David Loewenstein and Paul Stevens

Shakespeare on Film edited by Russell Jackson (second edition)

Shakespeare on Screen edited by Russell Jackson

Shakespeare on Stage edited by Stanley Wells and Sarah Stanton

Shakespearean Comedy edited by Alexander Leggatt

Shakespearean Tragedy edited by Claire McEachern (second edition)

Shakespeare's First Folio edited by Emma Smith

Shakespeare's History Plays edited by Michael Hattaway

Shakespeare's Language edited by Lynne Magnusson with David Schalkwyk

Shakespeare's Last Plays edited by Catherine M. S. Alexander

Shakespeare's Poetry edited by Patrick Cheney

Sherlock Holmes edited by Janice M. Allan and Christopher Pittard

The Sonnet edited by A. D. Cousins and Peter Howarth

The Spanish Novel: from 1600 to the Present edited by Harriet Turner and Adelaida López de Martínez

Textual Scholarship edited by Neil Fraistat and Julia Flanders

Theatre and Science edited by Kristen E. Shepherd-Barr

Theatre History edited by David Wiles and Christine Dymkowski

Transnational American Literature edited by Yogita Goyal

Travel Writing edited by Peter Hulme and Tim Youngs

The Twentieth-Century American Novel and Politics edited by Bryan Santin

Twentieth-Century American Poetry and Politics edited by Daniel Morris

Twentieth-Century British and Irish Women's Poetry edited by Jane Dowson

The Twentieth-Century English Novel edited by Robert L. Caserio

Twentieth-Century English Poetry edited by Neil Corcoran

Twentieth-Century Irish Drama edited by Shaun Richards

Twentieth-Century Literature and Politics edited by Christos Hadjiyiannis and Rachel Potter

Twentieth-Century Russian Literature edited by Marina Balina and Evgeny Dobrenko

Utopian Literature edited by Gregory Claeys

Victorian and Edwardian Theatre edited by Kerry Powell

The Victorian Novel edited by Deirdre David (second edition)

Victorian Poetry edited by Joseph Bristow

Victorian Women's Poetry edited by Linda K. Hughes

Victorian Women's Writing edited by Linda H. Peterson

War Writing edited by Kate McLoughlin

Women's Writing in Britain, 1660–1789 edited by Catherine Ingrassia

Women's Writing in the Romantic Period edited by Devoney Looser

World Literature edited by Ben Etherington and Jarad Zimbler

World Crime Fiction edited by Jesper Gulddal, Stewart King and Alistair Rolls

Writing of the English Revolution edited by N. H. Keeble

The Writings of Julius Caesar edited by Christopher Krebs and Luca Grillo

For EU product safety concerns, contact us at Calle de José Abascal, 56–1°, 28003 Madrid, Spain or eugpsr@cambridge.org.

www.ingramcontent.com/pod-product-compliance
Ingram Content Group UK Ltd.
Pitfield, Milton Keynes, MK11 3LW, UK
UKHW020340140625
459647UK00018B/2232

* 9 7 8 1 0 0 9 1 8 0 0 5 4 *